Modern Critical Views

Modern Critical Views

Gabriel García Márquez
Andrew Marvell
Carson McCullers
Herman Melville
George Meredith
James Merrill
John Stuart Mill
Arthur Miller
Henry Miller
John Milton
Yukio Mishima
Molière
Michel de Montaigne
Eugenio Montale
Marianne Moore
Alberto Moravia
Toni Morrison
Alice Munro
Iris Murdoch
Robert Musil
Vladimir Nabokov
V. S. Naipaul
R. K. Narayan
Pablo Neruda
John Henry, Cardinal
  Newman
Friedrich Nietzsche
Frank Norris
Joyce Carol Oates
Sean O'Casey
Flannery O'Connor
Christopher Okigbo
Charles Olson
Eugene O'Neill
José Ortega y Gasset
Joe Orton
George Orwell
Ovid
Wilfred Owen
Amos Oz
Cynthia Ozick
Grace Paley
Blaise Pascal
Walter Pater
Octavio Paz
Walker Percy
Petrarch
Pindar
Harold Pinter
Luigi Pirandello
Sylvia Plath
Plato

Plautus
Edgar Allan Poe
Poets of Sensibility & the
  Sublime
Poets of the Nineties
Alexander Pope
Katherine Anne Porter
Ezra Pound
Anthony Powell
Pre-Raphaelite Poets
Marcel Proust
Manuel Puig
Alexander Pushkin
Thomas Pynchon
Francisco de Quevedo
François Rabelais
Jean Racine
Ishmael Reed
Adrienne Rich
Samuel Richardson
Mordecai Richler
Rainer Maria Rilke
Arthur Rimbaud
Edwin Arlington Robinson
Theodore Roethke
Philip Roth
Jean-Jacques Rousseau
John Ruskin
J. D. Salinger
Jean-Paul Sartre
Gershom Scholem
Sir Walter Scott
William Shakespeare
  (3 vols.)
  Histories & Poems
  Comedies & Romances
  Tragedies
George Bernard Shaw
Mary Wollstonecraft
  Shelley
Percy Bysshe Shelley
Sam Shepard
Richard Brinsley Sheridan
Sir Philip Sidney
Isaac Bashevis Singer
Tobias Smollett
Alexander Solzhenitsyn
Sophocles
Wole Soyinka
Edmund Spenser
Gertrude Stein
John Steinbeck

Stendhal
Laurence Sterne
Wallace Stevens
Robert Louis Stevenson
Tom Stoppard
August Strindberg
Jonathan Swift
John Millington Synge
Alfred, Lord Tennyson
William Makepeace
  Thackeray
Dylan Thomas
Henry David Thoreau
James Thurber and S. J.
  Perelman
J. R. R. Tolkien
Leo Tolstoy
Jean Toomer
Lionel Trilling
Anthony Trollope
Ivan Turgenev
Mark Twain
Miguel de Unamuno
John Updike
Paul Valéry
Cesar Vallejo
Lope de Vega
Gore Vidal
Virgil
Voltaire
Kurt Vonnegut
Derek Walcott
Alice Walker
Robert Penn Warren
Evelyn Waugh
H. G. Wells
Eudora Welty
Nathanael West
Edith Wharton
Patrick White
Walt Whitman
Oscar Wilde
Tennessee Williams
William Carlos Williams
Thomas Wolfe
Virginia Woolf
William Wordsworth
Jay Wright
Richard Wright
William Butler Yeats
A. B. Yehoshua
Emile Zola

Modern Critical Views

FYODOR DOSTOEVSKY

WITHDRAWN

Edited and with an introduction by
Harold Bloom
Sterling Professor of the Humanities
Yale University

CHELSEA HOUSE PUBLISHERS
New York ◊ Philadelphia

Printed and bound in the United States of America

10 9 8 7 6 5 4 3

∞The paper used in this publication meets the minimum
requirements of the American National Standard for
Permanence of Paper for Printed Library Materials,
Z39.48-1984.

Library of Congress Cataloging-in-Publication Data
Fyodor Dostoevsky.
  (Modern critical views)
  Bibliography: p.
  Includes index.
  1. Dostoyevsky, Fyodor, 1821–1881—Criticism and
interpretation. I. Bloom, Harold. II. Series.
PG3328.Z6F96   1988   891.73′3   87–15766
ISBN 1–55546–294–4

Contents

Editor's Note

This book gathers together a representative selection of the best criticism available in English upon the fiction of Fyodor Dostoevsky. The critical essays are reprinted here in the chronological order of their original publication. I am grateful to Joyce Banerjee, Henry Finder, and Paul Barickman for their assistance in editing this volume.

My introduction offers brief readings of *Crime and Punishment* and *The Brothers Karamazov*, emphasizing both the strengths and the limitations of Dostoevsky's apocalyptic and transcendental stance as a novelist. Mikhail Bakhtin, legendary hero of Russian Formalist criticism, begins the chronological sequence with an analysis of how the apparently monological discourses of *Poor Folks* and *The Double* incorporate a debate with other voices.

Dostoevsky's best biographer, Joseph Frank, contextualizes *Notes from Underground* as a satire upon the Russian intelligentsia contemporary with Dostoevsky himself. *Crime and Punishment* is read by Donald Fanger as Raskolnikov's phantasmagoria, after which Gary S. Morson determines the genre of *The Diary of a Writer* as a kind of mixture of sensibility and the sublime, a personal apocalypse or "threshold art."

Dostoevsky's progression from his pre-exile *White Nights* to his post-exile *Notes from Underground* is chronicled by Michael Holquist as a gradual rejection of basing identity upon history. More complexly, Robert L. Belknap corrects the traditional misreading that Dostoevsky shares the ideas either of Ivan Karamazov or of Ivan's Grand Inquisitor, rather than the redeeming version of Father Zosima.

A. D. Nuttall, skeptically addressing himself to *Crime and Punishment*, sketches a possible psychological reduction of Raskolnikov's obscure motivations. In an astute psychoanalytical reading, Elizabeth Dalton traces patterns appropriate to epilepsy in *The Idiot* and its hero, Prince Myshkin. A related exegesis by Robert L. Jackson investigates the psychosexuality of gambling in the parodistic *The Gambler*, which inverts Christian cosmology, and hope for the Resurrection.

Zosima, spiritual ideal of *The Brothers Karamazov*, is analyzed by Sergei Hackel as a dialectical interplay of vision and evasion. An imaginative juxtaposition of Dostoevsky's notebooks and *The Possessed* is carried through by John Jones, who finds in Stavrogin the uncanny epitome of this visionary and "unsteady" novel, and so concludes our book in a properly Dostoevskian key.

Introduction

Rereading *Crime and Punishment*, I am haunted suddenly by a recollection of my worst experience as a teacher. Back in 1955, an outcast instructor in the then New Critical, Neo-Christian Yale English Department dominated by acolytes of the churchwardenly T. S. Eliot, I was compelled to teach *Crime and Punishment* in a freshman course to a motley collection of Yale legacies masquerading as students. Wearied of their response to Dostoevsky as so much more Eliotic Original Sin, I endeavored to cheer myself up (if not them) by reading aloud in class S. J. Perelman's sublime parody "A Farewell to Omsk," fragments of which are always with me, such as the highly Dostoevskian portrayal of the tobacconist Pyotr Pyotrvitch:

> "Good afternoon, Afya Afyakievitch!" replied the shopkeeper warmly. He was the son of a former notary public attached to the household of Prince Grashkin and gave himself no few airs in consequence. Whilst speaking it was his habit to extract a greasy barometer from his waistcoat and consult it importantly, a trick he had learned from the Prince's barber. On seeing Afya Afyakievitch he skipped about nimbly, dusted off the counter, gave one of his numerous offspring a box on the ear, drank a cup of tea, and on the whole behaved like a man of the world who has affairs of moment occupying him.

Unfortunately, my class did not think this funny, and did not even enjoy the marvelous close of Perelman's sketch:

> "Don't take any flannel kopecks," said Afya gloomily. He dislodged a piece of horse-radish from his tie, shied it at a passing Nihilist, and slid forward into the fresh loam.

1

Dostoevsky had his own mode of humor, but he might not have appreciated Perelman either. *Crime and Punishment* is less apocalyptic than *The Brothers Karamazov*, but it is apocalyptic enough. It is also tendentious in the extreme, which is the point of Perelman's parody, but Dostoevsky is so great a tragedian that this does not matter. Raskolnikov is a powerful representation of the will demonized by its own strength, while Svidrigaylov is beyond that and stands on the border of a convincing phantasmagoria. Until the unfortunate epilogue, no other narrative fiction drives itself onwards with the remorseless strength of *Crime and Punishment*, truly a shot out of hell and into hell again. To have written a naturalistic novel that reads like a continuous nightmare is Dostoevsky's unique achievement.

Raskolnikov never does repent and change, unless we believe the epilogue, in which Dostoevsky himself scarcely believed. Despair causes his surrender to Porfiry, but even his despair never matches the fierce ecstasy he has achieved in violating all limits. He breaks what can be broken, and yet does not break himself. He cannot be broken, not because he has found any truth, objective or psychological, but because he has known, however momentarily, the nihilistic abyss, a Gnostic freedom of what is beyond our sense of being creatures in God's creation. Konstantin Mochulsky is surely right to emphasize that Raskolnikov never comes to believe in redemption, never rejects his theory of strength and power. His surrender, as Mochulsky says, "is not a sign of penitence but of pusillanimity." We end up with a pre-Christian tragic hero, ruined by blind fate, at least in his own vision. But this is about as unattractive as a tragic hero can be, because Raskolnikov comes too late in cultural history to seem a Prometheus rather than a bookish intellectual. In a Christian context, Prometheus assimilates to Satan, and Raskolnikov's pride begins to seem too Satanic for tragedy.

Raskolnikov hardly persuades us on the level of Dostoevsky's Christian polemic, but psychologically he is fearsomely persuasive. Power for Raskolnikov can be defined as the ability to kill someone else, anyone at all, rather than oneself. I meet Raskolnikov daily, though generally not in so extreme a form, in many young contemporaries who constitute what I would call the School of Resentment. Their wounded narcissism, turned against the self, might make them poets or critics; turned outward, against others, it makes them eminent unrest-inducers. Raskolnikov does not move our sympathy *for him*, but he impresses us with his uncompromising intensity.

Svidrigaylov may have been intended as Raskolnikov's foil, but he got away from Dostoevsky, and runs off with the book, even as old Karamazov nearly steals the greater work away from the extraordinary Dmitri. Raskolnikov is too pure a Promethean or devil to be interested in desire, unless the object of desire be metaphysical freedom and power. He is a kind of ascetic Gnostic, while Svidrigaylov is a libertine Gnostic, attempting to liberate the sparks upward. If Raskolnikov portrays the madness of the Promethean will, then Svidrigaylov is beyond the will, as he is beyond the still-religious affirmations of atheism. He lives (if that can be the right word) a negativity that Raskolnikov is too much himself to attain. Raskolnikov killed for his own sake, he tells Sonia, to test his own strength. Svidrigaylov is light years beyond that, on the way downwards and outwards into the abyss, his foremother and forefather.

The best of all murder stories, *Crime and Punishment* seems to me beyond praise and beyond affection. Dostoevsky doubtless would impress me even more than he does already if I could read Russian, but I would not like him any better. A vicious obscurantism inheres in the four great narratives, including *The Idiot* and *The Possessed*, and it darkens *Crime and Punishment*. Only *The Brothers Karamazov* transcends Dostoevsky's hateful ideology, because the Karamazovs sweep past the truths that the novelist continues to shout at us. Tolstoy did not think that Dostoevsky's final and apocalyptic novel was one of the summits of the genre, but then he liked to think of Dostoevsky as the Russian Harriet Beecher Stowe, and would have wanted old Karamazov to have resembled Simon Legree.

What seems to me strongest in Dostoevsky is the control of visionary horror he shares with Blake, an imaginative prophet with whom he has absolutely nothing else in common. No one who has read *Crime and Punishment* ever can forget Raskolnikov's murder of poor Lizaveta:

> There in the middle of the floor, with a big bundle in her arms, stood Lizaveta, as white as a sheet, gazing in frozen horror at her murdered sister and apparently without the strength to cry out. When she saw him run in, she trembled like a leaf and her face twitched spasmodically; she raised her hand as if to cover her mouth, but no scream came and she backed slowly away from him towards the corner, with her eyes on him in a fixed stare, but still without a sound, as though she had no breath left to cry out. He flung himself forward with the axe; her lips writhed pitifully, like those of a young child when it is just beginning to be frightened and stands ready to scream, with its eyes fixed on the object of its fear. The wretched Lizaveta was so simple, browbeaten, and utterly terrified that she did not even put up her arms to protect her face, natural and almost inevitable as the gesture would have been at this moment when the axe was brandished

immediately above it. She only raised her free left hand a little and slowly stretched it out towards him as though she were trying to push him away. The blow fell on her skull, splitting it open from the top of the forehead almost to the crown of the head, and felling her instantly. Raskolnikov, completely beside himself, snatched up her bundle, threw it down again, and ran to the entrance.

Nothing could be more painfully effective than: "She only raised her free left hand a little and slowly stretched it out towards him as though she were trying to push him away." We think of the horrible dream in which Raskolnikov sees a poor, lean, old mare beaten to death with a crowbar, and we may reflect upon Nietzsche's darkest insights: that pain creates memory, so that the pain is the meaning, and meaning is therefore painful. Dostoevsky was a great visionary and an exuberant storyteller, but there is something paradoxically nihilistic in his narrative visions. The sublime mode asks us to give up easier pleasures for more difficult pleasures, which is altogether an aesthetic request. Dostoevsky belongs not to the sublime genre, but to the harsher perspectives of the apocalyptic. He insists that we accept pains that transcend aesthetic limits. His authority at apocalypse is beyond question, but such authority also has its own aesthetic limits.

II

For a critic who cannot read Russian, *The Brothers Karamazov* needs considerable mediation, more perhaps than *War and Peace* or *Fathers and Sons*. Much of this mediation is provided by Victor Terras, in his admirable commentary *A Karamazov Companion*, to which I am indebted here.

Dostoevsky's final novel, completed only two months before his death, when he was nine months short of sixty, *The Brothers Karamazov* was intended as Dostoevsky's apocalypse. Its genre might best be called Scripture rather than novel or tragedy, saga or chronicle. Dostoevsky's scope is from Genesis to Revelation, with the Book of Job and the Gospel of John as the centers. Old Karamazov is a kind of Adam, dreadfully vital and vitalistically dreadful. His four sons resist allegorical reduction, but William Blake would have interpreted them as being his Four Zoas or living principles of fallen man, with Ivan as Urizen, Dmitri as Luvah, Alyosha as Los, and the bastard Smerdyakov as a very debased Tharmas. On the model of this rather Hermetic mythology, Ivan is excessively dominated by the anxieties of the skeptical and analytic intellect, while Dmitri is culpable for "reasoning from the loins in the unreal forms of Beulah's night" and so is a victim of his own overly sensual affective nature. The image of imaginative and spiritual salvation, Alyosha, is thus seen as the true Christian visionary, while the natural—all-too-natural—Smerdyakov represents the drives or instincts turned murderously against the father and against the self.

That there may be affinities between English Blake and Great Russian Dostoevsky is itself surprising and ought not to be magnified, since the differences between the two seers are far more serious than any parallels in mythic projection. Despite his extraordinary powers of characterization and representation, the Dostoevsky of *Karamazov* is essentially an obscurantist, and Blake would have judged him to have been a greatly exalted version of his own Smerdyakov. Tolstoy entertained outrageous moralizations about the proper modes and uses for literature, but, compared to the author of *The Brothers Karamazov*, Tolstoy will seem an Enlightened rationalist to a Western reader at the present time. Perhaps that is only to say that Dostoevsky is less universal than Tolstoy in spirit, less the Russian Homer and more the Russian Dante.

The Brothers Karamazov is frequently an outrageous narrative and evidently has strong parodistic elements. Its narrator is faceless; John Jones calls him "a crowd in trousers." His story is told with a sly artlessness, which suits a novel whose burden is that we are all sinful, for even holy Russia swarms with sin, with the universal desire, conscious and unconscious, to murder the father. Old Karamazov is a monster, but a heroic vitalist, fierce in his drive for women and for drink. Dostoevsky evidently did not much care for Ivan either, and no one could care for Smerdyakov. Yet all the Karamazovs burn with psychic energy, all are true sons of that terrible but exuberant father. Freud's essay "Dostoyevski and Parricide" (1928) should be supplemented by his *Totem and Taboo*, because the violent tyrant-father murdered by his sons in the Primal History Scene is akin to old Karamazov, who also wishes to appropriate all the women for himself.

Old Karamazov is actually just fifty-five, though ancient in debauchery. He could be judged a Falstaffian figure, not as Shakespeare wrote Falstaff, but as moralizing critics too frequently view the fat knight, forgetting his supreme wit, his joy in play, and his masterful insights into reality. If Falstaff had continued the decline we observe in *Henry IV, Part 2*, then he might have achieved the rancid vitality of the father of the Karamazovs. Fyodor Pavlovich's peculiar vice however is non-Falstaffian. Falstaff after all is not a father, despite his longing to make Hal his son. Old Karamazov is primarily a father, the parody indeed of a bad father, almost the Freudian primitive father of *Totem and Taboo*. Still, this buffoon and insane sensualist is a fool in a complex way, almost a Shakespearean fool, seeing through all impostures, his own included. Fyodor Pavlovich lies to keep in practice, but his lies generally work to expose more truth. He lives to considerable purpose, doubtless despite himself. The largest purpose, in one of Dostoevsky's terrible ironies, is to be the inevitable victim of patricide, of his four sons' revenge for their abused mothers.

The image of the father, for the reactionary Dostoevsky, is ultimately also the image of the Czar and of God. Why then did Dostoevsky risk the ghastly Fyodor Pavlovich as his testament's vision of the father? I can only surmise that Dostoevsky's motivation was Jobean. If Old Karamazov is to be our universal father, then by identifying with Dmitri, or Ivan, or Alyosha (no one identifies with Smerdyakov!), we assume their Jobean situation. If your faith can survive the torment of seeing the image of paternal authority in Karamazov, then you are as justified as Job. Reversing Kierkegaard and Nietzsche, Dostoevsky persuades us that if we haven't had a bad enough father, then it is necessary to invent one. Old Karamazov is an ancestor-demon rather than an ancestor-god, a darkness visible rather than a luminous shadow. You do not mourn his murder, but as a reader you certainly miss him when he is gone. Nor can you hate him the way you despise the hideous Rakitin. Again, I admire John Jones's emphasis:

> The old man's complicity in his own murder gets carried by the book's master metaphor. His house stinks. His life stinks. Yet his mystic complicity never quite hardens into the judgment that he deserves to die. His nature is too broad to allow that.

By "broad" Jones means simply just too alive to deserve to die, which is what I myself would judge. So rammed with life is old Karamazov that his murder is a sin against life, life depraved and corrupt, yet fierce life, life refusing death. Even Dmitri falls short of his father's force of desire. Strangely like Blake again, Dostoevsky proclaims that everything that lives is holy, though he does not share Blake's conviction that nothing or no one is holier than anything or anyone else.

In his *Notebooks*, Dostoevsky insisted that "we are all, to the last man, Fyodor Pavloviches," because in a new, original form "we are all nihilists." A reader, but for the intercessions of his superego, might like to find himself in Falstaff, but hardly in Fyodor Pavlovich. Yet the honest reader should, and does, and no one wants to be murdered. As an apocalypse, *The Brothers Karamazov* forces identification upon one. The father in each male among us is compelled to some uncomfortable recognition in Old Karamazov; the son in each can choose among the three attractive brothers (Zosima is hardly a possibility). It cannot be said that Dostoevsky does as well with women;

Grushenka and Katerina Ivanovna may divide male fantasy between them, but that is all. Dostoevsky does not match Tolstoy as a portrayer of women, let alone Shakespeare.

Much of the permanent fascination of *The Brothers Karamazov* invests itself in the extraordinary differences between Dmitri and Ivan, and in Ivan's two phantasmagorias, his "poem" of the Grand Inquisitor and his mad confrontation with the Devil. Dmitri, though he yields us no phantasmagorias, is more endless to meditation than his half-brother, Ivan. Dostoevsky evidently saw Dmitri as the archetypal Great Russian: undisciplined, human—all-too-human, lustful, capable of all extremes, but a man of deep feeling and compassion, and an intuitive genius, a poet of action, an authentic comedian of the spirit, and potentially a Christian. Ivan is his father's son in a darker sense; turned inward, his ravening intellect destroys a sense of other selves, and his perpetually augmenting inner self threatens every value that Dostoevsky seeks to rescue. If Dmitri is the exemplary Russian, then Ivan is the Western intellectual consciousness uneasily inhabiting the Russian soul, with murderous consequences that work themselves through in his parody, Smerdyakov.

The legend of the Grand Inquisitor has achieved a fame that transcends *The Brothers Karamazov* as a whole, hardly a result Dostoevsky could have endured, partly because Ivan's parable tells us nothing about Dmitri, who is the authentic center of the novel, and partly because, out of context, Ivan's prose poem can be mistaken for Dostoevsky's, which is *The Brothers Karamazov*. Ivan's legend is one that Dostoevsky rejects, and yet Ivan also, like Old Karamazov, is Dostoevsky, even if Dmitri is more of Dostoevsky. The Grand Inquisitor stamps out human freedom because humans are too weak to endure their own freedom. If Dostoevsky really intended Zosima to be his answer to the Inquisitor, then he erred badly. Zosima, to an American ear anyway, is a muddle, and his interpretation of the Book of Job is the weakest failure in the history of theodicy. What is least acceptable about the Book of Job, its tacked-on conclusion in which God gives Job a perfect new set of sons and daughters, every bit as good as the old, is saluted by Zosima as the height of holy wisdom. It is difficult to answer the Grand Inquisitor with such sublime idiocy.

But then the Grand Inquisitor speaks a sublime idiocy, despite the grand reputation that the Legend has garnered as an excerpt. Dostoevsky is careful to distance himself and us, with the highest irony, from Ivan's dubious rhetoric. The Inquisitor rants on for too long, and just does not frighten us enough; he is more Gothic than we can accept, just as Ivan's Devil is too much a confused projection of Ivan. To be effective, the legend of the Inquisitor should have been composed and told by Dmitri, but then *The Brothers Karamazov* would have been a different and even stronger novel.

Freud, for polemical and tendentious reasons, overrated *The Brothers Karamazov*, ranking it first among all novels ever written, close to Shakespeare in eminence, and finding the rather lurid legend of the Grand Inquisitor to be a peak of world literature. That latter judgment is clearly mistaken; the status of the novel among all novels whatsoever is perhaps a touch problematic. The book's enormous gusto is unquestionable; the Karamazov family, father and sons, sometimes seems less an image of life, a mimesis, and more a super-mimesis, an evocation of a more abundant life than representation ought to be able to portray. There cannot be a more intense consciousness than that of Dmitri in a novel; only a few figures elsewhere can match him. Doubtless he speaks for what Dostoevsky could not repress in himself: "If they drive God from the earth, we shall shelter Him underground." If you wish to read "God" there as the God of Abraham, Isaac, and Jacob, the God of Moses and Jesus, you are justified; you follow Dostoevsky's intention. I am willing to read "God," here and elsewhere, as the desire for the transcendental and extraordinary, or Dmitri's and Dostoevsky's desire for the completion of what was already transcendental and extraordinary in themselves.

The Hero's Monologic Discourse
and Narrational Discourse
in Dostoevsky's Early Novels

Dostoevsky began with the epistolary form, a type of discourse in which the speech of the letter-writer refracts the anticipated speech of the recipient. Apropos of *Poor Folk*, he writes to his brother:

> They [the public and the critics—M. B.] have become accustomed to seeing the author's mug in everything; I didn't show mine. And it doesn't even occur to them that Devushkin is speaking, and not I, and that Devushkin cannot speak in any other way. They find the novel long-winded, but there is not a superfluous word in it.
>
> (Letter of February 1, 1846)

In this novel the main characters, Makar Devushkin and Varenka Dob-roselova, do the speaking; the author merely distributes their words: his intentions are refracted in the words of the hero and the heroine. The epistolary form is a variant of the *Ich-Erzählung* (first-person narrative). Discourse in this genre is oriented on the anticipated reactions of an auditor (*double-voiced discourse*), and in the majority of cases it acts as the compositional surrogate of the author's voice, which is absent here (*the uni-directional variant* of double-voiced discourse). We shall see that the author's conception is very subtly and carefully refracted in the words of the hero-narrators, although the entire work is filled with both obvious and hidden parodies, with both obvious and hidden (authorial) polemics.

But for the present we are interested in examining Makar Devushkin's speech only as the monologic utterance of a hero, and not as the speech of

From *Dostoevsky and Gogol*, edited by Priscilla Meyer and Stephen Rudy. © 1979 by Ardis Publishers.

a narrator in an *Ich-Erzählung*, a function which it in fact performs here, since there are no other speakers besides the heroes. The speech of any narrator, employed by the author for the realization of his artistic plan, itself belongs to some specific type of discourse, apart from that type which is determined by its function as narration. Of what type is Devushkin's monologic utterance?

The epistolary form in and of itself does not predetermine the type of discourse which will be found in it. In general this form allows for broad verbal possibilities, but it is most suited to the *active type* of double-voiced discourse, which reflects *the speech act of another person*. A characteristic feature of the letter form is the writer's acute awareness of his interlocutor, the addressee to whom it is directed. The letter, like a line of dialogue, is addressed to a specific person, and it takes into account his possible reactions, his possible reply. It can do this more, or less, intensively. In Dostoevsky's work this attention to the absent interlocutor has an extremely intensive character.

In his first work Dostoevsky develops a style of speech, characteristic of his entire oeuvre, which is determined by the intense anticipation of the other person's speech act. The significance of this style in his subsequent work is enormous: the most important confessional self-revelations of his heroes are permeated by a hypersensitivity to the anticipated speech acts of others about them and to others' reactions to their own words about themselves. Not only the tone and style, but also the internal conceptual structure of these self-revelations is determined by the anticipation of another person's speech, from the reservations and loopholes which stem from Golyadkin's easily offended nature to the ethical and metaphysical loopholes of Ivan Karamazov. The "servile" variant of this style began to develop in *Poor Folk*—speech which seems to cringe with timidity and shame at the awareness of another's possible response, yet contains a stifled cry of defiance.

This self-conscious awareness is manifested above all in the halting speech and the reservations which interrupt it that are characteristic of this style.

> I live in the kitchen, or, more correctly speaking, here next to the kitchen is a little room (and I would like to point out that our kitchen is clean and bright, a very good one), a little nook, a humble little corner . . . that is, to put it even better, the kitchen is large, with three windows, and along one wall there is a partition, so it is as if there were another room, a supernumerary one; it is all roomy and convenient, and there is a window, and it is all—in a word, it is convenient. Well, so, this is my little corner. Well now, my dear, don't think that there is anything strange here,

some mysterious significance—Aha, he lives in the kitchen!—that is, you see, I do live in this room behind the partition, but that doesn't matter; I keep to myself, away from the others, I live in a small way, I live quietly. I have a bed, a table, a chest of drawers, a couple of chairs, an ikon on the wall. True, there are better apartments, perhaps even much better ones, but then convenience is the main thing; I live like this for convenience's sake, and don't go thinking that it is for any other reason.

(Letter of April 8)

After almost every word Devushkin takes a sideward glance at his absent interlocutor, he is afraid that she will think he is complaining, he tries in advance to destroy the impression which the news that he lives in the kitchen will create, he does not want to distress his interlocutor, etc. The repetition of words results from his desire to intensify their accent or to give them a new nuance in light of his interlocutor's possible reaction.

In the excerpt which we have quoted, the speech act reflected is the potential speech of the addressee, Varenka Dobroselova. In the majority of instances Makar Devushkin's speech about himself is determined by the reflected speech of the "other person, the stranger." Here is how he defines this stranger. He asks Varenka Dobroselova:

And what will you do out there among strangers? Don't you know yet what a stranger is? . . . No, you've asked me a question, so I'll tell you what a stranger is. I know him, my dear, I know him well; I've had to eat his bread. He is mean, Varenka, mean, he is so mean, your poor little heart won't be able to stand the way he torments it with his reproaches and rebukes and his evil glance.

(Letter of July 1)

The poor, but "ambitious" man, such as Makar Devushkin, in keeping with Dostoevsky's intention, constantly feels other people's "evil glance" directed toward him, a glance which is either reproachful or—perhaps even worse in his eyes—mocking (for the heroes of the prouder type the worst glance of all is the compassionate one). Devushkin's speech cringes under this glance. He, like the hero from the underground, is constantly listening in on other people's speech about him.

The poor man, he is demanding: he looks at God's world differently, and he looks askance at every passerby, he casts a troubled gaze about him and he listens closely to every word—aren't they talking about him?

(Letter of August 1)

Makar Devushkin's sideward glance at the speech of the other who is
socially foreign to him determines not only the style and tone of his speech,
but also his very manner of thinking and experiencing, of seeing and
understanding himself and the little world which surrounds him. In Dostoevsky's artistic world there is always a profound organic bond between the
superficial elements of a character's manner of speech, his way of expressing
himself, and the ultimate foundations of his weltanschauung. A person's every
act reveals him in his totality. The orientation of one person to another person's speech and consciousness is, in essence, the basic theme of all of Dostoevsky's works. The hero's attitude toward himself is inseparably bound up with
his attitude towards the other and with the attitude of the other toward him.
His consciousness of self is constantly perceived against the background of
the other's consciousness of him—"I for myself" against the background of
"I for the other." For this reason the hero's speech about himself takes shape
under the continuous influence of the other's speech about him.

This theme develops in various forms in various works, with varying
content and on various spiritual levels. In *Poor Folk* the poor man's self-
awareness unfolds against the background of a socially foreign consciousness
of him. His self-affirmation has the sound of a continuous hidden polemic
or hidden dialogue with the other, the stranger, on the subject of himself.
In Dostoevsky's first works this is expressed rather simply and directly—the
dialogue has not yet been internalized, become part of the very atoms of
thought and experience, so to speak. The heroes' world is still small, and
they have not yet become ideologists. Their very social servility makes their
inner sideward glance and inner polemic direct and clear-cut, without the
complex internal loopholes which grow into the whole ideological construc-
tions that we see in Dostoevsky's final works. But the profoundly dialogic
and polemic nature of self-awareness and self-affirmation are already revealed
here with complete clarity.

> The other day in a private conversation Yevstafy Ivanovich said
> that the most important civic virtue is the ability to make a lot
> of money. He was joking (I know he was joking), it was a moral
> lesson that one shouldn't be a burden to anyone else, but I'm not
> a burden to anyone! I have my own piece of bread; true, it is a
> modest piece of bread, sometimes it's even stale, but it is mine,
> I win it with my own labor and use it lawfully and blamelessly.
> But what can one do? I know myself that my copying is not much
> of a job, but, still, I am proud of it: I work, I spill my sweat.
> Well, and really, so what if I just copy! Is it a sin to copy, or
> something? "He just copies! . . ." What is so dishonorable about

that? I realize now that I am needed, that I am indispensible, and that I shouldn't let their nonsense disturb me. Well, so I'm a rat, if they find some resemblance! But that rat is necessary, that rat accomplishes something, they're all supported by that rat, and that rat will get its reward—that's the kind of rat it is! But enough on this subject, my dear; I didn't want to talk about that, I just got a little carried away. All the same, it is nice to do oneself justice now and then.

(Letter of June 12)

Makar Devushkin's self-awareness is revealed in an even sharper polemic when he recognizes himself in Gogol's "The Overcoat"; he perceives it as the other's speech about him personally, and he seeks to destroy polemically that speech as being inapplicable to him.

But let us now take a closer look at the structure of this "speech with a sideward glance." Already in the first excerpt we quoted, where Devushkin anxiously informs Varenka Dobroselova of his new room, we notice the peculiar verbal counterpoint determining the syntactic and accentual structure of his speech. The other's replies as it were wedge their way into his speech, and although they are in reality not there, their influence brings about a radical accentual and syntactic reorganization of that speech. This other line of dialogue is not actually present, but casts a shadow on his speech, and that shadow is real. But sometimes the other's reply, in addition to its influence on the accentual and syntactic structure, leaves behind a word or two, and sometimes a whole sentence, in Makar Devushkin's speech:

Well now, my dear, don't think that there is anything strange here, some mysterious significance—Aha, he lives in the *kitchen*!—that is, you see, I do live in this room behind the partition, but that doesn't matter.

(Letter of April 8)

The word "kitchen" bursts into Devushkin's speech from out of the other's possible speech as it is anticipated by him. This word is presented with the other's accent, which Devushkin polemically exaggerates somewhat. He does not accept this accent, although he cannot help recognizing its power, and he tries to evade it by means of all sorts of reservations, partial concessions and extenuations, which distort the structure of his speech. The smooth surface of his speech is furrowed by ripples fanning out from the other's word, which has taken root in that speech. Except for this word, which obviously belongs to the other's speech and carries the accent of that speech, the majority of words in the quoted passage are chosen by the speaker from two points

of view simultaneously: as he himself understands them and wants others
to understand them, and as others might in fact understand them. Here the
other's accent is merely noted, but it already gives rise to reservations or hesita-
tions in his speech.

The embedding of words and especially of accents from the other's speech
in Makar Devushkin's speech is even more marked and obvious in the second
of the passages which we have quoted. Here the word containing the other's
polemically exaggerated accent is even enclosed in quotation marks: "He just
copies!" In the immediately preceding lines the word "copy" is repeated three
times. In each of these three instances the other's potential accent is present
in the word "copy," but it is suppressed by Devushkin's own accent; however,
it becomes constantly stronger, until it finally breaks through and takes on
the form of the direct speech of the other. Thus we are presented here with
the gradations of the gradual intensification of the other's accent: "I know
myself that my *copying* is not much of a job . . . [a reservation follows—
M. B.]. Well, and really, so what if I just *copy*! Is it a sin to *copy* or something?
'He just COPIES!'" We have indicated the other's accent, which gradually
grows stronger and finally completely dominates the word enclosed in quotation marks. Even so, in this last, obviously foreign word Devushkin's own
voice is present, too, as he polemically exaggerates the other's accent. To
the degree that the other's accent is intensified, Devushkin's counter-accent
is also intensified.

We can thus descriptively define all the phenomena which we have
discussed: the hero's self-awareness was penetrated by the other's consciousness of him, and the other's speech about him was injected into what
the hero had to say about himself; the other's consciousness of him and the
other's speech about him give rise to specific phenomena which determine
the development of the theme of Devushkin's self-awareness, its breaking
points, loopholes and protests, on the one hand, and the hero's speech with
its accentual counterpoint, syntactic breaking points, repetitions, reservations
and prolixity, on the other.

Or we can give another definition and explanation of the same
phenomena: let us imagine that two lines of very intense dialogue—a speech
and a counter-speech—instead of following one after the other and proceeding
from two different mouths, are superimposed one on the other and merge
into a *single* utterance coming from a single mouth. These lines of dialogue
move in opposite directions and collide with one another; therefore their
overlapping and merging into a single utterance produce a tense counterpoint.
The collision of entire, integral lines of dialogue is transformed within a new
utterance (which results from the merging of those lines) into a sharp counter-

point of voices which are contradictory in every detail and atom. The dialogic collision has been internalized into the subtlest structural elements of speech (and correspondingly—of consciousness).

The passage which we have quoted could be roughly paraphrased in the following crude dialogue between Makar Devushkin and the other, the "stranger":

> STRANGER: One must know how to make a lot of money. One shouldn't be a burden to anyone. But you are a burden to others.
>
> MAKAR DEVUSHKIN: I'm not a burden to anyone. I've got my own piece of bread.
>
> S.: But what a piece it is! Today it's there, and tomorrow it's gone. And most likely a stale piece, at that!
>
> M. D.: True, it is a modest piece of bread, sometimes it's even stale, but it is mine. I win it with my own labor and use it lawfully and blamelessly.
>
> S.: But what kind of labor! All you do is copy. You're not capable of anything else.
>
> M. D.: Well, what can one do! I know myself that my copying is not much of a job, but, still, I am proud of it!
>
> S.: Oh, there's something to be proud of, all right! Copying! It's disgraceful!
>
> M. D.: Well, and really, so what if I just copy! . . . etc.

It is as if this statement of Devushkin's about himself resulted from the overlapping and merging of the lines of this dialogue into a single voice.

Of course this imagined dialogue is terribly primitive, just as the content of Devushkin's consciousness is still primitive. For he is, in the final analysis, an Akaky Akakievich who is enlightened by a self-awareness and who has acquired speech and elaborated a "style." But on the other hand, as a result of its primitiveness and crudeness, the formal structure of his self-awareness and self-expression is extremely clear-cut and apparent. That is why we are examining it in such detail. All of the essential self-revelations of Dostoevsky's later heroes could also be turned into dialogues, since they all, as it were, arose out of two merged lines of dialogue, but in them the counterpoint of voices goes so deep, into such subtle elements of thought and speech, that to turn them into an obvious and crude dialogue, as we have just done with Devushkin's self-revelation, is, of course, completely impossible.

The phenomena which we have examined, produced by the speech of the other within the hero's speech, are in *Poor Folk* presented in the stylistic accoutrements of the speech of a Petersburg petty clerk. The structural characteristics of "speech with a sideward glance," of speech which is internally dialogic and conceals a hidden polemic, are refracted here in the strictly and skillfully sustained sociotypical verbal manner of Devushkin. For this reason all of these phenomena of language—reservations, repetitions, diminutives, diverse particles and interjections—could not appear in the same form in the mouths of other heroes of Dostoevsky, who belong to different social worlds. The same phenomena appear in a different sociotypical and individually characteristic form of speech. But their essence remains the same: the crossing and intersection in every element of a character's consciousness and speech of two consciousnesses, two points of view, two evaluations— the intra-atomic counterpoint of two voices.

Golyadkin's speech is constructed within the same sociotypical verbal milieu, but it has a different individually characteristic manner. The peculiar nature of consciousness and speech which we have examined above is found in *The Double* in a more extreme and clear-cut form than in any other of Dostoevsky's works. The tendencies which were already contained in the character of Makar Devushkin are here developed with extraordinary boldness and consistency to their conceptual limits on the basis of the same deliberately primitive, simple and crude material.

Dostoevsky himself, in a letter to his brother written while he was working on *The Double*, gave a parodic stylization of Golyadkin's speech and conceptual system. As is the case in any parodic stylization, the basic characteristics and tendencies of Golyadkin's speech are plainly and crudely made visible here.

> *Yakov Petrovich Golyadkin* holds his own completely. He's a terrible scoundrel and there's no approaching him; he refuses to move forward, pretending that, you see, he's not ready yet, that for the present he's on his own, he's all right, nothing is the matter, but that if it comes to that, then he can do that, too, why not, what's to prevent it? He's just like everyone else, he's nothing special, just like everyone else. What's it to him! He's a scoundrel, a terrible scoundrel! He'll never agree to end his career before the middle of November. He's already just spoken with his Excellency, and he just may (and why shouldn't he) announce his retirement.
> (Letter to M. M. Dostoevsky, Oct. 8, 1845)

As we shall see, *The Double* itself is narrated in this same style, parodying the hero. But we shall turn to the narration later.

The influence of the other's speech on Golyadkin's speech is completely obvious. We immediately feel that his speech, like Devushkin's, relates not just to itself and its referential object. However, Golyadkin's interrelationship with the speech and the consciousness of the other is somewhat different from Devushkin's. Therefore the phenomena in Golyadkin's style which result from the other's speech are also of a different sort.

Golyadkin's speech above all seeks to simulate total independence from the other's speech: "He's on his own, he's all right." This simulation of independence and indifference also leads to endless repetitions, reservations and prolixity, but here directed to himself, and not outside himself to the other: he tries to convince, reassure and comfort himself, playing the role of the other in relation to himself. Golyadkin's self-comforting dialogues with himself are the most widespread phenomenon in *The Double*. Along with the simulation of indifference goes another attitude to the other's speech: the desire to hide from it, to avoid calling attention to oneself, to get lost in the crowd, to become inconspicuous: "He's just like everyone else, he's nothing special, just like everyone else." But he is actually trying to convince not himself, but the other, of this. Finally, the third attitude to the other's speech involves Golyadkin's yielding to it, subordinating himself to it, and submissively adopting it, as if he himself were of the same opinion and sincerely agreed with it: "If it comes to that, then he can do that, too, why not, what's to prevent it?"

These are the three general lines in Golyadkin's orientation, and they are complicated by other secondary, but rather important, ones. Each of these three lines in and of itself gives rise to very complex phenomena in Golyadkin's consciousness and in his speech.

We shall concentrate above all on his simulation of independence and composure.

As we have said, the pages of *The Double* are full of the hero's dialogues with himself. One might say that Golyadkin's entire inner life develops dialogically. We quote two examples of such dialogues:

"But, still, will it be right?" continued our hero, alighting from the coach near the entrance to a certain five-storied house on the Liteynaya, beside which he had ordered his carriage to halt. "Will it be right? Will it be proper? Will it be appropriate? But really why all the fuss," he continued as he climbed the steps, catching his breath and checking the thumping of his heart, which was in the habit of thumping on other people's stairways. "Why the fuss? I'm on my own business, there's nothing reprehensible here at all.

. . . I would be silly to hide myself. I'll just pretend that nothing's
the matter, that I just happened by. . . . He'll see that everything's
as it should be."

(chap. 1)

The second example of interior dialogue is much more complex and
pointed. It takes place after the appearance of Golyadkin's double, i.e. after
the second voice has become objectified for him within his own field of vision.

Mr. Golyadkin's delight thus expressed itself, though at the same
time something was still tickling in his head, not exactly melancholy, but now and then it tugged so at his heart that he was
almost inconsolable. "Still and all, we'll wait until morning before
rejoicing. But really, why all the fuss? Well, we'll think it over,
we'll see. Well, let's think it over, my young friend, let's think
it over. Well, in the first place, he's a person just like you, exactly
the same. Well, what does it matter? Should I cry about it or
something, just because he's a person like that? What's it to me?
It doesn't involve me; I'll go my merry way, and that'll be all there
is to it! That's the way he wants it, and that's all there is to it!
Let him do his job! Well, it's a miracle and an oddity, they say
that there are Siamese twins. . . . Well, but why do they have
to be Siamese? Let's assume that they are twins, but great men
have sometimes been odd-looking, too. It's even known from
history that the famous Suvorov crowed like a rooster. . . . Well,
yes, that was for political reasons; and great generals . . . but
what are generals, anyway? I'm on my own, that's all there is to
it, I don't need anybody, and in my innocence I have nothing but
contempt for the enemy. I'm not an intriguer, and I'm proud of
it. I'm pure, I'm straightforward, orderly, pleasant, and gentle."

(chap. 6)

The first question to arise is that of the function in Golyadkin's life of
this dialogue with himself. The answer can be briefly formulated thus: *the
dialogue allows him to substitute his own voice for the voice of the other.*

The function of Golyadkin's second voice as a substitute is felt
everywhere. Without understanding this it is impossible to understand his
interior dialogues. Golyadkin addresses himself as if addressing another person ("my young friend"), he praises himself as only another person could,
he verbally caresses himself with tender familiarity: "Yakov Petrovich, my
dear fellow, you little Golyadka, you—you have just the right name!" and
he reassures and comforts himself with the authoritative tone of an older,

more confident person. But this second voice of Golyadkin's, confident and calmly self-satisfied, cannot possibly merge with his first voice, the uncertain, timid one; the dialogue cannot turn into the integral and confident monologue of a single Golyadkin. Moreover, that second voice is to such a degree unable to merge with the first one and feels so threateningly independent, that teasing, mocking, treacherous tones begin to appear in place of comforting, reassuring ones. With amazing tact and art, in a way almost imperceptible to the reader, Dostoevsky transfers Golyadkin's second voice from his interior dialogue to the narration itself: it takes on the sound of the voice of the narrator. But we shall speak of the narration a bit later.

Golyadkin's second voice must make up for the fact that he receives too little recognition from other people. Golyadkin wants to get by without such recognition, to get by on his own, so to speak. But this "on his own" inevitably takes on the form "you and I, my friend Golyadkin," i.e. it takes on the form of a dialogue. In fact Golyadkin lives only in the other, he lives by his reflection in the other: "will it be proper," "will it be appropriate?" And this question is always answered from the possible, conjectured point of view of the other: Golyadkin *will pretend* that nothing is the matter, that he just happened by, and the other will see "that everything's as it should be." Everything depends on the reaction of the other, on his speech and his answer. The confidence of Golyadkin's second voice cannot completely possess him and actually take the place of an actual other person. The other's speech is the most important thing for him.

> Although Mr. Golyadkin said all of these things [about his independence—M. B.] as clearly and confidently as could be, weighing and calculating every word for the surest effect, he was now looking uneasily, very uneasily, most uneasily at Krestyan Ivanovich. He was all eyes, and he timidly awaited Krestyan Ivanovich's answer with annoying, melancholy impatience.
>
> (chap. 2)

In the second quoted excerpt of interior dialogue the function of the second voice as a substitute is completely obvious. But in addition, a third voice appears here, the direct voice of the other, which interrupts the second, the merely substitute voice. Thus we have here phenomena which are completely analogous to those which we analyzed in Devushkin's speech—the other's words and words which partly belong to the other, with the corresponding accentual counterpoint:

> Well, it's a miracle and an oddity, they say that there are Siamese twins. . . . Well, but why do they have to be Siamese? Let's assume

that they are twins, but great men have sometimes been odd-looking, too. It's even known from history that the great Suvorov crowed like a rooster. . . . Well, yes, that was for political reasons: and great generals . . . but what are generals?

(chap. 6)

Everywhere, but especially in those places where ellipses appear, the anticipated reactions of others wedge themselves in. This passage, too, could be elaborated in the form of a dialogue, but here the dialogue is much more complex. While in Devushkin's speech a single, integral voice polemicized with the "other," here there are two voices: one is confident, too confident, and the other is too timid, it gives in to everything, capitulating totally.

Golyadkin's second voice—the one which serves as a substitute for that of another person, his first voice—the one which hides itself from the other's speech ("I'm like everyone else, I'm all right"), then gives in to it ("but if that's the case, then I'm prepared"), and finally the voice of the other which sounds constantly within him, are interrelated in such a complex way that they provide sufficient material for the entire intrigue and permit the whole novel to be constructed on them alone. The actual event, namely the unsuccessful courtship of Klara Olsufievna, and all the attendant circumstances are in fact not represented in the novel: they serve merely as the stimulus which sets the inner voices in motion, they merely intensify and make immediate the inner conflict which is the real object of representation in the novel.

Except for Golyadkin and his double, none of the characters takes any actual part whatever in the plot, which unfolds totally within the bounds of Golyadkin's self-awareness; the other characters merely provide the raw material, the fuel, as it were, necessary for the intense work of that self-awareness. The external, intentionally obscure plot (everything of importance has taken place before the novel begins) also serves as the barely discernible skeleton of Golyadkin's inner plot. The novel relates how Golyadkin wanted to get along without the consciousness of the other and without recognition by the other, how he wanted to avoid the other and to assert his own self, and what resulted therefrom. Dostoevsky intended *The Double* to be a "confession" (not in the personal sense, of course), i.e. the representation of an event which occurs within the bounds of the character's self-awareness. *The Double* is the *first dramatized confession* among Dostoevsky's works.

Thus at the basis of the plot lies Golyadkin's attempt, in view of the total non-recognition of his personality on the part of others, to find himself a substitute for the other. Golyadkin plays at being an independent person; his consciousness plays at being confident and self-sufficient. The new, violent collision with the other during the party when Golyadkin is publicly devastated intensifies the split in his personality. Golyadkin's second voice overexerts itself in a desperate simulation of self-sufficiency, in order to save face. Golyadkin's second voice cannot merge with him; on the contrary, the treacherous tones of ridicule grow louder and louder in it. It provokes and teases Golyadkin, it casts off his mask. The double appears. The inner conflict is dramatized; Golyadkin's intrigue with the double begins.

The double speaks in the words of Golyadkin himself, bringing in no new words or tones. At first he pretends to be a cringing, capitulating Golyadkin. When Golyadkin brings the double home with him, the latter looks and behaves like the first, uncertain voice in Golyadkin's interior dialogue ("will it be appropriate, will it be proper," etc.):

> The guest [the double—M. B.] was, obviously, extremely embarrassed, he was very timid, he submissively followed his host's every movement, he tried to catch his glances in order, so it seemed, to divine his thoughts from them. All of his gestures expressed something abased, downtrodden and terrified, so that, if the comparison will be permitted, in that moment he bore a fair resemblance to a person who, for lack of his own clothes, has put on someone else's: the sleeves crawl up his arms and the waist comes almost up to his neck, and he is constantly either straightening the tiny vest, shuffling sideways and getting out of the way, trying to hide somewhere, or glancing at people's faces and listening carefully to hear if they are talking about him or laughing at him or are ashamed for him—the fellow grows red, the fellow is flustered, and his pride suffers.
>
> (chap. 7)

This is a characterization of the cringing, self-effacing Golyadkin. The double also speaks in the tones and style of Golyadkin's first voice. The part of the second—the confident and tenderly reassuring—voice in relation to the double is played by Golyadkin himself, who this time as it were merges completely with this voice:

> "You and I, Yakov Petrovich, shall live like a fish with water, like blood brothers; we, my friend, shall be crafty, we together shall be crafty; we shall think up intrigues to spite them, to spite them we shall think up intrigues. And don't you trust any of them. Because I know you, Yakov Petrovich, and I understand your character: you'll go and tell everthing, you're a truthful soul! You must keep away from all of them, old boy."
>
> (chap. 7)

But subsequently the roles change: the treacherous double takes over the tone of Golyadkin's second voice, parodically exaggerating its tender familiarity. Already at their next meeting at the office the double takes on this tone and sustains it to the end of the novel; now and then he himself emphasizes the identity of his expressions with the words of Golyadkin (i.e. the ones Golyadkin said during their first conversation). During one of their meetings at the office the double, familiarly poking Golyadkin, "with the most venomous and broadly suggestive smile, said to him: "Oh no you don't Yakov Petrovich, old boy, oh no you don't! You and I'll be crafty, Yakov Petrovich, we'll be crafty' " (chap. 8). Or a little later, before their face-to-face confrontation in the café:

> "Well, so then, as you say, my good fellow," said Mr. Golyadkin Jr., getting out of the droshky and shamelessly patting our hero on the shoulder, "you're such a buddy; for you, Yakov Petrovich, I'd go through thick and thin (as you, Yakov Petrovich, once justly saw fit to remark). He is a rascal, though, he'll do to you whatever comes into his head!"
>
> (chap. 11)

This transferral of words from one mouth to another, in which their tone and ultimate meaning is changed, while their content remains the same, is one of Dostoevsky's basic devices. He causes his heroes to recognize themselves, their idea, their own speech, their orientation, and their gesture in another person, in whom all of these manifestations take on a different integral and ultimate meaning and a different sound, the sound of parody or ridicule.

As we have said, almost all of Dostoevsky's major heroes have a partial double in another person or even in several other people (Stavrogin and Ivan Karamazov). In his last work Dostoevsky again returned to the device of fully embodying the second voice, though on a more profound and subtle basis. In its externally formal plan Ivan Karamazov's dialogue with the devil is analogous to the interior dialogues which Golyadkin carries on with himself and with his double; despite the dissimilarity in situation and in ideological content, in both instances essentially the same artistic problem is being solved.

Thus Golyadkin's intrigue with his double develops as a dramatized crisis of self-awareness, as a dramatized confession. The action does not go beyond the bounds of his self-awareness since the characters are merely detached elements of that self-awareness. The actors are the three voices into which Golyadkin's voice and consciousness have dissociated: his "I for myself," which cannot do without the existence of the other and the other's recognition; his fictitious "I for the other" (reflection in the other), i.e. Golyadkin's second substitute-voice; and finally, the voice of the other which does not recognize Golyadkin, and which at the same time has no real existence outside him, since there are no other characters of equal stature in the work. (Other equal consciousnesses appear only in the big novels.) The result is a peculiar mystery play or, more precisely, a morality play, in which the actors are not whole people, but rather the spiritual forces battling within them, a morality play, however, devoid of any formalism or abstract allegoricalness.

But who tells the story in *The Double*? What is the position of the narrator and what is his voice like?

In the narration too we do not find a single element which goes beyond the bounds of Golyadkin's self-awareness, a single word or a single tone which could not be part of his interior dialogue with himself or of his dialogue with his double. The narrator picks up Golyadkin's words and thoughts, the words of his *second voice*, intensifies the teasing, mocking tones present in them, and in these tones depicts Golyadkin's every act, gesture and movement. We have already mentioned that Golyadkin's second voice, by means of imperceptible transitions, merges with the voice of the narrator; the impression is created that *the narration is dialogically addressed to Golyadkin himself*, it rings in his ears as the taunting voice of another person, the voice of his double, although formally the narration is addressed to the reader.

This is how the narrator describes Golyadkin's behavior at the most fateful moment in his adventures, when he tries to crash the ball given by Olsufy Ivanovich:

> We should better turn our attention to Mr. Golyadkin, the true and only hero of this our most veracious story.
>
> At the moment he is, to put it mildly, in a very strange situation. He, ladies and gentlemen, is also here, that is he is not at the ball, but he is almost at the ball; he, ladies and gentlemen, is all right; he may be on his own, but at this moment he is on a somewhat less than straight and narrow path; he is now—it seems strange even to say it—he is now standing in a passageway on the back stairs of Olsufy Ivanovich's house. But it's all right that he is standing here, it is nothing special. He is, ladies and gentlemen, standing in a corner, jammed into a little space, if not a very warm one, at least very dark, hiding partly behind a huge cabinet and some old screens, in the middle of all sorts of rubbish, trash and junk, waiting for the proper time, and at the moment just observing the general course of events in the capa-

city of a detached observer. He is, ladies and gentlemen, just observing now; but, ladies and gentlemen, he, too, could make an entrance . . . why shouldn't he make an entrance? He only has to step out, and he will make his entrance, and make it very adroitly, at that.

(chap. 4)

In the structure of this narration we observe the counterpoint of two voices, the same kind of merging of two lines of dialogue that we observed already in Makar Đevushkin's utterances. But here the roles have been changed; here it is as if the other's line of dialogue has swallowed up the hero's. The narration glitters with Golyadkin's own words: "He's all right," "He's on his own," etc. But the narrator gives these words an intonation of ridicule, ridicule and in part reproach, directed at Golyadkin himself and constructed in such a form as to touch his sore spots and provoke him. This mocking narration imperceptibly infiltrates the speech of Golyadkin himself. The question "why shouldn't he make an entrance?" belongs to Golyadkin himself, but it is spoken in the teasing, egging-on intonation of the narrator. But this intonation, too, is not in essence foreign to Golyadkin's own consciousness. All of these things could ring in his own head, as his second voice. Actually, the author could insert quotation marks at any point without changing the tone, the voice or the construction of the sentence.

Somewhat further on he does precisely that:

So, ladies and gentlemen, he is waiting quietly, now, and has been doing so for exactly two-and-one-half hours. And why shouldn't he wait? Villèle himself waited. "But what does Villèle have to do with it?" thought Mr. Golyadkin. "There's no Villèle here! But what should I do now . . . should I up and make my appearance? Ach, you nobody, you."

(chap. 4)

But why not insert quotation marks two sentences earlier, before the words "And why shouldn't," or still earlier, changing "So, ladies and gentlemen, he . . ." to "Golyadkin, old boy," or some other form of Golyadkin addressing himself? The quotation marks are, of course, not inserted at random. They are inserted in such a way as to make the transition particularly subtle and imperceptible. Villèle's name appears in the narrator's last sentence and in the hero's first. Golyadkin's words seem to continue the narration without interruption and to answer it in an interior dialogue. "Villèle himself waited." " 'But what does Villèle have to do with it?' " These are in fact lines from Golyadkin's interior dialogue with himself which have become separated, one going into the narration and the other remaining with Golyadkin. This is the reverse of the phenomenon which we observed earlier: the merging in counterpoint of two voices. But the result is the same: a double-voiced construction in counterpoint with all the accompanying phenomena. And the arena of action is the same: a single self-awareness. The difference is that this consciousness is ruled by the speech of the other which has taken up residence in it.

We shall quote another example with the same kind of vacillating border between the narration and the hero's speech. Golyadkin has made up his mind and at last entered the hall where the ball is going on; he appears before Klara Olsufievna:

> Without the slightest doubt, without batting an eye, he would at this moment have been most happy to fall through a hole in the earth; but what's done is done. . . . What could he do? "If it doesn't work out—stand firm; if it does—hold on. Mr. Golyadkin was, naturally, no intriguer, nor a master at polishing the parquet with his boots. . . ." So it happened. In addition, the Jesuits somehow had a hand in the affair. . . . Mr. Golyadkin was, however, in no mood for them!
>
> (chap. 4)

This passage is interesting because it contains no direct speech belonging to Mr. Golyadkin, and therefore there is no basis for the quotation marks. The portion of the narration included here in quotation marks was apparently mistakenly set off by the editor. Dostoevsky probably set off only the proverb, "If it doesn't work, stand firm; if it does, hold on." The following sentence is given in the third person, although it obviously belongs to Golyadkin himself. Further on, the pauses indicated by ellipses also belong to Golyadkin's inner speech. According to their accents, the sentences preceding and following these ellipses are related to one another as lines in an interior dialogue. The two adjacent sentences concerning the Jesuits are quite analogous to the above-quoted sentences about Villèle, which were set off by quotation marks.

Finally, one more excerpt in which, perhaps, the opposite mistake has crept in—quotation marks have been omitted where, grammatically, they should have been inserted. Golyadkin, having been ejected from the ball, runs home in a snowstorm and meets a passerby who later turns out to be his double:

> Not that he was afraid that he was a dangerous person, but then, perhaps. . . . "Who knows who this fellow is, out so late," flashed through Mr. Golyadkin's mind. "Maybe he's just out late like

I am, but then maybe he's not here for no reason, maybe he has
a purpose, to cross my path and bump into me."

(chap. 5)

Here the ellipsis serves as a divider between the narration and Golyadkin's
direct inner speech, which is given in the first person ("*my path*," "*bump
into me*"). But the two are so closely merged here that one really does not
want to put in the quotation marks. This sentence must be read as a sentence
which contains a single voice, although this voice is internally dialogized.
The transition from the narration to the hero's speech is executed with amazing success: we feel, as it were, a wave of a single current of speech which
carries us, with no dams or barriers, from the narration into the hero's soul,
and from it back into the narration; we feel that we are, in essence, moving
within the circle of a single consciousness.

It would be possible to cite many more examples proving that the narration is a direct continuation and development of Golyadkin's second voice
and that it is dialogically addressed to the hero, but the examples which we
have cited are sufficient. Thus the entire work is constructed as an interior
dialogue of three voices within the bounds of a single dissociated consciousness. Every essential element of the work lies in the point of intersection of these three voices and of their sharp, agonizing counterpoint. To make
use of our image, we can say that, while this is not yet polyphony, it is no
longer homophony. One and the same word, idea, phenomenon passes
through three voices, and has a different sound in each of them. One and
the same complex of words, tones and inner orientations passes through
Golyadkin's own speech, through the narrator's speech, and through the
speech of the double; these three voices are situated face to face and speak
not about one another, but with one another. The three voices sing the same
song, but not in unison—each has its own part.

But these three voices have not yet become completely independent, real
voices, they are not yet three full-fledged consciousnesses. That takes place
only in Dostoevsky's big novels. In *The Double*, monologic discourse, which
relates only to itself and its referential object, is not present. Every word is
dialogically dissociated, every word contains a counterpoint of voices, but
the genuine dialogue of unmerged consciousnesses which appears later in the
big novels is here not yet present. The rudiments of counterpoint are already
here: it is hinted at in the very structure of discourse. The analyses we have
made are, as it were, already contrapuntal analyses (figuratively speaking,
of course). But this counterpoint has not yet gone beyond the bounds of
monological material.

The provoking, mocking voice of the narrator and the voice of the double ring relentlessly in Golyadkin's ears. The narrator shouts his very own words and thoughts in his ear, but in a different, a hopelessly foreign, hopelessly censorious and mocking tone. This second voice is present in every one of Dostoevsky's heroes, but as we have said, in his last novel it again takes on the form of independent existence. The devil shouts Ivan Karamazov's own words in his ear in a mocking commentary on his decision to confess in court, repeating his intimate thoughts in a foreign tone. We shall not discuss Ivan's actual dialogue with the devil, since we will concern ourselves with the principles of the genuine dialogue later on. But we shall quote the story which Ivan excitedly relates to Alyosha immediately after his dialogue with the devil. Its structure is analogous to the structure of *The Double* as we have analyzed it. The same principle of the combination of voices is present here, though here everything is deeper and more complex. In this story Ivan passes his own personal thoughts and decisions through two voices simultaneously, he communicates them in two different tonalities. In the quoted excerpt we shall omit Alyosha's replies, since his real voice does not yet fit into our scheme. For the moment we are interested only in the intra-atomic counterpoint of voices and their combination only within the bounds of a single dissociated consciousness (i.e. a microdialogue).

> "He teased me! And cleverly, you know, cleverly: 'Conscience! What is conscience? I create it myself. Why do I torment myself? Out of habit. Out of a universal human habit seven thousand years old. When we get out of the habit, we will be gods.' That's what he said, that's what he said! . . .
>
> "Yes, but he is evil. He laughed at me. He was insolent, Alyosha," said Ivan with an offended shudder. "And he slandered me, he slandered me in many ways. He lied about me to my face. 'Oh, you are going to perform an heroic deed of virtue, you are going to announce that you killed your father, that you incited the lackey to kill your father. . . .'
>
> "That's what he says, he, and he knows it. 'You are going to perform an heroic deed of virtue, but you do not believe in virtue—that is what torments and enrages you, that is why you are so vindictive.' He told me these things about myself, and he knows what he is talking about. . . .
>
> "No, he knows how to torture, he is cruel," continued Ivan, not listening. "I always had the feeling I knew why he was coming. 'Let us assume that you went out of pride, but still there was

the hope that they would find Smerdyakov out and send him to
prison, exonerate Mitya, and only *morally* condemn you (he
laughed here, do you hear?), and others would praise you. But
then Smerdyakov died, hanged himself—well, now who is going
to take your word alone in court? but still you are going, you
are going, you will go anyway, you have resolved to go. But why
are you going now?' This is terrible, Alyosha, I can't endure such
questions!"

(Karamazov, pt. 4, bk. 11, chap. 10)

All the loopholes of Ivan's thoughts, all his sideward glances at the other's
speech and consciousness, all his attempts to avoid the other's speech and
to replace it in his soul with his own self-affirmation, all the reservations
of his conscience which create a counterpoint in his every thought, his every
word and experience, all these things are brought to a focus and intensified
here in the full statements of the devil. The difference between Ivan's words
and the devil's replies is not one of content, but merely of tone, of accent.
But this change of accent alters their entire ultimate meaning. The devil as
it were transfers to the main clause that which in Ivan's sentence was merely
a subordinate clause and which was pronounced in a low voice with no independent accent; he in turn transforms the content of the main clause into
an unaccented subordinate clause. The devil turns Ivan's reservation regard-
ing the main motif of his decision into the main motif, while the main motif
becomes a mere reservation. The result is a profoundly tense and extremely
eventful combination of voices, but one which at the same time is not based
on any opposition whatever in content or theme.

But, of course, this complete dialogization of Ivan's self-awareness is,
as is always the case in Dostoevsky's work, prepared gradually. The other's
speech stealthily, little by little, penetrates the speech and consciousness of
the hero: now in the form of a pause where none would occur in monologic-
ally secure speech, now in the form of an accent which is foreign to the speaker
and thus breaks up his sentence, now in the form of the abnormally raised,
exaggerated or hysterical tone of the speaker, etc. The process of the gradual
dialogic dissociation of Ivan's consciousness begins with his first words and
his whole inner orientation in Zosima's cell, and is drawn out through his
conversations with Alyosha, with his father, and especially with Smerdyakov
(before his departure for Chermashnya), and, finally, through his three
meetings with Smerdyakov after the murder; this process is more profound
and ideologically complex than in the case of Golyadkin, but structurally
the two are completely analogous.

The phenomenon of a foreign voice whispering the hero's own words in his ear (with a rearranged accent) and the resulting inimitable combination of vari-directional words and voices within a single word or a single speech and the intersection of two consciousnesses within a single consciousness are present—in one form or another, to one degree or another, in one ideological direction or another—in each of Dostoevsky's works. This contrapuntal combination of vari-directional voices within the bounds of a single consciousness also serves for him as the basis, the soil, on which he introduces other actual voices. But we shall turn our attention to this question later on. At this point we would like to quote a passage from Dostoevsky in which he presents with astounding artistic power a musical image of the interrelation of voices which we have analyzed. This page from *A Raw Youth* is all the more interesting since, except for this passage, Dostoevsky almost nowhere in his works discusses music.

Trishatov is telling the raw youth of his love for music and elaborates for him a plan for an opera:

> "Listen, do you love music? I love it terribly. I'll play you something when I come to visit you. I play the piano very well, and I studied for a very long time. I studied seriously. If I were to write an opera, I would, you know, take the plot from *Faust*. I like the theme very much. I am constantly creating the scene in the cathedral, just imagining it in my head. A gothic cathedral, the interior, choirs, hymns, Gretchen enters and, you know— medieval choirs, so that you can hear the fifteenth century. Gretchen is in anguish, first a recitative, a soft, but terrible, agonizing one, and the choirs thunder somberly, severely, without sympathy:
>
> Dies irae, dies illa!
>
> *And suddenly—the voice of the devil, the song of the devil. He is invisible, just his song, alongside the hymns, together with the hymns, almost coinciding with them, but still completely different from them—this would have to be done somehow.* The song is long, indefatigable—this is the tenor. It begins softly, tenderly: 'Do you remember, Gretchen, how you, still innocent, still a baby, would come with your mother to this cathedral and babble prayers from an old book?' But the song becomes ever stronger, more passionate and impetuous; the notes get higher: there are tears, hopeless, undying agony in them, and, finally, despair: 'There is no forgiveness, Gretchen, there is no forgiveness for you here!'

Gretchen wants to pray, but only shrieks burst from her breast—
you know, when the breast is convulsed from weeping—and
Satan's song goes on, piercing deeper and deeper into the soul,
like a spear, even higher, and suddenly it is nearly broken off by
a cry: 'It is the end, accursed one!' Gretchen falls on her knees,
wrings her hands—and then comes her prayer, something very
short, a semi-recitative, but naive, completely unpolished,
something utterly medieval, four lines, just four lines in all—there
are a few such notes in Stradella—and with the final note—she
swoons! Confusion. People lift her up and carry her—and then
suddenly a thundering chorus. It is like a clap of voices, an inspired, triumphant, overwhelming chorus, something like our
Dori-no-si-ma-chin-mi—so that everything rattles on its foundations, and then it all turns into a rapturous, exultant exclamation: Hosanna!—Like the cry of the entire universe, and she is
carried away, carried, and then the curtain falls.

(pt. 3, chap. 5)

A part of this musical plan, in the form of literary works, was, indis-
putably, realized by Dostoevsky, and realized more than once, using diverse
material.

But let us return to Golyadkin—we have not yet finished with him; more
precisely, we have not yet finished with the speech of the narrator. In his
article "Towards a Morphology of the Naturalist Style" V. Vinogradov gives
a definition of the narration in *The Double* which is analogous to ours, though
it proceeds from a completely different point of view—namely from the point
of view of linguistic stylistics.

Here is Vinogradov's basic assertion:

The introduction of the interjections and expressions of
Golyadkin's speech into the narrational *skaz* achieves an effect
whereby it seems at times that Golyadkin himself, hidden behind
the mask of the narrator, is relating his own adventures. In *The
Double* the convergence of Mr. Golyadkin's colloquial speech with
the narrational *skaz* of the storyteller is also intensified because
Golyadkin's style remains unchanged in "indirect" speech, thus
seeming to belong to the author. And since Golyadkin says one
and the same thing not only with his language, but with his glance,
his appearance, his gestures and movements as well, it is easy to
understand why almost all descriptions which underscore some
"perpetual custom" of Mr. Golyadkin's swarm with un-set-off
quotations from his speeches.

Citing a series of examples of the coincidence of the narrator's speech with that of Golyadkin, Vinogradov continues:

> There are many more examples, but those that we have quoted, which illustrate this combination of Mr. Golyadkin's self-definitions and the little verbal brush strokes of a detached observer, sufficiently emphasize the idea that the "Petersburg poem," at least in many parts, takes on the form of Golyadkin's story as told by his "double," that is, "by a person with his language and notions." The reason for the failure of *The Double* lay precisely in the use of this innovative device.

Vinogradov's analysis is sound and astute and his conclusions are correct, but of course he remains within the bounds of the method he has adopted, and the most important and essential points simply do not fit within these bounds.

It seems to us that V. Vinogradov was not able to perceive the real uniqueness of *The Double*'s syntax, since its syntactic system is determined not by the *skaz* in and of itself and not by the clerk's colloquial dialect or by the official bureaucratic jargon, but above all by the collision and the counterpoint of various accents within the bounds of a single syntactic whole, i.e. precisely by the fact that this whole, while being one, encompasses the accents of two voices. Furthermore, he does not comprehend or point out the fact that the narration is *dialogically addressed* to Golyadkin, which is made manifest by very clear external features, for example by the fact that the first sentence of Golyadkin's speech is very often an obvious reply to a preceding sentence in the narration. Finally, he does not understand the basic bond between the narration and Golyadkin's interior dialogue: the narration, after all, does not reproduce the general pattern of Golyadkin's speech, but rather, picks up only the speech of his second voice.

In general, it is impossible to approach the real artistic purpose of style while remaining within the bounds of linguistic stylistics. No one formal linguistic definition of a word can cover its artistic functions in a work. The true style-determining factors remain outside the field of vision of linguistic stylistics.

There is in the style of the narration in *The Double* yet another essential feature which Vinogradov correctly noted, but did not explain. "Motor images," he says, "predominate in the narrational *skaz*, and its primary stylistic device is the registration of movements, regardless of their repetitiveness."

Indeed, the narration registers with the most tedious exactness all the hero's minutest movements, not sparing endless repetitions. It is as if the narrator were riveted to his hero and cannot back far enough away from him to give a summarizing, integrated image of his deeds and actions. Such a generalizing, integrated image would lie outside the hero's own field of vision, and in general such an image assumes the existence of some firm external position. The narrator is not in possession of such a position, he does not have the required perspective for an artistic summation of the hero's image and his acts as a whole.

This peculiarity of the narration in *The Double* is retained, with certain modifications, throughout the course of all of Dostoevsky's subsequent creative work. Narration in Dostoevsky is always narration without perspective. To use a term from art criticism, we might say that in Dostoevsky there exists no "perspectival representation" of the hero and the event. The narrator finds himself in immediate proximity to the hero and to the event which is taking place, and he represents them from this maximally close, aperspectival point of view. True, Dostoevsky's chroniclers write their notes after the events have come to an end, i.e. from an apparent temporal perspective. The narrator of *The Possessed*, for example, quite often says, "now that all of this is over with," "now, as we recall all of this," etc., but in fact he constructs his narration without any significant perspective whatever.

On the other hand, in contrast to the narration in *The Double*, Dostoevsky's later narrations do not at all register the hero's minute movements, are not in the least long-winded, and are completely devoid of all repetition. The narration in Dostoevsky's later period is brief, dry, and even somewhat abstract (especially when it gives information about events that have already taken place). But the brevity and dryness of the narration in the later works, "sometimes equalling *Gil Blas*," stems not from perspective, but, on the contrary, from the lack of perspective. This deliberate lack of perspective is predetermined by Dostoevsky's entire artistic intention, for, as we know, a firm, finalized image of the hero and the event is excluded in advance from that intention.

But let us return once again to the narration in *The Double*. Along with its relationship to the speech of the hero, which we have already examined, we note yet another parodic tendency in it. Elements of literary parody are present in the narration of *The Double*, just as they are present in Devushkin's letters.

Already in *Poor Folk* the author made use of his hero's voice to refract his own parodic intentions. He achieved this by various means: the parodies were either motivated by the subject matter and simply introduced into Devushkin's letters (the excerpts from the works of Ratazyaev: the parody on the high society novel, on the historical novel of the time, and, finally, on the Natural School), or the parodic strokes were presented in the very structure of the novel (Teresa and Faldoni, for example). Finally, the author introduces into the novel the polemic with Gogol, which is refracted directly in the hero's voice; it is a parodically tinted voice—Devushkin's reading of "The Overcoat" and his outraged reaction to it. (The following episode, involving the general who helps the hero, contains an implied juxtaposition to the episode with the "important personage" in Gogol's "The Overcoat.")

In *The Double* a parodic stylization of the "high style" in *Dead Souls* is refracted in the voice of the narrator, and, in general, parodic and semiparodic allusions to various of Gogol's works are scattered throughout *The Double*. It should be mentioned that these parodic tones in the narration are directly intertwined with the narrator's mimicry of Golyadkin.

As a result of the introduction of the parodic and polemic element into the narration it becomes more multi-voiced and contrapuntal and has less relation to itself and its referential object. On the other hand, literary parody intensifies the element of literary conventionality within the narrator's speech, thus depriving it still more of its independence and finalizing power in relation to the hero. In Dostoevsky's subsequent works as well the element of literary conventionality and its exposure in one form or another always served to increase the full significance and independence of the hero's position. In this sense literary conventionality, in keeping with Dostoevsky's intention, did not only not reduce the ideational content and significance of his novel, but, on the contrary, could only increase it (as was, by the way, the case with Jean Paul and even with Sterne). The destruction in Dostoevsky's works of the ordinary monologic orientation led him to completely exclude certain elements of that monologic orientation from his structure, and to carefully neutralize others. One of the means of that neutralization was literary conventionality, i.e. the introduction of conventional discourse into the narration or into the principles of structure: stylized or parodic discourse.

The phenomenon of dialogically addressing the narration to the hero was still present, of course, in Dostoevsky's subsequent works, but it was modified and became more complex and profound. It is no longer the narrator's every word that is addressed to the hero, but rather the narration as a whole, its whole orientation. Speech within the narration is in the majority of cases dry and lustreless; "documentary style" is the best definition for it. But the basic function of this documentation is to expose and provoke; it is addressed to the hero, speaking as if to him and not about him, speaking with its entire mass, not with its individual elements. True, even in Dostoevsky's last novels certain heroes were presented in the light of a style which directly parodied and taunted them and which sounded like an exaggerated line taken from their interior dialogue. The narrator in *The Possessed*, for example, is so constructed in relation to Stepan Trofimovich, but only in relation to him. Isolated notes of this taunting style are scattered throughout the other novels, too. They are present in *The Brothers Karamazov*. But in general they are considerably weakened. Dostoevsky's basic tendency in his later period was to make his style and tone dry and precise, to neutralize it. But wherever dry, documentary, neutralized narration is exchanged for sharply accented tones colored with value judgments, those tones are in every case addressed to the hero and are born of the speeches in his potential interior dialogue with himself.

JOSEPH FRANK

Nihilism and Notes from Underground

*If philosophy among other vagaries were also to have the notion
that it could occur to a man to act in accordance with its teaching,
one might make out of that a queer comedy.*
—KIERKEGAARD, *Fear and Trembling*

Few works in modern literature are more widely read or more often cited
than Dostoevsky's *Notes from Underground*. The designation "underground
man" has entered into the vocabulary of the modern educated consciousness,
and this character has now begun—like Hamlet, Don Quixote, Don Juan
and Faust—to take on the symbolic stature of one of the great archetypal
literary creations. No book or essay on the situation of modern culture would
be complete without some allusion to Dostoevsky's figure. Every important
cultural development of the past half-century—Nietzscheanism, Freudianism,
Expressionism, Surrealism, Crisis Theology, Existentialism—has claimed the
underground man as its own; and when he has not been adopted as a prophetic anticipation, he has been held up to exhibition as a luridly repulsive
warning.

Indeed, *Notes from Underground* by now would seem to have been
discussed from every conceivable point of view—with one single but important exception. For this exception is the point of view of Dostoevsky himself.
Critics are ready to expatiate at the drop of a hat—amid an increasingly suffocating smokescreen of erudite irrelevancies and melodramatic pseudo-
profundities—on the vast "cultural significance" of *Notes from Underground*.
Meanwhile, the real point of Dostoevsky's fascinating little work has gotten
completely lost in the shuffle.

From *The Sewanee Review* 69, no. 1 (January–March 1961). © 1961 by the University of the South.

What was Dostoevsky himself trying to do? Everyone knows that *Notes from Underground* was originally begun as a polemic inspired by Dostoevsky's opposition to the Socialist radicals of his time (popularly called Nihilists as a result of the label affixed to them in Turgenev's *Fathers and Sons*). The outstanding spokesman for the Russian radicals at this moment was Nicolai G. Chernyshevsky, whose Utopian novel *What Is to Be Done?* had appeared in the spring of 1863 and had caused a sensation. *Notes from Underground* was intended as an answer to *What Is to Be Done?*; and the accepted account of the relation between them runs as follows.

Chernyshevsky and the radicals believed that man was innately good and amenable to reason, and that, once enlightened as to his true interests, reason and science would ultimately enable him to construct a perfect society. Dostoevsky, on the other hand, believed that man was innately evil, irrational, capricious and destructive; not reason but only faith in Christ could ever succeed in helping him to master the chaos of his impulses. This view of *Notes from Underground* was first advanced by the Russian religious philosopher V. V. Rozanov in his brilliant study, *The Legend of the Grand Inquisitor* (1890). And regardless of the differing explanations offered for the genesis of Dostoevsky's *Weltanschauung*, this interpretation of *Notes from Underground* has continued to reign unchallenged ever since.

Despite the hegemony it has enjoyed, however, Rozanov's theory is at best only a beguiling and misleading half-truth. Rozanov was not primarily concerned with interpreting Dostoevsky's art but with enlisting the awe-inspiring name of the novelist on the side of his religious philosophy; and he unduly emphasizes one pole of the actual dialectic of the work, bringing it to the foreground as the entire meaning of the whole with a total disregard for context. Worst of all, he sees the underground man only as the simple negative of what Dostoevsky was attacking—the irrational against reason, evil and moral chaos against purposive social activity.

If this interpretation were true, then we could only conclude that Dostoevsky was just about the worst polemicist in all of literary history. Could Dostoevsky really have imagined that any reader in his right mind would *prefer* the world of the underground man as an alternative to Chernyshevsky's idyllic Socialist Utopia? Hardly! Dostoevsky was by no means as simple-minded or as maladroit as admirers like Rozanov—though certainly without fully realizing it themselves—would make him out to be. In reality his attack on Chernyshevsky and the Nihilists is a good deal more insidious, subtle and effective than Dostoevsky ever has been given credit for.

Beginning with V. L. Komarovich in 1924, a number of Russian critics have explored in detail the relation between *Notes from Underground* and

What Is to Be Done? It is now clear that whole sections of Dostoevsky's novella—for example, the attempt of the underground man to bump into an officer on the Nevsky Prospect, or the famous encounter with the prostitute Lisa—were conceived entirely as *parodies* of specific episodes in Chernyshevsky's book. The uncovering of these parodies provided the first real glimpse into the inner logic of Dostoevsky's artistry; but the Russian critics themselves have never pressed their own insights home with sufficient rigor. What they have failed to realize is that *Notes from Underground* as a whole—not only certain details and episodes—was conceived and executed as one magnificent satirical parody.

This parody, however, does not consist merely in rejecting Nihilism and setting up a competing version of "human nature" in its place. Rather, since parody is ridicule by *imitation*, Dostoevsky assimilates the major doctrines of Russian Nihilism into the life of his underground man; and by revealing the hopeless dilemmas in which he lands as a result, Dostoevsky intends to undermine these doctrines from within. The tragedy of the underground man does not arise, as is popularly supposed, because of his rejection of reason. It derives from his acceptance of *all* the implications of "reason" in its then-current Russian incarnation—and particularly those implications which the advocates of reason like Chernyshevsky blithely preferred to overlook or deny.

Dostoevsky himself clearly pointed to his use of parody in the footnote appended to the title of his novella. "Both the author of the *Notes* and the *Notes* themselves," he writes, "are, of course, fictitious. Nevertheless, such persons as the author of such memoirs not only may, but must, exist in our society, if we take into consideration the circumstances which led to the formation of our society. It was my intention to bring before our reading public, more conspicuously than is usually done, one of the characters of our recent past. He is one of the representatives of a generation that is still with us." Dostoevsky here is obviously talking about the formation of Russian ("our") society, not—as has often been claimed—about the society of nineteenth-century Western Europe or of "modern culture." And Russian society, as Dostoevsky could expect all his readers to know, had been formed by the successive accretions of Western influence that had streamed into Russia since the time of Peter the Great. The underground man embodies and reflects the latest phases of this evolution in himself; he is a parodistic *persona* whose life exemplifies the serio-comic impasse of this historical process.

Only if we approach *Notes from Underground* in this way can we understand Dostoevsky's choice of subject matter and method of organization. The work consists of two tableaux selected from the life of the underground man—but each episode also, and more importantly, corresponds to a dif-

ferent and very crucial moment in the spiritual history of the Russian intelligentsia. The first section shows the underground man in the ideological grip
of the Nihilism of the sixties; the second, as a perfect product of the social
Romanticism of the forties. Each section of the work thus reveals the differing manner in which the personality of the educated Russian—depending
on the dominant ideology of the moment—had been disorganized and
disrupted by the attempt to live according to alien doctrines and ideals. This
also explains the peculiar construction of the work, which reverses
chronological sequence and proceeds backward in time. The Nihilism of the
sixties was uppermost in the consciousness of Dostoevsky's readers, and had
provided the immediate inspiration for the story. Since the underground man
was not primarily a private individual but a social type, Dostoevsky sacrifices
the natural biographical order of inner growth and development to obtain
as much polemical timeliness as possible from the very first page.

Notes from Underground, then, is not the self-revelation of a pathological personality, not a theological cry of despair over the evils of "human
nature," least of all a work expressing Dostoevsky's involuntary adoption
of Nietzsche's philosophy of "immoralism" and the will to power. On the
contrary, it is a brilliantly ironic Swiftian parody remarkable for its self-
conscious mastery, satirical control and Machiavellian finesse. But to prove
this contention we must set the work back in the context from which it came,
and endeavor to supply the framework of coordinates on which Dostoevsky
depended to obtain his effects.

II. THE DIALECTIC OF DETERMINISM

The famous opening tirade of *Notes from Underground* gives us an
unforgettable picture of the underground man stewing in his Petersburg "funk-
hole" and mulling over the peculiarities of his character—or rather, his total
inability to become a character. Nothing could be more abject, petty and
ridiculous than the image he gives of his life. He refuses to be treated for
a liver ailment out of "spite"; he remembers an attempt made in his youth,
when he was still in the civil service, to browbeat an officer for no reason
other than the assertion of petty vanity; he boasts of his honesty, and then,
when he realizes how "contemptible" such boasting is, he deliberately lets
it stand to degrade himself even more in the eyes of the reader.

The underground man, indeed, seems to be nothing more than a chaos
of conflicting emotional impulses; and his conflict may be defined as that
of a search for his own character—his quest for himself. "I did not even know
how to become anything," he says, "either spiteful or good, either a

blackguard or an honest man, either a hero or an insect." At the very moment when he feels most consc ous of "the sublime and the beautiful," he tells us, he was also "guilty of the most contemptible actions which—well, which, in fact, everybody is guilty of, but which, as though on purpose, I only happened to commit when I was most conscious that they ought not to be committed." Why, he asks plaintively, should this be so?

The answer to this question has invariably been sought in some "abnormal" or "psychopathic" trait of the underground man, which is then usually traced to the hidden recesses of Dostoevsky's own psychology. But the underground man's monologue provides a perfectly plausible answer to his question. "Whatever happened," he assures us, "happened in accordance with the normal and fundamental laws of intensified consciousness and by a sort of inertia which is a direct consequence of those laws, and . . . therefore you could not only not change yourself, but you simply couldn't make any attempt to." Dostoevsky, in other words, attributes to his underground man a belief in *scientific determinism*. The underground man, who remarks that he is "well-educated enough not to be superstitious," is quite well up on the most enlightened opinion of his time; he knows all about science and the laws of intensified consciousness; and he accepts the fact that whatever he does is inevitable and unalterable because it is totally determined by the laws of nature.

The moral impotence of the underground man thus springs directly from his acceptance of one of the cornerstones of Chernyshevsky's thought—absolute determinism. This aspect of Chernyshevsky's philosophy is mentioned only incidentally in *What Is to Be Done?*; and the behavior of some of the characters—as Chernyshevsky himself is embarrassedly forced to concede—can hardly be reconciled with this doctrine. Nonetheless, in his resounding article on *The Anthropological Principle in Philosophy* (1860), which was equally if not more famous than his novel, Chernyshevsky had flatly denied the existence of anything remotely resembling free will—or, for that matter, any kind of will. An act of will, according to Chernyshevsky, is "only the subjective impression which accompanies in our minds the rise of thoughts or actions from preceding thoughts, actions or external facts." Dostoevsky thus begins his parody of Nihilism by having the underground man use Chernyshevsky's philosophy as an excuse for his moral flaccidity. Under the magic wand of Chernyshevsky's determinism, *if taken seriously and consequentially*, all moral action has become impossible.

With skillful dialectical ingenuity, Dostoevsky displays the bewildered demoralization of his character before this unprecedented situation. The underground man, for instance, imagines that he wishes to forgive someone magnanimously for having slapped him in the face; but the more he thinks about it, the more impossible such an action becomes. "For I should most certainly not have known what to do with my magnanimity—neither to forgive, since the man who would have slapped my face would most probably have done it in obedience to the laws of nature; nor to forget, since though even if it is the law of nature, it hurts all the same."

Or suppose he wishes to act the other way round—not to forgive magnanimously but to take revenge. How can one take revenge when nobody is to blame for anything? "One look and the object disappears into thin air, your reasons evaporate, there is no guilty man, the injury is no longer an injury but just fate, something in the nature of a toothache for which no one can be blamed." That is why, as the underground man says, "the direct, the inevitable and the legitimate result of consciousness is to make all action impossible." Or, if any action is taken—say on the matter of revenge—then "it would merely be out of spite." Spite is not a valid cause for any kind of action, but it is the only one left when the "laws of nature" make any other response illegitimate.

In such passages, the moral vacuum created by the underground man's acceptance of scientific determinism is expressed with unrivalled psychological acumen. But while, as a well-trained member of the intelligentsia, reason forces him to accept determinism, it is impossible for him humanly to live with its conclusions. As a result of the laws of intensified consciousness, he writes sardonically, "you are quite right in being a blackguard, as though it were any consolation to the blackguard that he actually is a blackguard." Or, as regards the slap in the face, it is impossible to forget because "though even if it is the law of nature, it hurts all the same." Both these comments pose a total human reaction—a moral revulsion at being a blackguard, an upsurge of anger at the insult of being slapped—against a scientific rationale that dissolves all human responsibility and thus all possibility of a human response. "Reason" tells the underground man that feelings of guilt or even of indignation are totally irrational and unjustified; but conscience and a sense of dignity are not "reasonable"—happily for mankind—and they manage to assert themselves all the same.

It is this assertion of the moral-emotive level of the personality, striving to keep alive its significance in the face of the laws of nature, that is expressed by the underground man's so-called "masochism." He confesses, in a much-commented passage:

> I felt a sort of secret, abnormal, contemptible delight when, on coming home on one of the foulest nights in Petersburg, I used to realize intensely that again I had been guilty of some dastardly

action that day . . . and inwardly, secretly, I used to go on nag-
ging myself, worrying myself, accusing myself, till at last the bit-
terness I felt turned into a sort of shameful, damnable sweetness,
and finally, into real positive delight! Yes, into delight! . . . The
feeling of delight was there just because *I was so intensely aware
of my own degradation.*

Whatever a passage of this kind may reveal about Dostoevsky's psyche to
the trained clinical eye, in the context of *Notes from Underground* it does
not refer to Dostoevsky but to the underground man; and it has a specific
dramatic function. The ambiguous "delight" of the underground man arises
from the moral-emotive response of his *human nature* to the blank nullity
of the *laws of nature*. It signifies his refusal to abdicate his conscience and
submit silently to determinism, even though his reason assures him that there
is nothing he can really do to change for the better. The "masochism" of
the underground man thus has a *reverse* significance from that usually
attributed to it. Instead of being a sign of pathological abnormality, it is in
reality an indication of the underground man's paradoxical spiritual health—
his preservation of his moral sense.

III. THE MAN OF ACTION

It is only from this perspective, with its deceptive transvaluation of the
normal moral horizon, that we can grasp the underground man's relation
to the imaginary interlocutor with whom he argues all through the first part
of *Notes from Underground*. This interlocutor is obviously a follower of
Chernyshevsky, a man of action, *l'homme de la nature et de la vérité*; and
the underground man, as we see, *accepts* his theory that all human life is
simply a mechanical product of the laws of nature. But the underground man
knows what the man of action does not—that this theory makes all moral
action impossible, or at least meaningless. "I envy such a man with all the
forces of my embittered heart," says the underground man. "He is stupid—I
am not disputing that. But perhaps the normal man should be stupid." The
normal man, for example, the man of action, inspired by a feeling of revenge,
"goes straight to his goal, like a mad bull, with lowered horns." He does
not realize that what he thinks of as the basis for his action, i.e., justice,
is a ludicrously old-fashioned and unscientific prejudice eliminated by the
laws of nature. It is only his stupidity that allows him to maintain his complacency, and to look on the underground man's squirmings with unfeigned
contempt. Or conversely, the men of action "capitulate in all sincerity" before
the "stone wall" of scientific determinism and the laws of nature, which exert

"a sort of calming influence upon them, a sort of final and morally decisive influence and perhaps even a mystic one." The plain men of action simply do not understand that scientific determinism does not allow them to be "morally decisive" about anything; and they accept its conclusions with a smug awareness of being up-to-date, while they go on behaving exactly as in the past.

Very different is the response of the ignominious underground man, who knows only too well what the "stone wall" really means and, as a consequence, can only nurse a despicable resentment that he cannot justly discharge against anybody. But the underground man, with his well-known "masochism," cannot help behaving *as if* some sort of free human response were still possible and meaningful—"consequently there is only one solution left, namely, knocking your head against the wall as hard as you can." "Is it not much better to understand everything," cries the underground man,

> to be aware of everything, to be conscious of all the impossibilities and stone walls? Not to be reconciled to any of those impossibilities or stone walls if you hate being reconciled to them? To reach by way of the most irrefutable logical combinations the most hideous conclusions on the eternal theme that it is somehow your own fault if there is a stone wall, though again it is abundantly clear that it is not your fault at all, and therefore to abandon yourself sensuously to doing nothing, and silently and impotently gnashing your teeth?

Here, at first sight, the paradoxes of the underground man appear to reach a paroxysm of psychopathic self-accusation; but once we understand the logic of Dostoevsky's creation, it is quite clear that nobody in the world can be guilty of anything except the underground man. He knows that the idea of guilt, along with all other moral notions, has been abolished by the laws of nature; yet he persists in having moral responses just the same. And since there is nowhere else for him to assign moral responsibility, by the most irrefutable logic he and he alone is to blame for everything.

The portrait of the underground man we have been tracing is developed up through chapter 6 of the first part of *Notes from Underground*. And, as we have tried to show, it is based on an imaginative dramatization of a double movement: the acceptance of Chernyshevsky's determinism by the underground man's reason, but its rejection by his moral-emotive instincts. It is only from this point of view, indeed, that we can grasp the complex raillery of Dostoevsky's creation. The self-mockery of the underground man, the disgusted pejoratives he uses about himself, have usually been taken literally; but as we have seen in the case of "masochism," such a literal reading entirely misses Dostoevsky's meaning. In the same way, the continual self-derision of the underground man is intended to convey a consummate tragi-comic irony.

The underground man becomes what he is because his life is the *reductio ad absurdum* of the metaphysics of the man of action; and the more repulsive and hideous he portrays this life (and himself) as being, the more he underlines the incredible obtuseness of his self-confident judge. Far from wishing to portray the underground man as the embodiment of *evil*, the whole purpose of *Notes from Underground* is quite the opposite. Only in a world where human choice can make a difference, only where there is no absolute determinism, is any morality possible at all; and Dostoevsky adroitly defends the underground man's "capriciousness" as the necessary precondition for any morality whatsoever.

IV. THE CRYSTAL PALACE

Beginning with chapter 7 of *Notes from Underground*, Dostoevsky shifts his target of attack. Up to this point he has been aiming at Chernyshevsky's metaphysics in its most general formulation; but now he turns to his ethics of "rational egoism" on the one hand, and, on the other, to the ideal of the Crystal Palace. Both these doctrines are exploded by the use of the same strategy that Dostoevsky has already employed—his technique, as it were, of projection into the absolute. Dostoevsky, that is, places himself imaginatively at the position where the doctrine he wishes to attack has already achieved its goal; and then he demonstrates the moral-psychological incompatibility of this achievement with some aspect of the nature of man—in this case, man's need to feel spiritually free and morally responsible. This is what Dostoevsky meant when he spoke of the "fantastic realism" of his work—a realism of the possible and the extreme rather than of the median and the actual; and his first large-scale use of this "fantastic realism" occurs in *Notes from Underground*.

In the first part of this section, the underground man waxes merry over the "theory of the regeneration of the whole human race by means of the system of its own advantages." But what *is* man's true advantage? Can it only be found by "taking the average of statistical figures and relying on scientific and economic formulas"? "That's the trouble, gentlemen," says the underground man commiseratingly,

> that there exists something which is dearer to almost every man
> than his greatest good, or (not to upset the logic of my argument)

that there exists one most valuable good (the one, too, that is being constantly overlooked, namely, the one we are talking about) which is greater and more desirable than all other goods, and for the sake of which a man, if need be, is ready to challenge all law, that is to say, reason, honor, peace, prosperity—in short, all those excellent and useful things, provided he can obtain that primary and most desirable good which is dearer to him than anything in the world.

The tone and language of this passage, with its pretense of philosophical precision, is clearly a parody of some of the more laborious passages in *The Anthropological Principle*. Even more important, however, is to understand why Dostoevsky's "one most valuable good" is placed in such immitigable opposition to "reason, honor, peace, prosperity," etc. The ultimate goal of Chernyshevsky's ethics of "rational egoism" was the creation of a sanctified humanity which, out of sheer rational calculations of self-interest, had lost the very possibility of doing evil. A true "rational egoist," according to Chernyshevsky, "may say to himself: I will be wicked, I will do people harm; but he will not be able to do that any more than a clever man can be a fool even if he wanted to be one." Not Dostoevsky but Chernyshevsky had posed the alternative: either moral freedom, i.e., the freedom to *choose* between good and evil, or "reason" with all its material advantages. And the answer of the underground man is that man's need to feel himself free and morally autonomous is precisely the "one most valuable good" for which he is ready to sacrifice all the others. To obtain this "good" he will "deliberately and consciously desire something that is injurious, stupid, even outrageously stupid, just because he wants *to have the right* to desire for himself even what is very stupid and not to be bound by an obligation to desire only what is sensible." For at all events, however stupid and unreasonable this "good" may be, "it preserves what is most precious and most important to us, namely, our personality and our individuality."

The underground man's rejection of "rational egoism" paves the way for his reaction against its ultimate ideal in the future—the world of the Crystal Palace. In this future Utopia, described in *What Is to Be Done?*, all the laws of nature governing society will have been discovered. Here Dostoevsky is no longer dramatizing the moral-psychological impossibility of a purely deterministic world; the laws of nature are now seen in the light of their future triumphs, which will guide man's way to overwhelming material prosperity. The Crystal Palace was modelled, as all Chernyshevsky's readers knew, on the Fourierist phalanstery; and Fourier had calculated and combined all the details of life in the phalanstery with a precision that was not only mathematical but maniacal. The phalanstery, as Emile Faguet once pithily remarked [in *La Destinée Sociale*], "c'est l'Arcadie d'un chef de bureau."

The triumph of the Crystal Palace presupposes that science will have taught man that his free-will, in addition to being a regrettable speculative error, was also a positive hindrance to his welfare. For science proves that man "possesses neither will nor caprices, and never has done, and . . . he himself is nothing more than a sort of piano-key or organ-stop." (Fourier, it might be mentioned, spoke of the phalanstery as embodying the laws and principles of "harmony." His chief disciple, Victor Considerant, in a famous Socialist treatise mentioned anagrammatically in *What Is to Be Done?*, compared human passions to a "clavier" whose notes could be blended into such harmony: hence Dostoevsky's musical imagery.) The trouble is, however, that man is "phenomenally ungrateful. I'm even inclined," says the underground man, "to believe that the best definition of man is—a creature who walks on two legs and is ungrateful." For even if you "shower all the earthly blessings upon him, drown him in happiness, head over ears, so that only bubbles should be visible on the surface, or bestow such economic prosperity upon him as would leave him with nothing to do but sleep, eat cakes, and only worry about keeping world history going . . . even then he will, man will, out of sheer ingratitude . . . play a dirty trick on you." This "dirty trick" is precisely that he will throw everything overboard, will set his heart on the most uneconomic and positively harmful nonsense, "for the sole purpose of proving to himself (as though that were so necessary) that men are still men and not keys on a piano."

At this point, the underground man rises to a climactic vision of universal chaos which duplicates, on the socio-historical level, the chaos of the underground man's life in the earlier chapters. And in both cases, the cause of this chaos is the same—the revolt of the personality against the vision of a world in which personality and free-will will have no further reason for being. For even if such a world could really be created.

> even if he [man] really were nothing but a piano-key, even if this were proved to him by natural science and mathematically, even then he would refuse to come to his senses. . . . And if he has no other remedy, he will plan destruction and chaos, he will devise all sorts of sufferings. . . . If you say that this, too, can be calculated by the mathematical table—chaos, and darkness, and curses—so that the mere possibility of calculating it all before hand would stop it all and reason would triumph in the end—well, if that were to happen man would go purposely mad in order to rid himself of reason and carry his point.

Nothing in *Notes from Underground*, at first sight, seems more daring and shocking than this invocation to the gods of darkness—to destruction, chaos, and madness. And, not surprisingly, all interpreters of Dostoevsky have invariably taken it with the same literalness with which they took the underground man's "masochism" and "immorality." None have paid the slightest attention to the hypothetical and conditional form in which Dostoevsky cast these assertions, nor have they seen them in the light of his projection of the future ideal of the Crystal Palace. In fact, however, the senseless and self-destructive revolt of freedom is envisaged by Dostoevsky *only* as a last-ditch defense, in circumstances where man has no other way of preserving the autonomy of his personality. Indeed, the underground man himself makes abundantly clear that his frenetic harangue does not refer to man as he actually *exists* in ordinary "irrational" life; it applies to man as he might be forced to *become* if Chernyshevsky's Fourierist Utopia were ever realized. For after lividly declaiming in the name of curses, darkness and chaos, the underground man returns to reality for a moment and adds: "And how is one after that to resist the temptation to rejoice that all this has not happened yet and that so far desire depends on the devil alone knows what."

Once having envisaged the completion of the Crystal Palace, however, the underground man continues, in chapter 9, to question the confidence of Chernyshevsky and the Socialist radicals that such an ideal was what man really wanted. "Man likes to create and clear paths—that is undeniable," the underground man agrees; man wishes to accomplish useful and socially productive labor. But the underground man denies that man wishes to achieve the static secular Apocalypse of the Crystal Palace, to reach the literal end of history when all further striving, moral struggle, and inner conflict will have ceased. Perhaps man "is instinctively afraid of reaching the goal and completing the building he is erecting? . . . Perhaps he only loves building it and not living in it, preferring to leave it later *aux animaux domestiques* such as ants, sheep, etc., etc. . . . They [ants] have one marvelous building of this kind, a building that is forever indestructible—the ant-hill." The ideal of the "ant-hill" is suitable *aux animaux domestiques* exactly because they have no inkling of man's need to feel creative and free—because all they desire is to complete their appointed tasks in conformity with reason and the laws of nature through all eternity.

This comparison of the Socialist ideal to an "ant-hill" was a commonplace in the Russian journalism of the period, but the use of such an image here as a symbol for the secular end of history very probably derives from Alexander Herzen. "If humanity went straight to some goal," Herzen wrote in *From the Other Shore* (1855), "there would be no history, only logic; humanity would stop in some finished form, in a spontaneous *status quo* like the animals. . . . Besides, if the libretto existed, history would lose all interest, it would become futile, boring, ridiculous." Of all Herzen's works, Dostoevsky publicly expressed special admiration for *From the Other Shore;* and the similarity is too great to be accidental. Now Herzen, more than any other single individual, was responsible for the propagation of Socialist ideas in Russia; but he never accepted the Nihilist scientism and determinism of the sixties. Like Dostoevsky himself, Herzen was a member of the generation of the forties which had been nurtured on Schelling and Hegel; and no member of this generation, regardless of politics, ever succumbed completely to the lure of mechanical materialism. Dostoevsky here is thus using the forties to argue against the sixties, as he was to do later in *The Devils* (1871–72). And this interplay between the generations, as we shall see, is of first importance for understanding the meaning of *Notes from Underground* as a whole.

The ultimate argument of the underground man against the Crystal Palace is that it outlaws suffering. "In the Crystal Palace it is unthinkable; suffering is doubt, it is negation, and what sort of Crystal Palace would it be if one were to have any doubts about it? And yet I am convinced that man will never renounce real suffering, that is to say, destruction and chaos. Suffering! Why it's the sole cause of consciousness!" Within the ideological context of *Notes from Underground*, "suffering" clearly has the same function as "masochism" or as the underground man's inverted irony. It is the only way left of keeping alive his "consciousness" as a human being, of asserting his personality, individuality and moral responsibility. And in returning to the problem of "consciousness" at this point—the end of chapter 9—Dostoevsky brings his demolition of the Crystal Palace into relation with his earlier chapters, establishing the unity of what appears to be the underground man's spasmodic and disorderly tirade.

V. THE PALATIAL HENCOOP

In chapter 10, the penultimate section of *Notes from Underground*, the reader becomes aware of a new note being struck, or rather, of a note which had hitherto remained in the background suddenly ringing out above all the others. Up to this point, the self-torture and suffering of the underground man had been made amply evident. Still, the underground man's sacrilegious assertion that he had found "delight" in his suffering, and the sarcastic satisfaction with which he flaunts this "delight" before the horrified eyes of his interlocutor, somewhat mitigates our sense of his anguish. But in chapter 10, we become aware of how literally unbearable the situation of the underground man really is.

Torn between the convictions of his reason and the revolt of his conscience and feelings, the underground man cries out: "Surely I have not been made for the sole purpose of drawing the conclusion that the way I am made is a piece of rank deceit? Can this be the sole purpose? I don't believe it." The underground man is desperately searching for some solution to his racking dilemma; and he makes very clear that the underground revolt of the personality, valuable though it may be, is by no means a positive answer. "I rejected the Crystal Palace myself for the sole reason that one would not be allowed to stick out one's tongue at it" (again a self-mocking and derisive image for the revolt of moral freedom). "But I did not say that because I am so fond of sticking out my tongue. . . . On the contrary, I'd gladly have let my tongue be cut off out of gratitude if things could be so arranged that I should have no wish to stick it out at all."

Dostoevsky leaves us in no doubt that the underground man, far from rejecting all ideals, is desperately searching for one that would truly satisfy the needs of his spirit. Such an ideal would not spur his personality to revolt in rabid frenzy; on the contrary, it would lead to the willing surrender of himself in its favor. This alternative ideal obviously could only be one which, recognizing the autonomy of the will and the freedom of the personality, appealed to the moral nature of man instead of to "reason" and self-interest in the service of determinism. From a letter of Dostoevsky's we know that chapter 10 originally contained some clear indication that this alternative ideal was that of Christ; but this part of the text was mangled both by the censors and by the carelessness of the proofreaders.

"I am not at all happy about my article," Dostoevsky wrote after the publication of the first part of *Notes from Underground;*

> there are terrible proofreading errors, and it would have been better not to publish the penultimate chapter (the most important, where the very idea of the whole article is expressed) rather than to publish it this way, that is, with twisted sentences and contradictions. But what can one do? What swine the censors are! Where I derided everything, and sometimes blasphemed *for appearance*, they let it get by, but when from all this I deduced the necessity of belief in Christ, they cut it out. Why, are the censors perhaps conspiring against the government?

Dostoevsky, we may assume, corrected some of these errors when he revised the magazine text for publication in book form; but while the alternative ideal to the Crystal Palace is clearly enough indicated, some confusion still remains in the final text. This confusion arises when, in chapter 10, the underground man begins to compare the Crystal Palace to another structure that would be a "real" palace instead of a hencoop.

"You see" he says, "if it [the Crystal Palace] were not a palace but a hencoop, and if it should rain, I might crawl into it to avoid getting wet, but I would never pretend that the hencoop was a palace out of gratitude to it for sheltering me from the rain. You laugh and you tell me that in such circumstances even a hencoop is as good as a palace. Yes, I reply, it certainly is if the only purpose in life is not to get wet." It is not the usefulness of the hencoop that is impugned by the underground man, but the fact that it is mistaken for a palace, i.e., that in return for its practical advantages it has been elevated into mankind's ideal. But the underground man refuses to accept the hencoop-*qua*-palace as *his* ideal. "But what is to be done if I've got it into my head that that [i.e., not to get wet] is not the only purpose of life, and that if one has to live, one had better live in a palace?"

Here, as we can see, the undergound man poses a "true" against the "false" palace; and this is the point at which the confusion occurs. For the underground man develops this comparison as follows: "For the time being," he says, "I refuse to accept a hencoop for a palace. *The Crystal Palace* may be just an idle dream, it may be against all the laws of nature, I may have invented it because of my own stupidity, because of certain old and irrational habits of my generation. But what do I care whether it is against the laws of nature? What does it matter so long as it exists in my desires, or rather exists while my desires exist?" Now it is obvious that something is wrong here: the "Crystal Palace" mentioned in this passage is the *opposite* of everything it has stood for throughout the rest of the text.

This latter "Crystal Palace" is a structure that exists *against* the laws of nature instead of being their embodiment; it is an answer to man's desires and not their suppression. Moreover, the underground man's allusion to "certain old and irrational habits of my generation" reminds us that he is a member of the generation of the forties. This paves the way for part two of the work, and also indicates Dostoevsky's recognition that the forties—whatever else this era may have been guilty of from his point of view—still believed in the existence of the will and in the importance of feeling and desire. In any case, it is clear that the "Crystal Palace" of this citation refers to the "true" palace which is *not* a hencoop; but the fact that Dostoevsky allows the same designation to stand for both "palaces" cannot help but baffle the reader.

Despite Dostoevsky's indication of this alternative ideal, however, the essence of his conception of the underground man requires the latter to remain trapped in the negative phase of the revolt for freedom. He longs for another ideal, he knows that it must exist, but—accepting determinism and the laws of nature—he does not yet know how to attain it. All he can do is affirm despairingly: "I know that I shall never be content with a compromise, with an everlasting and recurring zero because it exists according to the laws of nature and *actually* exists. I will not accept as the crown of all my desires a big house with model flats for the poor on a lease of ninety-nine hundred and ninety-nine years."

And our last glimpse of the underground man, in the final chapter 11, masterfully depicts this state of mind, in which he both denies and affirms his underground revolt and his "dark cellar" in the space of a few lines.

> Though I have said that I envy the normal man to the point of exasperation, I wouldn't care to be in his place in the circumstances in which I find him (though I shall never cease envying him. No, no, the dark cellar is, at any rate, of much greater advantage to me!). In the dark cellar one can at least. . . . Sorry, I'm afraid I am exaggerating. I am exaggerating because I know, as well as twice-two, that it is not the dark cellar that is better, but something else, something else altogether, something I long for but cannot find. To hell with the dark cellar!

What that "something else" is, and why the underground man cannot attain it, forms the substance of the second part of *Notes from Underground*.

VI. IDEALISTS OF THE FORTIES

The second part of *Notes from Underground* is subtitled "Apropos of the Wet Snow." Since the snow plays no role whatever in the story, one may wonder why Dostoevsky chose to highlight it in this manner. The answer is: to heighten the symbolic atmosphere. This subtitle, along with the quotation from Nekrasov used as epigraph, serves to set this second part firmly in the ideological ambiance that Dostoevsky wishes to evoke. It had already been noted in the forties (by P. V. Annenkov) that writers of the "natural school" were fond of employing "wet snow" as a typical feature of the Petersburg landscape; and Dostoevsky uses it to summon up instantly an image of Petersburg in the forties—an image of the most "abstract and premeditated city in the whole world," whose very existence had become symbolic in Russian literature for the violence and unnaturalness of the Russian adaption to Western culture. In addition, the poem by Nekrasov also conjures up the moral and spiritual climate of the period.

Nekrasov's famous poem, to which Dostoevsky had also alluded ironically in an earlier work—*The Friend of the Family* (1859)—reproduces the pathetic confession of a repentant prostitute redeemed from her degraded life by the author:

> When with a word of fervent conviction,
> From the lowest dregs of dark affliction,
> A soul from eternal doom I saved;

Citing some further lines, Dostoevsky suddenly cuts it short with etc., etc.,—thereby indirectly indicating his feeling that the poem was completely conventional chatter. The redemption-of-a-prostitute theme, which runs from social Romantics like Eugène Sue, George Sand and Hugo right through to Tolstoy's *Resurrection* (1899), had become a commonplace in the Russian literature of the forties and also figures as a minor incident in *What Is to Be Done?* The climactic episode in the second part of *Notes from Underground*—the encounter between the underground man and the prostitute Lisa—is clearly an ironic parody and reversal of this social Romantic cliché.

The second part of *Notes from Underground*, then, is intended to satirize the sentimental social Romanticism of the forties just as the first part had satirized the Nihilism of the sixties. And a good deal of light is thrown on this second part by articles that Dostoevsky published in his magazine *Time* in the years immediately preceding the composition of his novella. The forties, Dostoevsky wrote in 1860, had been the moment when "the spirit of analysis penetrated into our intellectual classes. . . . Then everything was done according to principle, we lived according to principles, and we had a horrible fear of doing anything not according to the latest ideas." All spontaneity and unself-consciousness was lost; not to live by the light of "the latest ideas" was literally unthinkable. And under the influence of "the latest ideas" a new social type appeared among the Russian intelligentsia—the "Byronic natures," the liberal idealists of the forties.

As Dostoevsky describes them, these idealists were burning to help "humanity"; but they could find no occupation worthy of their powers. "They said it was not really worth the trouble to become angry and curse—that everything was so dirty that one hardly had the desire to wiggle a single finger, and that a good dinner was worth more than anything." All this was taken as the fine irony of despair, even when these idealists became fat and rosy-cheeked—or even when, as sometimes happened, they began to cheat at cards and were caught with their hands in someone else's pockets. But since these idealists were always longing to "sacrifice" themselves for "the good of humanity," Dostoevsky tauntingly pretends to take them at their word. Why, he asks, should they not really accomplish a sacrifice—and perhaps go so far as to teach a serf child to read? "Sacrifice yourselves, O giants," he bitingly enjoins them, "for the good of all. . . . Sacrifice yourselves completely, with your sublime temperament and your sublime ideas—lower yourselves, shrink yourselves, to this one particular child."

The social Romanticism of the forties, in Dostoevsky's opinion, had fostered an inflated "egoism of principle," which allowed the Russian intelligentsia to live in a dream-world of "universal" beneficence while actually nursing their own vanity with perfect moral complacency. And the moral task confronting these liberal idealists was to live up to their own pretensions, i.e., to turn their abstract love of "humanity," which chiefly served to heighten their own self-esteem, into a concrete act of self-sacrifice directed toward a particular, concrete individual. This is of course precisely the theme of the second part of *Notes from Underground*; and we find a corresponding shift of style and treatment to accord with the new atmosphere of the period. Earlier the irony had been harsh, grating, jarring; the final argument of the underground man against the world of the Crystal Palace could only be the rage of madness and self-destruction. But what now comes to the foreground is a lighter comic tone of burlesque and caricature.

The youthful underground man, as Dostoevsky conceives him, is stuffed full of bookish ideas culled from the European and Russian Romantics and social Romantics—"I could not speak," he says of himself, "except 'as though I was reading from a book.'" Describing his own life he writes: "At home I mostly spent my time reading . . . it [the reading] excited, delighted and tormented me." All through the second part there are constant allusions to the artificiality of his responses ("how paltry, *unliterary*, and commonplace the whole affair would be," he thinks at one point). Entire sections are nothing but an extended burlesque of the underground man's stilted and pedantic reactions to the simplest human situations; and it is a testimony to the power of received ideas that Dostoevsky's sharply derisive comedy should so long have gone unnoticed. This comedy predominates in all the episodes preceding the meeting with the prostitute Lisa; for in these the underground man is caught in what we may call a "dialectic of vanity," which parallels the "dialectic of determinism" in part one. The underground man's vanity convinces him of his own intellectual superiority and he despises everybody; but when he realizes that he cannot rest without *their* recognition of his superiority, he hates others for their indifference and falls into self-loathing at his own humiliating dependence. This is the inevitable dialectic of an egoism which cannot forget about itself for a moment, and, in seeking to wrest recognition from the world, only receives dislike and hostility in return. Psychologically, this dialectic duplicates the conflict of all against all that arises socially from the Western European principle of egoistic individualism. And Dostoevsky's implication is that the underground man—an "educated man, a modern intellectual," as he gleefully calls himself—has, as a result of imbibing the European culture popular in Russia in the forties, lost almost all capacity for undistorted and selfless moral feeling.

VII. LISA

The comedy changes into tragedy, however, when the underground man finally encounters another human being who fails to respond in the accustomed fashion. Dostoevsky was well aware of this alteration in texture, and, while working on the second part of his novella, wrote to his brother Mikhail: "You understand what is called a *transition* in music. Exactly the same thing happens here. In the first chapter, seemingly, there is just chatter; but suddenly this chatter, in the last two chapters, is resolved by a catastrophe." (In the final version the catastrophe is actually developed through chapters 5 to 10). This catastrophe is the incident with the prostitute Lisa, which resolves the conflict between imaginary sentimental idealism and ethical reality in dexterous fashion. And, by the ironic paradox of the conclusion, it reveals all the shabbiness of the intelligentsia's "ideals" when confronted with spontaneous and unselfish love.

The incident with Lisa begins on the underground man's arrival in the brothel. The proprietress treats him like any other patron and a girl enters. As he goes out with her, he catches sight of himself in a mirror: "My flustered face looked utterly revolting to me: pale, evil, mean, with dishevelled hair. 'It's all right, I'm glad of it,' I thought, 'I'm glad that I'll seem repulsive to her. I like that." Not having been able either to subdue his companions earlier or to insult them with sufficient weight to be taken seriously, the underground man characteristically anticipates revenging himself on the helpless girl. The more repulsive he is to her, the more his egoism and need for domination will be satisfied by forcing her to submit to his desires. It is not by physical submission alone, however, that the underground man attains his triumph over Lisa. For when he becomes aware of her hostile and resentful attitude, "a peevish thought stirred in my mind and seemed to pass all over my body like some vile sensation." This thought takes the form of an effort to play on Lisa's feelings, and to triumph over her not only physically but morally as well.

The underground man thus proceeds to break down the armor of indifference and assumed cynicism by which Lisa protects herself against the debasing circumstances of her life. Mingling horrible details of degradation with images of felicity whose banality makes them all the more poignant—and drawing on Balzac's *Le Père Goriot* in the process—the underground man succeeds in bringing to the surface Lisa's true feelings about herself and causing the total humiliation of her emotional breakdown. None of this was of course meant seriously; the underground man simply had been carried away by the power of his own eloquence. But this time his words hit home—Lisa is too young, naive and helpless to see through their falsity. "I worked myself up into so pathetic a state" he says, "that I felt a lump rising in my throat and—all of a sudden I stopped . . . and, bending over apprehensively, began to listen with a violently beating heart." Lisa's bosom was heaving spasmodically, and she was making harrowing efforts to contain her sobs. "She bit the pillow, she bit her arm till it bled (I saw it afterwards), or clutching at her dishevelled hair with her fingers, went rigid with that super-human effort, holding her breath and clenching her teeth."

The underground man, carried away by his victory, cannot resist living up to the exalted role of hero and benefactor that he had so often given himself in fantasy. When he leaves Lisa he gives her his address with a lordly gesture, inviting her to come and see him; and it is on this gesture that Dostoevsky turns the *dénouement* of the second part. For the moment the underground man emerges from the self-adulatory haze of his charlatanism, he is stricken with terror. He cannot bear the thought that Lisa might see him as he really is—wrapped in his shabby dressing-gown, living in his squalid "funk-hole," completely under the thumb of his manservant Apollon, immersed in all the exterior poverty and ignominy of his daily life. Never for a moment does it occur to him that he might help her nonetheless; he is so absorbed in himself that the only thought of her as a reality is an obscure sense of guilt. "Inside me, deep down in my heart and conscience, something kept stirring, would not die, and manifested itself in a feeling of poignant anguish."

After a few days pass and Lisa does not appear, the underground man becomes more cheerful; at times, he says, "I even began indulging in rather sweet day-dreams." These all concerned the process of Lisa's re-education, her confession of love for him, and his own confession that

> I did not dare lay claim to your heart first because I knew you were under my influence and was afraid that, out of gratitude, you would deliberately force yourself to respond to my love, that you would rouse a feeling in your heart which perhaps did not really exist, and I did not want this because it—it would be sheer despotism on my part—it would have been indelicate. . . . (Well,

in short, here I got myself entangled in a sort of European, George-Sandian inexpressibly noble subtleties).

Interspersed with these reveries—which are a slap both at Sand's importance in the forties, and the strong Sandian influence in *What Is to Be Done?*—is the low comedy of the underground man's efforts to bend the stubborn Apollon to his will. Dostoevsky, as it were, here uses the classical theatrical technique of two identical plots, one serious and the other farcical; and he interweaves them adroitly by having Lisa enter when the underground man is revealing all of his hysterical impotence in face of the imperturbable Apollon.

By this time, the underground man has reached a dangerous pitch of frustration and nervous exasperation. He breaks down completely before the bewildered Lisa, sobbing and complaining that he is "tortured" by Apollon. But all this is so humiliating that he cannot help turning on her in spiteful fury when, by stammering that she wishes to get out of the brothel, she reminds him of all that has taken place. And here he breaks into a famous tirade, in which he tells her the bitter truth about their relation: "To avenge my wounded pride on someone, to get my own back, I vented my spite on you and I laughed at you. I had been humiliated, so I too wanted to humiliate someone." With the typical inversion of his egoist's logic, he shouts: "I shall never forgive you for the tears which I was shedding before you a minute ago. . . . Nor shall I ever forgive *you* for what I am confessing to you!"

But at this point, a strange thing occurs—strange at least to the underground man. Instead of flaring up herself and hitting back—the only response the underground man is accustomed to—Lisa realizes that he too is unhappy and suffering. She throws herself into his arms to console *him*, and they both break into tears; but given the character of the underground man, who cannot respond selflessly to any feelings, such a moment cannot last very long. "It . . . occurred to me just then, overwrought as I was, that our parts were now completely changed, that she was the heroine now, while I was exactly the same crushed and humiliated creature as she had appeared to me that night four days before." And not out of love but out of hate, the underground man makes love to her on the spot to revenge himself on *her* for having dared to try to console him. Even more, to make his revenge complete and humiliate her further, he slips a five-rouble note into her hand; but though completely broken by this encounter, Lisa manages to fling the money on the table unnoticed before leaving.

All the moral depravity of the underground man is starkly revealed in this climactic scene—or perhaps not so much depravity as moral impotence. For he retains his moral awareness all through the novella, although his egoism prevents him from ever putting this awareness into practice. Even here, when he finds the five-rouble note, he distractedly rushes out after Lisa in the silent, snow-filled street to ask her forgiveness. But then, pulling himself up short, he realizes the futility of all his agitation. For he understands very well that "I could not possibly have loved anyone because, I repeat, to me love meant to tyrannize and be morally superior."

And as he turns slowly home, he conceives the most diabolic rationalization of all for his conduct.

> Will it not be better, [he thinks] suppressing the living pain in [his] heart . . . that she should now carry that insult away with her for ever? What is an insult but a sort of purification? It is the most corrosive and painful form of consciousness! . . . The memory of that humiliation will raise her and purify her by hatred, and, well, perhaps also by forgiveness . . . And, really . . . which is better: cheap happiness or exalted suffering? Well, which is better?

With this final stabbing irony, Dostoevsky allows his underground man to use the very idea of purification through suffering as a rationalization for his viciousness. In so doing, he returns to the main theme of the first part and places it in a new light. "Consciousness" and "suffering" were seen to be values when the underground man, out of a need to preserve his human identity, wished to suffer *himself* rather than to rationalize his conduct as an effect of the laws of nature. But so long as these values remain a function only of egoism, there is always the possibility that they will be devilishly interpreted primarily to cause *others* to suffer as a way of purifying *their* souls. And here, we might add, Dostoevsky has provided an inadvertent but prophetic parody on all those critics who have so often accused him of advocating an indiscriminate "salvation through suffering."

VIII. CONCLUSION

As the second part of *Notes from Underground* comes to an end, the underground man again returns to his frustrated isolation. For one moment he had caught a glimpse of the way out of his racking dialectic. Lisa's complete disregard of her own humiliation, her whole-souled identification with the underground man's torments—in short, her capacity for selfless love and self-sacrifice—is the only way to break the sorcerer's spell of egocentricity. When she rushes into the arms of the underground man, not thinking of herself but only of *his* suffering, she is at the same time illustrating that "something else" which his egoism will never allow him to attain. This "something else" is the ideal of the voluntary self-sacrifice of the personality out of love. In his encounter with Lisa, the underground man has met this ideal in the flesh; and his failure to respond to its appeal dooms him irrevocably for the future.

Nonetheless, if we look at *Notes from Underground* as a whole, we see that the idealistic egoism of the forties, with its cultivation of a sense of spiritual *noblesse* and its emphasis on individual moral consciousness, does not merely have a negative value. It was precisely because of such "old and irrational habits" of his generation that, as we noted, the underground man held out against the Nihilism of the sixties; and this is the relation between the forties and sixties that continues to prevail in Dostoevsky's work. Egocentric though it may have been, the sentimental idealism of the forties still stressed the importance of free-will and preserved a sense of the inner autonomy of the personality. Such a sense is the presupposition for any human world whatever; and this is the basis on which Dostoevsky defends "egoism." But so long as such egoism remains self-centered, it is not by itself a moral act; more is required, as we see in part two, for the underground man to achieve moral self-definition. Exactly the same relation between the two generations was later portrayed in *The Devils*, where the sentimental idealism of the old liberal Stepan Trofimovitch Verkhovensky is far superior morally to the utilitarian ruthlessness of Peter Verkhovensky; but Stepan Trofimovitch is himself morally impotent, and, like the underground man in part two, rhetorically longs for some contact with "reality."

As a coda to the entire work, Dostoevsky offers some remarks in which *both* ideologies of the radical intelligentsia are rejected; and in which we hear the same plea to return to the Russian "soil" that echoes in Dostoevsky's articles. For these ideologies have disoriented the natural, instinctive, spontaneous, spiritual reactions of the Russian intelligentsia to the point where, without such foreign ideas, they are totally helpless; but so long as they cling to such crutches, they can never learn to walk by themselves. "Leave us alone without any books," writes the underground man caustically, "and we shall at once get confused, lose ourselves in a maze, we shall not know what to cling to, what to hold on to, what to love and what to hate, what to respect and what to despise. We even find it hard to be men, men of *real* flesh and blood, *our own* flesh and blood." And to the reply that the underground man is only speaking for himself, Dostoevsky reaffirms the "typicality" he had stressed in the opening footnote, while at the same time defining the technique of satirical exaggeration and parodistic caricature that he had used. "For my part," remarks the underground man, "I have merely carried to extremes in my life what you have not dared to carry even half-way, and, in addition, you have mistaken your cowardice for common sense and have found comfort in that, deceiving yourselves." Nothing, it seems to me, could more amply confirm the interpretation of *Notes from Underground* offered in these pages.

DONALD FANGER

Apogee: Crime and Punishment

*Dismal, foul, and stinking summertime Petersburg suits my mood
and might even give me some false inspiration for the novel.*
—DOSTOEVSKY, letter of 1865

Crime and Punishment is the first—and arguably the greatest—product of that special realism toward which Dostoevsky had been groping for twenty years; it is unquestionably his greatest Petersburg work. *The Insulted and Injured* had given him the secret of uniting several plots into a single entity, and *Notes from Underground* the secret of transmuting his new ideological concerns into the stuff of fiction. The result, like *Hamlet,* is a metaphysical thriller, a point that critics writing in English cannot be accused of neglecting. What they have tended to neglect is the fact that this is also the first great Russian novel to deal with the life of the one city in Russia that could be compared to the capital cities of the West. A brief historical excursus will show how this is so.

The novel was originally conceived in terms that suggest Zola. Projected under the title of "The Drunkards," it was to deal "with the present question of drunkenness . . . [in] all its ramifications, especially the picture of a family and the bringing up of children in these circumstances, etc., etc." Once Dostoevsky conceived Raskolnikov and his crime, of course, this theme became auxiliary, centering in the story of the Marmeladov family. But even apart from them, it runs like a red thread through the novel. Marmeladov is the first and most important, but hardly the last, of the drunkards Raskolnikov meets, and he himself is taken for one more than once. The

From *Dostoevsky and Romantic Realism: A Study of Dostoevsky in Relation to Balzac, Dickens and Gogol.* © 1967 by the President and Fellows of Harvard College. Harvard University Press, 1967.

sympathetic Razumikhin meets his friend's mother and sister in a state of intoxication; Porfiry pointedly remarks that he does not drink; Raskolnikov's fateful interviews with Zametov and Svidrigailov take place in taverns. The reason for the prevalence of this motif is not far to seek: it was, like so much else in the novel, a particularly acute social problem of the day. In 1860 the government had projected a new system of excise taxes, hoping to control the consumption of alcohol more effectively. Its hopes proved illusory, but they were shared at the time by Dostoevsky's own journal, *Vremya* (*Time*), which in 1861 devoted a long article to drunkenness in France and particularly to the family side of the question. Again in 1865, when Dostoevsky was beginning work on the novel, the government set up a commission to review the whole question of the "excessive use" of alcohol among the people, provoking a whole series of journalistic comments. As Leonid Grossman has noted, "against the background of these numerous articles disclosing the connection of alcoholism with prostitution, tuberculosis, unemployment, destitution, abandoned children, and the physical dying-out of whole families, the main lines of the story of the Marmeladovs emerge with full clarity." Grossman goes on to say that, in contrast to the Falstaffian tradition of treating this theme in literature, Dostoevsky introduces for perhaps the first time its tragic side; in this, he parallels the innovation of his revered Pushkin, who similarly reversed a comic tradition in his "Covetous Knight," where he turned a tragic light on the figure of the miser (some three years before the appearance of Balzac's Grandet).

The theme of prostitution is closely connected with that of drunkenness, not only in the figure of Sonya but in a number of incidental figures— the seduced girl whom Raskolnikov rescues from her lecherous pursuer, the girl who attempts suicide in the canal, the procuress Louisa Ivanovna, the attractive Duclida. Here, too, he was exploiting an issue of immediate public concern. His own journal had printed in 1862 an article by one M. Rodevich entitled "Our Social Morality," which bespoke sympathy for "fallen women," tracing hunger and poverty as among the chief causes of prostitution and noting, "not infrequently even a mother will sell her daughter into vice because of oppressive poverty." The writer argues that one cannot condemn these daughters "of civil servants who are retired or have large families, or of rich men who have squandered their money": these are women "who have nothing to eat, who are consumed by need, pricked by the needle which provides a pitiful maintenance of pennies for laborious work." One recalls Marmeladov's pathetic account of Sonya's efforts to live as a seamstress. Equally striking in its pertinence to the novel is the point of another article in the same journal, entitled "Remarks on the Question of Social Morality" and signed only "P.S." Here the author goes beyond the question of sympathy for the prostitute. "The external manifestations of vice," he finds, "differ essentially from the internal, and one cannot combine them in one unbroken link. One can meet in a single evening a hundred prostitutes on any fine, brightly lighted street, and nevertheless have not the slighest notion of the state of their morality. To get this notion, it would be necessary to be transported into their internal world, and look at their behavior from there, from the new standpoint." The author sees this as a major literary problem and calls upon contemporary writers to produce "five or six stories of the life of prostitutes, honestly told with all the details and with psychological indications." Dostoevsky, whether deliberately or not, did answer this call: after Liza in *Notes from Underground* came Sonya; and after her the kept women, Nastasya Filippovna and Grushenka.

As it was with alcoholism and prostitution, so with the theme of crime. In the story of Raskolnikov, a number of impulses from the concerns of the day converge. There is, first of all, the fact that at this time Russian juridical thought, and especially criminology, was undergoing a renewal. Grossman thinks it likely that Dostoevsky himself was responsible for the editorial commentaries on a host of articles in his journals dealing with murder, robbery, and the efficacy of legal punishment. Besides theoretical pieces, moreover, he printed a long series entitled, "From the Criminal Affairs of France," which he commended as being "more engrossing than any possible novels because they [the trial accounts] illuminate such dark sides of the human soul, which art is not fond of touching on—so that if it does touch on them, it does so only in passing, in the form of episodes." Included in the series was the case of Lacenaire, whom Dostoevsky characterized in an editorial note as "a phenomenal, enigmatic, fearful, and interesting figure." What is more striking is a whole set of parallels between Lacenaire, as described in *Vremya*, and Raskolnikov. The young Frenchman is pictured as having features that were "fine and not without nobility. On his ironical lip there trembled constantly a ready sarcasm." He wanted to devote himself to the study of law and afterwards referred to himself, falsely, as a "student of law." Jailed in 1829 for killing Benjamin Constant's nephew in a duel, he dabbled in literature and on his release, along with a former fellow prisoner, used a three-edged rasp to kill one Chardon and his elderly mother. After the robbery—like Raskolnikov—he found two visitors asking for Chardon at the unlocked door, and with minor differences of detail he avoided being recognized in much the same way.

Finally, one more topical item, closer to home, may have contributed to the writing of *Crime and Punishment*. In the spring of 1865, just when

Dostoevsky was forming the idea of his novel, the Petersburg newspapers were filled with detailed stenographic accounts of the trial of Gerasim Chistov, who had killed two old women with a short-handled ax and robbed them of over eleven thousand rubles.

The very theme of money, moreover, struck so forcibly at the beginning and throughout the novel, was of particular pertinence just at this moment. It is true, of course, that Dostoevsky had always made the effects of money, or its absence, a key factor in his fiction, as the title of his first work indicates. But money plays a different role here—a role related as much to the world of *Le Père Goriot* as to that of *Poor Folk*. For the first time the figure of the predator becomes important (Alyona Ivanovna, Luzhin), and the temptation to quick riches immediate and compelling. As Paris and London had done some decades before, Petersburg was becoming a capitalist city, like them subject to new and severe financial crises. One such crisis was acute in the early sixties, and Dostoevsky's *Vremya*, along with the rest of the press, was full of articles about it; one of 1863 was entitled "Where Has Our Money Gone?" and discussed "the commercial, industrial, and financial crisis hanging over us." The situation reached its peak in 1865, the year Dostoevsky began *Crime and Punishment*. He felt the pinch himself, for he had to liquidate his publishing business, making for catastrophic losses in subscriptions. As Grossman sums it up: "Journals were closing down, general credit was falling improbably, the government was issuing loan after loan, the money market was overflowing with paper tokens, the government exchequer was 'oppressed' with a deficit. Such was the year when compassionate passers-by held out a penny on the street to the student Raskolnikov, and the titular councillor Marmeladov created his variation on the folk saying: 'Poverty is not a vice, but destitution, sir, destitution is a vice, sir.' "

Balzac had referred repeatedly to Rastignac as "one of those young men who . . ."—and Dostoevsky evidently intended Raskolnikov also to represent a trend. He was one of the "new men." Half a year before Dostoevsky began work on *Crime and Punishment*, his journal, *Epokha*, printed an article by Strakhov which claimed as the most striking feature of the time the fact that "Russian literature is troubled by the thought of the new men." Turgenev's Bazarov had been the first such, but many others followed. One expression of the trend that particularly exercised Dostoevsky was Chernyshevsky's *What Is to Be Done?* (which bore the subtitle, "From Stories about the New Men"). *Notes from Underground* had been an open argument with it, and *Crime and Punishment* only continued the polemic, incarnating the tragedy of nihilism in Raskolnikov and caricaturing it in Lebezyatnikov and, partially, in Luzhin. Dostoevsky's coworker Strakhov was quick to observe that the new novel was the first to show an unhappy nihilist, in whom life was struggling with theory—and the observation takes particular point against the contention of Chernyshevsky's hero Lopukhov that "a theory should be in its nature cold" and that "the mind should judge about things coldly." The story of Raskolnikov is Dostoevsky's answer by extrapolation to this notion.

Theory entered by another door as well. One of the calligraphic exercises in Dostoevsky's notebooks for *Crime and Punishment* consists of three carefully traced names: "Napoleon, Julius Caesar, Rachel." Whatever the last may mean, the first two are traceable to one of the sensations of early 1865, a book propounding the question of the role and rights of "extraordinary natures" that was widely discussed in the Western and Russian press— Louis Napoleon's *Histoire de Jules César*. It appeared in Paris in March and was already known from numerous reviews when it came out in Russian translation a month later. "When extraordinary deeds testify to a high genius," we read in the preface, "what can be more repulsive to common sense than to attribute to this genius all the passions and all the thoughts of an ordinary man? What can be more false than not to recognize the superiority of these exceptional beings, who appear in history from time to time like flashing beacons, dispelling the darkness of their times and lighting up the future?" In the widespread discussion attending this book, critics were quick to see that the defense of Caesarism was a defense of Napoleonism, that the book was not a history but a veiled self-justification. What is relevant to present concerns is the theory on which the self-justification was made to hinge, the theory that superior natures are beyond the morality that binds the mediocre mass of people. One passage from an article in *The Contemporary* (*Sovremennik*) setting out this theory has been found by a Soviet critic to match the summary Porfiry gives of Raskolnikov's own theory. "Borrowing" here is not in question; rather, we see once more the close correspondence between the concerns of Dostoevsky's novel and those of the day—indicative of a timeliness that must have struck contemporary readers and intensified the impact of the book with myriad relevancies now lost to us.

One last such relevancy—a literary one—calls for mention. The early sixties saw a flood of literature, sketches and feuilletons as well as stories and novels, devoted to the city. This literature was related, of course, to the "physiological sketches" of the forties, but its orientation and tone were already different. Here was no quest for an attitude toward the city, but the expression of one; and here one finds less the personal stylistic note than a concern with reportage. The new literature was a social literature, designed to record the facts of urban poverty, disease, and misery. These works bore titles like "Hell," "Silence," "A Ruined but Sweet Creature," "The Homeless," "The First Lodging," "In the Hospital and in the Cold," "A Day on a Barge, A Night in Lodgings (From the Notes of a Hungry Man)," "The Poor Lodgers (A Physiological Sketch)," *Petersburg Slums*, and so on. One popular subgenre was the description of city streets. In Krestovsky's *Petersburg Slums* a litterateur asks: "Have you read my 'Alley'? . . . Read it; it is really a Dickensian thing. Everyone is wild about it." Other popular subgenres were descriptions of taverns and the dwellings of the poor. Dostoevsky himself published a number of these works in his journals; of the sketch by Gorsky, entitled "In the Hospital and in the Cold," he wrote his brother: "This is not literature at all, and it would be stupid to regard it from that standpoint; it is simply *facts*, and useful ones."

In short, the whole social fabric of *Crime and Punishment*, many of its concerns and many of its figures and themes, attach to the immediate social and literary background of the middle sixties. Even the figure of Porfiry—like that of Dickens's Inspector Bucket—is directly connected with recent reforms in police administration and theory; even the title of the novel matches the title of an article by one V. Popov, published by Dostoevsky in his *Vremya* in 1863: "Crime and Punishment (Sketches from the History of Criminal Law)." All these elements, of course, are either transmuted in the novel or made auxiliary to the main drama; they acquire a predominantly psychological significance and are used to point questions of personal rather than social morality. Yet their background should not be overlooked; it gives the work added weight of reference precisely because so much of the reference was familiar to Dostoevsky's readers and could be taken for granted by the writer, so that a simple allusion might conjure up a whole social context. Dostoevsky's novel was a topical one, and the very evidence of topicality suggests how solid was the realistic ballast he put into it.

In the light of all this, the transition from the original plan of "The Drunkards" to the final version of *Crime and Punishment* becomes clearer. Dostoevsky did not completely abandon the idea of a social novel, but evolved it. In fact, the seeds of that evolution are implicit in his idea of a social novel. Soon after its appearance, he had praised Victor Hugo's *Les Misérables* as an outstanding treatment of the great theme of nineteenth-century literature: the resurrection of the fallen man. This he found a "Christian and highly moral" theme, and in it, right up to the end of his life, he saw also the principal greatness of his favorites, Dickens and George Sand. A social novel, in other words, was unthinkable for him except as it touched on moral resurrection: resurrection was the rationale, the rest important but subsidiary. So the story of the Marmeladovs comes to counterpoint that of Raskolnikov, and the social—which is to say, the urban—background is used to lend perspective and immediacy to these individual dramas. The question must now be confronted more precisely: Just what is the role of the city in Dostoevsky's novel?

ROLE OF THE CITY

Crime and Punishment is, as a recent Soviet critic has said, the first great Russian novel "in which the climactic moments of the action are played out in dirty taverns, on the street, in the sordid back rooms of the poor." What is true of the climactic moments is true of a strikingly high proportion of the others as well. Add the police stations and the shabby hotel where Svidrigailov spends his last night, and you have almost all the set changes this drama requires. Where Balzac, for contrast, alternates the scenes of *Le Père Goriot* between the Maison Vauquer and the various haunts of the aristocracy, Dostoevsky achieves a grimmer and equally effective contrast by alternating his scenes between stifling rooms and the often no less stifling streets. So the book opens with Raskolnikov hurrying downstairs from his fifth-floor cubicle, "which he rented from lodgers," out onto the street, where the July heat and "the closeness, the crush, and the plaster, scaffolding, bricks, and dust everywhere, along with that peculiar summer stench, so familiar to every Petersburger" all irritate his already overworked nerves. "The truly intolerable stench from the saloons, which are particularly numerous in that part of town, and the drunks he kept running into, although it was a weekday, gave a finishing touch to the repulsive and melancholy atmosphere of the picture" (pt. 1, chap. 1). The neighborhood is carefully specified in order to explain why Raskolnikov's extreme shabbiness goes unremarked: "Because of the proximity of the Haymarket, the abundance of a certain kind of establishment, and the preponderance of the artisan and working-class population crowded in these streets and alleys of central Petersburg, the general panorama was sometimes enlivened with such types that it was hardly possible to imagine the sort of figure that might cause surprise" (pt. 1, chap. 1).

Here, then, assailing the nose, eyes, and nerves, is the general scene of the action, carefully and closely observed in innumerable details. If Dostoevsky has been sometimes thought to slight this background, it is because, unlike Balzac, he tends to avoid bald exposition whenever possible; instead of a preliminary scene setting, he begins with action, and the reality of the scene is built in passing, by a host of details called forth in the order of their relevance to what is going on. The setting is a function of the action. To collect these details here would be a pedestrian task, and an unnecessary one:

an attentive reading even of the first few pages suffices to discover them. But we may note that distances, too, are indicated with revealing exactitude: Raskolnikov has an even seven hundred and thirty paces from the gate of his building to the huge house fronting on the canal where Alyona Ivanovna, the pawnbroker, lives; seeing Marmeladov home from the tavern where he first meets him is a matter of two or three hundred paces. These distances set up a unity of place that is not artificial. Here is the heart of Petersburg, a neighborhood that is also a microcosm. Its compactness facilitates and rationalizes coincidence, as well as the swift accumulation of the action, just as its social nature underlines the irony of Marmeladov's reference to "this capital, magnificent and adorned with innumerable monuments" (pt. 1, chap. 2).

There is nothing monumental about these teeming streets and alleys except the quantity of life they contain. Raskolnikov wonders in a moment of reverie "why in all great cities men are not just impelled by necessity, but somehow peculiarly inclined to live and settle in just those parts of the city where there are no gardens or fountains, where there is most dirt and stench and all sorts of filth" (pt. 1, chap. 6). Yet he himself is drawn to them, as if by an instinctive and obscure fellow-feeling that is a refutation of his intellectual theory about himself. Here, for all its squalor, is quintessential urban life, and its forms, as Dostoevsky had shown in *Notes from Underground*, are liable to be sordid. "I love to hear singing to a street organ," Raskolnikov confesses to an alarmed stranger, "on a cold, dark, damp autumn evening—it must be damp—when all the passers-by have pale green, sickly faces, or better still when wet snow is falling, straight down, when there's no wind—you know what I mean? and the street lamps are shining through it."

Chapter 6 of part 2, from which the above incident is taken, is a fair specimen of the world of the streets as this novel presents it. Raskolnikov slips down from his room at sunset and "greedily" drinks in "the stinking, dusty, city-infected air." From habit he walks toward the Haymarket. He passes the organ-grinder with his fifteen-year-old singer, "dressed up like a lady in a crinoline, gloves, and a straw hat with a flame-colored feather in it, all old and shabby," and makes inquiry of "a young fellow in a red shirt who stood yawning at the entrance to a corn chandler's shop." Dostoevsky's account is crammed with the sort of detail that makes it a physiological sketch par excellence:

> Now he entered the alley, thinking of nothing. At that point there
> is a long building, entirely occupied by saloons and other
> establishments for eating and drinking; women kept running in
> and out of them every minute, bareheaded and without coats. In

two or three places they crowded the sidewalk in groups, chiefly around the ground-floor entrances, where one could walk down two steps into various houses of pleasure. From one of them at that moment there came a racket that filled the whole street—the strumming of a guitar, voices singing, great merriment. A large group of women were crowded around the door; some sat on the steps, others on the sidewalk; still others were standing and talking. Alongside, in the street, a drunken soldier with a cigarette was swearing loudly; he seemed to want to go in somewhere, but to have forgotten where. One beggar was quarreling with another, and a man, dead drunk, was lying right across the road. Raskolnikov stopped by the throng of women. They were talking in husky voices; all of them were bareheaded and wearing cotton dresses and goatskin shoes. Some were over forty, but there were others not more than seventeen; almost all had black eyes.

It is here that he meets the good-looking prostitute Duclida, to whom he gives fifteen kopecks for a drink, observing at the same time her "quiet and earnest" coworker, "a pock-marked wench of thirty, covered with bruises." "Only to live," he reflects, "to live and live! Whatever sort of life—only life! . . . Man is a scoundrel! . . . And a scoundrel is the man who calls him one for that." In the tavern called the Crystal Palace he has his fateful conversation with Zametov in which he all but confesses to the murders, runs into Razumikhin, then goes out to stand on the X—Bridge to witness the attempted suicide of the drunken woman. The sordidness of his earlier encounters had reflected his own spiritual state; this one anticipates an impulse to suicide. He feels disgust at the ignobility of what he has witnessed: "No, that's loathsome . . . water . . . not that," he mutters. He goes back to the scene of his crime, again all but confesses, and returns once more to the street— where he will find Marmeladov, crushed by a carriage and dying.

The streets are Raskolnikov's contact with life; it may seem tautological to add, with urban life, but his walk to the islands gives the addition a special point. Here is Nature and, as might be expected, "the greenness and freshness were at first pleasing to his tired eyes, accustomed to the dust of the city and the huge houses that hemmed him in and oppressed him. Here there were no taverns, no closeness, no stench. But soon even these new, pleasant sensations turned morbid and irritating" (pt. 1, chap. 5). The world of nature offers no lasting solace and no way out because Raskolnikov's whole world is the man-made one of the city; there and there alone his drama arises, and there it must be played out. Theories, like cities, are made by men and their creators must come to terms with them; escape cannot remove the problem of reconciling "living life" with the conditions of city life. So even amid the sickly life of the streets, Raskolnikov finds a kind of tentative community. His own is a tragedy of the garret, and it is kept significantly apart from his experience out of doors. There his generosity comes instinctively into play, in his quixotic attempts to save the seduced and drunken girl from her pursuer, in his disinterested gift of money to Duclida, in his helping the injured Marmeladov and lavishness to his family; and there, too, if a coachman whips him for getting in the way, a passer-by will slip him a small charity "for Christ's sake."

The real city, in short, rendered with a striking concreteness, is also a city of the mind in the way that its atmosphere answers Raskolnikov's spiritual condition and almost symbolizes it. It is crowded, stifling, and parched. All the more significant, then, is the single contrasting "spiritual landscape" evoked in describing Svidrigailov's last night. Svidrigailov's element is absurdity and chaos. After the abandonment of his designs on Dunya, he wanders through a series of taverns to wind up in a "pleasure garden" whose claim to the title is "one skinny three-year-old spruce tree and three little bushes," accompanied by "two little clerks" who attract him because they both have "crooked noses, one slanting to the right and the other to the left" (pt. 6, chap. 6). Even the tentative communication Raskolnikov finds possible in public places is impossible here. Svidrigailov is chosen to decide a dispute, but though he listens to them for a quarter of an hour, "they were shouting so that there wasn't the slightest possibility of understanding anything." As his suicidal intention ripens, the rain begins: "The water fell not in drops, but beat on the ground in streams. Lightning flashed every minute and one could count to five in the space of each flash." Drenched to the skin, he goes about settling his affairs and exactly at midnight, in a roaring wind, crosses the river and wanders in a bleak and "endless" street in search of the shabby Hotel Adrianople. There, in a cramped and filthy room, he watches a sordid argument through a crack in the wall and undergoes his nightmares. He hears (or dreams he hears) the cannon shots signaling a flood—the primal chaos, the revolt of the element on which the city stands. Raskolnikov's symbol is aridity; Svidrigailov's is water. The landscapes in which they make their fateful moves reflect this. Svidrigailov goes out to kill himself (as Dostoevsky had originally planned for Raskolnikov to do). In a thick mist, he walks along a "slippery dirty wooden sidewalk," "picturing the waters . . . which had risen high during the night, Petrovsky Island, the wet paths, the wet grass, the wet trees and bushes and at last the very bush [under which he plans to kill himself]." The streets are empty (Raskolnikov never encounters empty streets); the houses look "despondent and dirty." "A dirty, shivering dog" crosses his path "with its tail between its legs." In such a setting, he chooses a sour-faced Jewish doorman wearing an incongruous "Achilles helmet" as witness of his suicide, and with him he holds his last, absurd human conversation. They stare at each other for a long moment. Then "Achilles" breaks the silence with his caricatured Russian:

> "Vot you vont here?" . . .
> "Nothing at all, my friend," replied Svidrigailov. "Good morning!"
> "Dis ain't no place."
> "I'm leaving for foreign parts, my friend."
> "Foreign parts?"
> "To America."
> "To America?"
> Svidrigailov took out the revolver and cocked it. Achilles raised his eyebrows.
> "Vot's diss? Dese chokes (jokes) ain't no place here."
> "And why not, pray?"
> "Chust becoss it ain't de place."
> "Well, friend, it makes no difference to me. The place is good enough. If they ask you about it, tell them he said he'd gone to America."
> He put the revolver to his right temple.
> "You kent here, dis ain't de place!" Achilles gave a start, his pupils growing bigger and bigger.
> Svidrigailov pulled the trigger.
>
> (pt. 6, chap. 6)

Svidrigailov's last hours are spent on the outskirts of the city, in symbolically different weather, yet the "atmosphere" here, for all its difference from that of Raskolnikov's heart of Petersburg, is one with it in emotional tonality: it is, in Svidrigailov's own characterization, "gloomy, harsh, and queer."

The atmosphere of the interiors is no less so. From the anonymity of the labyrinthine alleyways to the secrecy of the labyrinthine stairways is only a step. Scenes of a comparable intensity are played out on them—most often of flight and evasion. The book opens with a description of Raskolnikov's creeping down the stairs of his own building "like a cat" to avoid a humiliating meeting with his landlady. On the pawnbroker's "back staircase, dark and narrow," he suffers agonies of fear as he tries to leave the scene of his crime. Staircases are (despite the confusion of directions) a kind of entrance to the underworld, linking the public with the private. They are, as it were, the tendrils of the city, half-public, half-private, uniting into great and artificial groups the various closed worlds of rented rooms and apartments. Already enclosed, they inspire a kind of claustrophobia, but the rooms do this to an even greater extent.

At the beginning of chapter 3 (part 1), Raskolnikov awakens and looks about with hatred at "a tiny hencoop of a room about six paces in length" with "dusty yellowish paper peeling off the walls" and "so low-ceilinged that a man of more than average height would feel uneasy in it and seem at every moment to be about to bump his head on the ceiling." And the room is in keeping with his state of mind: "He had positively withdrawn from everyone, like a tortoise in its shell, and even the face of the servant girl who was obliged to serve him and sometimes looked into his room provoked him to irritation and convulsions." Here is the extreme of isolation and the fitting birthplace of his theory. His mother notices immediately when she enters. "What a terrible room you have, Rodya, it's just like a coffin," she remarks; "I'm sure it's half from your room that you've become such a melancholic." And Raskolnikov, thinking of the murder he has just committed, takes up the point. "Yes," he answers, "the room had a lot to do with it . . . I thought of that, too. . . . If you only knew, though, what a strange thing you said just now, mother" (pt. 3, chap. 3). Later, in his confession to Sonya, he repeats: "I hid in my corner like a spider. You've been in that hole, you've seen it. . . . And do you know, Sonya, that low ceilings and tiny rooms cramp the soul and the mind?" (pt. 5, chap. 4). What is worse, they take on an attraction of their own: "Ah, how I hated that garret! And yet I wouldn't go out of it! I purposely wouldn't" (pt. 5, chap. 4). Like all of Dostoevsky's dreamers, from Ordynov through the underground man, Raskolnikov "preferred lying still and thinking" (pt. 5, chap. 4). The difference is that his dreams are rational dreams—not a substitute for the world but a plan for mastering it. "You don't suppose," he asks Sonya, "that I went into it headlong like a fool? I went into it like a wise man, and that was my downfall" (pt. 5, chap. 4). For such wisdom his airless and sordid little cubicle is a telling symbol.

The only other room in the book comparable to this in its extremity is the room taken by Raskolnikov's quasi-double, Svidrigailov, in the Adrianople. The parallels are striking: "It was a little cell with one window, so low-ceilinged that even Svidrigailov could barely stand up in it; a very dirty bed, together with a plain painted chair and table, took up almost all the space. The walls, which seemed to consist of a few planks knocked together, were covered with worn paper, so dusty and tattered that the pattern was indistinguishable, though one could still divine the color (yellow). One part of the wall and ceiling was angled, as is customary in attics, though in this case it was a stairway that went over the sloping portion" (pt. 6, chap. 6). For the rest, the apartment of the Marmeladovs, the room into which Luzhin first puts Dunya and Raskolnikov's mother, Razumikhin's room, and those of the pawnbroker all share a depressing poverty, depressingly itemized, and function on the social and realistic, rather than on the personal and symbolic, level. The single exception is Sonya's, "a large but extremely low-ceilinged room . . . [that] looked like a barn; it was a very irregular quadrangle and this added a grotesque note. A wall with three windows opening on to the canal ran aslant so that one corner, forming a very acute angle, was a deep recess, hard to descry in the weak light; the angle of the other corner was monstrously obtuse. In all of this large room there was hardly any furniture" (pt. 4, chap. 4). The room of the sacrificial prostitute, like that of the murderer, is low and poor: but though irregular, it is spacious. His is like a coffin; hers, Dostoevsky reports, is like a desert: but even in a desert life is possible. And where his has a single window facing inward, on the courtyard, hers has three windows, looking out onto the canal. Sonya's room, like its mistress, is oriented toward austerity, but outward—toward life.

Of these streets and rooms is the Petersburg of *Crime and Punishment* made up. It is the city of unrelieved poverty. The wealthy are depraved and futile, like Svidrigailov, or silly and obnoxious, like Luzhin. Magnificence has no place in it, because magnificence is external, formal, abstract, cold. The striking scene where Raskolnikov, returning home from his visit to Razumikhin, pauses to take in the majestic panorama along the river, suggests this: "When he was attending the university, he had stopped at this same spot, perhaps a hundred times, to gaze at this truly magnificent spectacle and almost always to wonder at the vague and elusive impression it produced in him. This magnificent panorama always seemed to exude an inexplicable coldness: this splendid picture was for him the embodiment of some blank and dead spirit. He wondered every time at his somber and enigmatic impression, and, mistrusting himself, put off seeking an explanation" (pt. 2, chap. 2). In its mysterious intensity, this recalls the sunset vision on the Neva of "A Weak Heart" and "Petersburg Visions." But where, in the earlier context, the city seemed to be invested with magic, here it is divested even of life. This beauty is rare, as is the sunlight itself. The real city lies not along the majestic river but by the narrow canals, and it is closer to Svidrigailov's characterization: "This is a city of half-crazy people. If we were a scientific people, doctors, lawyers and philosophers could make the most valuable investigations in Petersburg, each in his own field. There are few places where you'll find so many gloomy, harsh and strange influences on the soul of man as in Petersburg. Consider the influence of the climate alone" (pt. 6, chap. 3). The real city is here, where for all its distortion there is life—which means people and suffering. Raskolnikov had bowed to Sonya, saying that he was bowing "to all the suffering in the world"; at the end he kneels in the middle of the Haymarket, "bow[s] down to the earth, and kiss[es] that filthy earth with joy and rapture" (pt. 6, chap. 8). "He's bowing down to all the world and kissing the great city of St. Petersburg and its pavement," a drunken workman comments. The pavement is as holy as the earth; it, too, in its terrible way, bears life.

In this scene, a magnificent touch follows the workman's comment: "Quite a young fellow, too!" another bystander remarks.

> "And a gentleman," someone observed in a sober voice.
> "These days there's no telling who's a gentleman and who isn't."

Here to the exalted emotional reality is added a reminder of the mundane social reality—its constant foil in this work. The role of "the great city of St. Petersburg" as it existed, concretely and socially, in the middle of the 1860s, is fundamental in *Crime and Punishment*. Only once this is recognized can the significance of that role be fully and truly assessed.

SIGNIFICANCE OF THE CITY

If much of Dostoevsky's social detail can be called naturalistic, his point of view cannot. There is, in the last analysis, small interest shown in the determining role of social forces, and no description of the city that betrays any quasi-scientific interest in how its life is lived. By quasi-scientific I mean a detached interest in the phenomenon as such. Detachment in this sense was foreign to the premises of Dostoevsky's art, and Vyacheslav Ivanov's remark [in *Freedom and the Tragic Life: A Study in Dostoevsky*] about his attitude toward nature is equally true of his attitude toward the city: "It is as though he had taken an oath never to become what the lyrical poet Fet calls 'an idle spectator of Nature.'" The static surface of things leaves him as cold as the panorama on the Neva leaves Raskolnikov: for him, significant action is all, and the significance of any action inevitably establishes the relevant point of view. In a notebook passage planned for the narrator of *The Possessed*, he makes clear his general policy:

> I do not describe the city, the setting, the customs [*byt*], the people, the occupations, the relations and curious fluctuations in those relations, of the strictly private . . . life of our city. . . . I have no time to occupy myself directly with a picture of our parts. I consider myself the chronicler of a single private and curious event,

> which took place among us suddenly and unexpectedly of late, and struck us all with astonishment. It goes without saying that since the thing happened not in the sky but among us, it is impossible for me not to touch sometimes on the purely pictorial and customary side of our . . . life; but I forewarn [the reader] that I shall do this only to the exact extent that the most unavoidable necessity requires. I shall not concern myself specially with the descriptive part of our contemporary ways.

These words, designed for a different book and a different locale, still fit the narration of *Crime and Punishment*—in fact, all of Dostoevsky's Petersburg works. Here the "single private and curious event" is, of course, the murder: this is what determines the relevance of everything else in the novel. The fact that Dostoevsky was able to make good his stated intention to "re-explore [*pereryt*] all questions" in the book only demonstrates his skill in using this sort of concentration.

His notebooks make clear the enormous difficulty he had in deciding on a point of view. Originally this was to be a retrospective confession, by Raskolnikov himself, but the plan was dropped as too constricting. What we have instead is a compromise of genius: third-person narration, which allows the inclusion of scenes (like Svidrigailov's suicide) otherwise impossible, and yet is so close to Raskolnikov's point of view as to approach interior monologue. The only perspective on Raskolnikov comes from his own actions, his own words, and those he inspires in the other characters. His is the only mind into which we penetrate, his the only thoughts we read—and his the guiding perception of the city.

The last may be new in degree, but not in kind. It is a perception based on isolation, that isolation which comes finally to define so much of Dostoevsky's myth of Petersburg. It is first of all symbolized by the tiny and sordidly furnished rooms and apartments: Raskolnikov's "coffin," Alyona's spotless and characterless den, the crowded pigsty of the Marmeladovs—and before them the underground man's "mouse hole," the cubicle Ivan Petrovich takes over from old Smith, the room of the narrator of "White Nights," "into which a different sun shines," Golyadkin's refuge, and Devushkin's side of the kitchen. Located often at the top of dark and dirty stairways, in huge blocks of apartment buildings, these are the discrete cells of which the city is made, and their trapped inhabitants are a product or outgrowth of the fantastic city.

It is possible to dream in such places, but hardly to live, as the physical and spiritual health of Dostoevsky's characters plainly testifies. (In *Crime and Punishment*, Razumikhin and Dunya alone among the principal characters are conspicuously healthy, and their lives alone survive

Raskolnikov's tragedy unchanged.) Dostoevsky's characters so regularly suffer
from some unnamed fever—the product of poverty and climate, as well as
the emblem of their spiritual states—that this becomes a feature in its own
right of the fantastic city. Disease for Dostoevsky, as for the romantics,
"represented the negation of the ordinary, the normal, the reasonable and
contained the dualism of life and death, nature and non-nature, continuance
and dissolution, which dominated their whole conception of life (Arnold
Hauser, *The Social History of Art*). Added to isolation, it creates fear.
"Petersburg is hell for me," Dostoevsky had written his brother Mikhail at
the very beginning of his career: "It is so miserable, so miserable to live here.
And my health, it appears, is worse. Moreover, I am terribly afraid."

Crime and Punishment is unusual among Dostoevsky's novels in that
it is set entirely in the summer. Twenty years before, in the fourth installment of his "Petersburg Chronicle," he had spoken of the need to get away
from the city in the summer, to "quench with the variety of natural
phenomena our eternal unsated thirst for direct, natural life." Here we see
the alternative. From the stultifying closeness of his room Raskolnikov, ill
and weak, is driven into the stinking, no less stifling streets. There is, of
course, an obvious symbolism in the state of airlessness that surrounds him—
but, as will be shown, his situation is only an extreme form of the general
Petersburg condition. After reading his mother's letter, Raskolnikov feels
"stifled and cramped in that little yellow room that was like a cupboard or
trunk." His eyes and mind "seek space" and he hurries down to the street,
where he walks, "as usual, without noticing his way, whispering and even
speaking aloud to himself" (pt. 1, chap. 3). This walk—and the others like
it—can be plotted in detail on a map: Dostoevsky's directions are precise.
Yet the city through which he walks fades and reappears as his attention
rests on it or takes flight. And since the narration adheres so closely to his
point of view, something of a sporadic solipsism results, creating a city that
is fantastic in its evanescence and showing that the streets, far from dispelling isolation, only underline it. Nor do they offer relief from oppression.
Raskolnikov's love for them is a perverse one: "I like it," he says, "when all
the passers-by have pale, green, sickly faces"; he goes out "to feel even more
nauseated." He is in this respect, as in others, like the underground man,
who liked to walk along some of the same crowded streets "at dusk just when
they become more crowded with people of all sorts, merchants and artisans
going home from their day's work, with faces worried to the point of looking malicious"; what attracts him is "just that cheap bustle, that blatant pro-
saic quality" (pt. 2, chap. 8). (So too will Arkady Dolgoruky, the narrator
of *A Raw Youth*, find fascinating "the faces of poor people hurrying back

home to their corners from work and trade," each with "his own sullen anxiety in his face"—and "perhaps not one common uniting thought in the crowd.") This is a petty, masochistic pleasure, the paradoxical community one atom of the city can feel at observing the separateness of the other atoms.

Individuals, then, are the basic units of Dostoevsky's myth of the city—not, as in the case of Balzac's professed intention and Dickens's practice, families. By and large, Dostoevsky's families tend to be parodies of what is usually understood by that word. Marmeladov is the head of his family in an ironic sense only, and Katerina Ivanovna shows her motherliness by goading her stepdaughter into prostitution and, in her madness at the end, making grotesque street performers of her children. Raskolnikov's family is without a father. It may be taken as a general rule that, when families do appear in Dostoevsky's fiction, they tend to be shown in process of dissolution. The city, sociologically speaking, is largely responsible for this dissolution; and so, for literary purposes, it makes the ideal background for dramas of isolation. In this respect, Dickens's treatment is exceptional, for he still follows tradition—the double tradition here being the sentimental one (exemplified in *The Vicar of Wakefield*) and, even more important, the comic one that finds its happy ending par excellence in a wedding. Tolstoy, the more thoroughgoing realist, knew better, noting in his plans for *War and Peace* that marriage seemed to him a starting point, rather than a denouement. And in his novels of Paris, despite his programmatic statement that he regarded the family as the essential unit of society, Balzac also either omitted it or showed its disintegration.

Dostoevsky's novels from *Crime and Punishment* on show an increasing concern with the family as a theme—but always in the light indicated above. He is most explicit on the subject in *A Raw Youth*, in which he goes into the theme of "accidental families" (*sluchaynye semyi*)—a term whose significance is obscured by Constance Garnett's translation, "exceptional families." In his *Diary of a Writer*, Dostoevsky takes issue with Tolstoy precisely on this point:

> Never has the Russian family been more shaken, disintegrated, unsorted, and formless than at present. Where will you find today "Childhoods and Boyhoods" that could be represented in such clear and harmonious fashion as that, for example, of Count Leo Tolstoy, in his depiction of *his own* epoch and his own family, or in his *War and Peace*? All these creations are now *no more than historical pictures of the distant past.* . . . The contemporary Russian family is becoming more and more an *accidental* family.

Precisely *accidental*—there you have the definition of the contemporary Russian family.

(July–August 1877, chap. 1)

In a similar sense, the city is accidental—not in its founding, but in the
"abstract" results of that intentional founding. Petersburg becomes "the most
fantastic city, with the most fantastic history of all the cities of the earth"
in terms of the abnormality of the life that is lived there. The absence of roots,
frequent changes of apartment, precariousness of employment—these are further signs. And so, of course, is the absence of nature: the only vegetation
in the city of *Crime and Punishment* are the pathetic geraniums in
Raskolnikov's room and the pitiful young spruce tree and two bushes of the
"pleasure garden." Even the climate is inimical to normal life, producing those
"pale, green, sickly faces" that Raskolnikov professes to love and provoking
a kind of reciprocal action in coloring the Petersburgers' own perception of
their city: it can be seen as early as *Poor Folk* and *The Double*. This reciprocity
very often issues in action that is hallucinatory, or seems to be.

Preceding the doubt about what is or is not hallucination, and giving
it foundation, are actual illness and fever. The illness is often—as with
Raskolnikov—unspecified, apparently a generally run-down condition that
leaves the body weak and the mind dangerously active. This is the natural
state of the dreamer, his physical debility reflecting his alienation from "normal life," his feverish mental freedom representing both a contributing cause
and a compensation. The fever is the badge of alienation, poverty,
malnutrition—the mark of the Petersburg hero or antihero in Dostoevsky's
heroically antiheroic Petersburg. Dreams are born of it, which represent
themselves as spiritual illness, and they move the dreamer "to see the fantastic in everything." The earliest essays in this direction are the most extreme: *The Double* deals, confusingly, with the psychopathology of hallucination, as does, less obviously, "The Landlady." Bem, in fact, has explained
the latter as an experiment in "the dramatization of delirium." Neither of them
was fully appreciated until the twentieth century—though it is only fair to
add that this latter-day appreciation was prompted by a desire unknown to
earlier critics, the desire to see their place in the process that led to the later
works. In any event, *Crime and Punishment* is the supreme example of this
technique. Where the actual goings-on of the earlier work were too obscure,
here they are made clear. Through the filter of Raskolnikov's fever and distrac-
tion, objective time, place, and situation shine through; their color is that
of the filter, but the outlines are their own.

Thus Raskolnikov's movements at the scene of the murder are described
as mechanical, and afterwards he moves about the pawnbroker's apartment

in a state "of blankness, even dreaminess." Returned home, he spends the night on his sofa, *seeming* to wake up from time to time. Walking the streets, he falls into meditation, talking to himself, noticing only what obtrudes upon his reverie or what catches his attention in the brief pauses between meditation. The scene on K—Boulevard where he tries to rescue the drunken and seduced young girl from her pursuer is an excellent case in point. He has not yet committed murder; he is still contemplating it, spurred on by the knowledge of his sister's imminent self-sacrifice on his behalf. When the subject recurs to him, he feels "a hammering in his head, and there [is] a darkness before his eyes." Looking for a place to sit, he notices a woman walking in front of him, and his attention fastens on her, "at first reluctantly and, as it were, with annoyance, and then more and more intently" (pt. 1, chap. 4). From a scrutiny of her dress and manner, Raskolnikov reconstructs the circumstances of her seduction and even imagines the scene of her return home. The incident is a telling one, not only for what it indicates about Raskolnikov, and not only as an incident characteristic of the Petersburg of this book, but because it also exemplifies the general manner in which the city is seen. What, after all, do we know of this girl's affecting story? The answer is, only what Raskolnikov observes and imagines. His deductions are certainly plausible, given the objective facts (which a policeman confirms). But we shall never know if his version is true. We have the girl's situation, but only Raskolnikov's notion of its meaning, only Raskolnikov's projection of its pathos.

Of the characters most intimately involved in Raskolnikov's fate, something similar is true. Sonya, for instance, is seen only in his company, only in reaction to him and through his reaction to her. And Svidrigailov, of whom this cannot be said, nevertheless appears so abruptly in Raskolnikov's room that the latter wonders pointedly and repeatedly whether he is only a continuation of his dream. (Svidrigailov himself—as befits the double of Raskolnikov—is subject to the same doubts about what is real and what is hallucination; these terrible doubts are the substance of his last night at the Adrianople.) This centrality of Raskolnikov's point of view extends even to Porfiry the detective, whose intimate probings of Raskolnikov's conscience (in the double French sense) entitle us to say of him, as Voltaire said of God, that if Porfiry did not exist it would have been necessary for Raskolnikov to invent him. And, in a special sense, the suspicion is permissible that he did.

That sense is not a literal one, of course. R. P. Blackmur, who first made this point in print, offers no convincing justification for slighting the detective as "that thirty-five-year-old roly-poly of the disengaged intellect called Porfiry," but he is right in insisting that "he is a fancy of the pursuing intellect whom Raskolnikov must have invented had he not turned up of his own accord" and in pointing out further:

> As Svidrigailov and Sonya between them represent the under-part, and the conflict in the under-part, of Raskolnikov's secret self, so Porfiry represents the maximum possible perfection of the artificial, intellectual self under whose ministrations Raskolnikov *reasons* himself into committing his crime, and who therefore is the appropriate instrument for driving him to the point of confessing it. It is Porfiry . . . who whenever he comes to sack Raskolnikov leaves him in a state of collapse, just as it is either Svidrigailov or Sonya who gives him strength.

What Blackmur does not credit is the full force of Raskolnikov's attraction to Porfiry, which—despite his resistance, by turns fierce and weary—represents an attraction to confession; before he ever meets Porfiry he displays this in his talk with Zametov in the tavern. The police stand for the retribution Raskolnikov yearns for and resists at the same time. They too—almost as an institution—represent an impulse of Raskolnikov's own fevered psyche.

In what could well be an epigraph to the whole novel, Dostoevsky writes:

> In a morbid state, dreams are often distinguished by an unusual vividness and clarity, and by an extraordinary resemblance to reality. Sometimes a monstrous picture will take shape, but the setting and the whole process of presentation are nevertheless so plausible and contain details so subtle, unexpected, yet artistically consonant with everything else in it, that the dreamer could never have invented them while awake, were he even such an artist as Pushkin or Turgenev.
>
> (pt. 1, chap. 5)

In the light of this statement, and reinforced by many clear hints, the fact is unmistakable: this whole novel is like a bad dream, and the social and physical Petersburg in which the action takes place is no less so.

Poverty also seems like a bad dream in the extremity of its depiction in the Marmeladov family. Is not having "nowhere to go" the mark of the most terrifying nightmares? Dostoevsky, as Arnold Hauser has noted, is "one of the few genuine writers on poverty, for he writes not merely out of sympathy with the poor, like George Sand or Eugène Sue, or as a result of vague memories, like Dickens, but as one who has spent most of his time in need and has literally starved from time to time." But this valid observation needs to be taken a step further, for otherwise it might appear to leave Dostoevsky among the humanitarian novelists, the fighters for social justice—as, from his early work, he was judged to be. The fact is that from *Poor Folk* on, he is developing a special and different theme of his own—the revolt of the poor man—which is based on the protest of an individual against an unjust fate. Poverty is thus considered as the destruction of the right of individuality, as the suppression of its potentialities.

The result of all the factors discussed so far—isolation, fever, dreaming, rootlessness, the unnatural city, poverty—is crime. This is by no means to say that Raskolnikov's crime is the socially determined effect of these abstract causes. Dostoevsky had a streak of the naturalist in him, but it was always subsidiary to other conceptions. What can be said, rather, is that all these factors furnish together *the perfect theater* for Raskolnikov's crime, at once providing the opportunity and feeding the impulse. Berdyaev justly points out [in *Dostoevsky*] that Dostoevsky "shows the ontological consequences of crime," but he overstates his case in claiming that "this spiritual nature [refuses] to explain evil and wickedness by reference to social environment." It would be truer to say that he refuses to explain these things by reference to social environment alone, for Dostoevsky's notebooks make clear his own increasing uncertainty about the real motive for Raskolnikov's crime—as does the final text of the novel. In the last analysis, the motives are plural, just as the causes are antecedent to motive.

With the story of Raskolnikov, crime enters Dostoevsky's world, and none of the novels that follow will be without its murder (or, in the case of *A Raw Youth*, its near-murder). This fact alone is important. It is not crime in general that interests Dostoevsky, but only crime against life: how negligible are questions of property can be seen from Raskolnikov's characteristic neglect of what he has stolen. As a result, there can be no correspondence between Dostoevsky's myth of the criminal and Balzac's, for the glamor that suffuses the Balzacian criminal is essentially a military glamor: his brilliance is the brilliance of a strategist at war with society, a sui generis pursuer of *la carrière ouverte aux talents*. In prison Dostoevsky had met criminals, and in his report of those years he treats his fellow convicts by and large in the traditional Russian way, as "unfortunates." What they have done anyone, in principle, might do; their crimes are frequently crimes of passion; their common humanity is only too evident. There is, however, another class of criminal that fascinated him, represented by one Orlov, "a criminal such as there are few, who had murdered old people and children in cold blood":

> This was not at all an ordinary man. . . . I can positively assert
> that never in my life have I met a man of such strength, of so

> iron a will as he. . . . His was literally a full victory over the flesh.
> It was evident that the man's power of control was limitless, that
> he despised every kind of torture and punishment, and feared
> nothing in the world. We saw in him only infinite energy, a thirst
> for action, a thirst for vengeance, a thirst to achieve his chosen
> end. Among other things I was struck by his strange haughtiness.
> He looked down on everything with incredible disdain, but
> without any effort to raise himself above others—just, somehow,
> naturally. . . . He was very sharp-witted, and somehow strangely
> open, though by no means talkative.
>
> (*The House of the Dead*, pt. 1, chap. 4)

Orlov is a healthy and spontaneous specimen of what Raskolnikov would make himself through will and intellection. Dostoevsky shows an awed fascination for him. But he goes no further than this and never really takes the "exceptional nature" as a problem to investigate. In the major novels, the problem that occupies him is that of the man who is not quite exceptional but seeks to be, who spurns the obscure promptings of his real nature to follow a theory, to act on an idea. The Russian word for crime means "transgression" or "overstepping"—and one of Dostoevsky's main themes, from *Crime and Punishment* onward, becomes the tragedy of overstepping the proper bounds of intellect by taking it alone as a sanction for action. Raskolnikov's intellect sanctions his crime (just as Ivan Karamazov's intellect will sanction Smerdyakov's crime); his punishment and his hopes for salvation come through the discovery that intellect is insufficient, that it cannot prevent moral suffering, that the holiness of life is a fact impermeable to reason. Dickens's late realization that the criminal does not struggle away from his crime but toward it is the essence of Dostoevsky's practice. His criminals are all amateurs—a fact that underscores their similarity to Everyman. This is why we cannot feel the excitement of the detached spectator in reading *Crime and Punishment*, as we do in reading *Le Père Goriot*. "All of us without exception," as Blackmur comments, are "deeply implicated in the nature of the Crime."

We are in the same way implicated in the moral crime of Sonya's enforced prostitution, and this robs her profession of any vestige of the excitement that a Balzac might find in it. Here again the sense is plain in which Dostoevsky can be called the inheritor of romantic realism. Alone among the major Russian writers of his time, he deals in large measure with the themes of romantic realism—and consistently he reinterprets them, gives them a new sense and a quite new drama by detypifying them, removing them from social categories, and returning them to the undifferentiated fund of common humanity whose mark is, above all, suffering. In his notebooks, this is spelled out:

> THE IDEA OF THE NOVEL. The Orthodox view[;] in what does Orthodoxy consist. There is no happiness in comfort; happiness is purchased by suffering. Man is not born for happiness. Man earns his happiness, and always with suffering. There is no injustice here, for the title and consciousness of life (i.e., directly sensible by the body and the spirit, i.e., by the whole vital process) is acquired by experience *pro* and *contra*, which one must take upon oneself.

The burden of suffering, then, is to be assumed by experience *pro* and *contra*—which means, in Raskolnikov's case, experience of the intellect and the contrary experience of the spirit. The form is that of a debate. The experience pits the deepest irrational sources in him against the highest refinements of dialectical skill. Here again Dostoevsky the inheritor shows his innovation; it is, as Arnold Hauser formulates it, "the fact that he is a romantic in the world of thought, and the movement of thought has the same motive power and the same emotional, not to say pathological, impetus in him as the flood and stress of the feelings had in the romantics." This can already be seen in the morbid dialectics of the man from underground, and it persists throughout the subsequent novels: this, more than anything else, separates his early period from his late. His novels are, as the Soviet critic Bakhtin has shown, "polyphonic," in the sense that they are peopled with incarnate points of view which the author allows full and independent play, and which he neither complements nor resolves as do traditional omniscient narrators. Viewpoints clash in the open, as it were, outside of any governing moral convention or *parti pris*.

The polyphonic novel, Bakhtin says [in *Problems in Dostoevsky's Poetics*], was possible only in the period of capitalism—a statement equally true of the romantic realism of Balzac and Dickens. But he goes on to suggest that the development of capitalism in Russia (and especially in Petersburg) peculiarly favored this new literary mutation, because capitalism had come suddenly "and caught intact a variety of social worlds and groups which had not, as in the West, begun to lose their distinct apartness." (Compare Balzac's lament about the disappearance of social distinction in his time.) For aristocratic writers with their roots in the relatively changeless countryside, a stable and inclusive point of view might still be possible; but in the cities, the contradictions of a time of transition were "bound to manifest themselves especially sharply, while at the same time the individuality of those worlds that had been thrown off their ideological balance and into collision was bound to be especially full and clear." In this way, Bakhtin argues, "the objective preconditions were created for the essential multilevel and multivoice structure of the polyphonic novel." It remains only to add that this historical picture lent a symbolic plausibility (if not an actual one) to the way in which Dostoevsky managed to bring characters from different social classes into contact with one another on a footing of essential equality. It is not that he erases class barriers; what he does is to concentrate on certain déclassé aristocrats whose fortunes or tastes have led them out of their conventional circles and into the arena of free-floating atoms, the heart of Dostoevsky's mythical city where a common rootlessness does make for a common human destiny—and where the very absence of conventional norms can suggest to a mortally sick Katerina Ivanovna and a dangerously isolated Raskolnikov that all, indeed, is permitted.

In Bakhtin's analysis, then, we have the particularization of Lewis Mumford's general observation [in *The City in History*]: "Perhaps the best definition of the city in its higher aspects is to say that it is a place designed to offer the widest facilities for significant conversation." "The dialogue," he goes on, "is one of the ultimate expressions of life in the city: the delicate flower of its long vegetative growth," and he adds: "Not by accident, then, has more than one historic city reached its climax in a dialogue that sums up its total experience of life. In the Book of Job, one beholds Jerusalem; in Plato, Sophocles, and Euripides, Athens; in Shakespeare and Marlowe, Dekker and Webster, Elizabethan London. In a sense the dramatic dialogue is both the fullest symbol and the final justification of the city's life." Mumford's list of literary monuments to particular cities, if extended in time, would have to include Balzac's Paris, Dickens's London, and Dostoevsky's Petersburg. All of them, most notably the last, fit and illustrate his definition.

We are in a position to see now why it is that Dostoevsky's myth of the city—the third great one in the nineteenth century—has about it such an unrivaled sense of modernity in the mid-twentieth century. Is it not, in the first place, because his myth divests the city of any facile glamor, removes from it the happy ending of "success," informs it with a spirit of searching and anguish? He presented for the first time the life of the city in all its sordidness—not simply to show what these conditions automatically did to people, as the naturalists would show, but to raise the problem of how, within them, sentient human beings might pursue the quest for dignity. And on a less literal level, he raised the chaotic city to the position of a symbol of the chaotic moral world of man, so that the contradictions of the second find their counterpart in the contrasts of the first. He showed, without abstraction, bare human consciousness striving in a world where there were few of the usual categories of normality, striving with a terrible and unsought freedom, isolated and rootless, together without community, to rediscover the conditions for "living life." The nature of the struggle is ultimately intellectual, the seductions ideological, the goal a new or an old morality—something to fill the void. With two devastating world wars behind us and a last one threatening in the offing, with a displacement of persons unparalleled in modern times, amid a technological revolution that makes tradition more an object of nostalgia than something that can be lived, with nations acting on principles that are Raskolnikov's raised to the nth power, it is Dostoevsky's city and his alone that prefigures our dilemma. In any present-day metropolis can be found pieces from Dickens's myth or from Balzac's. But our private and collective fears and uncertainties, our besetting struggles with what the existentialists term absurdity, are engaged only by the myth of "the most abstract" and "the gloomiest city in the world," whose heroes are forever wandering the streets, aimless and distracted.

Crime and Punishment introduces the great themes that fill the later books—questions of transgression, guilt, and suffering, of freedom and authority, of "new men," positivism, socialism, the difficulties of belief and the tragedy of unbelief. In Raskolnikov's story we see Dostoevsky not only discovering these themes, but refining his myth of Petersburg to accommodate them. The city, here and henceforth, is "gloomy, harsh, and queer" in ways quite absent from the earlier works; he had regarded it from the very beginning as a symbol, but only here does the symbol take on its full freight, with all the implications of its abstract origins explored in the contemporary cultural context. This new fullness of his use of the city contains a kind of transcendence: when "The Drunkards" had metamorphosed into *Crime and Punishment*, the artist, too, had metamorphosed, "found himself," as we say retrospectively. And it was precisely his developing myth of the city that had led him to the discovery.

After this, the possibilities of the city no longer called for the same exploration. Among the remaining novels of his major period, only *A Raw Youth* re-creates the essentially Dostoevskian Petersburg—and then, significantly, the result is a potpourri of familiar motifs and an engaging failure. In the others, the symbolic presence of Petersburg is of fundamental importance, but it operates as a fixed quantity. This is most strikingly seen in *The Possessed* and *The Brothers Karamazov*, where theories related to Raskolnikov's and matured, like his, in the Petersburg ambience, result in murder. Stavrogin and the young Verkhovensky were both educated in the capital and tasted their first corruption there; Ivan Karamazov is the Petersburg intellectual par excellence.

There is, finally, another sense in which *Crime and Punishment* inau-

gurates Dostoevsky's major period. This fullest treatment of the Dostoevskian city, this first presentation of the major themes, is also the first full
example of the peculiar realism associated with his name. In *Crime and
Punishment* Dostoevsky brought a technique to maturity, and the great novels
all reflect the poetics we have seen him fashioning through his Petersburg
works. One might speak with full justice in this connection of a Dostoevskian "poetics of the city."

GARY S. MORSON

Dostoevsky's Writer's Diary as Literature of Process

Dostoevsky wrote to A. E. Vrangel' in 1865 that he had in mind a new "periodical publication, but not a journal." This new publication eventually matured into *The Diary of a Writer*, which Dostoevsky intended as an original art form. "I dream of starting a new weekly journal, one of my own type, which I have invented," he wrote in his correspondence. "Without fail I wish to publish something like a newspaper . . . and now the form and the purpose have become completely clear." By 1877, Dostoevsky was fully satisfied that "the *Diary* has matured to the point where even the slightest change in its form is impossible." But critics, perplexed by this strange mixture of journalism and fiction, have largely ignored the work to which Dostoevsky attached such great importance.

So, too, the *Diary*'s central idea—the prediction of the apocalypse and the millennium—has not been taken literally, as it was meant. The *Diary* repeatedly asserts that the millennium will not only be realized on earth, but that it is actually imminent. Quoting from a wide range of prophetic writings, the *Diary* itself becomes a work of "prophecies" of "the end of the world." Insisting on a "Utopian Understanding of History," the *Diary* is written in "expectation" of the immediate establishment of "the brotherhood of men, the universal reconciliation of the nations . . . and, finally, in the very renewal of men on the true principles of Christ. And if the belief in this 'new word,' which Russia, at the head of a united Orthodoxy, could say to the world, is a 'utopia,' worthy only of ridicule, then let me, too, be counted among these utopians, and let me be ridiculous." Like St. John of the Apocalypse,

From *Russian Literature* 4, no. 1 (January 1976). © 1976 by North-Holland Publishing Co.

the author reveals the "denouement," the "last battle" that is *"inevitable and near."* "Now for everyone in the world already 'the time is at hand,' " the diarist applies the line from Revelations to the present. "And it is about time, too."

But while Dostoevsky constantly insists that he is speaking "without any exaggeration" and that he believes in the apocalypse "in reality," critics have tended to treat Dostoevsky's beliefs as "the hallucinations of an epileptic" (to quote his proofreader at *The Citizen*) or, in E. H. Carr's phrase, as a "jingoistic" series of "outrageous lapses from good sense and good taste." Yet it is precisely the concept of the apocalyptic transformation of history into utopia that explains the *Diary's* peculiarly fragmented form.

In the days when all is being made new, art itself, it would seem, must assume a new form; Dostoevsky called this form *The Diary of a Writer, A Monthly Publication.* If we consider the implications of this, the work's full title, we will see the relation of its form to its task. For the sake of analysis, consider the three parts of the title separately.

I. THE SEARCH FOR A VOICE

The work is, first of all, a *diary*, a *personal* record of a subject written by the author to himself, where the central figure is the self—either as theme or, at least, as observer. "This will be a diary in the literal sense of the word" and will treat "the impressions I have lived through each month," the author writes in the brief explanation of his new form that appears at the close of the January 1876 issue. Though it traces political and social history, the *Diary* is not a chronicle, Dostoevsky declares; and he repeatedly insists that in his descriptions "primarily of actual events" the authorial "I" is of central importance.

This subjectivity of the *Diary* also points to the nature of its essential speech act. In it, the reader is also the author, what is said is already known. In this sense, a *Diary* is Platonic, seeking self-knowledge through *anamnesis*; it is a recollection of the self. In other words, as Dostoevsky puns on the title of a rival publication, his work is a search for a "voice." As the presence of strictly autobiographical articles stresses, a diary is, if nothing else, an act of self-consciousness, and the voices of the speaker are self-consciously spoken. They are experimental; he is trying them out. Constantly re-examined, they have a *tentative* quality, in the attempt to discover the voice of the real self. On this level, therefore, the work takes on a tone of questioning and uncertainty. It is an ongoing search, an exploration in process, and neither its direction nor its goal is ever perfectly clear. It is part of the nature of a diary to be indefinite.

Uncertainty is also implicit in a second characteristic of a diary. As its etymology implies, it is *periodic*, day to day. The narrator has no knowledge of the future of his work, and its unity is one of recurrent concerns rather than conscious plan. The author speaks to us in the present, because we are—like the readers who so frequently interrupt his editorial work—present at the *Diary*'s continuous creation. Always awaiting the outcome of the events he describes and "lives through," the author resembles the "I" of a novel, a narrator-protagonist who does not know his own fate in the story he tells. Fortune may literally play tricks on him, since the external world of contingency is formative of his work. The "plot" is unintentional.

Stated negatively, therefore, a diary lacks both an audience and foreseen sequentiality. There is sequence, rather than consequence. "My position is in the highest degree undefined," writes Dostoevsky in his introduction to the 1873 *Diary*. "But I will be speaking to myself and for my own pleasure, in the form of this diary, and let come what may. About what will I speak? About everything that strikes me or makes me think." "Here there is even caprice," he declares. Caprice, whimsy, surprise—these words recur throughout the *Diary*'s self-referential passages. Characteristically, the titles of several articles contain the word "apropos" ("po povodu") or refer to their contents as "Unsubstantiated Assertions" or "Inappropriate" ideas. So, too, the length of the titles—which often run into several sentences—implicitly stresses the arbitrariness of "everything that strikes" the author. The diarist repeatedly insists on the absolute, whimsical freedom to shape a purely personal work as he wishes. "The point is that I am sometimes writing my *Diary* not only for the public, but for myself," Dostoevsky reminds us at the beginning of one particularly capricious, "personal and private," passage. "This is probably why there is so much roughness and so many surprises in it, i.e. thoughts perfectly familiar to me, which have long been working themselves out within me, but which, to the reader, seem to be something which has suddenly leaped out of somewhere, without any connection with the preceding." Guided by the association of ideas, the diarist emphasizes the pure spontaneity of his "impressions."

As a diary, therefore, the work is ultimately related to its themes of solipsism and insanity. The diarist frequently refers to the frenzied, disconnected quality of his speech, and he explicitly stresses the thematic significance of his subjective form. "I strongly suspect that for a long time the *Citizen* will have to speak only to itself and for its own pleasure," Dostoevsky coyly declares in the introduction to the 1873 *Diary*; and he immediately concedes that "according to medical science, conversation with oneself signifies a predisposition to insanity." So, too, Dostoevsky cites the diary of Gogol's madman as a precedent for his own.

This subjective level of the work is epitomized by the story constructed on an inner monologue, "The Meek One." The story is subtitled "fantastic," the author explains in his foreword, because of its formal similarity to personal "notes" ("zapiski") when there was no opportunity for making a record. The story resembles a "stenographer's" transcript more than an ordinary, finished narrative, the foreword insists; and the story's narrator seems to echo this characterization when he concedes in his first paragraph that "I am not a literary man" and will relate his thoughts as they occur to him. As in a diary, the speech is immedite and the speaker is the listener; the narrator, says Dostoevsky, "talks to himself" and (like his creator, it would seem) "contradicts himself. . . . Sometimes he justifies himself, sometimes accuses her, and sometimes embarks on extraneous explanations." As in the whole *Diary*, speech to oneself is "a series of reminiscences" and reminiscence takes on a therapeutic, self-analytic function in the speaker's search for "order." "The point is that now I wish to recall everything," the hero explains the function of his narrative. "I wish to clarify it to myself."

The stream of the speaker's consciousness is the only formal rule of these notes, Dostoevsky stresses in his foreword. Each statement is tentative, spoken "to gather his thoughts into focus." Like the diarist, this narrator also digresses, rebukes himself, and returns to the topic. "Faster, faster," he exclaims, "this is not the point at all!" But as the reminiscence progresses, "little by little . . . truth reveals itself to the unhappy man." The reader witnesses the evolution of tone and voice from their incoherent beginning (the story starts on an ellipsis) to the last line of the monologue: "No, seriously, when they take her away tomorrow, what will I do?" "Seriously"—he now says—because this line, unlike its predecessors, is *not* tentative.

Like the diarist, the narrator of "The Meek One" is constantly changing his stance. "Now he speaks to himself, now he addresses, as it were an unseen listener—some kind of a judge." For as an emblem of the whole, the story is a work in process, and, as such, subject to all the vicissitudes of temporal being, all the "surprises" which may be "working themselves out." "The process of the narrative," says the foreword, "lasts several hours, with interruptions and interludes, in a confused form." And the form of these notes, like that of the *Diary* as a whole, is designed precisely to stress this narrative *process*.

II. PRODUCT AND PROCESS

Dostoevsky's "new publication," however, is not simply a diary; it is *The Diary of a Writer*. If we stress the second term of the title, we emphasize the literary quality of the work. Now, since a diary is precisely an unpolished and purely private work, there is an implicit tension between these two levels. A "writer's diary" borders on contradiction, as Dostoevsky seems to indicate when he introduces an editor to go over the spontaneous monologue of "The Meek One." Though he does not interfere with the psychological order of these "notes," the editor polishes the record of the imagined stenographer; indeed, the stenographer, too, is a purely literary device, and Dostoevsky cites a literary precedent for it in Victor Hugo. The writer, therefore, is doubly present, and the work is an author's creation with a foreword "From the Author." It cannot be the spontaneous product it strives to be; it must lie, as Dostoevsky says, somewhere between a story and notes. Spontaneity and the absence of authorial intent cannot be completely achieved.

If there is a writer, there must also be a reader, and the presence of an audience modifies the nature of the speech. If the word "diary" emphasizes the speaker, the "writer" implicitly calls attention to the listener. "I directly consider my many correspondents to be my co-workers," Dostoevsky writes in "To the Readers" (December 1877); and their formative role achieves symbolic representation when, in such stories as "Bobok" and the "Plan for an Accusatory Story," they are fully personified.

For the character of the "I" changes by having an addressee. His tone by necessity becomes more public, therefore less spontaneous and more given to irony and indirection. "I too naively thought that this would be a *genuine* 'diary' " writes Dostoevsky, instead of one "only for show, for the public." No longer a purely private act, his speech becomes material, contrivance. It is now self-consciously art, and as art—artificial. In addition to the self-consciousness of a diary, therefore, we now have the new self-consciousness of an actor before an audience.

Self-conscious spontaneity—this is the result of the tension between a diary and a literary work. Now, a literary work that denies its status as a finished product is what Northrop Frye has called "literature as process" (as opposed to "literature as product") and Frye's terms suggest that, in fact, the idiosyncrasies of Dostoevsky's creation draw on an essential moment of the literary act. "Some languages," writes Frye in his essay "Towards Defining an Age of Sensibility,"

> use verb-tenses to express, not time, but the difference between completed and continuous action. And in the history of literature we become aware, not only of periods, but of a recurrent opposition of two views of literature. These two views are the Aristotelian and the Longinian, the aesthetic and the

psychological, the view of literature as product and the view of literature as process.

It is characteristic of "process" literature that the "plot" is not in the events, but in the development of the work itself. "All the great story-tellers," continues Frye,

> have a strong sense of literature as a finished product. The suspense is thrown forward until it reaches the end, and is based on our confidence that the author knows what is coming next. . . . But when we turn to *Tristram Shandy* we not only read the book but watch the author at work writing it; at any moment the house of Walter Shandy may vanish and be replaced by the author's study. . . . here we are not being led into a story, but into the process of writing a story; we wonder, not what is coming next, but what the author will think of next.
>
> Sterne is, of course, an unusually pure example of a process-writer, but even in Richardson we find many of the same characteristics. Johnson's well-known remark that if you read Richardson for the story you would hang yourself, indicates that Richardson is not interested in a plot with a quick-march rhythm. Richardson does not throw the suspense forward, but keeps the emotion at a continuous present. Readers of *Pamela* have become so fascinated by watching the sheets of Pamela's manuscript spawning and secreting all over her master's house . . . as she fends off assault with one hand and writes about it with the other, that they sometimes overlook the reason for an apparently clumsy device. The reason is, of course, to give the impression of literature as process, as created on the spot out of the events it describes.

The periodic nature of the *Diary* quite literally makes it, too, literature created on the spot out of the events it describes; and a "continuous present" is maintained by the nature of the form. Here, *The Diary of a Writer* follows the example of *Tristram Shandy* (which also came out in installments), as well as that of Boswell (with a diary). And in Dostoevsky's running correspondence with his readers, the epistolary technique comes into play.

Since the diarist creates as he goes along, his work does not have an end, in the Aristotelian sense; it simply stops when its author dies. Here, again, the *Diary* resembles *Tristram Shandy*, which was also to continue indefinitely, and ends simply by breaking off arbitrarily at the end of an installment. For in process literature, the unity is not achieved by throwing the suspense forward until it reaches the end: instead of an end in the sense of completion, we have an end in the sense of an organizing purpose.

In literature of process, therefore, the seeming lack of ordered sequentiality is an essential part of the form. The author *allows* his material to get out of hand, and makes himself a victim, as well as a creator, of his work. Thus we have the time-honored device of digressions—in Sterne, Byron, and Pushkin—a device which the *Diary* continually uses. In the opening article of the first chapter of the January 1881 issue, for instance, the diarist promises to discuss the Russian economy, but immediately digresses into his usual themes of idealism, popular principles, and the Jews. Both the promise and its violation are repeated in each of the chapter's essays, as the author plays on his "Inability" to keep to the topic. "Instead of a Firm Financial Tone I Am Lapsing into Old Words," proclaims the very title of one article; and the avowedly mistitled essay, "Is It Possible among Us to Ask for European Finances?" immediately "lays bare" the *Diary*'s recurrent device:

> "Well, what about finances? What about that financial article of yours?"—they (the readers) will say to me. But, again, what kind of an economist, what kind of a financier am I? I do not dare to write about finances at all. Why then did I dare and why do I intend to write such an article? Precisely because I am sure that, having begun to write about finances, I will immediately deviate to something altogether different, and thus I will produce not a financial, but some wholly different article. And this alone encourages me.

Deliberately breaking his own rules, the diarist thus creates as he goes along. For "such is my nature," he coyly admits at the beginning of this chapter's third article, "that I must write impatiently, directly, without preparations."

So, too, the device of fortuitous "interruptions" creates the illusion of composition at a continuous present. Readers protest the author's conclusions before they are even clearly formulated; and, like the narrator of "Bobok," they may at any moment invade the editor's office itself and demand that their contributions be included in the text. Voices clash, prose lacks "measure," articles are misshapen. Indeed, in the attempt to create the illusion of immediate creation, Dostoevsky even uses Sterne's favorite device of physically mangling his text. The "Certain Person's 'Half-Letter' " is exactly that because it was cut in half, it seems, during a dispute in the editor's office—and so must be printed as it stands, beginning with the conjunction "and."

Of course, the spontaneity here is highly self-conscious; this is, again, not a diary, but *The Diary of a Writer*. For it is precisely the *illusion* of spontaneity that characterizes process literature. In Sterne, the humor derives from our knowledge of the intentionality behind the ramblings, of the control to which the chaos is subject. The form, in other words, works by playing on its essential contradiction of contrived freedom.

Like the personae of *Onegin* and *Tristram*, the author of the *Diary* is constantly *posturing*. His caprice is willed. Marvelling at the spontaneous generation of his own text, he makes the reader aware of the laboratory of his creation as well as its product; and the *Diary*'s headlines often call more attention to the process of the author's composition than to his conclusions ("Because of Inability I Lapse into Something Spiritual," "An Altogether Special Word about Slavs, Which I Meant to Say Long Ago," "I Lapse into Old Words"). So, too, the inclusion of advertisements and information about subscriptions in the text (like Tristram's lectures on printing and pagination) reminds us of the mechanics of the ongoing process of publication. Above all, the motif of "apologies"—like indulgences for sins still to be committed— stresses the conscious manipulation of the supposedly spontaneous text. Implicitly and explicitly, they remind us of the directing hand of the creator, that the free play of inspiration is itself a well-wrought artifice.

"The Boy at Christ's Christmas Tree" corresponds to this level of *The Writer's Diary*. In contrast to the narrator of "The Meek One," this narrator repeatedly emphasizes his formative role in the action he describes. Rather than direct "stenography," this tale is self-conscious contrivance, and the creator is present from the first sentence. "But I am a novelist," the opening paragraph begins, and the authorial "I" who has "composed" the tale, constantly reappears in its few pages to construct situations and find explanations for them. "It seems to me that the boy was in a basement" with his mother, he introduces his characters; but he soon interrupts his description to return to the laboratory of his creation. "How did she happen to be here?" he abruptly asks his "co-worker," the reader. "She may have come from some other town." The alternation of narrative and authorial commentary on its "composition" continues throughout the tale; and the ending—which is almost literally a *deus ex machina*—stresses the unmistakable, controlling hand of the author. Speaking directly to the reader about the text, the narrator repeatedly intercedes to keep the action going. He is always "pulling strings," and perhaps the exhibition of manikins that the boy sees could serve as an emblem for the tale. "At first the boy thought that they were alive, but at last . . . he guessed that they were only little puppets." "They look at each other, their lips move, they speak, they really speak—only one can't hear them through the window."

In the story, too, the reader is not allowed to see the action directly, but only through the glass of the author's consciousness; he witnesses both the story and the act of its composition, as the author continually stresses that his work is artifice. "And why did I compose such a story, one that is so inappropriate to an ordinary, reasonable diary, and especially a writer's diary?" Dostoevsky returns to his laboratory in his conclusion. And his final apology (like the opening one) calls attention to the process of creativity as well as to the created product. "That is why I am a novelist," he explains, "in order to invent things."

III. THRESHOLD ART

These "inventions," however, are part of "A Monthly Publication," and the third element of the title suggests the journalistic intent of the work. On this level, the *Diary* is frankly publicistic, advocating courses of social and political action that will (the author believes) achieve utopia. And as propagandist, the speaker once more changes character. Now he is most public, least given to doubt, introspection, or indirect and ironic speech. Rather than the diarist as flâneur, or the writer speaking through a conventional literary persona, we now see the public prophet forecasting doom, the apocalypse, and the millennium.

The speaker has, at last, found his voice: he is herald of the End. Diction is now pre-diction and, even, inter-diction. The nature of speech itself changes: its function is not conviction, but persuasion. Its goal is to motivate to the concrete action that will bring on the millennium, the universal reconciliation. The implicit reader also changes. Rather than addressee, he is now an object to be activated. The narrator's tone is no longer confiding, but hostile or partisan; he seeks to overcome the reader's resistance and scepticism. Here again, therefore, the active response of reader's published correspondence becomes an integral part of the work. The reader is co-author of the work, as he is co-builder of utopia.

It is here that we reach the central problem of the working aesthetics of the *Diary*. How can the forms of process literature be used for chiliastic propaganda? What happens when *Tristram Shandy* must serve the purposes of the Revelations of St. John, or Boswell's journals the aims of *The Republic*?

The answer is essentially this: for Dostoevsky, the forms of a literature of process correspond to the moment when existence itself is in the process of changing its essential character. The constant transformations of journalism into fiction, which constitute the rhythm of the *Diary*, also re-enact the transformation of reality into the Idea. For in the moment of "messianic woes," reality becomes fantastic—just as in the *Diary* raw journalism turns

into art before our very eyes. Uncertainty of genre in fact reflects a moment
of metaphysical uncertainty. The themes of individual creativity and universal creation merge; in the work, as in the world, all is on the threshold of
the fantastic. The issue of the day is yielding to that of the Day.

Therefore, *The Diary of a Writer* is also the diary of the Last Days, when
all is undergoing ontological change. As such, it reflects a moment when all
fixed forms are in question. Now the indefinite forms of process literature
take on universal symbolic meaning: only they are adequate to an art of the
Coming of the End. The dominance of the unexpected in a process novel,
where we wonder "not what is coming next, but what the author will think
of next," reflects the historical moment as well. The writer truly does not
know what is coming next. So, too, the author's manipulations of the forms
and events of the text correspond to his formative influence as prophet of
the Last Days; he is creator and victim simultaneously. Violated chronology
and lack of sequence now become emblematic of the end of history itself,
when there will be no more time, when all things will be made new. "The
ends and beginnings" no longer constitute to men a realm of the fantastic,
at odds with the everyday. We see the author in the process of composition
because the work and the world are being formed together. The *Diary* is,
must be, endless, because its end would be history's.

But if the *Diary* adapts process literature, it also develops the loose forms
that specifically characterize Russian literature. Here the Russian tradition
of annual reviews of literature and society is speeded up to monthly installments, monitoring the very pulse of transformation. And we sense that
the pulse is quickening: "there are new and strange facts; they are appearing
daily" and "Europe is changing from hour to hour." The closeness of the
writer in time provided by a periodical emphasizes the sense of immediacy
of events: fresh war despatches interrupt the monthly reports, and predic-
tions and their confirmations occur within a single chapter. The proximity
of the end also allows Dostoevsky to develop the genre of "zapiski" ("notes").
Now the tentative, unfinished quality of notes is dictated by the rapidity of
the transformation of existence itself. Art, therefore, must be written at a
continuous present, directly from the events it describes. Otherwise it will
necessarily be anachronistic.

The *Diary*, in short, is threshold art. The work is the dramatization of
the chiliastic moment, the process of metamorphosis, when reality is in flux
between an old and a new identity. *The Diary of a Writer* is the birth pangs
of the Idea. Or, to use Frye's verbal analogy, it is the literature of the progressive tense, the genre of the Russian imperfective.

MICHAEL HOLQUIST

The Search for a Story: White Nights, Winter Notes on Summer Impressions, *and* Notes from Underground

It is customary to regard *Notes from Underground* as a key to under-standing the thematic concerns of the novels Dostoevsky wrote in his sub-sequent career, as a kind of Rosetta stone for such hieroglyphs of the major phase of *Crime and Punishment* or *The Brothers Karamazov*. While there is much to recommend such an approach, it is perhaps no less interesting if we try to focus on the work from the other end of the telescope: that is, if we regard it in the light of works *preceding* it in the Dostoevskian canon. One of the preconceptions of what follows is that *Notes from Underground* differs from Dostoevsky's earlier work—and is therefore significant in inter-preting his later work—insofar as it makes use of a new basis for the various conflicts out of which all the fiction, early and late, is spun. In such works as *Poor Folk* or *White Nights* the characteristically Dostoevskian dichotomies of self/other, dream/waking, validity/self-deception, etc., are already pre-sent. But the scope of such conflicts is—relative to his own post–1864 phase, at any rate—comparatively narrow: what is often advanced as the best argu-ment for Dostoevsky's importance—that he is a great psychologist—is perhaps most true of these early works, where he is frequently *only* a psychologist.

The Double, that extraordinary inscape of schizophrenia, may be regarded as the early text that arguably comes closest to the novels of the major phase; it nevertheless ultimately avoids the metaphysical dimension present in the later period. At the heart of such early fictions is a conception of character that is more limited (or "merely personal" in the sense of that late Neoplatonist, Jay Gatsby) than it will be later. Another difference is that,

From *Dostoevsky and the Novel.* © 1977 by Princeton University Press.

while Dostoevsky already knew in these early works that St. Petersburg was a fantastic city, the how and why of its ontology have not yet been grasped by him in such a way that he can use it as a cosmological space, a very special sort of planetarium, as he will do in *Crime and Punishment* or *The Idiot*. In the early work St. Petersburg is still one of those countries of the mind, of which there are so many in the nineteenth-century novel that one frequently has the sense of reading psychological gazeteers (Balzac's "Paris," Dickens's "London"). The space of Dostoevsky's earlier works is more confined because it is cut out of a bolt of temporality differing from that extensive sense of time which gives shape and locality to the later novels.

I am assuming that the central concern of all Dostoevsky's work is a series of questions about identity; not only "who am I?" but "how can I be?" or "if I am *that*, who, then, are others?" It is further assumed that such questions are grounded in time. Thus the difference between earlier and later work springs not from a change in themes but rather from a different structuring of the same questions that results from Dostoevsky's increasingly complex sense of time and history. The specific way in which the experiences of mock-execution, Siberian exile, and his first trip to Western Europe affected Dostoevsky's work from 1864 on, was more and more to exacerbate those questions of identity he had always asked, as he more and more deeply explored that relationship between self and time which can be grasped in something like the following terms: "Man first existed in space, but he first became aware of himself in time. Thinking is an activity performed in time, for it is only in terms of time that thought becomes conscious of itself. *The discovery of the self and the experience of temporality occurred simultaneously since it is the self that posits, separates, and mediates the dimensions of past and future"* (John G. Gunnell, *Political Philosophy and Time*; emphasis added). The sense of time is more complex in Dostoevsky's later novels, and, therefore, so is the sense of self. Such a statement should not be let to stand on its own, so before plunging into an interpretation of *Notes* itself, I will first contrast it with a pre-exile story, *White Nights*.

II

White Nights (1848) was one of the last pieces Dostoevsky wrote before his arrest on April 23, 1849. Its subtitle, "From the Reminiscences of a Dreamer," is significant: this is a tale about *dreams*, and not about nightmares. The organizing contrast is one between a conventional conception of dreaming, on the one hand (the distinction between night or day dreams is lost in the mysterious half light of St. Petersburg's midsummer white nights) and a conventional conception of reality, on the other, symbolized in the contrast between the soft nights of the poet's *past* that are used to divide the various sections of the tale ("1st night," "2nd night," etc.) versus the harsh morning of his *present* ("morning" is the title of the final section, when the poet must face the fact that Nastenka has gone off with her boarder). Thus, instead of probing for reality in a quotidian (a modifier that must in this context have a special resonance) waking experience that is more fantastic than dreams, as he will in his later works, Dostoevsky in 1848 assumes an opposition between unexamined dream and unquestioned reality that limits the frontiers of both. However, insofar as its basic contrast is one of conflicting ontologies, *White Nights* is similar to *Notes from Underground*, where such a conflict, intensified and re-structured, is crucial. In this and other ways we must now explore, the earlier work reads like a sentimental parody of the later work (and in this its other subtitle "A Sentimental Novel" is justified).

Both tell the tale of a duel between lonely, unhappy men who seek to capture young women by means of a self-consciously "literary" eloquence. Both are told in the first person, in the form of notes, with the eccentric dreamers making frequent asides to the reader. The poet in *White Nights* begins by admitting he is "prey to a peculiar melancholy. I suddenly fancied that everyone was forsaking me in my loneliness, that everyone was casting me off. . . . It frightened me to be left alone, and for three whole days I wandered up and down the streets in deep dejection." Like the underground man, too, he is a *boulevardier-voyeur*, who walks about the city studying others: "Of course they don't know me, but I know them." His room has many of the characteristics of the underground: "green, grimy walls hung with cobwebs." And the awful rigidity, the fear of change that the underground represents is also here: "If I see a single chair standing differently from where it had stood the day before, I grow restless; I gazed at the windows, but all to no avail." The suggestion of prison here is another parallel with the later story, as is the vexed relationship between the poet and his servant: "It even occurred to me to summon Matryona and give her a fatherly scolding about the cobwebs and the untidiness generally, but she only looked at me in surprise and left the room without a word, and so the cobwebs remain undisturbed to this day."

Like the underground man the poet "*has no story (istorija*—an ambiguity Dostoevsky will not in the 1864 work neglect) *of* [*his*] *own*" (emphasis added). He calls himself a "Type," meaning individual, but it is clear he is also a "type" in the sense of a generic example. Since he has no story that is his to *experience*, he makes up stories about himself to *tell*—referring to himself in the third person. He quotes the poet Zhukovsky, his speech is always lofty, taken from books. Just as Liza says to the underground man that he "sounds like a book," so Nastenka tells the poet: "couldn't you somehow make your speech less splendid? Because you sound as if you were reading it out of a book." He depends on literature in this way for two reasons, both similar to those which explain the underground man's literariness. First, because it is part of his—hesitating—campaign to win Nastenka, to seduce her with words: just after he tells her a pathetic story about himself, he admits: "I shivered with pathos, having come to the end of my pathetic utterances. I remember how hard I strove to bring myself to laugh just then, for I could already feel some hostile imp stirring in my heart." He knows the girl feels "a certain respect for the pathos of my speech and my lofty style."

Second, he needs literary clichés to provide him with a plot, things to *do* and *say* in the absence of any more substantial ground for action: "I am a dreamer. I have so little actual life, moments like this [his meeting with Nastenka] come to me so rarely that I cannot but live through them again and again in my dreams." Later he says "Do you know what I have come to, Nastenka? Do you know that I now have to mark the anniversary of my past emotions . . . this anniversary, too, has to be observed according to the same foolish, incorporeal dreams; I am driven to it because the foolish dreams themselves are no more, for *I have nothing to support them with*" (emphasis added).

Beyond likenesses between the character of the two major protagonists of *White Nights* and *Notes from Underground* there is an even more convincing structural parallel between the two plots. Each is a collection of notes, focussing on an encounter with women in the past. The poet looks back over fifteen years to his meeting with Nastenka; the underground man writes sixteen years after his duel with Liza. Thus, in the case of each there is an attempt to understand the present by interpreting a key moment in the past, a moment that has had the effect of shutting the one in amidst his cobwebs, for the other of sealing his underground forever. Just as the underground man's fine words of part 1 are undercut by his actions in part 2, so the conclusion of *White Nights* serves to indict the dreamer: "The vista of all my life to come stretched before me so bleakly and so sadly, and I saw myself the way I am now, exactly fifteen years since, an aged man, in the same old room, as lonely as ever, with the same old Matryona."

But he immediately resorts to his habit of not facing the truth, of obscuring it with fine words and "exalted emotions," as if he were a bookish squid surrounding himself with inky rhetoric as he addresses the memory of Nastenka in the best Sentimentalist tradition: "that I should ever mar your pure and blissful happiness with a cloud of sorrow . . . that I should ever crush a single one of those exquisite flowers you wore in your dark curls when you walked up to the altar with him," etc. This purple patch, following as it does his recognition of the prison erected around him by his dreams, adds an unintended pathos to the poet's last question (and the tale's last line) "Good Lord! A Whole Minute of Bliss! Why, isn't it enough, even for a lifetime?" The answer for the dreamer, of course, is that it is *not* enough for a lifetime, and we can see the genesis here of all those characters in Dostoevsky's later novels who will seek to correct the poet's error, will seek to find a moment that *will* be enough to guarantee a lifetime.

Up to this point we have emphasized parallels between *White Nights* and *Notes from Underground*. However, each of the similarities listed contains also, on closer examination, a difference. The character of the poet in *White Nights* is that of a merely embryonic (or so we should say were we to forget that the latter springs from a test tube) underground man. We remarked on the poet's melancholy, his loneliness; but, as he says himself, the reason he feels cut off from others is merely because it is summer and everyone else has left town to go to their *dachas*: "And finally, only this morning [of the tale's first night], I understood what was the matter. Why, they were skipping from me into the country." He recognizes his proclivity to dream rather than to act is potentially dangerous ("A new dream—a new dose of happiness! A new dose of poison, subtle and sensuous," he says; but his analysis of why this should be so never gets beyond the level of psychological common sense, beyond a received wisdom that is content to use such small change as "shyness" as a technical term for the farthest reach of its speculation. The most complex metaphor the poet succeeds in finding for his condition is a "miserable little kitten" tormented by thoughtless children, so that it must "spend a whole hour [under a chair] bristling and snorting, washing its hurt little face with both paws."

The plot, no less than the character of the major protagonist in both stories, differs not so much in details as in the *scope* of their various contexts. The poet reflects on his personal past, the one moment of potential change in an otherwise uninterrupted stasis, in order to insure the present out of which he writes his notes. The underground man also, of course, reflects on a past encounter with a woman, but the interest has shifted from the encounter itself, from a *personal* event, to the very act of analysis. Thus the underground man must ultimately combine not just two moments cut out of his own biography; he must re-think the possibility of "past" and "present" as it has traditionally been understood in the European historical imagination.

While the grammar of Dostoevsky's concerns—the morphology of character-type and in large measure even the syntax of plot-shapes—remains surprisingly uniform in works written before and after his decade of prison and exile, the semantics of those elements go through an enormous change, as he constantly expands the context of his novelistic gestures. *White Nights* is limited by the generic possibilities of the feuilleton. Dostoevsky wrote a series of these for the *St. Petersburg Gazette*, beginning in April 1847; it is out of these sketches that *White Nights* developed. The parallels between the story and the *Petersburg Chronicle* (generic name for the feuilletons Dostoevsky wrote during this period) have been pointed out often enough not to need comment, except to remind the reader that whole chunks of the feuilleton material are present, virtually unmodified, in the short story.

The feuilleton had, by 1847, become, under the influence of Eugène Sue's example in *Les Mystères de Paris* (1842), a complex literary form in its own right. But the emphasis was overwhelmingly on *description* rather than on analysis, a distinction caught in the very name of what became its most influential form in Russia, the physiological sketch. It was the journalistic equivalent of time-lapse photography; the typical author of such a piece would find a perspective point on the city (for Nekrasov, *The Corners of St. Petersburg*, for Krestovsky *The Squares of St. Petersburg*, for Butkov *The Upper Stories of St. Petersburg* [all in 1845]) and then describe what went on in his chosen *tranche de ville*, usually, over a twenty-four hour period, as in Kovalevsky's *Petersburg by Day and Night* (also in 1845), or in the opening discourse on Nevsky Prospect in Gogol's story of that name. The aspect of the city such an author would choose had as its ultimate function much the same purpose that monuments of nature or antiquity had for sentimental travelers—such as Karamzin—in the eighteenth century; their importance was in proportion to the degree they could spark an emotional response. They were, in effect, essays in the rediscovery of what already was there, and therefore occasions for demonstrating the writer's sensibility or wit. Thus such feuilletons had built into their generic presuppositions a limited sense of time and personality. As the titles above suggest, they were overwhelmingly *local*.

In order for the *Problemstellung* of *White Nights* to become what it is in *Notes from Underground*, in order for "Petersburg" to become the "underground," an analytical impulse deeper than that provided by an expansion of the feuilleton was necessary. And of course in the years between *White Nights* and *Notes from Underground*, everything in Dostoevsky's biography was conducive to a deepening of that impulse: imprisonment, "execution," hard labor in Siberia, exile. It is a decade of returns for Dostoevsky: return to the living after that day in 1849 on Semyenovsky Square when he was certain he would surely die in the next moment; return to Petersburg after nearly a decade of prison and exile; and, after his first trip abroad in 1863, a return to Russia. Each of these returns would give rise to at least one book: return from death and exile resulted in *Notes from the House of the Dead*; return from Europe (after his first visit to the West), in *Winter Notes on Summer Impressions*. The first book is Dostoevsky's discovery of that particular *Russia* he will intend from now on when invoking that name; the second is his discovery of that particular sense of *Europe* he will deploy in his later writings. From 1864 on, these two poles will serve as major categories for organizing the shifting patterns of opposition that constitute the core of his subsequent works. In order to understand the underground notes (which were published in the following year) we must first take a closer look at these winter notes.

III

Winter Notes on Summer Impressions is the first sustained treatment of the contrast between Dostoevsky's "Russia" and his "Europe." It is an account, published first as a series of articles in his journal *Vremja* (*Time*, [1863]), of two months he spent in the summer of 1862 in several West European countries (Italy, Switzerland, Germany, as well as England and France). The whole emphasis of the book, however, is on London, and especially Paris. In Dostoevsky's portrayal of the French bourgeois, in particular, we can see him discovering the most extreme form of all that the West would come to mean for him. I mean by this not only the static characteristics of national type (egoistic, sanctimonious, materialistic, etc.) but the dynamic *temporal* model that explains such characteristics. That is, "East" and "West," in Dostoevsky's use of the terms, are merely convenient tags for two kinds of temporality; each stands in for a space where different conceptions of time have resulted in different anthropologies. Thus the opposition that generates all the others in *Winter Notes on Summer Impressions*, from the contrasting seasons of the title to the contrasting political and religious theories of the text, is one between a merely human time in which the end of history is contained *in* history (change and upheaval, the West), on the one hand, and, on the other, a transcendent time (slow evolution, Russia), in which the making of history is extra-historical, i.e., derives from a God outside time.

How does space, and the national character that is peculiar to it, function as a temporality? Consider the anecdote Dostoevsky introduces as a newspaper article that he had read under the headline, "Vestiges of Barbarism." The anecdote is also a good illustration of his humor, which often results from the contrast between a ridiculous or embarrassing event and a philosophical purpose in the service of which he immediately enlists the event. The anecdote tells of how a Moscow matchmaker was seen taking a package one morning from the apartment of two newlyweds, a package that contained the bride's bloody nightgown, proof of her virginity to be shown to the parents: "The newspaper indignantly, conceitedly, blusteringly reported this unheard-of barbarism 'existing even today, in spite of all the progress of civilization.'" Dostoevsky sarcastically agrees that this custom is "savage," "Slavic," possible only because "of ignorance of anything better, higher, European." He contrasts this unconscious Russian concern with the "dainty garments" and "minute calculation" of society women as they "add padding to a certain part of their enchanting European clothing."

In other words, the difference between East and West, Russia and Europe, is not that the one is more advanced than the other; by questioning such a possibility Dostoevsky points to what he feels the real difference is: "Are these cares, these worries, these *conscious* [Dostoevsky's emphasis] preoccupations about additions of padding—are they purer, more moral . . . than 'the bloody nightgown taken to the parents of the bride'?" The word he stresses here, "conscious," is key to the differences: West Europeans are offended by the gown because the custom does not accord with their prejudices, prejudices that have been erected into a theory of history. Such "vestiges of barbarism" occur "even *today*, in spite of all the *progress* of civilization." That is, the West sees itself as farther along toward a definite goal in history than the Russians, who are still trapped at a stage the Europeans have previously experienced, but have now gone beyond. Thus the Russians, in this view, exist in a brute chronological synchrony with the West, but in a *historical* diachrony. France and Russia may share the same continent, but each has a different time. The Russians have experienced less "history" than the French during the same amount of time.

Dostoevsky is concerned to attack this historicism, choosing the French bourgeoisie as the supreme example of its power to corrupt. The first sentence of the chapter in *Winter Notes* he calls "Essay on the Bourgeoisie" is a question he spends the rest of the book answering: "Why are they ill at ease here?" [in Paris]. Why should the nineteenth-century Frenchman—envied even by other Europeans as the heir of all the ages, secure in a rich culture, great wealth, and the trappings of imperial power—lack confidence? Because while he proclaims himself to be the most advanced product of human progress he must—insofar as he believes such a claim—recognize that he is, *therefore*, "alone on earth, that there no longer is anything superior to him, that he is the ideal." Dostoevsky presents him as the logical outcome of Abbé Sieyès's

1789 prophecy: " 'What is the third Estate? Nothing! What ought it to be? Everything!' Well, everything happened just as he said." But to have achieved "the perfect terrestrial paradise," to live at the *end* of history so conceived—is to experience its meaninglessness. It is to experience that which was foretold to be *everything*, actually to be, when realized, *nothing*. The Frenchman knows that while others may seek to re-enact his historicism, to achieve the end of progress the French already have reached is in fact a goal not worth pursuing. It is this knowledge that defines his loneliness: all others are deceived; he alone knows the awful truth. What defines his unease is the need to keep up the appearance of paradise to which his progressive historical model condemns him. So the bourgeois is forced to labor mightily to deny the particular kind of meaninglessness his historically achieved paradise results in. Thus all the lies that are institutionalized in his government, sexual mores, newspapers, the very clothing (padded, deceptive) of his women: all are aimed at concealing the inadequacy of an historical scheme that posits bourgeois values as its supreme goal.

The various strategies for deception developed by the bourgeois grow out of his sense of void: "I do not exist. I absolutely do not exist. I have hidden myself!" He doubts his existence, not as did the dreamer of *White Nights*, but because he conceives it as a radical individuality: "In Western nature in general 'fraternity' is not present; you find there instead a principle of isolation, of intense self-preservation, of personal gain, of self-determination, of the I, of opposing this I to all nature and the rest of mankind." As a result of this solipsism, language loses its power to communicate, to bind together, a condition Dostoevsky examines in his study of the bourgeois love of eloquence.

Eloquence is conceived by Dostoevsky not as forceful expression, but as bombast; the characteristic trait of language so used is a disparity between event and expression: eloquence is a term used by him to indicate language's power to deceive; it is form put into the service of *concealing* content. A French politician will know that "nothing at all will come of his speech, that it is all one big farce and nothing more, . . . a masquerade. And nevertheless he speaks; he speaks for several years on end." Together with his frequent references to French spies, it is the overinflated language of the bourgeoisie more than any other aspect of their existence that Dostoevsky uses to condemn the deceptiveness of the West. "The bourgeois is eaten up with eloquence to the very bone." Since the bourgeois defines his individuality as a radical uniqueness, he *is* alone: he cannot share language with others, and so language loses its ground of meaning. The only thing one bourgeois shares with another is the concern to cover up the void at the center of their existence; thus the dominant mode of their discourse is eloquence, hyperbole. And thus it is, too, that the dominant art form of the bourgeois in Dostoevsky's scheme is not—as later historians have argued—the novel; rather it is melodrama, institutionalized theatricality: the bourgeois "needs something lofty, he needs ineffable nobility, he needs emotion, and melodrama contains all of these. . . . Melodrama will not die as long as the bourgeois lives." Just as eloquence (as Dostoevsky uses it in this essay) is conceived as something more than a particular situation demands of ordinary language, so is melodrama more extreme than ordinary drama. Between the norms of language and eloquence, between drama and melodrama, there is a distance, and it is that disparity which defines the space where the bourgeois has his being.

IV

In Dostoevsky's analysis of the French bourgeois one can see for the first time the particular meaning that "the West" will have in the works to follow. He has discovered a way to think about, to conceive—if not yet to novelize—that opposition of Russia versus the West that will fuel the dialectical structure of the later works. *Winter Notes* is an important element, then, in the development of the Dostoevskian mythology, if we assume that one of the major functions of myth is "to stabilize and extend classification itself . . . myth explains not so much what to think about events and objects, but in what directions and with what degree of force to think—and how precisely to situate the constituents of the thinkable" (Warner Berthoff, in *The Interpretation of Narrative Theory and Practice*, edited by Morton Bloomfield). That is to say that the major elements present in *Notes from Underground* were also present in Dostoevsky's earlier work. But the exercise of *Winter Notes* has taught him into what directions such elements as past and present might be extended, with what degree of force to analyze such topics as dreaming and eloquence.

In *Winter Notes* Dostoevsky discusses the predicament that will figure so largely in all his later works. It is given as the unease of the French bourgeois who lives at the end of history. In *Notes from Underground* that unease has become the anxiety of modern man: the underground man is Dostoevsky's French bourgeois raised to the level of a phenomenological type. The shape of the plot is itself a metaphor for the dilemma of the underground man, which is to live the unease of a brutally oversimplified historicism: where there are no supra-historical values, all values are merely historical phenomena that are valid only in a certain time in a certain place.

Since all order is relative, how create a system to live by? In this scheme literary plot (or the underground man's use of plot) equals history, and the plotlessness of the notes themselves is a structural metaphor for the failure of history, or at least the failure of history understood as the principle that the meaning of existence will come to light progressively in the course of its own process.

In his analysis of the French bourgeois, Dostoevsky defined the Westerner as a man who feels he has come to the end of a history. The bourgeois, with his faith in progress, then, is the telos of his own theory of history, and his intellectual defenders, such as the Abbe Sieyes in the eighteenth century or Henry Buckle in the nineteenth, try to convince their less reflective fellows that they should—as the crown stone in the pyramid of time—feel happiness. It is what Nietzsche had in mind when he wrote that, "the belief that one is a late-comer in the world . . . frightful and devastating when it raises our late-comer, by a neat turn of the wheel [*mit Kecker Umstülpung*] to the level of a God as the true meaning and object of all past creation and his conscious misery is set up as the perfection of the world's history." The pride of the bourgeois is a result of theory; their uneasiness is a result of experience. They do not *feel* like the end; therefore they resort, as we have seen in our reading of *Winter Notes*, to strategies for deceiving themselves and others that the theoretical conclusion—they are the end, the highest—is true. Thus the melodrama, with its overdone gestures, its appeal to the coarsest emotions, its insistence on nobility, is Dostoevsky's essential metaphor for the bad theater of their lives.

In the underground man we see both poles of this dilemma—the theoretical and experiential—being examined from the inside: that is, the underground man is conscious of the theoretical conclusion that modern man must be the pinnacle of history as it has come to be understood in the nineteenth century (its meaning will be revealed in its own process); but he is also aware that he does not *feel* like the heir of the ages. He not only, like the bourgeois, recognizes the incompatibility of such a history with his own experience, but he goes beyond the bourgeois in seeing clearly what the implications of the conflict are. He does not try to keep the old, organic sense of history—history as guarantor of identity—alive by deception, as does the bourgeois. Rather, he abandons it as an inadequate source for understanding himself. And he does so because in his rejection of any system (science as well as history) as a means by which to understand himself, he abandons the primary assumption of older conceptions of identity based in history.

The old sense of history, the history that the underground man casts off, has been characterized by Michel Foucault as one in which it was felt that "by ordering the time of human beings upon the world's development . . . or inversely by extending the principle and movement of a human destiny to even the smallest particles of nature . . . human destiny was conceived of as a vast historical stream, uniform in each of its points, drawing with it in one and the same current, in one and the same fall or ascension, or cycle, all men, and with them things or animals, every living or inert being even the most unmoved aspects of earth" (*The Order of Things*).

That is to say that all things were felt to be moving within the same all-encompassing sea of time. While nature had its own rhythms (rocks and stars, or insects with a life span of only a few hours), those rhythms shared with the rhythm of human life a *developmental* aspect. Everything had the same temporality: you could understand the present by viewing it as the sum of past developments. In this conception there is nothing—from the point of view of time—that will serve to distinguish the uniqueness of man's status in the universe (what Max Scheler has called his *Sonderstellung*). Laws proper to the explanation of physical phenomena, therefore, will be proper to explain the human phenomenon as well. What men shared with nature was an etiological time: the present came out of the past at different speeds, but, whether rock or man, each was to be understood historically, as the present product of a process begun in the past.

This prejudice is obvious enough in those works we conventionally call histories; but the connection such a temporality has with personal identity is perhaps more clearly charted in autobiography, which is, after all, a narrative of events occurring in time, a kind of history in its own right. At least since Rousseau, the historical bias has been particularly strong in autobiography, a genre in which "formal continuity is a principle of philosophic, not merely narrative, coherence. It is in some sense the real subject of the work, the gradual evolution of an always-identifiable self" (John N. Morris, *Versions of the Self*). This is what John Stuart Mill means when he calls his autobiography a "mental history." That is, there is not only chronological continuity, but a conceptual continuity. The parallel with conventional history is in this, "that there are at least two levels of interpretation in every historical work: one in which the historian constitutes a story out of the chronicle of events and another in which, by a more fundamental narrative technique, he progressively identifies the *kind of story* he is telling, comedy, tragedy, romance, epic, or satire." (Hayden White, "Interpretation in History," *New Literary History* 4, no. 2[1973]). This "more fundamental narrative technique" is what F. M. Cornford in his study of the tragic structure of Thucydides' history has called "mythistoria," history cast in a literary or philosophical form that was already inwrought in the structure of the mind, part of its unreflecting assumptive world, before the work was even contemplated.

In what has been called the first biography, we can see both elements, the chronological and conceptual (E. M. Forster's "story" and "plot," the Russian Formalist distinction between *"fabula"* and *"sjužet"*) separated off: Xenophon divided his encomium to Agesilaus "into two parts. The first was written in . . . chronological order . . . the second part was a non-chronological, systematic review of Agesilaus' virtues. As Xenophon explains at the beginning of chapter three, after having given the record of the king's deeds he is now attempting to show the virtue that was in his soul" (Arnaldo Momigliano, *The Development of Greek Biography*). In other words, Xenophon writes as if he can tell the life, and *then* explain it.

In subsequent biography, however, the need is felt to fuse the two elements—the chronology of a life *with* its meaning. The narrative continuity of the text asserts the unity of the self, and it does so by stressing a temporally continuous personality. We may call this self "historical," in that its basic premise—that its essence is contained in its temporal shape—is one that historians have always felt: the assumption that there is an elective affinity between the modes of explanation and the modes of emplot-ment, and that by means of such an affinity they may achieve a particular kind of explanatory effect, an overarching interpretive grasp of the historical field under study.

The historical self, then, is the subject of a biography whose events are arranged as a function of the author's attempts to *explain* those events. The belief that past, present, and future constitute a causal relationship is so deeply ingrained in historical accounts that historians have used this chronology even in societies and at times when philosophers were speculating on radically different conceptions of what might be the shape of time. Among fifth-century Greeks, for instance, philosophers might argue that time is cyclical, and even though contemporary religion tended to support this view, Herodotus—as a working historian—knew that "on the human level there was real change. Later historians were quite aware of this fact. They also knew the present came out of the past; and . . . were aware of [the future] as well. . . . Historians move now, as always, in their own path with respect to time; perhaps this is inevitable inasmuch as history is [a discipline] . . . by which men account to themselves for their nature" (Chester G. Starr, *History and the Concept of Time*).

While historians may have continued to operate with this sense of history, there were, of course, others in the nineteenth century who challenged the validity of such past-present-future models to "account to themselves for their nature," and the underground man is one. The bourgeois was still operating with an historical sense of self, not only in his individual life, but in his assumptions about the world at large. Just as he at age, let us say, of fifty was the sum of all his previous life, he *was* his biography, so was, let us say, France in 1863 the sum of the *world's* biography. That is why, in Dostoevsky, the French are said to be at the end of a history.

But in the nineteenth century, as Michel Foucault has recently reminded us, others were becoming aware of a separation between the history of things—the world—and men: "It was discovered that there existed a historicity proper to nature . . . it became possible to show that activities as peculiarly human as labor or language contained within themselves a historicity that could not be placed within the great *narrative* [emphasis added] common to things and to men . . . [language, economics, etc.] have internal laws of functioning, and . . . their chronology unfolds in accordance with a time that refers in the first place to their own particular coherence." It was seen that linguistic history had a shape that did not correspond to the shape of economic history, for instance, and, furthermore, that *none* of the subjects of these disciplines (what Foucault calls "positivities") had a privileged shape that could, in itself, define a history of man:

> Things first of all received an historic proper to them, which freed them from the continuous space that imposed the same chronology upon them as upon man. So that man found himself dispossessed of what constituted the most manifest contents of his history: nature no longer speaks to him of the creation or the end of the world, of his dependency or his approaching judgment. . . . The human being has no history: or, rather, since he speaks, works, and lives, he finds himself interwoven in his own being with histories that are neither subordinate to him nor homogenous with him. By the fragmentation of the space over which classical knowledge extended in its own continuity . . . the man who appears at the beginning of the nineteenth century is "dehistoricized."

It is precisely the domains of classical knowledge (the sciences, even mathematics, as well as "history") that the underground man specifically rejects—and he does so in his attempt to find a history that is validly *his own*, and not simply a template superimposed upon the alien chronologies that such *other* histories represent. This is the "consciousness" that he identifies as his sickness, the consciousness that traditional ways of organizing histories and biographies no longer avail. He is conscious of the *myth* in mythistoria as merely a fiction. Previous attempts to organize chronology had behind them unexamined assumptions about what might properly constitute an explanatory model, such as "God," "Kingship," or "Science." Such authors either were *unconscious* that their histories were a function of belief, of ideology or religion, or they consciously attempted to synchronize their narrative of events with a pre-existing conception of order, such as the ancient Chinese historians, who would "determine the facts or the dates, establish texts, lop off interpolations, classify works, not with objective detachment, but in the hope of rendering more acute and purer, in themselves and their readers, the consciousness of an ideal that history cannot explain, for it precedes history" (Marcel Granet, *Chinese Civilization*). There was something out there that was *true* and events could be referred back to whatever it was— God or the clockwork order of the physical universe—for a valid order of reckoning. The underground man cannot find a way to order events because there is no ground back to which he can refer them, because there is *no* order he will bring himself not to question. The condition of history becomes for the underground man the condition of contingency.

V

Contingency is not only what *Notes from Underground* is about— it is the condition that is dramatized in its own unique plot. Dostoevsky gives the illusion of contingency by systematically subverting the traditional literary expectation of a neat beginning, middle, and end. Almost all literary plots meet the conditions for plot outlined by Aristotle for tragedy, something that:

> is an imitation of a whole, that is, it has a beginning, a middle, and an end. A beginning is that which does not itself follow anything by causal necessity, but after which something naturally is or comes to be. An end, on the contrary, is that which itself naturally follows some other thing, either by necessity or as a rule, but has nothing following it. A middle is that which follows something as some other thing follows it. A well-constructed plot, therefore, must neither begin nor end at haphazard, but conform to these principles.

The high degree of abstraction in such a definition permits endless interpretations of what might constitute a beginning, middle, or end. But two things are clear: Aristotelean plot is *ordered*, and it has *movement*. Later in the *Poetics* he says: "the tragic plot must not be composed of irrational parts. Everything irrational should, if possible, be excluded."

The parallel between this view of plot, on the one hand, and what we have been discussing as a historical sense of self, on the other, should be clear. The order of events in Aristotelean plot is determined by its ability to define the whole; it, once again, is an *explanatory* chronology. The principle that excludes the irrational is a principle of order pre-existing any attempt to give coherence to a specific set of events. The Aristotelean plot is achieved through rules of exclusion governed by the principle of the tale's unity; thus we begin by assuming the tale *has* a unity, and further that it is defined by its chronology in such a way that any *other* order will appear irrational. Plot, then, ignores what is gratuitous to itself, and in these terms its movement is logical. Now let us recall that the underground man is opposed to logic, the syllogism. It should come as no surprise that the plot in which he is caught, the plot that defines him, is itself anti-historical, is not *linear* or Aristotelean. It is, in fact, the underground man's twisted formula of $2 \times 2 = 5$ expressed in architectonics.

Aristotelean plot also has parallels with the metaphor, which is defined in classical rhetoric, since at least Quintilian, as also having three parts: a metaphor is a comparison of two things, based on a third element common to both, the *tertium comparationis*. By subverting the assumptive world of order behind classical plot structure, Dostoevsky put in jeopardy the neat proportional relationship of classical metaphor. As Bede Alleman has pointed out [in *Interpretation: The Poetry of Meaning*, ed. S. R. Hopper and Daniel Miller]: "For Aristotle analogy is something easily expressed mathematically, that is by a proportional equation: the proportion of a to b equals the proportion of c to d. . . . But modern poetry no longer recognizes the essential prerequisite for this act of combination: namely the idea of a rational order of the universe that can be represented adequately by a network or relationship." In the case of the underground man we can be more specific about the way in which this breakdown of "the rational order of the universe" stands in: it is not the breakdown of a single, ordered cosmology. Rather, what has collapsed is the idea of *order* itself. Thus the inability of the underground man to account for his self in historical terms; he cannot find a chronology that is *in itself* explanatory of what he feels he is. His dilemma is structurally dramatized in the collapse of linear plot (historical development) in the *Notes*, considered as a literary text.

Before turning to the text of *Notes from Underground*, let me very quickly recapitulate what I understand to be the specific qualities of traditional plot against which Dostoevsky is working. Most dictionaries give four definitions of plot: it is (1) an area marked off on a surface, usually ground; (2) a chart, diagram, or map; (3) the plan of action of a play, novel, poem, short story, etc.; (4) a secret project or scheme, a conspiracy. All of these meanings bear on the history of our subject. A plot is, above all, a thing marked off, something that has boundaries, that is distinctly itself and not some other thing. In order to achieve this quality of boundedness it must work by rules of exclusion; certain things must be left out. What plots leave out, of course, is various degrees of contingency, the state in which events may occur by chance, accidentally, fortuitously. This is the irrational against which Aristotle inveighs, the messiness of ordinary lived experience with its confusions, its half-finished sentences, its daily eruptions of the absurd. Plots are a means to cut all that out, and are thus like maps, which turn stormy oceans into neat, still designs, or the chaos of a jungle into a geometric patch of green ink. Thus plot is bounded, purged of contingency, and therefore available to linearity.

It is the fourth definition that we must invoke in connection with *Notes*: a conspiracy. *Notes from Underground* is in this sense a plot against plots, at least of the sort Aristotle—and the dictionary in the first three of its definitions—intended.

The basic pattern of the *Notes* is a cycle of well-made stories that—in themselves—make sense, have traditional, *literary* plots. The structure of these stories is then subverted, one by one, as they are shown in the face of reality, in the face of the very contingency they abjured to achieve their shapely form—to be just that: shapely forms. They are only *tales*, and nothing more. This configuration, which defines the *several* stories the underground man tells about the world and himself, is subsumed by the same pattern, as it is bodied forth in the movement from part 1 of the *Notes* to part 2. In part 1 the underground man makes himself a character in a philosophical parable, which, for all its acerbity, has the effect of turning him into an Existentialist hero. That is why part 1 is included in Existentialist anthologies without part 2, because the Liza episode—reality, events, contingency—gives the lie to the rhetoric of part 1, which is merely talk.

This movement from part 1 to part 2 has the same function as the Scheherezade story in *The Arabian Nights*; it is the story of stories, the structural model for all the other stories it contains. And, like Scheherezade, the underground man must keep telling stories in order to stay alive. As he says: "I used to invent my own adventures. I used to devise my own life for myself, so as to be able to carry on somehow."

He must make up plots for himself to figure in, because none of the available systems used by others to structure their lives are for the underground man acceptable, believable. He specifically attacks Darwinism: "When . . . it is proved to you that you are descended from a monkey, then it's no use pulling a long face about it: you just have to accept it." Of course, he does *not* accept it. Darwin must be a special target for the underground man, Darwin who found a whole new system for shoring up the connection between the history of nature and the history of man; who posits a developmental theory for rocks and humans, each of which is to be explained by the shape of its chronology: "I look at the geological record as a history of the world . . . written in a changing dialect." While attempts have been made to dissociate Darwin from the doctrine that has become known as "cultural Darwinism," it is difficult not to hear the voice of Dostoevsky's French bourgeois of the *Winter Notes* in such lines as the following (from *The Descent of Man*): "Man may be excused for feeling some pride at having risen . . . to the very summit of the organic scale." The underground man rejects Darwin because the evolutionary plot is too neat, is too homogenous, for him. Darwin may, with his system, be able to write the biography of coral atolls and perhaps even of the human *species*—but he cannot provide a biography for the underground man; he cannot account for the sense of unique selfhood that is the underground man's curse and pride.

It is important here to grasp that the underground man is not merely objecting to the indignity of being descended from an ape—his capacity for self-disgust can absorb much more than this—what he is opposing is the attempt to employ *History* as an explanation: "you can say anything you like about world history, anything that might enter the head of a man with the most disordered imagination. One thing, though," he says, "you cannot possibly say about it: you cannot say that it makes sense." What the underground man means by "world history" becomes more explicit if we keep in mind that he uses Henry Thomas Buckle (1821–62) as his symbol of the historian par excellence. Buckle ascribed to the workings of time the rational order of a well-played game of chess (he was an internationally famous player before reaching the age of twenty): "the progress of every people is regulated by principles . . . as certain as those which govern the physical world," he wrote in his *History of Civilization in England* (vol. 1, 1857; vol. 2, 1861). What Buckle shared with Darwin was the sense that the present grew out of, was explained by, the *past*; and thus while the present might represent a height not previously achieved by men, men could not be *separate* from those who had gone before, could not be radically *themselves*.

It is the need to attack the dependence of part to whole that also accounts for the underground man's rejection of mathematics: "Twice-two-makes-four is in my humble opinion, nothing but a piece of impudence. Twice-two-makes-four is a farcical, dressed up fellow who stands across your path with arms akimbo and spits at you. Mind you, I quite agree that twice-two-makes-four is a most excellent thing [*prevosxodnaja vešč'*]; but if we are to give everything its due, then twice-two-equals-five is a most charming little thing, too [*premilaja inogda veščica*]." The underground man rejects the formula

$2 \times 2 = 4$ because it—like Aristotelean plot, like Darwin's conception of nature or Buckle's conception of human history—emphasizes the whole over the parts: four is seen as the product, the sum of what has gone before, 2×2. What is equally significant here is the way he turns the two philosophical systems represented by $2 \times 2 = 4$ and $2 \times 2 = 5$ into personalities: the diminutive used to evoke the latter system makes it almost a literary character. By making the conflict into a little tale he suggests that there is no ground for it, that it is therefore fiction, merely another story.

This insistence on the fiction-making process as the basis of all his understanding is extended in the same section. The underground man collapses the pet ideas of nineteenth-century positivism into a simple metaphor: the crystal palace. He then compares it to a musical comedy. But he does so in a particular way: "In vaudevilles, for instance, suffering is not permitted. . . . In the crystal palace it is unthinkable." Just as the invalidity of the French bourgeois was said, in *Winter Notes*, to have found its best representation in melodrama, here it is argued that the perfect order (the system of parts to whole) of the Utopian Socialists is no more related to experience than is the vaudeville: both operate by the law of plot; they achieve their shape by excluding contingency; each is systematic only to the degree that they exclude the pressure of events. Well might he say in the concluding section of part 1 that he is pleased with the "*literary* quality" of his jokes.

The first movement from part 1 into part 2 is full of ironies. There is first of all the underground man's admission that "I assure you most solemnly, gentlemen, there is not a word I have just written I believe in!" That is to say, none of the various positions he has attacked *or* supported in the course of his long polemic on systems satisfied his needs to believe. They are *all* mere fictions—the system of mathematics, on the one hand, and the underground man's own plea for *freedom* from systems, on the other. It is programmatically necessary that he state at the outset of part 2 its discontinuity with part 1: the structure he presents in his text is not sequential in the way $2 \times 2 = 4$ is, or a *progressive* history is, or in the way that most literary plots are arranged.

There is, of course, a central ambiguity in his use of literary plot: its neat order may be used as a damaging metaphor for systems that seek a neat order outside literature, and thus it is stressed that insofar as history or social reform or scientific thinking seek to impose a homogenous order on the world, they are *fictive*, like literature: the harmonious schemes of Utopian Socialists, for instance, have the ontological status of vaudeville. On the other hand, however, since he has abandoned the possibility of *any* system as a privileged source in which to ground his selfhood, he is condemned to a world where *nothing* is real, and therefore the strategies of fiction provide the only workable means of giving shape—if only momentarily, from story to story—to experience. Recognizing that the history of rocks, the history of things, does not suggest a shape for his self, he is forced into the recognition that time is not something we invent as a construct—it is, rather, what we are. But what *kind* of time are we? If "History is the systematic science of that radical reality, my life" (Ortega y Gasset, *History as System*, tr. Helene Weyl), what separates it from the "systematic sciences" of geology or physics and the histories *their* "radical reality" constitute? Or, as Foucault puts the question:

> Can [man's] history ever be anything but the inextricable nexus of the different times [of the positive sciences] which are foreign to him and heterogeneous in respect to one another? Will the history of man ever be more than a sort of modulation common to changes in the conditions of life (climate, soil fertility, methods of agriculture, exploitation of wealth), to transformations in the economy (and consequently in society and its institutions) and to the succession of forms and usages in language?

As we have seen, it is these systems which the underground man rejects; to accept them would be to chart a temporal course for himself by maps that pictured the wrong ocean. He seeks rather to evaluate his *own* progress of things. The uniqueness of what is human would be lost if humans were perceived as merely the nodal point for the various histories of things that are *not* human. If he is merely a way to tell the time of things, then, "in that case, man is not himself historical: since time comes to him from somewhere other than himself, he constitutes himself as a subject of history only by the superimposition of the history of living things [biology], the history of 'things' [geology, physics] and the history of words [linguistics]."

But if the coordinates of these progressions will not serve to shape the life of an individual man, where may one turn to find a clock that will validly tell the time of self? The underground man's answer is to plots from literature, plots of several familiar kinds. He is attempting to forge a continuity for his identity, to experiment with what would constitute a true history of his self. Therefore, as does any historian, he "must draw upon a fund of culturally provided 'mythoi' [or standard plot schemes] in order to constitute the facts as figuring a story of a particular kind, just as he must appeal to that same fund of 'mythos' in the minds of his readers to endow his account of the past with the odor of meaning of significance" (White, "Interpretation"). Such a view assumes that the power of history to explain things resides in its story, and, further, that there can be no story without a plot by which to make of it a story of a particular kind.

We must keep these points in mind as we read the underground man's reasons for attempting a biography, a biography, moreover, he does not intend to be read by anyone else. He is attempting to write a biography, a history of continuous identity for himself—and the fact that his attempt breaks down into mere disconnected notes from underground is only one of the ironies he dramatizes. He quotes Heine, who "says that true biographies are almost impossible, and that a man will most certainly tell a lot of lies about himself. . . . But Heine had in mind a man who made his confessions to the public. I, however, am writing for myself." The form of biography is always false to the essence of life it tells; it gives that life a shape that is recognizable to *others*, but what others grasp as a meaningful form must be a *common* form, and insofar as it is common the uniqueness of its subject is lost. The underground man several times attempts to answer why he writes down his biography: "I am imagining an audience on purpose so as to observe the proprieties [*vesti sebja priličnee*] when I write . . . it will look more dignified on paper . . . the whole style will, I'm sure, be better." By imagining an audience, he can imagine what they will expect of a biography and he can in turn use those conventional demands as parameters for a self he cannot otherwise historicize. He cannot find his *own* mode of emplot-ment, so he will use the conventional one. He seeks to make a coherent story out of his life by imposing on it a literary pattern. The process is dramatized in the closing lines of part 1 as he seeks to create a bridge—to make a coherent connection—with part 2: "moreover, I may feel easier in my mind if I write it down. I have, for instance, been oppressed lately by the memory of some incident that happened to me long ago . . . it has been annoying me like some tune you cannot get out of your head. And yet I simply must get rid of it, I have hundreds of such memories." Like Max Frisch's Gantenbein, he "has had an experience and is looking for a story with which to match it; for one cannot live with an experience that has not found outlet through a story."

The predicament of the underground man is, stated simply, that the only way he can organize a self is through stories that fit into existing literary categories, shapes that pre-exist his own life, are as outside his experienced sense of self as the temporal shapes of Darwinian progressions or mathematical sequences. He writes his memoirs to achieve the coherent effect of literary plot for his biography. And yet he knows such plots are made up, fictive, have no ground: they can be manipulated by himself but are *not* of himself. We can see this dilemma in the structure of the story that makes up part 2, the encounter with the prostitute Liza.

The fact that what he is about to relate is a *fiction*, a story in the sense that the order of his plot is secured through the exclusion of *chance*, is revealed in two ways: one, the event that triggers the underground man's memory of the Liza episode is in itself fortuitous: "Snow is falling today, almost wet snow, yellow, dirty. It was snowing yesterday, too, and the other day. I think it is because of the wet snow that I remembered the incident which gives me no rest now." The second way in which the empty order, the bad literariness of the underground man's method is undercut, is in the epigraph to part 2 that follows immediately. It is a passage from Nekrasov's 1845 poem "*Kogda iz mraka zabluždenja*," the story in verse of what happens when a "decent man" brings home a reformed prostitute. It is a poem full of the worst literary clichés, all served up with a mind-numbing sentimentality. Dostoevsky gives the lie to the whole thing by cutting the poem off at a particularly pathetic moment with a series of "and so forth and so forths."

It has often been pointed out that, in so doing, Dostoevsky has dramatized a contrast between Nekrasov's sentimental version of the prostitute and his own realistic picture. But the way in which Dostoevsky explodes the literariness of Nekrasov's poem in the last line is, more specifically, another structural metaphor for the pattern of the story—neat plot—which is then destroyed by contact with reality. In other words, the debunked sentimentalism of the poem catches the basic morphology not only of movement from part 1, "The Underground," to part 2, "Apropos of the Wet Snow," but for *all* the stories that the underground man makes up to give himself an identity and that are later invalidated by contingency.

The underground man has no organic coherence, no systems for ordering experience that he can believe in; existence does not come naturally to him. His life is an inversion of the Cartesian cogito: instead of, "I think, therefore I am," the underground man, whose sickness is an overdeveloped consciousness, thinks, therefore he is *not*. Sprung from a test tube, he must act like a man born of woman. But with no patterns to fall back on, he is forced to invent his own, with no rules to guide him except for those which derive from his reading. He is constantly making experiments in ontology, a mad scientist in the cluttered laboratory of his own identity.

At the beginning of part 2 he says: "I even used to make experiments to see whether I could meet without flinching the look of one or another of my colleagues." This experiment is characteristic of several others the underground man makes. It is the first of several encounters that define the only way the underground man can confront other people or events in real life: he can do so only as *combat*, as an unending series of skirmishes. But these battles for existence are not the sort one encounters amid the unpredictability of actual warfare: they always have the choreographed, ritual quality of duels, which are all very literary, of course.

The initial section of part 2 bristles with references to the underground man's wide reading: "At home I mostly spent my time reading," or "Apart from reading I had nothing to occupy me." His literariness operates at several levels. There is the obvious one of specific reference to well-known works by Pushkin, Lermontov, Byron, Balzac, and very frequently to Gogol. But the essential meaning of the underground man's literariness is the one we have already remarked in connection with plots: it is his way of establishing a continuous self, of giving shape to the events that constantly threaten to overcome him. Consider the first sustained story of part 2: one night the underground man sees some men quarreling in a billiard parlor. He goes inside, but is picked up and set down by an army officer, who wishes to get him out of the way in order to make his exit. The underground man is mortified, moved about "as if I were a piece of furniture. I would have given anything at that moment for a real, a more regular, a more decent, and a more, so to speak, *literary* [Dostoevsky's emphasis] quarrel." He considers haranguing the other men in the place who have witnessed his humiliation, but decides, "they would jeer at me if I protested and began addressing them in literary language. For even today we cannot speak of a point of honor . . . except in literary language." He himself recognizes the artificiality, the contrived "literary" nature, of the duel.

He does two things—he actually *writes* a story about his encounter and sends it off for publication, but it is rejected. So he falls back on his more usual literary variant: "At last I resolved to challenge the officer to a duel." He writes a "most beautiful, most charming letter" of challenge, but does not send it. Instead, he resolves on a duel of another sort: he will meet the officer on Nevsky Prospekt—and not move aside. "I shall only knock against him as much as he knocks against me." But he leaves nothing to *chance*—all must go according to the script he has prepared in his mind. And like a good actor/producer, he considers the setting and his costume. Of the former he says, "there was sure to be quite an audience there; a countess, out for a walk, Prince D. taking a walk," and then he adds what is even more important for him, "the whole *literary* world taking a walk." He prepares his costume by buying a new fur collar for his overcoat, plagiarizing here, as he does in other places, from Gogol's story *The Overcoat*. When all is prepared—two years after his first meeting with the officer—the underground man does confront his unwitting antagonist on the Nevsky, only to be ignored by him. But he is not daunted by this—*he* was true—if not to any generally held code of honor, then at least to his own plot. This shows another way that he uses his stories: not only as blueprint for future raids on reality, but as a kind of narrative therapeutic after life has squashed him once again—as he says so accurately of himself—like a fly.

This leads naturally into the opening of subchapter 2 in the second half of *Notes*, where he reveals that he would dream "for three months on end, skulking in his corner." Freed from reality, he says, "I suddenly became a hero." It is at this point that he reveals one of the primary meanings of life as single combat: in life he is lowest of the low, in his dreams he is a hero. As he says: "Either a hero or dirt [*grjaz'*], there was no middle way." Which is to say that there is no middle way between his dreams and reality. His is an impossible either/or; the order of daydream, with perfect plots, is totally removed from reality, where there is only the complete chaos of contingency. It is this lack of dialectic, of a middle, that makes the duel so crucial a metaphor for the underground man: it too is a polar opposition, an either/or, you or me—to the death.

The underground, then, can be understood as a kind of literary grace, that place in the mind where good stories can happen. The underground man reveals here some of his more imaginative plots: he will become a millionaire; everyone will love him; he will preach new ideas; a general amnesty will be declared; the Pope will agree to leave Rome and move to Brazil; Lake Como will be transferred to the outskirts of Rome, where, in the Villa Borghese, a ball for the whole of Italy will be held. This impulse to turn everything into a story is best expressed by the underground man himself: "Everything, however, always ended most satisfactorily in an indolent and rapturous transition to art, that is, to the *beautiful* forms of existence, all ready-made, snatched forcibly from the poets and novelists and adapted to every possible need and requirement."

It should be noted in passing, by the way, that the remarkable plot he hatches about the Pope's removal to Brazil, etc., follows the pattern of *all* his stories: it is marvelous, but it cannot last. The line that ends this particular story is: "this would be followed by the scene in the bushes, and so on and so forth—don't tell me you don't know it!"

We now move into chapter 2 of part 2, in which the essential story of that whole cycle, the Liza episode, begins. The underground man invites himself to a dinner given by some former schoolmates, an occasion for revealing certain facts of his childhood, two of which are significant from the point of view we are pursuing here: one, even at a tender age he, not surprisingly, "was already reading books which [the other boys] could not read." More importantly, he says of himself "Whether it was because I was not used to change or for some other reason, all through my life I could not help feeling that any extraneous event, however trivial, would immediately bring about some radical alteration in my life." Precisely: since it lacks any coherence of its own, his biography is helpless to resist the effect of "extraneous events." That is why he makes up stories that are viable only when uncontaminated by reality. It is also why he cannot lift his glass when, at dinner, Zverkov proposes the toast: "To our past, gentlemen, and to our future!" The underground man cannot share in this toast because it presupposes a continuum in biography that he does not share—his life has no organic beginning, middle, and end.

He offends his friends, finally, challenging one of them to a duel. When the others scoff at this, he says "you can't possibly refuse me. I want to show you I'm not afraid of a duel. You can fire first, and I'll fire in the air!" It goes without saying that such nobility is one of the most overworked clichés of duels in literature, and another hint at the Pushkin story of a duel that the underground man mentions specifically, *The Shot*.

His schoolmates leave him as they go off to the bordello. The underground man decides to follow them. The duel mechanism is now extended: he says that everything depends on another encounter with his former friends, "my whole future. . . . Either they'll implore me for my friendship on their knees—or I'll slap Zverkov's face!" He creates a situation in which everything turns on one act—sets up an either/or; that is the meaning of the duel at one level. Its meaning at another is indicated in the underground man's words as he speeds to the confrontation: "So this is it—this is it at last—a head-on clash with reality." Once again it is literature versus life. As the sledge drives him to Olympia's he tells himself more stories about what will happen—he knows it all in *advance*, his compulsive making of plots evaporates reality. He sees himself as Pushkin's Silvio, but this tale, too, is debunked by events. When he rushes into the bordello, there is no one there, "everything had vanished, everything had changed!" as he says.

Now begins the real duel he is to fight at the bordello. He makes love to the prostitute Liza, and, as they are lying in the bed later, he starts telling stories. At first things are a bit jumbled. "The events of the previous day passed disjointedly through my mind, as though of themselves and without any effort on my part." But he very quickly works out a strategy, a story, a plot. He tells of a burial in Volkovo cemetery, of a grave that had a foot of water in it. It is all a lie, as he admits: "I had never seen [the ground] there, nor have I ever been in Volkovo cemetery." But he wishes to hurt his opponent, Liza. He embroiders his tale: the coffin buried in the marshy ground was that of a prostitute who had come to a sorry end. As he goes on, he says, "Suddenly something flared up in me, a sort of aim had appeared." He decides to incorporate Liza into the story of his own life; he seeks to gain power over her by getting her to act out a part he shall write. It is a plot *against* the girl that is advanced by means of the *plots* in the stories the underground man now tells her. The next tale—of a self-sacrificing father's love for his daughter—is cribbed from Balzac's *Père Goriot*. The underground man—whose considerable gifts for rhetoric have been demonstrated in the eleven chapters of polemic in part 1—now warms to his task; nobility shines in the scenes he draws for the girl. He introduces some more plots: he tells the story of how happy Liza would be "if she had a rosy little baby boy sucking at [her] breast"; he creates a touching domestic scene with an adoring husband. "It is with pictures, with pictures like these you will beguile her," he thinks to himself.

But his tone is so literary that even the prostitute recognizes it for what it is: "Why you—you're speaking as though you were reading from a book." This only spurs the underground man on to even more *complex* stories. He tells of how once, on a New Year's eve, he saw another prostitute turned out into the cold night, shrieking at the top of her lungs and beating the steps with a salt fish. He is a great author for details! Since his tale of Liza's future with a child and husband left her unmoved, he spins out another plot for her future: she will die a horrible death of consumption, and be buried in a grave of wet blue clay, covered with dirty snow. This, too, is a tale full of literary clichés: "I knew I was speaking in a stiff, affected, even bookish manner . . . but this did not worry me . . . for I knew . . . that this very bookishness would assist rather than hinder weeping." The underground man has his opponent at his feet, destroyed by stories just as surely as if she had been wounded by a pistol in a duel. He cannot resist one last, grand gesture of nobility—he gives her his address. He knows he has triumphed when she shows him her greatest treasure—a declaration of love from a medical student who did not know she was a prostitute. She has her stories, too.

But his sense of achievement is short-lived. Just as the Lake Como dream-story was destroyed by the scene in the bushes, this victory of fantasy is undercut as he thinks on the way home: "But the truth was already blazing through my bewilderment. The disgusting truth!"

The next day he writes a masterly letter of explanation to the former schoolmates he had so offended at the dinner party. It shows again how the underground man is able to take chaotic events and force them into a neat pattern, flattering to himself: it is another of his plots, this time imposed on the past instead of the future. He knows it is all a lie, but "the main thing is that I got out of it."

At any rate, he has new worries. What if Liza takes him at his word and comes to his shabby apartment: once again one of his stories will be destroyed by life's refusal to accept his plots. At first he is angry at the girl for believing him. But, then, as days pass and she does not show up, he starts telling himself a different story of what would have happened had she, in fact, visited him. It is another idyll—he educates her, she falls in love with him, he is tender, noble. It is all, as he says, very "George Sandian." When he thinks her coming is a *reality*, there is no room for stories, and he is *angry*; when it appears she will *not* come, he is freed to make up a story about what *would* have happened *had* she come—and it is a much more Aristotelean tale.

But of course Liza does come to his room. He is thrown into a towering rage: he tells her he did not wish to save her; he spun those tales he told her for the sake of the telling. "For all I wanted was to make the few fine speeches, to have something to dream about." She is dream fodder. In other words, he was merely telling more of the stories that keep him alive, that give shape to the unconnected minutes of his disjointed biography.

However, instead of being crushed, Liza pities him, understands that he is unhappy. He cannot believe this at first: "I was so used to imagining everything and to thinking of everything as it happened in books, and to picturing everything in the world as I had previously made it up in my dreams, that at first I could not all at once grasp the meaning of this occurrence." But when he does understand her pity, he is even more furious: "our parts were now completely changed . . . she was the heroine now, while I was exactly the same crushed and humiliated creature . . . she had appeared to *me* that night—four days before." Because his capacity to come to terms with the world outside his own plots has long since atrophied, he cannot accept even the girl's selfless love—accept, in other words, the thing for what it is. He smothers this reality with another plot. She has refused to accept the role he has assigned her. Even more, by pitying him she has turned the tables; he has been outflanked, *wounded* in this duel. But even as she holds him in her arms, he forces her back into his plot, that plot that says she is not a woman, but merely a category, a prostitute. He has sex with her again—that is, he insists she act out the attribute of her role, remain in her dramatic *emploi*.

She becomes aware that he has used her for purposes of revenge, and is about to crawl away. For the underground man she cannot leave soon enough—she has brought too much reality into his schematic underground. "I wanted her to disappear. I longed for 'peace.' I wanted to be left alone. . . . 'Real life' [*živaja žizn'*]—so unaccustomed to it was I—had crushed me so much that I found it difficult to breathe." In other words, he almost expires from reality.

As she goes out the door, he presses a five-ruble note into her hand as the ultimate reminder that she is still the character he has invented—only a prostitute. But just after she has gone out he thinks, "This cruelty was so insincere, so much thought out, so deliberately invented, so *bookish*, that I couldn't stand it myself even for a minute." But he is too late to catch the girl—who has disappeared into the wet snow that is always, in the *Notes*, part of a semantic field associated with death.

Returning to his room he discovers she has left the money on a table—once again reality thwarts his plot. He dashes out after her again, but she is gone. At first he regrets he was unable to apologize to her—but this emotion is soon surrounded and devoured by the narrative pseudopod of yet another story: it is all for the best that he did *not* catch her, what he has done will help her somehow, his insult will purify her—he has done a good deed, etc. Sixteen years later, as he is writing all this down in his memoirs, it is the style of the story, not its substance, he remembers: "I may as well add that I remained for a long time pleased with the *phrase* about the usefulness of insults." This emphasis on style as language used in the service of concealment is only one more way in which the underground man reveals himself as an avatar of Dostoevsky's French bourgeois (who used "eloquence" in the same end) in *Winter Notes*.

In the closing lines of the *Notes*, the meaning of the underground man's literariness is made explicit. He presents himself as typical of modern man: "We have all lost touch with life, we are all cripples, every one of us . . . we have gone so far that we look upon 'real life' almost as a sort of burden, and we are all agreed that 'life' as we find it in books is much better." That is, since there is no dialectic between imagination and reality, what results is the either/or of neat plots in fantasy, on the one hand, and threatening chaos in real life, on the other. Since there is no middle, how can there be a beginning or an end that makes sense: there is no center in the underground, how can it have boundaries? Since there is no natural, no organic way to end, the *Notes* simply peter out: "But enough—I don't want to write any more 'from the underground.' " But of course he does *not* end, as the "editor's note" that Dostoevsky appends makes clear: "He could not resist, and continued further."

The underground man will continue to spin his web of stories until the ultimate contingency—death—puts a stop to them. Because there is *nothing to hold the stories together*: there is no plot of plots. Because there is no comprehensive *end* toward which each of the stories is directed, the story they comprise all together can have no ending: the breakdown of teleology in the plot of *Notes* is an attempt by Dostoevsky to expand the meaning of plot beyond what are traditionally thought to be merely literary bounds; it is plot understood as the problem of the possibility of a meaningfully coherent series at all. Thus the underground man's hostility to all that is merely literature. His position is the polar opposite to Matthew Arnold's exaggerated claims for the role of literature in an age of disbelief: "The future of poetry is immense, because in poetry our race . . . will find an ever surer and surer stay. There is not a creed which is not shaken, not an accredited dogma which is not shown to be questionable, not a received tradition which does not threaten to dissolve. Our religion has materialized itself in the fact . . . and now the fact is failing it . . . the strongest part of our religion today is its unconscious *poetry*" [emphasis added]. Even *this* last hope is dashed by the underground man. For not only does he not believe in systems born of reason—logic, history, mathematics, science—as has been pointed out so many times; he *also* doubts systems born of fantasy—dreams, stories. Not only has the *adequati rei et intellectus*, the adequation of mind to things, broken down, but so has the adequation of imagination and things: the underground man knows that his stories are only stories.

But Dostoevsky's counterplot serves not only to characterize the underground man. It is a technique he will employ again and again: in *Crime and Punishment* he explodes that most syllogistic of all plot structures, the detective story; in *The Possessed* he subverts several plots familiar to all readers of utopian fiction; in *The Brothers Karamazov* he sets up the life of Zosima along the familiar lines of saintly biography, only to provide a most unhagiographic twist in the monk's stinking corpse.

The calculated inversion of plots familiar to readers from other books is a major structural device of the whole Dostoevskian *oeuvre*. It is this device which provides the illusion of that enormous contingency one senses in the Dostoevskian novel. This is why Walter Kaufmann [in *Existentialism from Dostoevsky to Sartre*] has called *Notes from Underground* "the best overture for existentialism ever written." He has in mind only the themes to which the underground man gives expression in part 1 of the *Notes*. It has remained to another philosopher, who is also significantly a novelist, to locate the structural importance of the story, to isolate the meaning of Dostoevsky's attack on conventional plot. Sartre, in his programmatic work *Nausea*, provides the theory behind Dostoevsky's structural practice. Roquentin says:

> I have never had adventures. Things have happened to me, events, incidents, anything you like. But no adventures . . . for the most banal event to become an adventure, you must . . . begin to recount it. This is what fools people: a man is always a teller of tales, he lives surrounded by his stories and the stories of others, he sees everything that happens to him through them; and he lives

his own life as if he were telling a story. But you have to choose: live or tell.

The underground man, too, is aware that man—whether he be scientist, politician, or historian—is "always a teller of tales." But his conclusion is less optimistic: there is no choice; perhaps it is the case that *in order* to live, men are condemned to tell.

ROBERT L. BELKNAP

The Rhetoric of an Ideological Novel

This paper treats the ways in which Dostoevsky's social and ideological intentions interacted with certain of his sources in the genesis of Ivan Karamazov and Ivan's Grand Inquisitor. These intentions have eluded some of the best literary minds that have written about Dostoevsky—at least these minds differ so sharply that they cannot all be right. Let me quote two statements bearing on Dostoevsky's intention. The first is from D. H. Lawrence's introduction to a separate edition of the Grand Inquisitor chapter, translated by S. S. Koteliansky:

> If there is any question: who is the Grand Inquisitor? surely we must say it is Ivan himself. And Ivan is the thinking mind of the human being in rebellion, thinking the whole thing out to the bitter end. As such he is, of course, identical with the Russian Revolutionary of the thinking type. He is also, of course, Dostoevsky himself in his thoughtful as apart from his passional and inspirational self. Dostoevsky half-hated Ivan. Yet after all, Ivan is the greatest of the three brothers, pivotal. The passionate Dmitri and the inspired Alyosha are, at last, only offsets to Ivan.
>
> And we cannot doubt that the Grand Inquisitor speaks Dostoevsky's own final opinion about Jesus. The opinion is baldly, this: Jesus, you are inadequate. Men must correct you. And Jesus gives the kiss of acquiescence to the Inquisitor, as Alyosha does to Ivan.

From *Literature and Society in Imperial Russia, 1800–1914*, edited by William Mills Todd III. © 1978 by Stanford University Press.

Lawrence had not read Bakhtin's remarks about the polyphonic novel, but he knew better than to assume that a character is a spokesman for the author. He offered three reasons for identifying Ivan and the Grand Inquisitor with Dostoevsky: Ivan's greatness, his pivotal position in the novel, and the kiss of acquiescence the Inquisitor receives. Ivan's greatness generates a rhetorical and a genetic argument. First, one may ask why an author would select such an attractive mouthpiece for ideas he hopes to crush. Second, one can deny the possibility of creating a truly great character without real sympathy at some level. Lawrence argues this explicitly with respect to Tolstoy.

These are persuasive arguments, but many readers take the diametrically opposite view of Dostoevsky's intent, though they may agree that Ivan is identical with the Russian revolutionary of the thinking type. The most concise and authoritative statement of their position comes from Dostoevsky's own letter to his editor Liubimov on May 10, 1879.

> [Ivan's] convictions are precisely what I accept as the *synthesis* of Russian anarchism in our day, the denial not of God, but of the meaning of his creation. All socialism had its origins and beginnings in the denial of the meaning of historical actuality [*deistvitel' nosti*], and progressed to a program of destruction and anarchism. The original anarchists were in many cases men of sincere convictions. My hero takes up a topic I consider irrefutable [*neotrazimuiu*]—the senselessness of the suffering of children— and deduces from that the absurdness [*absurd*, not *nelepost'*] of all historical actuality. I don't know whether I managed it well, but I know that the figure of my character is in the highest degree real [*real'noe*]. (In *The Possessed* there were a multitude of figures whom I was attacked for as fantastic, and then, can you believe it, they all were justified by actuality, so they must have been imagined correctly.)
>
> All that is said by my character in the text I sent you is based on actuality. All the stories about children happened, were printed in the papers, and I can show where; nothing was invented by me. . . . As for my character's blasphemy, it will be triumphantly confused [*oprovergnuto*] in the next [June] issue, on which I am working now with fear and trembling and veneration, considering my task (the crushing of anarchism) a patriotic exploit. Wish me success, my dear Nikolai Alekseevich.

Although Dostoevsky's statement carries more authority than Lawrence's, the mere existence of Lawrence's presents a curious disjunction.

Either Lawrence's article is correct, and Dostoevsky was consciously or unconsciously lying, or Dostoevsky's letter is correct, and Dostoevsky was a rhetorical incompetent. If rhetoric is language that makes the reader feel, judge, or act in accord with the author's intent, its success can be measured like that of the most primitive communication system, in which the sender, whether a telegrapher or an author, encodes a message into a form that can be transmitted through a channel, anything from a telegraph wire to a line of letters folded into a book. The receiver decodes the message, and the measure of success is the degree to which the reconstituted message coincides with the sender's. Lawrence's letter is a fair example of one major line in Dostoevsky criticism. In fact, an enormous number of readers have sided with the Grand Inquisitor, and many, like V. V. Rozanov, who do not side with him have stated that Dostoevsky did.

To accept Lawrence's arguments, however, one must reject the testimony of Dostoevsky's letter. The letter, of course, is a good example of a somewhat suspect literary form, one that has been studied little, although cultivated by many masters of European prose—the letter requesting the extension of a deadline. Anti-anarchism would have appealed to Liubimov and his chief, Katkov, whose journal, *The Russian Messenger*, was well to the right of center. Still, Dostoevsky's letter summarizes a position he had taken often in his journalism, and it cannot be summarily dismissed. Instead it may provide additional insights on close inspection.

Except for one rather puzzling sentence about the sincerity of the anarchists, the passage quoted falls into three parts, only the last of which promises to confute Ivan's argument. The first part traces Ivan's anarchism to the senselessness of the suffering of children, by way of the concept of the absurd that was to become so fashionable three generations later. Between this statement about the text's ideology and the statement of his intention to refute it, Dostoevsky claims absolute fidelity to his sources. Thus, where Lawrence moves directly from the author's text to his intention, Dostoevsky disconcertingly moves from the text through the sources on his way to the opposite intention.

In calling Ivan's convictions the "synthesis" of contemporary anarchism, Dostoevsky is already preparing his reader for the middle part of the passage, where the phrases "all socialism had its origins" and "the original anarchists were in many cases" actually imply that Ivan is the highest artistic achievement under the realist aesthetic of his day—a literary type, an accurate representation of an identifiable segment of society. The ambitiousness of this claim explains the modest beginning of a following sentence, "I don't know whether I managed it well," which at first glance conflicts with Dostoevsky's fear that he had done Ivan too well. Of course, the word "well" means two different things here. I use it to mean "persuasively," "appealingly," "powerfully," as Lawrence would, whereas Dostoevsky is using it to mean "typically." He offers two different kinds of evidence to support his claim to typicality. The reference to *The Possessed* expresses pride in the subsequent confirmation of a reality that did not exist at the time he wrote, whereas the sentences around it claim that every detail about Ivan is based on prior reality. The implicit paradox is real and important, but for all his love of paradox, Dostoevsky did not invent it. He merely voiced the standard doctrine of the prosaists of his day, that artists were artists precisely because they could perceive reality more sharply and subtly than other men, and could select and assemble details whose firm basis in reality explained their crystallization into accurate types, even if the author himself did not realize their implication. This paradoxical dependence of special, even prophetic, insight on photographic fidelity to reality rests on a metonymic faith in the capacity of the parts of a reality to generate a representation of the whole.

Dostoevsky's claim that his fidelity to reality has produced an accurate ideological type justifies Ivan's attractiveness and also draws attention to Ivan's sources. Ivan, as Dostoevsky and Lawrence agree, has his origins in the reality of Russian radicalism. Belinsky's letters to Botkin and Gogol, and Herzen's *From the Other Shore* provided Dostoevsky with much of Ivan's language and ideology. Indeed, these sources offer a simple answer to Lawrence's question about producing a great character without personal sympathy. A writer like Lawrence tends to equate greatness with eloquence, and others [like A. Rammelmeyer] have already shown that a substantial part of Ivan's eloquence is borrowed from these authors. More important, however, Dostoevsky had adored Belinsky, had participated in the Petrashevsky circle, and had talked with Herzen and possibly Bakunin enough to feel their magnetism, sometimes simultaneously with his doubts about their doctrines. At the Petrashevsky interrogations Dostoevsky said that he read Belinsky's letter to Gogol for its language, not its ideas. He was desperate for excuses, of course, but Maikov's memories suggest that his testimony might by coincidence have been true. For Dostoevsky in the seventies, Herzen and Belinsky might be wrong, but they were noble in their eloquence, in their willingness to sacrifice their happiness, and in that sincerity of conviction whose relevance seemed puzzling at first in the letter to Liubimov. Dostoevsky's fidelity to this aspect of his sources could have made Ivan Karamazov more attractive in his desperate love than seems fitting or strategic if Dostoevsky's letter expressed his real intent.

This conservation of rhetorical power and moral persuasiveness alters the model of the primitive communication system in a novel of this sort. Dostoevsky is in part the sender, but he also is a channel through which the qualities of his sources are transmitted intact. Jakobson, Lotman, and many others have discussed the limitations and complications of this sender-channel-receiver model. We realize, for example, along with the fact that the sender does not generate the message ex nihilo, that the codes of the sender and the receiver may not coincide, and that data outside the text may enter the interpretation. Dostoevsky's letter to Liubimov introduces the crucial question for this paper, the interdependence of the sender and the channel. Whether we think of the input into the system as a body of information Dostoevsky had gathered from his reading, his conversation, and his other experiences, or as a body of intentions generated out of these experiences, we must consider the central element in his experiment in 1879—*The Brothers Karamazov*. We do not have the traditional, straightforward communication diagram of sender → message in channel → receiver, but rather this:

As it comes into being, the message in the channel is a constant source of feedback to the sender, just as the sound of one's own voice crucially affects the way one speaks. The letter to Liubimov begins with a description of Dostoevsky's fidelity to his prior experience and ends with his reaction to *The Brothers Karamazov* as it was emerging—fear and trembling, or negative feedback. Here the sources, the intention, and the emerging text shape each other. Physicists are hard put to it to solve a three-body problem where the bodies are mathematical points and the only influence is gravitational. I do not aspire to such a solution here, but to an indication of the kind of interaction among these three entities in Dostoevsky's mind.

II

This formulation of our task suggests an obvious way to test the authenticity of Dostoevsky's fear and trembling. If Ivan's greatness is an accidental side effect of Dostoevsky's fidelity to his sources, we should find in the text a series of efforts to destroy one of the most eloquent and convincing arguments in all literature, an argument whose starting point Dostoevsky himself had called irrefutable. Indeed, it has been said that Ivan's fate in the novel is designed to show what happens to an atheist and a socialist. He is desperately unhappy; he is rejected in love; and he becomes diseased in the part of him on which he depends excessively, the brain. His suffering and his incapacity at the end of the novel are taken as Dostoevsky's vision of the just punishment of unbelief.

A more sophisticated way of refuting Ivan's position involves not what happens to him but what he does and is. Valentina Vetlovskaia has catalogued enough unpleasant actions and features of Ivan's to make a convincing case that Dostoevsky intended to discredit Ivan's argument by discrediting its spokesman. Her study underlines the problem this novel presents. She shows Dostoevsky using one of the classical rhetorical techniques, the *argumentum ad hominem*, and leaves us with the evidence of Lawrence and scores of other able readers that the technique did not work. I should like to look at one of Vetlovskaia's points more closely, Dostoevsky's effort to discredit Ivan by associating him with devils.

As long as men have talked about sin, they have acknowledged its attractiveness, but in the Middle Ages evil, unlike sin, was presented as unattractive, and its embodiment, devils, tended to be represented as repulsive, filthy, stinking, vicious, and subhuman. Dostoevsky needed such devils if he intended to discredit Ivan by association with them, but the literature of his day offered a very different figure; as early as Milton, but insistently since Blake, Byron, and Baudelaire, various elements of the diabolic had had a good press. The Grand Inquisitor's devil is not a stupid and disgusting torturer, but a dire and fearsome spirit whose very name is taboo. This romantic fascination with the diabolic had weakened a literary resource Dostoevsky needed, the old devil who could provoke instant hostility. Indeed, within a few years of the creation of the Grand Inquisitor, Swinburne, Strindberg, Raspisardi, and Lautréamont had written major glorifications of the diabolic in four differing languages.

To counteract this loss of prefabricated repulsiveness, Dostoevsky has to train his readers to associate scorn or revulsion with the word "devil." Except for the biblical demons in *The Possessed*, devils play little part in Dostoevsky's works. Demonic figures like Murin in "The Landlady" are not connected with any particular supernatural being. But in *The Brothers Karamazov* a multitude of devils appear. Old Fyodor Karamazov introduces these creatures early in the novel, setting the stamp of his own savage weirdness on them:

> You see, it's impossible, I think, that the devils should forget to drag me down with hooks when I die. Well, then I think: Hooks? And where do they get them? Made of what? Iron? Forged where? Is there a factory of some sort they've got there? Now, over there in the monastery, the monks probably believe that in hell, for example, there's a ceiling; but I'm willing to believe in hell, only without a ceiling. It works out sort of neater, more enlightened, more Lutheran, that is. . . . Well, if there's no ceiling, therefore there

can't be any hooks, and if there's no hooks and all that's cast aside, that means—implausibly again—who'll drag me in with hooks, because if they don't drag me, then what will happen, where's there any justice in the world?

With or without hooks these devils could not be made grand or attractive. Even where a larger spirit is involved, Fyodor's presence makes him the mocker of mankind:

> "Does God exist or not? For the last time."
> "And for the last time, no."
> "Then who is laughing at mankind, Ivan?"
> "The Devil, probably," grinned Ivan.
> "And the Devil exists?"
> "No, the Devil too doesn't."

Such talk of the Devil as a mocker and of devils as torturers shapes our response to the devil who is the Grand Inquisitor's mentor. Sometimes the torture is explicit and the devils implicit, as in the story of the Virgin's descent into hell; sometimes the reverse, as with the devils Ferapont encounters. And sometimes both the torture and the devils are explicit, as with the devils Ferapont, Lize, and even Alyosha vanquish with a cross. Ferapont and Lize share the devils' love of pain. Ferapont sees one hiding

> behind the door from me, a full-sized one, too, a yard and a half or more tall; its tail was thick and brown and long, and the tip of the tail had slipped into the crack of the door; and I'm nobody's fool, so I suddenly slammed the door to, and caught its tail. And it got to squealing and started thrashing around; I took and put the sign of the cross on it, three times I crossed it. And then it died, like a spider that had been crushed.

Ferapond savors the agonized extinction of this devil just as he takes physical delight in the idea of heroic fasting, and the nastiness of his twisted sensuality becomes linked with that of his imagined victim. Ivan picks up this vision of the demonic and reinforces it, in the most moving linkage of the Devil with evil that we find, his adaptation of Voltaire's remark, in response to his own catalogue of the sufferings of children: "If the Devil does not exist, and man in fact created him, then he created him in his own image and likeness." Dostoevsky drew these various devils in large part from his readings in old Russian literature, and their antiquity reduces their rhetorical usefulness. Their association with the devil the Grand Inquisitor quotes remains largely verbal.

The most elaborate picture of an unlovely devil has different sources, and a far more intimate relation to Ivan. This is the devil who appears in Ivan's nightmare at the moment of Smerdyakov's suicide. Consider the following passage:

> Ivan felt that he was unwell, but from some dread of telling himself quite clearly that he was sick, he turned from the light and tried to go to sleep. His sleep was heavy and fitful; he was incessantly waking up, tossing restlessly on the bed, and again dozing off for a minute.
>
> Waking up one time, Ivan thought he would not get to sleep any more. He wanted to get up. His head was leaden; in his arms and legs there was some sort of dull pain. With an effort, he sat up on the bed leaning with his back on the corner of the room. He sat sometimes with no thought at all, sometimes there awakened in his head a turbulent and hazy consciousness that he felt bad. He would sit, would say "I feel bad," and again would senselessly focus his eyes on the opposite corner of the room. Suddenly it seemed to him as if something was stirring there. He gazed there. Just so, something was effortfully crawling out of the corner crack, shifted clumsily, and began to grow. It was some sort of likeness of a human. . . . Ivan rubbed his eyes, and then opened them again; there was no monster there any longer.

This apparition of a very personal demon to a sick man comes from a novel called *Likho* (The Evil Spirit) by Dmitry Vasilievich Averkiev (1836–1905), who had been a writer for Dostoevsky's journals in the 1860s. This passage appeared in issue no. 5 of the weekly *Ogonek* five months before Dostoevsky published Ivan's scene with the devil. Dostoevsky tended to read as many journals as he could, and had made a note to himself to look at that issue.

Ivan Karamazov's devil appears in much the same way. The passage that follows contains extensive ellipses, but no change of order.

> Ivan [Karamazov] was sitting on the couch and feeling his head spinning. He felt that he was sick and feeble. He was about to doze off, but got up restlessly and paced the room to keep off the sleep. At moments he imagined that he must be delirious. But it wasn't his sickness that preoccupied him most: when he sat down again, he began to glance around occasionally, as if he was looking for something. It happened several times. Finally, his gaze was fixed on one point. . . . He sat a long time in his place, firmly supporting his head on both hands and still glancing obliquely

at the same point as before, at the couch by the opposite wall. Evidently something was disturbing him, some object, distracting, bothering. . . .

He knew that he was unwell, but detested being sick at that time with revulsion. . . . So he was sitting now, almost conscious of being delirious . . . and fixedly staring at some object by the other wall on the couch. Suddenly, someone was sitting there.

Both passages begin with a presentation of sickness and go on to describe restless sleep, weakness and pain, and then a confusion of mind to which Dostoevsky gives the label delirium. Finally, both Ivans fix their gaze more and more firmly on a single spot, where an apparition occurs. Averkiev's Ivan expresses his incredulity with a gesture, and the creature disappears. Ivan Karamazov's hallucination remains for the entire chapter, and so does Ivan's incredulity. Dostoevsky's passage is longer, but except for the fear to admit sickness, the parallel elements appear in the same order, as if the Averkiev passage served as a framework. Dostoevsky, however, has elaborated a very different hallucination: he has retained none of the medieval qualities that Averkiev's creature shares with the devils Fyodor, Lize, Ferapont, and Grushenka describe. Dostoevsky no longer needs the little, subhuman medieval devils, but instead a being close enough to Ivan to debase Ivan's arguments, his rhetoric, and, most of all, that "dire and fearsome spirit of self-annihilation and nonbeing" with whom the Grand Inquisitor had so romantically associated himself. Indeed, as Ivan says repeatedly in this chapter, this devil *is* Ivan.

This ideological need works together with the interplay of sources to explain why Dostoevsky preserves so much of Averkiev's apparition scene but so little of his apparition. Averkiev was writing a historical novel and, like Dostoevsky, had plainly been reading folklore and nineteenth-century editions of the Russian saints' lives, which contain many demonic creatures. He would certainly have been brought up on *Faust* and E. T. A. Hoffmann, and very probably would have encountered the Nordic tradition of the personal fetish that normally appeared just before one's own death. He had apparently learned what Freud learned from reading Hoffman, that the sense of the uncanny comes from the reintrusion of long-abandoned beliefs. But Averkiev's background and his technique plainly mark another, more important source for his apparition scene. He had learned from his old associate Dostoevsky, most specifically from the appearance of a hideous arthropod to the dying radical Ippolit in *The Idiot* and the first appearance of Svidrigailov in the room of the delirious Raskolnikov in *Crime and Punishment*. Svidrigailov not only is mistaken for a hallucination; he has hallucinations—of the three victims of his unpunishable murders, his servant, his wife, and the little girl he raped. Averkiev's apparition scene combines rhetorically appealing elements shared by four of Dostoevsky's favorite sources, the lives of the saints, Goethe, Hoffmann, and Dostoevsky himself. When Ivan Karamazov, like Svidrigailov, blunders feverishly and beneficently through a storm on his way to his final hallucination, Dostoevsky is returning in his last great novel to the pattern of his first one to describe the ultimate collision between the rational intellect and the moral imperative. Like Svidrigailov and Raskolnikov, Ivan is conscious of blood guilt which the law cannot touch without his confession; his dreams, like theirs, reflect his victim, in this case his father, that shrewd, insolent, sophistical, insinuating, provincial mocker and hanger-on who resembles Ivan's devil and, to Ivan's distress, Ivan himself. In short, Ivan Karamazov's embodiment of evil diverges from Averkiev's because Averkiev's sources fitted Dostoevsky's literary taste and ideological purpose better than Averkiev's text.

In fact, the interesting question is not why Dostoevsky abandoned Averkiev's hallucination as a source, but why he adhered so faithfully to the order of details in a second-rate novel when he had a multitude of sources in better literature. Here, Dostoevsky was really using the same technique he used when he presented the despicable devils of antiquity: the desophistication of a figure whose current identity offered ideological complications. This technique was certainly not Dostoevsky's invention; it seems to come from the same source as the devil's tawdry gentility. Likhachev has pointed out that medieval devils can be cruel and dirty, but that this *poshlost'* can appear only in an age of social mobility and collapsing structures. Mephistopheles has this quality at times, with Martha, for example; but here, as in Averkiev, the richness of *déjà lu* goes deeper, to a source that Goethe and Dostoevsky both quoted extensively in their texts, the Book of Job. Many scholars believe the Book of Job was written at the high point of Hebrew culture, very likely in the reign of David, when the urban sophisticates toyed like pastoral poets with the figure from their folklore of a God whose sons presented themselves subserviently before him. One of those sons was a hanger-on who spoke to God when spoken to, but a tempter at the same time, challenging goodness with cynicism—"Doth Job fear God for naught?"—and prompting the most spectacular display of innocent suffering in literature before Ivan's catalogue of tortured children.

The letter to Liubimov explains why Dostoevsky would want to use the Book of Job as a source for the most notable character traits of Ivan's devil, as well as for the technique of desophistication, which led him to such other sources as the Russian saints' lives and Averkiev's historical novel. Ivan's argument rests on the senselessness of the world, according to that letter, and the task of the novel is to confute Ivan's argument: to justify the ways of God to man. The Book of Job is the oldest and the greatest theodicy Dostoevsky knew. It begins with the argument Dostoevsky considered unanswerable, the meaninglessness of innocent suffering. Job's children are destroyed, and the full authority of the biblical narrator declares Job innocent before his suffering begins. Bildad the Shuhite and his friends have the scholarly clear-sightedness that Ivan has, and like Ivan they enunciate the tempter's argument with the most insistent eloquence the rhetoric of their time afforded. In the Book of Job as it stands (some scholars think its sources ended differently), these massively elaborated arguments are destroyed by a theophany. In Dostoevsky's most immediate source for the encounter between Christ and the Inquisitor, *Le Christ au Vatican* by Cabantous, Christ is launched like a rocket into the empyrean before the eyes of an evil, astonished pope. But Dostoevsky's ideology excluded miracles or theophanies to justify or prove God. As Lia Mikhailovna Rozenblium has so clearly shown, Dostoevsky had very little of the mystic about him. In his notebooks he specifically rejected mysticism as a trait for Alyosha. Dostoevsky could draw his tawdry, subservient devil from the Book of Job, but in an antimystical age, with a nonmystical mind, he could not invoke the voice of God out of the whirlwind to refute the position argued by the devil and those associated with him.

III

Perhaps because some of his sources were too elequent and others conflicted with his ideology on miracles, Dostoevsky resorted to a series of rhetorical maneuvers to carry out the confutation he had promised Liubimov. One such maneuver deflates the Grand Inquisitor with a simplicity so transparent as to be invisible.

Ivan Karamazov says at the start of the legend that it belongs to a literary genre in which the Son of God can visit earth. The Grand Inquisitor sees Him resurrect a little girl, asks Him, "Is this Thou, Thou?" and then adds that he does not want an answer. Ivan comments that it would not matter for the account if the Grand Inquisitor was mistaken or delirious, so long as he spoke out. In any case, the Inquisitor addresses Christ as a being who has the power to save or doom mankind, to defy gravity, to turn stones into bread, to rule the kingdoms of the earth or else provide for the salvation of an elect. He also says that men are too feeble to obey the commandments of Christ, that in their disobedience they will suffer pangs of guilt, as well as practical misfortunes on earth, and will inevitably earn misfortunes in the hereafter: "Your great prophet in his vision and his allegory says he saw all the members of the first resurrection, and that there were twelve thousand of them from each of the Twelve Tribes. . . . But remember that there were only a few thousand of them in all—and gods at that—but the remainder? And what are the remaining feeble people to blame for, that they could not endure what the mighty could?"

By resort to miracle, mystery, and authority, the Inquisitor's church has imposed certain of Christ's laws on mankind and has concealed those laws demanding a moral heroism of which mankind is incapable. The Inquisitor says that disobedience to laws suppressed by the church cannot earn damnation for these unknowing sinners:

> We shall tell them that every sin shall be redeemed if it has been committed with our permission. . . . There will be thousands of millions of happy children and a hundred thousand sufferers who have taken upon themselves the curse of the knowledge of good and evil. Quietly they will die, quietly will expire in Thy name, and beyond the grave will find only death. But we will preserve the secret, and for their own happiness we will entice them with a heavenly and eternal reward. For if there were something in the other world, it is surely not for such as they. They say and prophesy that Thou wilt come and triumph anew, wilt come with Thy elect, with Thy proud and mighty, but we shall say that those have only saved themselves, while we saved all. . . . And we who have taken their sins upon us for their happiness, we shall stand before Thee and shall say, "Judge us if Thou canst and darest."

This intercession between man and Christ resembles Christ's intercession between man and God more than it resembles the Virgin's intercession between man and Christ in the medieval story Ivan tells about the Virgin's visit to hell. The Grand Inquisitor feels he is substituting his own punishment for that which divine justice would otherwise certainly inflict on mankind. Certainly he has incurred great sin—not only the suppression of Christ's truth, but the taking of all the lives in the autos da fé. The Grand Inquisitor believes he is doing great good on earth, preventing war and famine and despair, but his supreme exploit is more romantic than anything in Herzen: he has sacrificed the happiness of his immortal soul to save mankind from damnation.

Dostoevsky deflates this magnificent gesture with a very simple one. Christ says nothing, but kisses the Grand Inquisitor. The kiss is obviously a blessing; it burns in the Inquisitor's heart as holy things do in this novel.

And if Christ can bless the Grand Inquisitor, who has imprisoned Him, concealed His word, and killed hundreds of His followers, then obviously none
of the lesser sinners are cut off from Christ's salvation. The Grand Inquisitor
is unable to sacrifice his immortal soul, because Christ still can pardon him,
and he has no reason to do so, because mankind need not be damned. In
a later chapter, indeed, Zosima reduces damnation to eternal regret at having failed to love actively during the one life that a soul is given in all eternity. Here, in a single kiss, the most absolute and most appealing part of
the Grand Inquisitor's exploit becomes an empty, unnecessary gesture. He
has simply miscalculated the dimensions of God's mercy. He believes that
he believes in God and Christ, but actually he believes in a more Euclidean,
less merciful being.

Only one commentator on this passage has asked, "What are these sins
of people taken on oneself? . . . It's really just godlessness; that's the whole
secret. Your Inquisitor doesn't believe in God; that's his whole secret!"
Alyosha Karamazov says this before he hears about the kiss, and Ivan's answer
raises several of the same questions as the kiss: "Even though it were! You've
guessed at last. And really it is so, the whole secret is just in this, but really
isn't this suffering?" Ivan accepts Alyosha's deflation of the Grand Inquisitor
before offering his own. From Dostoevsky's point of view this willingness
to see a magnificent construct vitiated makes sense, if the Liubimov letter
expresses his real intention. From Ivan's point of view the Grand Inquisitor
might seem to deserve better. But the legend is not offered as a simple exposition of Ivan's belief. Ivan has said, "You're my kid brother; you're not the
one I want to debauch and shift from your position; I'd maybe like to heal
myself through you." Ivan's ambivalence makes his destruction of his own
argument psychologically reasonable; but this affectionate, hesitant candor
helps to make him so attractive that among all the commentators on this
passage, only Alyosha with his own kiss caught the ideological irony embodied
in the kiss of Christ. The rhetorical failure is almost absolute.

Dostoevsky continues this argument in the teachings of Father Zosima,
and there gives an answer to the problem of evil as telling in its way as Job's
theophany. Zosima doubts the reality of hell as Fyodor envisions it, with
or without hooks. He agrees with the Grand Inquisitor that the teachings
of Christ will fill men with guilt at their failure to live up to them, but he
sings a virtual hymn of rejoicing at this guilt. Indeed, he takes one of the
central doctrines of the materialists whom Dostoevsky claimed to be opposing, and turns this doctrine to his account. I mean the doctrine of universal
causal connections, the belief that all things in the world are interconnected,
that no event occurs without its causes in this world, that if we knew enough

we would see the world as a seamless web of causes and effects. As Zosima puts it, "The world is like an ocean, and if you push at one place, it gives at the opposite end of the world." In Zosima's doctrine of evil this universal causal linkage is central. He holds that every one of us at some time in his life has acted out of spite or failed to act with full goodness. If this is true, and if the world is really one, then every one of us is implicated in every sparrow's fall. Ivan had asked, "Why does God permit innocent suffering?" Instead of answering that question, Zosima turns it on the questioner and asks, "Why do you cause innocent suffering?" In a totally determined world each of us has had a part in every evil thing that happens. In this sense, Zosima proclaims, all men are guilty of all things; but unlike those who try to escape guilt, he rejoices in it as his bond with the whole of being.

In short, Zosima offers a rhetorical answer to the problem of children's suffering, which Dostoevsky in his letter had considered unanswerable. Zosima does not justify such suffering; he simply calls on the reader to share the blame. But even this did not seem to satisfy Dostoevsky. He had still another resource for the destruction of Ivan, the reductio ad absurdum, the carrying of Ivan's nature and doctrines to the logical conclusion that would discredit them. This involves the introduction into the novel of a body of characters whose analogy to Ivan is made distinct, and whose ridiculousness is made more distinct.

IV

Several characters in *The Brothers Karamazov* have closely marked doctrinal, personal, and even verbal ties with Ivan Karamazov. In ["The Origins of Alesa Karamazov"] I showed how such characters could be seen as repositories for elements in a character's sources which were not needed for that character, but which some conscious or unconscious fidelity to his sources led Dostoevsky to preserve in the novel. In this section and the next, I will try to show how this collection of genetically related characters evolved into an instrument of Dostoevsky's polemic with the righteousness of Schiller, Herzen, and Belinsky as manifested in the attractive traits of Ivan and the Grand Inquisitor.

Rakitin, the seminarian on the make, is probably the most repulsive character in *The Brothers Karamazov*, though his full loathsomeness does not emerge until the chapters after the legend of the Grand Inquisitor. In his first appearance only his eyes and his exaggerated humility hint at something distasteful: "A young fellow, apparently about twenty-two, in a layman's frock coat, a seminarian and future theologian, for some reason the protégé of the monastery and its members. He was rather tall, with a fresh face, broad cheekbones, and shrewd, alert, narrow brown eyes. His face expressed utter respectfulness, decent but without any evident fawning." The narrator hints that Rakitin has some thoughts of a different sort, but a Russian reader would only begin to recognize Rakitin when he speaks:

> "You're hurrying to the father superior's. I know; he has a spread. Since that time he received the archpriest and General Pakhatov, remember it, there hasn't been a spread like that. I'll not be there, but go ahead, serve the sauces. But tell me one thing, Aleksei: What means this dream? That's what I wanted to ask you."
>
> "What dream?"
>
> "Why prostrating himself before your brother Dmitry. And he gave his forehead a real bump, too."
>
> "You mean about Father Zosima?"
>
> "Yes, about Father Zosima."
>
> "His forehead?"
>
> "Oh, I expressed myself disrespectfully! Well, all right, it was disrespectful. So what's the meaning of this dream?"
>
> "I don't know what it means, Misha."
>
> "Just as I expected—he wouldn't explain it to you. There's nothing mysterious in this, of course; I guess it's just the usual 'benignorance' [blagogluposti]. But the trick was done on purpose. And now all the dévots in town will get talking and spread it through the district: 'What can be the meaning of this dream?' I think the old boy really is sharp-eyed: he sniffed crime. Your house stinks with it."
>
> "What crime?"
>
> Rakitin plainly wanted to express something.
>
> "It's going to happen in your fine family, this crime. It'll be between your dear brothers and your Daddy with his bit of a fortune. So Father Zosima banged his forehead just in case. Later, if anything happens, '—oh, the holy elder foretold and prophesied it,' though what's prophetic about banging his forehead on the floor?"

From this first speech any of Dostoevsky's original readers would have recognized Rakitin as a type, a certain kind of theological student, the quick, shrewd, observant son of a Russian priest, whose lively language and cynical insight into the establishment led to power, position, and sometimes wealth in the world centered about the radical journals of the time. The invented word *blagogluposti* ("benignorance") has been connected with Shchedrin, but Dostoevsky certainly intended it to suggest a far more plebian type like Dobroliubov. The quick, facile logic, the materialistic or social explanation of the religious, the special awareness of monetary and sexual concerns, the expectation of the criminal, the use of diminutives and words like "stinks," "sniffed," and "dévots," and the short, hard sentences all call to mind the articles in *The Contemporary* and, after it closed, the *Fatherland Notes* and other journals of the Russian radicals. In short, the style of this first dialogue has already implied a tie between Rakitin and Ivan that later would be made explicit. Both were setting out on careers in journalism, but Ivan was starting with the simplicity, sincerity, and intelligence of Belinsky, whereas Rakitin's style already reflected the nasty polemics of the writers in the sixties, whom Dostoevsky looked on as living parodies of Belinsky.

Though in the early part of the novel Rakitin is nothing worse than an ill-natured and somewhat sophomoric gossip, in the pages following the legend of the Grand Inquisitor, he is quickly established as a vicious parody of Ivan. Finding Alyosha crushed by the unjust mockery of Zosima's stinking corpse, he adopts the double role of tormentor and tempter as Ivan, the Grand Inquisitor, and the Devil had done, but instead of being tortured himself, he is complacent:

> "Can you really [be in this state] simply because your old boy made a stench? Can you really have seriously believed he'd start throwing miracles? . . . Why, what the hell, why nowadays a thirteen-year-old schoolboy doesn't believe that. Still, what the hell—so it's your God you're mad at now, you've mutinied; they passed him by for a promotion, and didn't give him a medal on honors day. Oh, you people." . . .
>
> "I'm not mutinying against my God; I simply 'don't accept His world!'"

Aloysha's quotation from Ivan's "mutiny" makes explicit the parallel. Rakitin has replaced Ivan as the tormentor and tempter of Alyosha. Ivan tormented Alyosha with stories of cruelty, and tempted him to the "absurdity" of advocating vengeance. The Inquisitor tortured Christ with the woes of humanity and dared Christ to destroy him; and the Devil, the chief torturer, tempted Christ in the wilderness. All these tortures are vicarious, and the temptations are toward altruism. Rakitin offers a debased version of these trials: he exacerbates Alyosha's personal hurt, and he tempts him with food and drink and sex, the cheap materialist's equivalent for the earthly bread offered by the Grand Inquisitor, the Devil, and the Russian radicals.

Having established the parallel with Ivan, Dostoevsky proceeds to destroy Rakitin. He uses Rakitin's own denials to suggest the things denied. In two sentences he indicates not only what two people think of Rakitin, but also the petty vengefulness of his reactions: "Your dear brother Ivan once upon a time proclaimed me a 'talentless liberal bumpkin.' And you too one fine time couldn't stand it and gave me to understand that I was 'dishonorable.' All right! Now, I'll have a look at your talent and honor." In the next chapter Rakitin's destruction continues, as we learn that he brought Alyosha to Grushenka not on a whim, but because she had offered him twenty-five pieces of silver to do so. The reference to Judas is made explicit, and we are able to say initially that Dostoevsky's invention took the form of a systematic distortion of the Judas story in a simple direction. Alyosha and Rakitin eat together, not a religious feast, but a snack that breaks the dietary rules of the monastery. Like Christ Alyosha realizes his tempter's intent, and tells him to carry it out, but a seduction not a crucifixion is involved, and this fails instead of succeeding. The reduction of the sum from thirty to twenty-five pieces of silver is thus consistent with Dostoevsky's lightening of all the other elements in his fictionalized version.

Elsewhere in the novel the same depreciation of currency takes place when Smerdyakov kills his father and then hangs himself after returning the thirty pieces of paper—hundred-ruble notes—for which he has committed the crime. Another piece of nonfiction probably enters the picture here. Dostoevsky had received a letter asking for "30 rubles in silver," a normal phrase in a period when a silver ruble would purchase far more than the inflated paper ruble. The letter came from a relative he disliked, and is dated five months before the appearance of the book "Alyosha" in *The Russian Messenger*. I would suggest the following chain of associations. The thirty silver rubles for the disliked relatives suggested the thirty pieces of silver for Judas. This essentially literary association aroused a feeling of distaste in Dostoevsky, the same feeling he had for the radical journalists of his day. That complex of radicals, relatives, revulsion, and Judas—an ideological, a personal, an emotional, and a literary stimulus—suggested a rhetorical device to Dostoevsky, the use of the familiar Judas figure as a means of stimulating in the reader a prefabricated revulsion for Rakitin. This use of the name of Judas was a commonplace, of course. In Russian literature Dostoevsky could haved found it from Avvakum in the seventeenth century to his contemporary Saltykov-Shchedrin, whose most famous villain is nicknamed little Judas. But the letter is the most plausible core about which this particular complex of biblical, political, and rhetorical sources crystallized.

The connection with Ivan's promising career in journalism leads to more elaborate patterns of association for Rakitin, who plans to marry a rich idiot, grow richer as a radical journalist, and build himself a stone house on the Liteinii avenue in St. Petersburg. When he takes the witness stand at Dmitry's trial, he is asked: "Are you that same Mr. Rakitin whose brochure published by the episcopal authorities I recently read with such pleasure, *The Life of the Elder Father Zosima, who rests in the bosom of the Lord*, full of profound and religious thoughts, with a superb and devout dedication to his Eminence? . . . With the sponsorship of his Eminence, your invaluable brochure has circulated and done considerable good." Rakitin is embarrassed and claims that he never expected publication, obviously afraid that such a background will affect his reputation in radical circles. That is all. The subject is dropped.

It has been pointed out that Dostoevsky's readers would consider this passage realistic not only because the Russian radicals tended to emerge from the theological seminaries—one of the few places they could obtain a free education, places by their nature conducive to revolt—but because one of them, Grigory Zakharevich Eliseev, had indeed enriched himself as a radical journalist and owned a large stone house on the Liteinii avenue. Eliseev's first book was called *The Biography of the Saintly Grigorii, Herman, and Varsonofii of Kazan and Sviiazhsk*. The dedication read as follows:

> Your exaltedly eminent Lordship, benevolent Father and Arch-pastor! From your archpastoral benediction I started upon these labors, with your unceasing attention continued them, and to you I now offer this small item of my making. Your exaltedly eminent Lordship! Accept with your habitual condescension my meager offering, and with your condescension the unworthiness of the laborer will take heart for the great work. Your exalted Eminence, benevolent Father and Archpastor's humblest servant, student in the Kazan Theological Academy, Grigory Eliseev.

Since a major Russian author, Leskov, had called attention to this passage eight years before *The Brothers Karamazov* in a major work called *An Enigmatic Man* (chap. 38), Dostoevsky could count on most of his readers to catch the reference, but he was plainly not using the example of Eliseev's sycophancy merely to discredit Rakitin. A direct transcription of his source would have been much more damning than the sharply abbreviated version he does offer. Rather he seems to be using Eliseev's life simply as source material, to provide the kind of data that will anchor his fiction in reality and give it that treasured capacity to fit even subsequently revealed fact which Dostoevsky claimed in the Liubimov letter. The episode is in *The Brothers Karamazov* because it happened and because Rakitin's character demanded it. It is brief because the trial was already threatening to overbalance the novel, and because the mere discomfiture was enough. In this case what started as a source became a resource, a literary reference that would identify Rakitin as a caricature of a radical, in contrast to Ivan, the apotheosis of the radical.

A similar discovery of a real-life caricature of a Russian radical led Dostoevsky to build into Rakitin parodies of one of the greatest parodists of his time, Dmitry Minaev. Here the polemic cuts both ways. The reference to Minaev's parodies would have been clear to contemporary readers, and Dostoevsky was essentially using this recognition to say both that Rakitin was a Minaev, and that Minaev was a Rakitin. Since he had already linked Rakitin with Ivan, he was creating a careerist parody for the independence and ambition with which Ivan was arranging his career. Eliseev and Minaev, in Dostoevsky's mind, were to Belinsky and Herzen as Rakitin was to Ivan.

Like any respectable Russian radical of his day, including Ivan, who had written a work on the geological revolution, Rakitin was much involved with the natural sciences, especially with the materialist claim that science could explain everything. Mitya Karamazov reports on Rakitin's beliefs:

> You see, there in the nerves, in the head, that is, there in the brain these nerves—to hell with them!—there are these little tails; those nerves have little tails, now as soon as they wiggle there, that is, you see, I look at something with my eyes, like this, and they wiggle, these little tails, and as they wiggle there appears an image and it doesn't appear immediately but a certain instant passes, a second, and something like a moment, that is, not a moment, damn the moment, but an image, that is, an object, or an event, now then, damn it, that's why I observe, and then I think—because of the tails.

With the care he frequently displays, Dostoevsky footnoted this passage with references to Claude Bernard, the French neurologist, materialist, and proponent of the scientific method of discovery who had been made a literary symbol in a book Dostoevsky had parodied fifteen years earlier, Chernyshevsky's *What Is to Be Done*. Dostoevsky had apparently mocked Chernyshevsky so viciously in his "Crocodile" (1865) that Dostoevsky later denied the allusion. Here I would suggest that the articles on physiology and neurology in many contemporary journals provide more than adequate sources for Rakitin's teachings as Mitya recounts them. One element, however, is missing. The articles in the journals were sometimes pedantic, sometimes superficial, often arrogant, but they were not stupid. Dostoevsky's ideological enemies were his intellectual equals, and he knew it.

Can we find a source for the sarcastic scorn Mitya heaps on Rakitin in this passage? Dostoevsky's correspondence may provide a clue, for he received letters from readers of every persuasion and every level of intelligence. Let me cite a letter that can serve as an example of a genre. It came late in December 1876 from a Kharkhov businessman named Ballin, whose letterhead proclaims that he was a dealer in sewing machines, materials, aids, incidentals for writing, educational games, scales, and disinfectant substances. S. V. Belov, who is probably the greatest storehouse of Dostoevskiana alive, informs me that these dealerships were the cover for an illegal printing press. Dostoevsky would have had no way of knowing the level of his correspondent's commitment to radical causes, but he would have felt some evidence of it in his passionate and fuzzy materialism. Ballin begins with praise for Dostoevsky's short story "The Gentle Creature," and goes on to admit that he has not read the second half, adding "Oh well, you don't get everything read." Of all Dostoevsky's works "The Gentle Creature" depends most on the climactic realization presented on the very last page. Without that it is a totally different work of art. Dostoevsky could only have responded to this opening with annoyance. The letter goes on to elucidate certain of Ballin's theories about consciousness:

> Concerning spiritualism, I am fully convinced of the realness of ideas. Thought and feeling I cannot conceive otherwise than as an aggregate of organized molecules appearing in our brain as a result of external influences, and these external influences I consider to be the external expression of the life around us. I cannot conceive an individual otherwise than humanly, and therefore accept as individuals also such beings as the earthly sphere and the sun. By consciousness I mean a complicated interaction of the parts of the individualized substance in various places and at various times. Understanding consciousness in this way, it appears incontrovertible to me that consciousness develops proportionally with the cooperation of the mass. Hence I deduce a vicious conclusion—that the consciousness of the sun, for example, must exceed human consciousness by a million times, the more so because the individual psychic activity is in specific relation to the size of the surface of the individual and the surface of the sun is also very great. It's plain that in saying the consciousness of the sun, I have in mind something altogether uncomprehended by me, and not a human consciousness made great.

This portentous and disconnected fabric of fashionable phrases would have become linked in Dostoevsky's mind with the materialism that underlies it,

and with the self-satisfaction at the beginning of the letter, to form a real-life
parody of the radical style and doctrine.

For Dostoevsky, Rakitin is related to Ivan in much the same way as the
Eliseevs and Minaevs and Ballins are related to Herzen and Belinsky. The
greedy, vicious, foolish epigones become the sources for Rakitin, just as the
great figures become the sources for Ivan.

V

The finest parody of Ivan and his Inquisitor is Kolya Krasotkin, the
thirteen-year-old schoolboy who can strike terror into the hearts of his
mother, his teachers, and his classmates. Like Ivan, Kolya is very intelligent,
is incessantly tortured by self-consciousness, quotes Voltaire, and has a
breadth of reading that astonishes those around him. But his intelligence is
a schoolboy's smartness, amusing to watch, and his self-doubt and self-
consciousness involve his appearance and his wits, not his moral position.
He quotes Voltaire but does not understand him, and his reading is in trivial
school compendiums.

When Ivan meets Alyosha, he says he wants to see him very much: "I
want to get acquainted with you once and for all, and to get you to know
me. . . . I've finally learned to respect you; it's plain this man stands firm.
. . . I love these firm ones, whatever they may stand on, even if they're little
galoots like you." The intensity of the affection overrides the patronizing
words, and Alyosha responds in kind: "You're just the same sort of young
man as all the other 23-year-olds, the same young, youthful, fresh, and won-
drous boy, a weanling, and to sum it up, a boy. Tell me, did I hurt your
feelings badly?" When Kolya summons Alyosha, he also "very, very much
wanted to get acquainted." Later he says, "I'm glad to know you, Karamazov.
I've wanted to know you for a long time. . . . I learned long ago to respect
you as a rare being. . . . I have heard that you are a mystic and were in the
monastery. I know you are a mystic, but—that didn't stop me. Contact with
reality will cure you." Kolya here constitutes the realization of Ivan's
metaphors. He is a real, not a figurative, boy, and at the simplest level he
believes the patronizing words he is using. At the same time, his respect and
affection for Alyosha emerge in close parallel to Ivan's.

One puzzling moment in the novel is Kolya's long account of the goose,
a lame story of a piece of boyish cruelty. He had asked a stupid peasant
whether a cartwheel would decapitate a goose that was pecking under it.
Watching from the side where the goose was pecking, Kolya winked at the
right moment, and the peasant made the cart move, cutting the goose's neck
in two. "You did that on purpose," people cry. "No, not on purpose," Kolya

answers; but the stupid peasant says, "It wasn't me, that's the one who got me to do it." Kolya's answer has the hauteur of his intellectual superiority: "I hadn't taught him at all; I had simply expressed the basic idea and only spoke hypothetically." This guiltily rationalized account seems overly expanded in the novel, until it takes its place with Ivan's struggle to avoid admitting that his basic idea has seduced Smerdyakov into killing, and with Smerdyakov's teaching of little Ilyusha to torture dogs by feeding them bread with pins in it. The vicarious assaults on the animals remind readers of Ivan's place in the murder, and rob him of much of the sympathy that might attach to him as a misunderstood manipulator.

Kolya's behavior trivializes the ideas of the Grand Inquisitor and the Devil, as well as those Ivan expresses himself. Kolya trains the dog Zhuchka to play dead and resurrect itself, and then stages the reappearance of the dog as a miracle for Ilyusha. He exploits the mysterious secret about the founding of Troy, and crushes the boy who divulges it. He performs an exploit that is the modern child's equivalent of Christ's second temptation in the wilderness, casting himself between the tracks of an oncoming train. And he uses authority, deception, and force for the good of the little group of schoolboys, whom he treats as the Grand Inquisitor treats all humanity. The Inquisitor said:

> Oh we shall finally persuade them not to be proud; . . . we shall show them that though they are feeble, though they are only pitiable children, childish happiness is the sweetest of all. They will grow timid and will start to look up to us and press against us in fear, like fledglings to their mother. They will feel wonder and terror at us. . . . Yes, we will make them work, but in the hours free from work, we will arrange their life like children's play . . . and they will worship us as their benefactors.

Kolya realizes some of these metaphors. He actually arranges childish games and commands the obedience of the boys "like a god." He even says:

> And, generally, I love the small fry. I have two fledglings on my hands at home right now; even today they delayed me. So [the boys] stopped beating Ilyusha, and I took him under my protection. I can see that he's a proud boy. I tell you that: he's proud, but in the end he has entrusted himself to me like a slave, fulfills my slightest commands, obeys me like a god, and tries to imitate me. . . . So now you too, Karamazov, have gotten together with all these fledglings?

Everything here echoes Ivan and cheapens Ivan. The pride of sinful humanity becomes the stubbornness of a pathetic child. The children or fledglings shrink, from the whole of humanity whom the Inquisitor loves and serves, to a couple of groups of children who reinforce Kolya's ego. The Inquisitor's godlike dominion becomes a child's bossiness. And Kolya's resurrection of the dog becomes a comment on Ivan's dreams of resurrecting the dead and all the talk of miracles, because we can see the effect of this miracle: "If the unsuspecting Krasotkin had understood how torturingly and murderously such a moment could influence the health of the sick boy, he would not have thought of playing a trick like the one he played." The word "murderously" here removes Kolya from the world of real mockery and makes him an involuntary killer in his blind superiority.

Radicalism in Dostoevsky's day was almost a club, and membership required certain attitudes. Various novels and journalistic pieces, friendly, hostile, and ambivalent, ranging from Turgenev's *Fathers and Sons* to Chernyshevsky's *What Is to Be Done?*, had canonized the list: materialism, scientism, positivism, atheism, socialism, internationalism, realism, feminism, and in the 1870s populism, all coupled with hostility to sentiment, tradition, prejudice, manners, the aesthetic, the establishment, and the government. Except for feminism and internationalism Kolya manages to take every pose demanded of a radical. In the chapter "A Schoolboy," he begins: "They're scum . . . doctors and the whole medical filth, speaking in general and, of course, in detail. I reject medicine. It's a useless establishment." This remark might not seem scientistic, but in the tradition of Russian radicalism the deliverers of medical care received none of the honor accorded to the investigators of medical truth.

Kolya goes on to attack Alyosha and the boys for sentimentalizing in their visits to Ilyusha, and later, after an "impressive silence," he makes an excursion into scientism and utopian political positivism:

> "I love to observe realism, Smurov. Have you observed how dogs meet and sniff each other. They obey some common law of nature there."
>
> "Yes, it's sort of funny."
>
> "No, it's not funny. You're wrong about that. In nature there's nothing funny, however, it might seem to a man with his prejudices. . . . That's a thought of Rakitin's, a remarkable thought. I'm a socialist, Smurov."
>
> "And what's a socialist?" . . .
>
> "That's if all are equal and own common property, and there

are no marriages, and religion and all the laws are the way each person wants, and, well, and so on. You're still young for that; it's early for you. It's chilly, though." . . .

"Have you noticed, Smurov, the way in the middle of winter, if it's fifteen or even eighteen degrees, it doesn't seem so cold as now, for example, at the beginning of winter. . . . With people everything's a matter of habit, even in governmental and political relationships."

Kolya then pauses to tease a benign peasant he passes, concluding, "I love to talk with the people, and am always prepared to give it its due. . . . With the people, you have to know how to talk."

The picture of the young radical pontificating to a devotedly receptive follower had become ironic at least as early as *Fathers and Sons* and savage in Leskov's *An Enigmatic Man*. The catalogue of shibboleths recurs two chapters later in another setting, also as old as Turgenev, with the young man patronizingly enlightening the older about radical doctrine. The indoctrination of Alyosha also starts with the statement that medicine is villainy. After an interruption by concerns involving Ilyusha, Kolya expounds on his schoolboy cynicism toward history, which parodies Ivan's sense of the meaninglessness of history as described by Dostoevsky to Liubimov. Kolya says:

I don't ascribe much importance to all those old wives' tales, and in general haven't too much respect for world history. . . . It's the study of the series of human stupidities, and that's all. I respect only mathematics and natural science. . . . Again, these classical languages . . . classical languages, if you want my opinion about them, are a police measure. . . . They're introduced because they're tiresome and because they dull our capacities. . . . It was pointless, so how could it be made more pointless? And that's when they thought up the classical languages.

At this point, one boy in the group shouts out, "And he's the top student in Latin." In enunciating one of the standard doctrines of the practical and scientistic radicals, Kolya displays his disinterestedness. This rejection of what he labels "baseness" (*podlost'*) offers a child's equivalent of the nobility with which the Grand Inquisitor rejects the salvation he has the ability to earn, or with which Ivan returns his ticket. The gesture is the same, and the love for the oppressed is the same, but the schoolboy's showing off infects the reader's recollection of the Inquisitor's magnificent self-sacrifice.

Dostoevsky's central quarrel with the radicals may well have involved their attitude toward religion. Kolya follows his splendid thirteen-year-old statement that contact with reality would cure Alyosha's mysticism with this definition of mysticism: "Well, God and all." He elaborates his ideas about God, which turn out to be a travesty of Ivan's ambivalent abstention from denial.

> "I don't have anything against God. Of course, God is only a hypothesis—but—I admit that He is necessary for order—for the order of the world and so on—and if He did not exist, it would be necessary to invent Him," added Kolya, starting to blush. . . . "Even without believing in God, it's possible to love mankind. . . . I've read *Candide*, in Russian translation. . . . I'm a socialist, Karamazov, an incorrigible socialist. . . . The Christian faith has served only the rich and noble, to hold the lower class in slavery, isn't that true? . . . I am not against Christ. That was a really humane person, and if He had lived in our time, He would have joined the revolutionists right away and maybe played a prominent role—that's certain, even."

The talk about hypotheses, the order of things, the necessity for God, and the possibility of love without God all plainly reminds the reader of Ivan. The talk about socialism, the sins of Christianity, and Christ's need to join the revolutionists recalls the Grand Inquisitor. Ivan has observed, "Everything that in Europe is a hypothesis is immediately an axiom for the Russian boy." His frequent use of the word "boy" (*mal'chik*) prepares the reader for the repetition of these doctrines by a real boy, culminating in the word-for-word repetition of Voltaire's aphorism about the invention of God. But this aphorism is the highest reach of Kolya's sophistication, whereas for Ivan it is the starting point for two passionate statements about a single vision of humanity. We have already noted the first: "I think that if the Devil does not exist, and man in fact created him, then he created him in his own image and likeness." The second is so powerful that it needed Kolya's parody:

> And indeed, man did invent God. It would be nothing strange and nothing wondrous for God to really exist, but the wondrous thing is that such a thought, the thought of the necessity of God, could creep into the head of such a savage and evil animal as man; it is so holy, so touching, so wise, and does such honor to man.

Through this entire catalogue of shibboleths, Ivan's doctrines become associated with the conceit and embarrassed self-consciousness that are Kolya's most visible traits. The rhetorical function of Kolya's conceit is curiously related to the best-known source for Kolya. George Chulkov has shown that many of Kolya's doctrines coincide closely with statements made by Belinsky. And we know that in the early seventies Dostoevsky found conceit to be a central feature of Belinsky's character. Arkady Dolinin has summed up Dostoevsky's attitude toward Belinsky at that time by using a series of quotations from Dostoevsky's letters:

> "Belinsky, that most rotten, dull, and shameful phenomenon of Russian life." "A stinkbug, Belinsky was just an impotent and feeble little talent." "Belinksy cursed Russia and knowingly brought upon her so much woe." "In Belinsky there was so much petty conceit, viciousness, impatience, exacerbation, baseness, but most of all conceit. It never occurred to him that he himself was disgusting. He was pleased with himself in the highest degree, and that was already a stinking, shameful, personal stupidity." "He related to Gogol's characters superficially to the point of meaninglessness. . . . He scolded Pushkin when Pushkin casts off his false pose. . . . He rejected the end of *Eugene Onegin*. . . ." "He didn't even understand his own people. He didn't even understand Turgenev."

Perhaps here, in this vision of Belinsky, is a source for some of the conceit in Kolya, for some of the littleness and incomprehension. Of course, the nastiness that is such a conspicuous part of these letters has disappeared. Kolya can be cruel, arrogant, conceited, but there is no stinking, shameful talentlessness in him. These qualities seem to survive in two places. One is Kolya's vision of himself: "Tell me, Karamazov," he asks, "do you despise me terribly?" And the other repository for these unpleasant qualities is Rakitin, who embodies them superbly.

Dolinin argues, however, that Dostoevsky's view of Belinsky and his political attitude as a whole underwent a revolution in 1876, and that by the time *The Brothers Karamazov* began to emerge, he was expressing some of the old ardor he had felt for the Belinsky who had honored and befriended him in 1846. He refers to him as "the most honorable and noble Belinsky," and echoes Apollon Grigor'ev's claim that "if he had lived longer, Belinsky would necessarily have joined the Slavophiles." The chronological lines may not be so neat as Dolinin makes them, but the ambivalence is certainly there. If the vile and nasty traits Dostoevsky saw in Belinsky went to make Rakitin, we should look in a novel of the 1870s for some expression of the magnificent eloquence and true self-sacrifice Dostoevsky also attributed to him. Here the most obvious repository is Ivan himself. Indeed, an excellent critic of Dostoevsky, Alfred Rammelmeyer, considers Belinsky a chief source for the

Grand Inquisitor, documenting his case primarily with Belinsky's letters to Botkin, which Pypin had published not long before the writing of *The Brothers Karamazov*.

If Kolya and Ivan both derive from Belinsky, one from the noble vision and one from the little, conceited vision, with Rakitin as the repository for all the vilest traits, at first glance it might seem that Chulkov had over-simplified the pattern, and that Kolya resembles Belinsky because Ivan does and Kolya is a parody of Ivan. On the basis of the notebooks for *The Brothers Karamazov*, I would suggest another pattern of development. For years Dostoevsky had been working on two projects, the life of a great sinner and a book about children. Earlier he had planned two other great novels, "Atheism" and the Russian Candide. The great sinner, whose life was to be traced from childhood, was to fall into radicalism and eventually to be saved. This career coincides not with Ivan's, not with Alyosha's, both of which have been connected with the plan, but with Kolya's. If this formulation is right, in the mid-1870s the plans for the Russian Candide, for "Atheism," for the life of the great sinner, and for the novel about children all became focused on the figure of little Kolya Krasotkin. The earliest surviving notes we have for *The Brothers Karamozov* relate to him. The figure of Ivan the radical emerges only later. Ivan then, like Rakitin, would have come into existence as a repository for traits Dostoevsky could not incorporate into a child when he merged the heroes of these four unwritten novels into a single youthful figure.

Once the character of Ivan had been spun off, it assumed the residual loveliness of Belinsky and of Aleksandr Herzen. Indeed, it might perhaps be argued that the ideological revolution in Dostoevsky's thinking which Dolinin dates to the mid-1870s was the result and not the cause of the emergence of Ivan from the mass of materials that were to become the novel. About the figure of Ivan would gather the noble doubts, the mighty pity, the love of life, of humanity, of family that were later to make him so dangerous to the ideological intentions Dostoevsky described in his letter to Liubimov. In this case, I would suggest that the child is father of the man.

VI

We no longer need Dostoevsky's letter to Liubimov or any other state-ment as evidence in our evaluation of Lawrence's argument that Dostoevsky agreed with Ivan and the Grand Inquisitor. We have been looking at what Dostoevsky did, not what he said. We have ascribed his eloquence not to his sincerity but to his borrowings. We have ascribed the kiss of Christ not to acquiescence but to ideological irony. We have ascribed the pivotal position of Ivan in part to the parodic figures clustering around him. And we have offered the rhetorical energy Dostoevsky expended on the deprecation of Ivan as evidence of his good faith in promising to confute Ivan's doctrines.

In this final section we must return to the disjunction we started with and ask why Dostoevsky's rhetoric failed to convince Lawrence and many others. Lawrence, of course, was writing an introduction to a dubious enterprise, a separate edition to the legend of the Grand Inquisitor. The isolation of the passage could explain Lawrence's misreading, but not the widespread prevalence of his view. One could say that many readers read badly or read with preestablished conclusions because certain early errors have been immortalized. But major writers should have a rhetoric that will preclude such errors about the central issues of a work. The final explanation for the failure of Dostoevsky's rhetoric to communicate his intent may involve a technical truth he had mastered early in his career.

There are a number of connections between *The Brothers Karamazov* and *Crime and Punishment*. Let us consider the passage in *Crime and Punishment* where Raskolnikov has just committed the double murder and stands poised for his getaway. He opens the door and listens at the head of the stairs. Someone goes out of the building. He is about to leave when he hears someone entering the building, and he grows convinced that the person is coming to visit his victims. At the last minute he slips back and silently bolts the door, then listens, holding his breath, while this visitor and another discuss how to get in. And at some point in these three pages, the reader suddenly realizes that he too is holding his breath. The descriptions of Raskolnikov have been contagious, and without willing it or even knowing it at first, the reader has concentrated his entire poised attentiveness and desire on the escape of this murderer. In short, Dostoevsky manipulates the reader into the experience of having just committed a murder.

He uses this device many times in *Crime and Punishment*. It is not original with him, for it is a common trick in the picaresque to involve the reader's attention in the escape of a first-person narrator he deplores. Stanley Fish suggests, for example, that in *Paradise Lost*, Milton inspires sympathy with Satan as a way of letting the reader experience Adam's fall, then destroys this sympathy step by step, until all the fallen angels turn to snakes; according to this interpretation, Blake's belief that Milton favored Satan rests on the beginning, not the whole work (*Surprised by Sin: The Reader in* Paradise Lost). Dostoevsky abandons this technique in the novels after *Crime and Punishment*; he never again shows us the mind of a murderer from the inside. But in *The Brothers Karamazov* he does take us inside the mind of a vicarious criminal, Ivan, whose "all is lawful" stimulates or liberates Smerdyakov's murderous proclivities.

By carrying his reader through a genuine experience of what it means to be a Russian radical—a compassionate, noble, generous, tortured, loving one—Dostoevsky implicates the reader in the feelings of guilt, self-consciousness, stupidity, and even savagery to which he makes radicalism lead Ivan, Kolya, Rakitin, and several other characters. The epigraph of the novel comes from the Gospel according to St. John: "Except a corn of wheat fall upon the ground and die, it abideth alone, but if it die, it bringeth forth much fruit." The seed here is the grace of God, which John says will bear fruit only if it dies. By this reckoning the Grand Inquisitor's effort to isolate mankind from evil is actually making grace sterile by not letting it die. Dostoevsky prefers to tempt his readers, as Rakitin and Ivan tempted Alyosha and as the Devil tempted Christ. He tries to carry his readers through a death of grace as dangerous as Zosima's in his youth, or Alyosha's when his faith is shaken, hoping he can bring them out beyond as fertile disseminators of grace. Dostoevsky thus is engaging not in communication but in manipulation. Instead of the semiotic model we struggled with, we need a cybernetic one.

This use of the novel for the propagation of active grace entails the danger that the process may stop at the first step, and the less grave but more likely danger that readers may interpret the author's intention as stopping at the first step. Dostoevsky took this risk, and a substantial, but I think decreasing, number of his readers have justified his fear and trembling.

A. D. NUTTALL

Crime and Punishment:
The Psychological Problem

The interrogative word "Why?" has many uses. It can invite a rational answer, in terms of purpose and design: "Why are you treading on his hand?" Answer: "To make him let go." Or it can seek a merely causal explanation: "Why did he tread on that man's hand?" Answer: "His childhood in Alaska made him into a very aggressive person." Notice that "Why" with the second person and the present tense is almost always used in the first way whereas "Why" with the third person more easily allows the second, bleaker sort of explanation; which shows how mere courtesy can, in certain quarters of our lives, still keep a reductive philosophy at bay.

So with Raskolnikov. "Why did he kill the old woman?" has so far been treated as a question of type A, that is, what was his reason for doing it? Will it bear consideration as a question of type B? In so far as psychology has over the years gradually disengaged itself from mere gossipy "insight into human nature" by an austere subordination of rational motives to unacknowledged causes, and in so far as *Crime and Punishment* is allowed on all hands to be a psychological novel, it would seem that an exploration of unacknowledged causes is unavoidable, especially as the explanation we reached by the other route is so manifestly incomplete.

We determined that beneath Raskolnikov's professed utilitarianism lay a more naked existentialism, but then conceded that the existentialist profession was in a manner refuted by the actual conduct of the crime. Raskolnikov could find no better reason than that he murdered to be free, but we watched him do it, and he never once looked like a free man. We

---

From Crime and Punishment: *Murder as Philosophic Experiment.* © 1978 by A. D. Nuttall. Sussex University Press, 1978.

therefore ask again, but with the emphasis appropriate to type B, why *did* he do it?

The simplest answer was given more than a hundred years ago by Dmitry Pisarev: Raskolnikov was driven to crime by poverty and malnutrition, which upset his nervous system. This explanation will do very well as long as we notice that it leaves out the difficult part of the problem, for we must immediately ask the further question, why was his nervous system upset in that particular way, and with that result? Why, for example, did he not withdraw into a catatonic stupor, or become an alcoholic? In other words, the inadequacies of Pisarev's ostentatiously materialist explanation immediately propel us forward into obscure questions concerning the individual psychology of Raskolnikov himself. Dostoevsky foresaw all this, and disarmed the reductive, materialist critic in advance, not by denying his thesis, but by instantly admitting that it has a part to play—but a modest part. The young doctor Zossimov, whom Razumikhin fetches to attend to Raskolnikov, says that Raskolnikov's condition has both a material origin (the squalid circumstances in which he lives) and a moral one. There is no question of assimilating the second to the first. Zossimov is a lightly drawn character, but he is firmly credited by the author with a shrewdness equal to Porfiry's—and considerably more benevolent. Later in the book Raskolnikov's mother says that the meanness of his lodging must have caused his melancholy; Raskolnikov answers, listlessly, "yes, the lodging had a great deal to do with it." The reader cannot help but see that the mother in accepting this explanation as total is grasping at a delusive comfort, and that Raskolnikov's abstracted reply can only deepen her anxiety.

We must advance, then, into the darkened terrain of Raskolnikov's personality. It has become fashionable in recent years to seek out, in circumstances like these, the subject's family, to smell out the variously crushing pressures of his home environment: *Cherchez la mère*. But if we try this we meet once more with the special frustration of an immediate yet trivialising confirmation of our hypothesis. Raskolnikov's family, evidently, subject him to a constant torture of devotion. His sister and mother both sacrifice themselves to him over and over again. At the point where the novel opens they are in extreme poverty, and their poverty is largely occasioned by Raskolnikov himself, who is living the idle life of a student. When he compounds his guilt towards them by not only taking their money but by not even troubling to pursue his studies, the pressure exerted by the mere thought of his mother may reasonably be supposed to have reached an intolerable pitch. She, in an agony of uncomprehending love, urges him to read his Bible, but, for fear of offending him, cannot tell him with a proper candour to get off his backside and work. Instead, her spaniel eyes look up at him in unappeasable, merciless, mindless love.

The situation is a familiar one. Once again Dostoevsky presents it with a crispness and force which shows that he understands every aspect of it, and shows equally that he understands how little it explains. First, let us make sure our moral judgements are in order. No doubt Pulcheria Alexandrovna is at fault in not communicating in a more forthright fashion with her son (though can we really expect her ever to have encountered intellectually the nihilist theories he espoused?—one of the crueller ironies of the book is her obsessive touting of his article as if it was a new Gospel after her wits have gone). Nevertheless, we may agree, a cooler approach on her part might have been more salutary. A strict judge might well determine, on grounds like these, that a measure of fault lies with the mother. But where will such strictness leave Raskolnikov, who sponged on his mother and his sister when they were in real need? Whose fault is the greater? When we say, enforcing sympathy for Raskolnikov, that he was tortured by guilt, let us remember that he had something to feel guilty about, and when we blame his mother for her failure to reach him, let us not forget that she too has claims upon our sympathy.

In fact, the whole "family pressure" thesis has only to be stated in bald terms for its inadequacy to be plain: Raskolnikov's family wrought upon his guilt feelings so much that he became seriously disturbed; and so he went off and cut up two old women with an axe.

The hiatus between the explanation and the thing to be explained would seem to be as great as ever. Other men have suffered the torment, both economic and moral, that Raskolnikov suffers, but they have not committed murder. Razumikhin like Raskolnikov is poor; unlike Raskolnikov he keeps himself by working.

It seems that we are not going to find an answer easily. We must drop premature theorising and attend to detail. Raskolnikov, socially isolated, becomes fascinated by a theory according to which freedom consists in total emancipation from convention. He is violently excited by a conversation he overhears in which someone who holds a theory like his puts the theory in the form of a practical challenge: Kill this socially harmful person. The person is, by chance, known to Raskolnikov. He plans and carries out the murder in a sort of mechanical stupor, proceeding methodically and yet uncomprehendingly, with just enough consciousness of what he is doing to experience inarticulate terror when the real world presents him with awkward, accidental features not formulated in his plan. We have already noted the irony whereby a crime conceived as a grand stroke of freedom becomes in practice a kind of slavery, in which any hope of not after all having to carry it through appears to the subject as liberating. Despite the fact that the crime according to his theory was to provide a financial basis for an ambitious future, Raskolnikov does not even count the money he takes from the old woman, and, having hidden it away, makes no further use of it. Similarly, when Razumikhin offers him money Raskolnikov gives it back though his need is dire. Lest the reader should take this for some sort of chivalry, Dostoevsky has Raskolnikov mistaken for a beggar a page later and given twenty copecks; this time he has no opportunity to return the money. If Raskolnikov's plight was merely economic he would obviously have lost no time in buying himself a square meal. Instead he throws the money in the Neva. When after the murder Raskolnikov is able to help the Marmeladov family, he finds that his nervous condition is greatly improved; he says that his life has become "real." Further, when his mother and sister visit him in his lodgings, after their long arduous journey, he speaks to them in a disconnected fashion, breaks out in great anger against the proposed marriage of Dounia to Luzhin, and then lies down on a sofa and turns his face to the wall. The next day he appears much calmer and his friends are delighted. He soberly apologizes to his mother and sister and his language is somewhat more orderly. However we perceive almost at once that things are if anything worse than at the first conversation. There his indignation against Luzhin, though intemperately expressed, commanded moral respect. Now his apology, though seemingly rational, is somehow horribly divorced from reality. Raskolnikov speaks with a ponderous care which suggests a mind focussing with difficulty upon a distant object. Dounia is terribly distressed. She wonders, "Is he being reconciled and asking forgiveness as though he were performing a rite or repeating a lesson?" We are reminded of the Underground Man's inability to talk to Liza otherwise than through a sort of intervening glass of artifice, as if he was telling a story. Later in the same conversation Raskolnikov says "I seem to be looking at you from a thousand miles away." In the course of his confession to Sonia, Raskolnikov musingly observes that whereas Napoleon would have killed without thinking about it, he, Raskolnikov *stopped* thinking about it—and killed.

These scraps and fragments combine to make up a picture of a disturbed personality, certainly, but not a personality so strange as to be psychologically unclassifiable. At the beginning of this book I drew a distinction between that kind of art which wilfully frames contradictions merely to frustrate the reader and that which feels itself obliged to consult, in all the puzzles it offers, the world of possibility. If the character of Raskolnikov had been constructed by an artist of the first type, it would be idle to seek any sort of unitary conception of his nature; but the very recognizability of Raskolnikov suggests that Dostoevsky is an artist of the second type. His intention is not merely wilful or spell binding; it is also seriously cognitive. And, if Raskolnikov is, palpably, a possible person, it is fair to ask, "What sort of person is he?"

Clearly, he is under some sort of compulsion. Equally clearly, he is to some extent what we today call schizophrenic. I have already imported into the discussion of *Crime and Punishment* one ponderously anachronistic term: "existentialism." My excuse has been simple; though Dostoevsky never heard the term, the historical connexions between him and professed existentialists are numerous and established: moreover as soon as we define "existentialism" we find that many of his ideas conform instantly to the definition. With "schizophrenia" the situation is somewhat different. My use of this word commits me to the following propositions: There are certain features which sometimes combine in a single personality, producing a strange but not unique result; psychologists have produced a term for this type of personality, namely, "the Schizophrenic"; Dostoevsky, though he lacked the term, noticed the phenomenon—which after all could hardly be supposed to have first appeared on the face of the earth simultaneously with the writings of Kretchmer. In these circumstances it would be unthrifty to avoid the obvious term which posterity has provided.

But let us look first at the element of compulsion in Raskolnikov's behaviour. Raskolnikov speaks like one repeating a lesson; one he taught himself. At the moment of the killing his body seems to perform independently of his mind:

> He pulled the axe quite out, swung it with both arms, scarcely conscious of himself, and almost without effort, brought the blunt side down on her head. He seemed not to use his own strength in this but as soon as he had once brought the axe down, his strength returned to him.

His state seems in a manner *hypnotic*.

Once more, the word is perhaps more accurate than it seems. Many features of Raskolnikov's behaviour recall the phenomena produced by hypnosis. In post-hypnotic suggestion, for example, the hypnotist tells his subject while the latter is still in a trance, that after he has returned to consciousness he is, say, to stand up and blow his nose when the hypnotist mentions the Queen. The power of such suggestion is very great, as is shown by an anecdote told by H. J. Eysenck:

The subject of the experiment was a well known psychologist, deeply interested in the phenomena of hypnosis, and himself an experimentalist of considerable standing in this field. His personality was very stable and strong, with no traces of neurotic weakness. He expressed a desire to experience the phenomena of hypnosis at first hand, and was accordingly hypnotized, falling into a reasonably deep trance. In the trance it was suggested to him that upon a pre-arranged signal he would get up from his chair, walk across the room, and sit down in another chair. He was awakened from the hypnosis, and after half an hour or so the prearranged signal was given. He became a little agitated, began to look across the room at the other chair, and finally said "I feel a strong tendency to go across the room and sit on that chair. I am sure you have given me a post-hypnotic suggestion to this effect. Well, I'm damned if I'll do it!"

He continued taking part in the conversation, but became more and more distracted and monosyllabic, until finally he jumped out of his chair, crossed over and sat down in the designated chair, and exclaimed, "I couldn't stand it any longer!"

What happens to Raskolnikov is like a protracted and attenuated version of this story, with the difference that in a curious yet credible way he is, so to speak, his own hypnotist. First we have the inducing of the "trance." This is accomplished over a period of months, by solitude, poor food, and the monotonous, obsessive reiteration of certain sentences and words: "Everything is permitted," "Exceptional Man," "destruction of the present for the sake of the better," "Napoleon." And together with all this comes the self-addressed imperative: "Dare." Of course the proximity of Raskolnikov's condition to one of trance varies considerably from day to day, and from hour to hour, but that does not matter; the groundwork has been laid. The suggestion introduced during trance, will produce effects when the trance has passed off. But for that, of course, you need some sort of signal, a "trigger."

This comes to Raskolnikov, quite fortuitously, in the form of the overheard conversation. After months spent in a sort of private dream, Raskolnikov, indeed no free man but rather a solidly programmed being, hears quite objectively from another's lips the imperative which has before existed only within the dream. Hardly knowing why, he finds himself moving into action. Our analogy with hypnotism thus provides us with an admissible word for the function in the novel of this episode. We call it "the Trigger."

And perhaps our analogy is more than just an analogy. The phenomena of hypnotic compulsion are mysterious, but not without parallel in ordinary life. There is an unmistakable affinity between, for example, the hypnotic subject, compelled by suggestion, and the pathologically superstitious subject, who must never walk under a ladder. The latter case, indeed, may be said to bring us a step nearer to Raskolnikov, since such compulsive behaviour can be self-induced. The man who avoids walking under ladders presumably received his suggestion from others, but the man who must count every railing in the street before he can enter his own house is, in a hideously inverted sense, master of himself. Part of the horror of these mental states consists in the fact that a process is started in the mind which then continues in a sort of disengagement from the rest, independent of the subject's control. One is reminded of the interesting example given in Sartre's *L'Imaginaire* to combat those who said mental imagery was always entirely controllable; it consists of a challenge: "Imagine a turning wheel. Now stop it turning." This, it turns out, is very difficult, and the experience of trying produces a special sort of nausea, like the nausea experienced by a man trying to break free of a compulsive suggestion. Of course different people vary in their susceptibility to this kind of pressure. For the reader who would like to test his own degree of susceptibility, I offer the following test: suppose that you are lying in bed in the morning; say to yourself "I am going to count to ten. When I reach ten I must get up." Then count to ten. If the completion of this ritual would leave you as comfortably somnolent as before, you are not susceptible. If on the other hand you could not continue to lie still without an obscure inward discomfort, Raskolnikov is your kinsman. Sartre in a self-parodying passage which might well excite the envy of Paul Jennings, says the function of alarm clocks is to relieve us of the *angoisse* of deciding when to get up. Plainly, he is one of us.

The notion of disengagement brings us naturally to our second special concept: "schizophrenia." The etymology of this word gives us "split mind" but the term has come to be used, not of the sort of multiple personality discussed about the turn of the century by Pierre Janet and William James, but of those persons in whom rational processes are oddly disengaged from the emotions, or in whom certain consecutive lines of thought are grotesquely disjoined from the normal humane context. Thus schizophrenic utterance is not always irrational; on the contrary it can exhibit formal rationality of a high order, together with a crass incapacity to notice the material context. Apparently a good question to ask if you wish to elicit symptoms of schizophrenia is the following: "What would you do if you were in a cinema and you saw a fire starting?" The ordinary person usually goes through two mental stages in response to this question: Stage one, "Shout

Fire!"; Stage two, "No, that would cause a panic; better approach a responsible official who could cause a suitable form of words to be flashed on the
screen." There is a textbook account of a typical schizophrenic answer given
by H. H. Kendler: "Finally he smiled shyly and commented 'I know the
answer. I'd yell fire in such a way that it would not cause a panic.' When
asked to show how he would do this, the patient rose to his feet slowly and
whispered 'fire.' " There is a certain similarity between this picture of the
schizophrenic and the academic philosopher. After all, philosophers, if they
are not to be confined to the endless repetition of commonplaces, must
occasionally pursue an idiosyncratic train of reasoning into unfamiliar country. Indeed, a resolute loyalty to the formal implications of one's statements,
together with an ability to set aside "material accidents" might be reckoned
part of the essential equipment of a philosopher. It is perhaps not so very
surprising that in the pages of R. D. Laing's study of schizophrenia, *The
Divided Self*, one can find a schizophrenic latter-day Descartes who believes
himself disjoined from his body. In practice, the line between the concentration of the philosopher and the mental isolation of the speculative thinker
can be almost invisible.

Raskolnikov illustrates the difficulty perfectly. On the one hand he is
a real systematic thinker, whose thought has brought him into strange ter-
ritory and stranger company. On the other hand he is manifestly sick, the
victim rather than the controller of his mental processes, seriously cut off
from reality. It follows that although this chapter is concerned not with the
intellectual debate, but with the psychic pressures upon Raskolnikov, we must
still refer to his theories. But the theories must now be considered not so
much as bodies of doctrine of which the inner logic must be explored but
rather as movements in a mind, mental events, having causal consequences
for the psyche in which they occur. After all it is not as if, while theories
exist in books, real minds contain only images and drives, so that the subject
matter of intellectual history overlaps at no point with the subject matter of
psychology. On the contrary this overlap is precisely what interests Dostoevsky. He was interested both in theories and in men who theorize. Freudian
psychoanalysis in general ascribes to theory a merely epiphenomenal status;
it is the inadvertent product of simpler, blinder forces. Of theory as itself
this cause or agent of psychosis Freud has little to say. Once more then we
find that the approach invited by the greatest of psychological novelists is
not the psychoanalytic one.

Of course the degree of Raskolnikov's schizophrenia is mild. Let us look
more closely at the apology he makes to his mother and sister. The conversation begins with what appears to be a warm show of friendliness and com-

punction on Raskolnikov's part. Only Dounia is aware that something is amiss. With great skill, Dostoevsky makes her most perceptive where Razumikhin (whom she loves) is involved. Raskolnikov says, pointing to Razumikhin, that he hardly knows how to thank him, that he will say nothing about the matter, "though he has had nothing from me either but insults and trouble." Razumikhin answers, "What nonsense he is talking! Why, you are in a sentimental mood today, are you?" And then follows one of Dostoevsky's rare explanatory interventions: "If he had had more penetration he would have seen that there was no trace of sentimentality in him, but something indeed quite the opposite. But Avdotya Tomanovna [that is, Dounia] noticed it." What he is telling us is precisely what the psychologists tell us of schizophrenia: the appropriate accompaniment of feeling is in fact absent. It may be thought that Dostoevsky ought not have needed to tell us that Raskolnikov's behaviour was peculiar; that he should have been able to exhibit it in the dialogue. The answer to this is two-fold; first, Dostoevsky, in the dialogue which follows, does exhibit perfectly the peculiar effect of dissociation which Raskolnikov's language betrays; secondly, the effect in question is so subtle that he may perhaps be forgiven for warning us in advance. Since the whole point about this sort of mild schizophrenic language is that its oddity consists precisely in its inhuman purity, so to speak, of logical or conventional form—an oddity that is picked up in real life from those minute physical signals (the unfocussed pupil, the misplaced hesitation, the almost imperceptible retardation) to which the human organism is so finely attuned—its communication on the printed page through printed dialogue presents a technical problem. The thing can be conveyed gradually to the reader, who cannot hear the timbre of the voice and the rest, but an intelligent participant (such as Dounia) in the real conversation will get there sooner. And Dostoevsky wants us to know that Dounia is perceptive in this way. It seems that the only course open to him is to disclose authorially what she noticed before we discern it for ourselves.

Pulcheria Alexandrovna, of course, is less intelligent than her daughter. She is overjoyed to find her son himself again (as she supposes) and unguardedly expresses her delight, though subconsciously she finds herself afraid. This again is in profound accord with what we learn of her elsewhere in the book, and affords a beautiful illustration of the craft of a great novelist. Pulcheria Alexandrovna, if you like, is the hostage we give to psychoanalysis; she really has a conscious and an unconscious mind, and it is the unconscious which connects more firmly with reality. When at the end of the novel her conscious mind gives way, the "free association" of her delirium betrays the fact that she had always understood far more of her son's fate than anyone had supposed. Again, the Freudian term presents itself: the knowledge had been *repressed*.

Pulcheria Alexandrovna begins to tell Raskolnikov how utterly alone and without support she and Dounia are, and then, suddenly flinching away from the subject of Luzhin (since it so agitated Raskolnikov last time it came up) reverts to saying, from a full heart, "We are quite happy again." What follows must be quoted:

> "Yes, yes. . . . Of course it's very annoying. . . ." Raskolnikov muttered in reply, but with such a preoccupied and inattentive air that Dounia gazed at him in perplexity.
>
> "What else was it I wanted to say?" He went on trying to recollect. "Oh, yes; mother, and you too, Dounia, please don't think that I didn't mean to come and see you today and was waiting for you to come first. . . .
>
> . . . I've only just waked up, and wanted to go to you, but was delayed owing to my clothes; I forgot yesterday to ask her. . . . Nastasya . . . to wash out the blood . . . I've only just got dressed.

Notice first the heavy punctuation suggesting an unnatural degree of hesitation, as if the speaker was grappling with a difficult intellectual problem. "What else was it I wanted to say?" suggests a person in a quite different situation from Raskolnikov's, a man drafting a report, or issuing a set of impersonal instructions. Then there is the complete failure to meet, with a properly human response, the last words of Pulcheria Alexandrovna. Finally although the inner meaning of the words is, so to speak, "reasonable" there is the lack of a proper "contextual" awareness, that is of the ordinary human instinct for what needs to be explained and what does not, for the effect one's words will have on the particular person to whom they are addressed. Raskolnikov refers uninformatively to the lodging house servant as "her" and then dimly perceives the need to explain and adds "Nastasya"; the dreadful word "blood" he lets fall with complete unconcern and then only dimly perceives the need to allay anxiety in his listeners.

This lack of contextual awareness, though not yet disabling, is, identifiably, schizophrenic in character. It is interesting that the insanity of such language lies not in its content but in its form and presentation. This has some bearing on recent attempts, such as R. D. Laing's, to argue that the schizophrenic is really sane. The argument goes something like this: The advanced schizophrenic (far more advanced than Raskolnikov) says, "My mother sticks pins in my head"; the ordinary world dismisses this as mere nonsense, but an investigation of the family situation reveals that the mother's importunate treatment of her son is admirably described by the metaphor of "sticks pins in my head." The argument turns, it will be noticed, on rescuing the content of the schizophrenic's words. But the whole point about schizophrenia is that the subject often gets the content right and the form wrong. In the present example, the subject is insane not because he says his mother maltreats him, but because he says it metaphorically *without knowing that he has employed metaphor.*

I have said that the communication of this peculiar terror of incipient schizophrenia, at once so elusive and, once noticed, so overwhelming, constitutes a technical problem for the novelist. Dostoevsky overcomes this problem and the overcoming is a feat of creative imagination. Here we have a feature of our mental lives which, though aberrant, is in its milder forms very widespread. The subtle and horrible malaise of the dissociated intelligence is one of our more familiar demons. Yet it is hard to think of a single literary artist before Dostoevsky who brought it off. Perhaps this is an area where only the very greatest can succeed. I think Euripides caught it in the *Hippolytus* and I am sure that Shakespeare did, in *Richard II* and *Hamlet.* But who else?

The conversation with his mother and sister gives us Raskolnikov's sickness, so to speak, in microcosm. But its long term, major expression is the pursuance of the theory to the execution of the crime. In the confession to Sonia, we find:

> "I thought you would cry out again! Don't speak of it, leave off!" Raskolnikov gave a laugh, but rather a forced one. "What, silence again?" he asked a minute later. "We must talk about something, you know. It would be interesting for me to know how you would decide a certain 'problem' as Lebeziatnikov would say." (He was beginning to lose the thread.) "No, really, I am serious. Imagine, Sonia, that you had known all Luzhin's intentions beforehand. Known, that is, for a fact, that they would be the ruin of Katerina Ivanovna and the children and yourself thrown in—since you don't count yourself for anything—Polenka too. . . . for she'll go the same way. Well, if suddenly it all depended on your decision whether he or they should go on living, that is whether Luzhin should go on living and doing wicked things, or Katerina Ivanovna should die? How would you decide which of them was to die? I ask you!"

This passage brilliantly conveys a mind struggling between the schizophrenic and the rational pursuance of an idea. The signals of schizophrenia are the reductive words, the words which suggest a merely frivolous, loosely speculative status for the whole idea (and jar on the ear because of their wanton disregard of real context). They are "interesting" and "problem." This is reinforced by his forced laugh and by the fact that he loses the thread of the sentence. But then the rational element grows stronger and this is signalled by the vocative, "Sonia," now honestly acknowledging the real urgency of the context.

That the whole programme of reason leading to murder is schizophrenic in character seems clear. When Raskolnikov comes to commit the crime he proceeds almost mechanically but his progress is repeatedly pulled up short by the gratuitous, accidental, unforeseen features of the real context of his action. This at once stamps him as subtly different from the more straightforward criminal who acts, so to speak, without blinkers. Raskolnikov's extreme shock and bewilderment on finding that he must hide the trinkets he has picked up marks quite clearly the unnaturally obsessive character of his thought up to that point. Both the slow, impeded behaviour of the typical schizophrenic and the exclusion from the mental world of all contextural or accidental features are found in Raskolnikov. This becomes clearer and clearer as the theory becomes progressively entangled in fact.

For the most brilliant stroke of *Crime and Punishment* is the way in which the theory is first yoked by its own profound logic to action and is then so to speak mocked and betrayed by the actual. The ingredients of the situation as we have so far analysed them are: first, a mildly schizophrenic mind, endlessly reiterating to itself a given formula; secondly, consequent upon this reiteration, a state of quasi-hypnotic subjection to a suggestion; thirdly, triggered by a fortuitously corroborative overheard conversation, a compulsive action. To all these we must now add the fact that the theory itself can produce this result precisely because it is itself contemptuous of theory and committed to violent action. Hence the "triggering" conversation has at the rational level the character of a challenge. "If you mean what you say, you must kill," and then the intellectual acceptance of a necessary consequence transforms itself into a peremptory command: "Kill!"

Here, then, is a considerable irony. Raskolnikov in carrying through the murder meets the challenge and satisfies the internal canons of consistency. But then because action is—actually—action, the performance of the crime involves a great many accidental features, a great deal, in short, of *mess*, which the theory, for all its ostentatious realism, never predicted. We thus have a curious system of overdetermination operating upon Raskolnikov. It was only because the theory required action that it resulted in a crime; it was only when the actual crime occurred that it became clear that the original doctrine had been maintained by Raskolnikov with the blinkered intensity of the schizophrenic. But had he not so maintained it, he would never have been able to carry it out (since he would have been vividly aware beforehand that the smashing of an old woman's skull would be much too horrible a thing). And so he would never have maintained his consistency and met the challenge to his theory.

There remains the larger question whether the mere fact of murdering on rational grounds is not itself, paradoxically, a form of madness. The idea is not altogether absurd. I imagine that most people would find something disquieting in a person who, say, fell in love on purely rational grounds. The same code, though in a lesser degree, governs our view of the way marriages should come about (though, note, women are conventionally allowed to be two or three degrees more rational about marriage than men, perhaps because a woman's economic future is commonly at stake in marriage as a man's is not).

It may be that this strange situation in which it becomes possible to call reason madness and unreason sanity is partly due to David Hume, together with that great movement of eighteenth-century thought which increasingly confined "reason" to ratiocinative deduction and inference, and ascribed all else to feeling. Roughly speaking, before Hume reason was habitually thought of as the organ of moral perception as well as the ratiocinative faculty. Thus a man who shot his neighbour because he did not like the colour of the roses he grew is, according to the older usage, irrational; that is, his rational *perception* of what is and is not just is at fault. In the philosophy of Hume such a man is not irrational—since he makes no error of reasoning. What is at fault is his system of moral sentiments. In a famous passage Hume wrote:

> 'Tis not contrary to reason to prefer the destruction of the whole
> world to the scratching of my little finger.

The sentence is clearer if we italicize "reason." The argument is on its own terms entirely sound. And the conclusion is clear. A man who would blow up the world to stop his finger itching is mad. Such a man (we have agreed) is not irrational, makes no error in reasoning. Therefore reason and madness are perfectly compatible.

Of course it would be foolish to claim that a single technical passage of Hume's philosophy modified the consciousness of posterity. Rather, we would say that Hume gave a special force and extreme clarity to a subtle change in the general sense of what was meant by "reason." And this movement has in any case never gone so far as to obliterate the older use of "reason." It remains possible in present usage to speak of the man who shot his neighbour as irrational. At the same time, however, the idea that a given action might be at the same time both rational and mad—an idea which would have simply baffled Dante or Chaucer—found increasingly fertile soil.

And of course Dostoevsky never read a word of Hume. But it would seem obvious that he was exposed to a similar modification of consciousness. Moreover in a curious way he is actually like Hume; that is, he excelled at bringing to a final and shattering clarity the ideological impulses of the age. It is perfectly clear that Dostoevsky while he was writing *Crime and Punishment* followed for a moment at least a track of thought curiously like Hume's. The young doctor Zossimov and Razumikhin are discussing the case of Raskolnikov in particular and monomania in general; Zossimov remarks "Why, I know one case in which a hypochondriac, a man of forty, cut the throat of a little boy of eight, because he couldn't endure the jokes he made every day at table." The case is parallel to the example advanced by Hume of the man with the scratched finger. But, in an astonishingly brief space, Dostoevsky has succeeded in investing his example with the special additional eeriness of schizophrenia: the word "hypochondriac" and the fact that the speaker is a doctor predisposes us to look for a pathological explanation, and the general context of "monomania" suggests the peculiar exclusiveness of the schizophrenic consciousness. Nevertheless the philosophic structure of the example is clear: here is a man who knew clearly why he did what he did, acted for a given end and accomplished it, and yet, to any outside observer, is plainly insane.

Zossimov's brief anecdote works as a sort of thumbnail caricature of Raskolnikov. He, too, acts not from violence or passion but from an absurdly isolated process of reason. Of course there are distinctions to be drawn. Hume's example is designed to show the independence of reason and morals. Zossimov's story could be made to illustrate the same point, but Raskolnikov's reasoning proceeds from ethical premises, and so the contrast set before us is not so much that between moral sentiment and morally neutral reasoning as that between a narrowly rationalised morality and one properly receptive to ordinary intuitive data. However, the basic connexion between the Humian example and Raskolnikov remain strong: what is wrong with Raskolnikov is not his reasoning but his faculty of moral apprehension. He is rational and, mildly, insane.

Of course neither the term (of course!) nor the concept of schizophrenia is present in Hume, largely because he does not trouble to consider his example as involving a possible psychopathology. Nevertheless the relevance of "schizophrenia" as a concept to such examples is immediate. It is as if it alone, in the vocabulary of psychology, allows a place for a mode of insanity of which the inner structure is highly rational. Other clinical terms seem firmly wedded to the ancient assumption of the essential sanity of reason and of the necessarily passional character of psychosis. It is as if psychology, apart from this single concept, were a Manichaean discipline: matter is evil, spirit good: insofar as a subject is rational he cannot be insane. "Schizophrenia" alone accommodates the notion of an essentially rational insanity.

Yet there will always be war between the speculative thinker and the psychologist on this point. To diagnose a man as schizophrenic will always imply an element of patronising dismissal. Your mild schizophrenic can be diagnosed as such if his reasoning departs from common sentiment. But how if his reasoning were designed to do just that? The check on the reasoning, the check which enables us to say "insane" is never itself rational; rather it is plain man's intuition. We *know* he's crazy, and there's an end to it. In such contexts the word "obviously" is used with a repellently hearty emphasis. The man who shot his neighbour is *obviously* mad; Zossimov's hypochondriac was *obviously* insane. Raskolnikov's programme of murder was *obviously* deranged. "Obviously"? Yes, perhaps, but the rationalist will want to know *why*.

It is by now clear that there are two quite different reasons one might want to give for saying that Raskolnikov's plan is insane. The first is personal: Raskolnikov is manifestly not up to the task, temperamentally unfitted for it. This reasoning, notice, allows the Raskolnikov *theory* to stand, its status unimpaired. Raskolnikov adopts this view in his confession to Sonia: "I want to prove one thing only, that the devil led me on then and he has shown me since that I had not the right to take that path, because I am just such a louse as all the rest." Even as he plunges into the most primitive language of Christianity, he leaves the vital implication: someone exceptional, someone who was not a louse would have the right to do this thing. The second reason for calling Raskolnikov deranged implies that the theory is itself wrong, not because the reasoning is incorrect, but because the premise is unsound: the quantification of human happiness and misery, and the use of this as a sufficient basis for all moral decisions is itself grotesque *because it is inadequate to the real richness and complexity of moral experience*; the morality of murder immediately defies analysis in terms of a hedonic calculus; for example, a man can kill another man and cause him no pain, while across the street a mother brushing her child's tangled hair can cause considerable pain; to say that the mother is morally worse than the man is self-evidently absurd; the value we attach to human life is not expressible in terms of the calculus. The implication of the second account is that the exceptional man, no less than the louse has an impaired view of reality. And it is with this second account that our own picture of Raskolnikov begins to slip away into an unmanageable ambiguity. For the second argument will be seen by some people as rationalist and by others as a piece of plain-man's dismissal of reason, the routing of reason by a mass appeal to the "obvious." Thus there will be those who will believe that Raskolnikov could conceivably have been saved by rational argument, and others who will believe that he could only be saved by a good shaking up of his psyche (electric shock?), and yet others who will think that he never needed saving at all. Lebeziatnikov, the foolish snapper-up of trifles dropped from the high table of new thought, tells Raskolnikov that according to the latest medical opinion madness is essentially a logical mistake and can be cured by logical argument. The applicability and at the same time the inapplicability of this to Raskolnikov is curiously poignant. Of most madness it is patently, indeed, comically untrue. Yet Raskolnikov's disorder may be the one kind that can be said to consist originally in an unacceptable theory. But to combat that theory what "arguments" do we use? Was penal servitude an argument or a mode of therapy, or some third thing? Which of these was Sonia's love?

Why, then, did Raskolnikov murder the old woman? The psychological answer is as follows: a particular theory of heroic action found in Raskolnikov a peculiarly unstable and suggestible subject. The reason why Raskolnikov, unlike all the other young men who thought the same thoughts and yet never broke a law, committed murder, is that an original tendency to schizophrenia made him capable of the kind of obsession necessary to carry the theory into action. Neither the theory alone, nor his particular temperament alone would have resulted in murder. It was the combination that proved fatal to Alyona Ivanovna.

Yet how much, still, is unexplained? In effect our psychological argument has run: Raskolnikov did it because he was the kind of person who in those circumstances would do that. Thus far something has been achieved but not very much. When we ask "Why was he that sort of person?" we find ourselves at a stand. The concept "schizophrenic," as we have employed it, itself explains nothing. Those who think the entire matter cleared up by such language are victims of what might be called the "give it a Greek name and consider it explained" fallacy. Moreover it would be foolish to pretend that the precise position of the frontier between sanity and insanity in Raskolnikov's presentation of his theory is ever finally determined. Other writers make such things easier for their readers.

ELIZABETH DALTON

The Epileptic Mode of Being

One has the sense in reading *The Idiot* that the action of the novel is balanced quite perilously, that just beyond or beneath its precarious coherence is a kind of maelstrom or abyss in which emotion might lose its connection with intelligible form and manifest itself in some unimaginably direct, "raw" state; here ordinary coherent speech and gesture might give way to frenzy or blankness. And indeed the novel does present us with the image of this extremity in the epileptic seizure. In fact, the seizure is a sort of paradigm of the emotional progression in the book's great scenes. In most of these scenes there is a pattern of rising excitement focused upon one central figure whose consciousness becomes more and more strained or exalted, until a moment of unbearable tension, when there is a loss of control, followed by physical and mental collapse.

This is the emotional pattern of the climactic episode at Nastasya's birthday party, when Nastasya throws the hundred thousand roubles into the fire and Ganya, torn between greed and pride, falls in a faint. It is also the pattern of Ippolit's confession, read to the guests at Myshkin's party at Pavlovsk in a state of growing delirium that reaches a climax in Ippolit's suicide attempt. This sequence also appears, of course, in the two episodes that end with Myshkin's epileptic attacks, the first on the hotel staircase and the second at the Epanchins' party; moreover, the second attack is preceded by a separate incident in which Myshkin, after a long and increasingly euphoric tirade about the greatness of Russia, swings his arm in an

From *Unconscious Structure in Dostoevsky's* The Idiot: *A Study in Literature and Psychoanalysis.* © 1979 by Princeton University Press.

171

uncontrolled gesture and breaks Mme Epanchin's precious Chinese vase. The last scene of the novel, in which Rogozhin leads Myshkin to the body of Nastasya, ends with a total loss of control, the collapse of Myshkin into idiocy and blankness. In lesser forms, the same phenomenon appears throughout the novel, in the constant tendency to frenzied and uncontrolled behavior and in many scenes of wild emotion.

The novel also shows this "epileptic" pattern in its larger structure: the action seems to progress unevenly, in waves of tension that gather and burst in climactic scenes of spectacular emotional violence, leaving the narrative energy of the novel depleted and for a time directionless, until a new wave of tension begins to accumulate. The first break of this kind occurs after Nastasya's birthday party, which ends part 1; the opening of part 2 is almost like the beginning of a new novel. The next episode is Myshkin's long day in Petersburg, ending in the climactic scene on the staircase. Once again there is a sort of break in the narrative, and then a new action begins at Lebedyev's villa at Pavlovsk, with the gathering at which Antip Burdovsky and the "nihilists" confront Myshkin. The narrative connection from one of these climactic scenes to the next is rather tenuous. In the intervals between them there is a kind of "forgetting"; the action wanders, the novel appears not to remember what it is about. Highly charged material crucial to the plot seems submerged under the effects of repression, as in the six-month lacuna between parts 1 and 2, in which significant episodes in Nastasya's relationships with both Rogozhin and Myshkin are presented so sketchily as to be virtually lost. *The Idiot* does not have the tightly integrated plot structure of *Crime and Punishment* or of *The Brothers Karamazov*, with their relentless forward motion and evenly calibrated tension, nor the complex intrigue of *The Possessed*. Its dramatic scenes are not strongly connected by the thread of continuous narrative. Each scene, instead of being generated by the preceding one on the horizontal plane of the plot, seems to be derived directly from the explosive emotional experience at the center of the novel.

We know from the notebooks that Dostoevsky had great difficulty in projecting the plot of *The Idiot*. And because of his commitment to his editor and his terrible financial plight, each section had to be submitted for publication before the next had been written or even sketched out. In these desperate circumstances, it would seem that Dostoevsky was forced back upon the spontaneous images and rhythms of his mental life to a greater extent than in any other work. It is perhaps because the novel reveals so openly the nature of that life that its author's feelings about it were peculiarly intense. The progress of the novel was intimately linked in Dostoevsky's mind to the course of his epilepsy. The excitement that informs the climactic scenes with their fury and brilliance expressed itself in life in the epileptic seizures, and Dostoevsky reckoned the cost of the great scenes in fits: "I wrote this finale [Nastasya's birthday party] in a state of inspiration, and it cost me two fits in a row." Dostoevsky expressed parts of himself in all of his characters, but to Myshkin alone among his principal heroes he gave the ambiguous gift of his illness. The novel is in some sense Dostoevsky's exploration of the meaning of his epilepsy, a study in the epileptic mode of being. [I have taken this phrase from Robert Lord (*Dostoevsky: Essays and Perspectives*), who entitles his chapter on *The Idiot* "An Epileptic Mode of Being."]

Myshkin's disease appears so much a condition of the soul that one almost forgets its connection with the body. Medically, epilepsy remains a complex and little understood disorder; the term itself designates a configuration of symptoms rather than a single clinical entity. The symptoms may come from a number of quite different sources, including a physiological alteration of the central nervous system such as a lesion or chemical imbalance, a psychological cause such as a traumatic incident or hysteria, or some combination of physical and psychological elements. The facts of Dostoevsky's illness are unclear and difficult to interpret; however, even if his epileptic pattern of response was based on an organic predisposition, as seems likely, the disease certainly assumed a psychological meaning for him in the context of his experience and personality, as it must for anyone who suffers from such a condition. Whatever the organic basis of his epilepsy, he seemed always to conceive of it primarily as a psychological and moral phenomenon. In his presentation of Myshkin's epilepsy, there is virtually no interest in it as an organic disorder; it is treated almost entirely as a mental and spiritual condition.

In "Dostoevsky and Parricide," Freud argues that Dostoevsky's epilepsy was probably "affective" and hysterical in character. The epileptic reaction, whatever its organic basis, was available for the expression of his neurosis; thus the psychological function of the seizure was to get rid, by somatic means, of masses of stimuli that could not be dealt with psychically. From information about Dostoevsky's later life and personality, Freud concludes that the Oedipus complex was resolved in the negative form, and that there was a strong bisexual predisposition and an element of latent homosexuality in his character. Thus the hatred of the father and the fear of castration implicit in the normal Oedipus complex received a pathogenic reinforcement from the fear of being made to play the castrated "feminine" role in relation to the father, leading to the intensification of parricidal wishes. The guilt attendant upon such wishes was disastrously reinforced in Dostoevsky's case by their fulfillment in reality; the death of his father, whom Dostoevsky and the rest of the family always believed to have been murdered by his serfs, could have been construed as a kind of parricide. Freud sees Dostoevsky's epileptic attacks as self-punishment for the parricidal wishes; in the seizure he became temporarily dead, like the murdered father, for whose death he unconsciously held his own guilty wishes responsible. Accounts of Dostoevsky's illness suggest that the attacks did not assume a definitely epileptic character until some time after his father's death.

In *The Idiot* the epileptic seizure is overdetermined in an extremely complex way; it is a sort of nodal point at which all the strands of sexual and aggressive feeling are tied into a single expression. It has a clearly sexual meaning as a substitute for and symbolic representation of erotic contact with the father, which implies the terrifying corollary of castration. But the suffering or deathlike aspect of the attack also serves as a punishment for the parricidal wishes aroused by the fear of castration, here reinforced by the homosexual wish. Thus pleasure and pain are united, the pleasurable fantasy supplying its own pain and punishment, and the punishment taking an erotically gratifying form. The suffering and humiliation of the epileptic attack is thus a somatic version of the internal drama of self-punishment played out in the novel on the moral plane, the vengeance of the sadistic superego upon the masochistic ego, which keeps alive within the personality the erotically gratifying suffering of the old relationship with the punishing father.

As it is represented in the novel, then, the epileptic personality is one in which sexual and aggressive drives have assumed a particularly dangerous character, involving homosexual and parricidal wishes so threatening to the ego that they must be entirely repressed. In the epileptic seizure these energies erupt periodically in the form of a violent attack in which the ego does indeed lose all control.

But Myshkin's epilepsy also has another dimension, a powerfully positive aspect that makes it the fundamental enigma of his being, the point of transformation at which disease may become sanctity. Epilepsy is what sets Myshkin apart from other men in every way: it is weakness, idiocy, illness. But if it is illness, it is the *morbus sacer*, the sacred disease of shamans and prophets who are torn by the rough hand of God, who see through this rent in the fabric of their beings into another world, a luminous reality free of the limitations and ambiguities of ordinary experience. This mystical aspect of Myshkin's epilepsy is concentrated in the aura, the momentary alteration of consciousness that precedes the fit, which is described in the following passage:

> He remembered among other things that he always had one
> minute just before the epileptic fit (if it came on while he was

awake), when suddenly in the midst of sadness, spiritual darkness
and oppression, there were moments when it seemed as if his brain
had caught fire, and with extraordinary impetus all his vital forces
would be intensified. The sense of life, the consciousness of self,
were multiplied almost ten times at these moments, which passed
like a flash of lightning. His mind and heart were illuminated with
extraordinary light; all his uneasiness, all his doubts, all his
anxieties were relieved at once; they were resolved into a kind
of lofty calm, full of serene, harmonious joy and hope, full of
understanding and the knowledge of the ultimate cause of things.
But these moments, these flashes, were only the presage of that
final second (it was never more than a second) with which the
fit itself began. That second was, of course, unendurable.
Thinking of that moment later, when he was all right again, he
often said to himself that all these gleams and flashes of a higher
self-awareness, and therefore also of "a higher form of existence,"
were nothing but disease, the violation of the normal conditions;
and if so, it was not at all a higher form of existence, but on the
contrary must be reckoned the lowest. And yet he came at last
to an extremely paradoxical conclusion. "What if it is disease?"
he decided at last. "What does it matter that it is an abnormal
intensity, if the result, if the minute of sensation, remembered and
analysed afterwards in health, turns out to be the acme of harmony
and beauty, and gives a feeling, unknown and undivined till then,
of completeness, of proportion, of reconciliation, and of ecstatic
devotional merging in the highest synthesis of life?" These cloudy
expressions seemed to him very comprehensible, though too weak.
That it really was "beauty and prayer," that it really was the
"highest synthesis of life" he could not doubt, and could not admit
the possibility of doubt. It was not as though he saw abnormal
and unreal visions of some sort at that moment, as from hashish,
opium, or wine, destroying the reason and distorting the soul.
He was quite capable of judging of that when the attack was over.
These moments were precisely an extraordinary quickening of self-
consciousness—if the condition was to be expressed in one
word—and at the same time of the direct sensation of existence
in the most intense degree.

(pt. 2, chap. 5)

   The features repeatedly stressed in this account of the aura are the flashes
of light, the heightened intensity and directness of the sensation of self and

of existence, and above all the ecstatic sense of harmony in which qualities of reconciliation, synthesis, and merging are emphasized. In this "ecstatic devotional merging" Myshkin, like others who have had the mystical revelation, experiences a sudden resolution of doubts and conflicts and a sense of oneness with something outside of himself, with "the highest synthesis of life." This sense of oneness with the universe seems to be the "oceanic feeling" described by Freud in *Civilization and Its Discontents*, where he explains it as a dissolution of the boundaries of the ego, a regression to the primordial state of the infant at the breast, who "does not as yet distinguish his ego from the external world as the source of sensations flowing in upon him."

The "extraordinary quickening of self-consciousness" in the aura may seem inconsistent with the *loss* of a sense of self suggested by the oceanic feeling and by Myshkin's sense of ecstatic merging. However, the "self" in this passage is not Myshkin's everyday self, which is often beset by doubt and guilt, but a quite different self free of any sense of limitation, open to "the direct sensation of existence in the most intense degree." This euphoric sense of self is quite compatible with the oceanic feeling. Freud writes,

> originally the ego includes everything, later it separates off an external world from itself. Our present ego-feeling is, therefore, only a shrunken residue of a much more inclusive—indeed an all-embracing—feeling which corresponded to a more intimate bond between the ego and the world about it. . . . There are many people in whose mental life this primary ego-feeling has persisted . . . side by side with the narrower and more sharply demarcated ego-feeling of maturity. . . . The ideational contents appropriate to it would be precisely those of limitlessness and of a bond with the universe.

Myshkin's quickened consciousness of self in the aura is not the "sharply demarcated ego-feeling of maturity," but rather a return to the all-embracing "primary ego-feeling." The effect of this regression is to restore the boundless narcissism of the infant; thus the often painful and alienating feeling of separation between the self and the external world is overcome in the mystical ecstasy.

This dissolution of boundaries affects the ego's relationship not only with the external world but also with the other parts of the mind. With the decrease in repression comes increased access to the contents of the id. Freud writes, "certain mystical practices may succeed in upsetting the normal relations between the different regions of the mind, so that, for instance, perception may be able to grasp happenings in the depths of the ego and in the id which were otherwise inaccessible to it."

This change in the functions and relations of the different parts of the mind in mystical experience can also be understood through a comparison with manic-depressive illness. Although the behavior and the personality of the mystic and the manic-depressive are different in obvious ways, interesting resemblances suggest that the underlying pattern of sudden changes in the distribution of energy within the mental systems may be similar. In manic-depressive illness, the personality is dominated for long periods by a severe superego, which prohibits instinctual expression. At the onset of the manic phase, the dammed-up instinctual energy erupts explosively, overthrowing the superego and producing a feeling of elation and fantasies of omnipotence. The ego, no longer obliged to repress, is flooded with the instinctual energy of the id; this collapse of the structures of personality is experienced as a narcissistic triumph, producing a brilliant sense of euphoria.

The personality of the mystic, at least that typical of the great Catholic mystics of Europe, is also dominated by superego: the mystic lives under a severe regime of mortification of the flesh, fasting, and chastity. But this instinctual deprivation is apparently compensated by the joy of the mystical experience, for which denial of the senses is the preparation. The mystical vision is often preceded by a terrible period of intellectual and sexual temptation, doubts and obscene visions, not unlike the ordeal of Myshkin's long day in Petersburg before the first fit. After enduring this torment, the mystic is rewarded by the mystical revelation. This revelation may include the apparition of Christ, the saints, or the Virgin, often described in intensely sexual language. Or it may be a more generalized experience—an ineffable sense of beatitude or absorption into the radiance of the divine being such as Myshkin has during the aura. As in mania, there is an eruption of long-repressed instinctual energy, the superego is overthrown, and the ego is free to experience the gratification of id impulses, although in a form disguised by and consonant with religious beliefs.

Thus the sense of merging, reconciliation, and synthesis in the mystical experience refers not only to the ego's feeling of oneness with the external world but also to the annihilation of internal conflict and the merging of psychic structures as the repressive superego is overthrown and id energy rushes into the ego. The "extraordinary light" that floods the mind and heart of Myshkin appears to be an image of this surge of energy. The successful rebellion against the superego represents a narcissistic victory for the ego, producing the intensely heightened feeling of self-consciousness and of "the direct sensation of existence." The infantile oral union with the world, in which the infant at the breast feels as though he incorporates everything into himself, is restored. The reality principle is deposed by the pleasure principle of the primitive ego, which seeks immediate gratification. The sense of time, a function of the mature ego associated with the delay of gratification, is suspended during the mystical experience, which is always described as somehow outside of time. Myshkin understands during the ecstatic moment the saying "there shall be no more time"; it is this moment, he says, "which was not long enough for the water to be spilt out of Mahomet's pitcher, though the epileptic prophet had time to gaze at all the habitations of Allah" (pt. 2, chap. 5).

Thus the brilliant, unlimited, harmonious vision that comes to Myshkin during the pre-epileptic aura is a regression to the timeless world of the primitive ego, buried in the oldest layers of the mind and illuminated during the instant of the aura like a dark landscape in a flash of lightning. The vision occurs during the moment when the structures of the differentiated personality collapse under the pressure of unconscious instinctual impulses and the mind regresses to an earlier and simpler mode of function, which is remembered after the experience as a sort of radiant prelapsarian paradise in contrast to the fallen world of the reality principle and the adult ego.

The moment of the aura is virtually the only point in *The Idiot* at which instinctual impulses break through the barriers of repression with sufficient force to be felt in direct, unmodified form as pleasurable and gratifying. At this point the sexual and aggressive feelings usually experienced by Myshkin in the disguised masochistic form of suffering rush into the ego with an effect of ecstatic and joyful release. But the ego cannot tolerate the force of these energies in their original unmodified form, nor can it allow their meaning to rise into conscious awareness. The moment of orgiastic release is followed by the total eclipse of the ego in the epileptic seizure. The fit is also the revenge of the superego, which can be deposed only temporarily; for the uninhibited release of sexual and aggressive energy it exacts the talion penalty of symbolic castration and death. The instinctual drives are once more experienced under the negative sign of superego, in the form of asceticism and suffering.

There is another kind of episode in *The Idiot*—related in form and meaning to the scenes of epilepsy—in which this negative form of instinctual excitement is most fully expressed, and in which mental experience and the sense of existence reach the same unbearable intensity as in the epileptic seizure. Myshkin describes several times the thoughts of a condemned man on the scaffold; these passages present a kind of inversion and counterpart of the epileptic seizure, and complete its meaning. There are two such descriptions, which are really two versions of the same scene. In one version, Myshkin relates a story based on Dostoevsky's own mock execution: a friend of Myshkin, sentenced to be shot for a political offense, is led out to the scaffold fully convinced that he is about to die, and then at the last moment is given a reprieve. When Myshkin's friend believed that only five more minutes remained to him before his execution,

> "those five minutes seemed to him an infinite time, a vast wealth; he felt that in those five minutes he could live through so many lifetimes that there was no need yet to think about himself for the last time, so much so that he divided his time up. He set aside time to take leave of his comrades, two minutes for that; then he kept another two minutes to think for the last time; and then a minute to look about him for the last time. [. . .] Then [. . .] the two minutes came that he had set apart for *thinking about himself*. He knew beforehand what he would think about. He wanted to realise as quickly and clearly as possible how it could be that now he existed and was living and in three minutes he would be *something*—someone or something. But what? Where? He meant to decide all that in those two minutes! Not far off there was a church, and the gilt roof was glittering in the bright sunshine. He remembered that he stared very persistently at that roof and at the rays of light flashing from it; he could not tear himself away from the light. It seemed to him that those rays were his new nature and that in three minutes he would somehow melt into them. . . . The uncertainty and feeling of aversion for that new thing which would be and was just coming was awful. But he said that nothing was so dreadful at that time as the continual thought, 'What if I were not to die! What if I could go back to life—what eternity! And it would all be mine! I would turn every minute into an age; I would lose nothing, I would count every minute as it passed, I would not waste one!' He said that this idea turned to such fury at last that he longed to be shot quickly."

(pt. 1, chap. 5)

In the second version, a man condemned to the guillotine experiences a similar intensification of perception and self-consciousness:

> "It's strange that people rarely faint at these last moments. On the contrary, the brain is extraordinarily lively and must be racing, racing, racing, like a machine at full speed. I fancy that there is a continual throbbing of ideas of all sorts, always unfinished and perhaps absurd too, quite irrelevant ideas: 'That man is looking at me. He has a wart on his forehead. One of the executioner's buttons is rusty.' . . . and yet all the while one knows and

remembers everything. There is one point which can never be
forgotten, and one can't faint, and everything moves and turns
about it, about that point. And only think that it must be like
that up to the last quarter of a second, when his head lies on the
block and he waits and . . . *knows*, and suddenly he hears the
iron slithering down above his head!"

(pt. 1, chap. 5)

In these execution scenes, the threat of punishment implicit throughout
the novel and enacted symbolically in the epileptic attack appears undisguised.
The man who rebels against the paternal authority of state or society is to
be shot or guillotined. Once again, however, the idea of punishment is juxta-
posed with tremendously heightened mental awareness. Both here and in the
pre-epileptic aura, the sense of self-conscious existence reaches its highest pitch
at the very moment when the ego is actually threatened with annihilation.
In the epileptic seizure, the repressed impulses are first released directly in
positive unmodified form, producing an instant of ecstatically heightened consciousness in the aura, which is then followed by retaliation and punishment
in the seizure. Here the sequence is reversed. The idea of punishment comes
first, arousing excited thoughts and feverish mental activity comparable to
the mental intensity of the aura and suggesting the release into the ego of
instinctual excitement. It is as if these impulses may justifiably be released
now, since they are certain to be punished; in fact, the punishment is finally
longed for, as though to end the intolerable tension of instinctual excitement:
"this idea [of the value of every minute] turned to such fury at last that he
longed to be shot quickly."

The execution is described three times, as if there were a compulsion
to repeat it again and again. Each successive repetition contains an increasingly minute attention to the most painful details. The last description of
the man on the guillotine ends in this way:

"And only think that it must be like that up to the last quarter of
a second, when his head lies on the block and he waits and . . .
knows, and suddenly he hears the iron slithering down above his
head! You would certainly hear that! If I were lying there, I should
listen on purpose and hear. It may last only the tenth part of a
second, but you would be sure to hear it. And only fancy, it's
still disputed whether, when the head is cut off, it knows for a
second after that it has been cut off! What an idea! And what
if it knows it for five seconds!"

(pt. 1, chap. 5)

This passage creates and then elaborates upon an unbearably vivid image of the conscious experience of suffering. As if the idea of the head's knowing for one second that it has been cut off were not sufficiently dreadful, the interval is expanded to five seconds, as though to stimulate and increase to the highest possible intensity the terror and the masochistic excitement associated with pain and punishment.

It is significant too that the scene before the firing squad here becomes an execution on the guillotine, a form of death suggestive of castration. This transformation reveals more clearly the meaning of the punishment fantasy that unites the scenes of execution and of epilepsy. Castration would of course be the punishment for wishing to replace the father; but it would also represent a reconciliation with him, a way of at last placating this terrible father and being loved by and united with him in final passivity. At the intrapsychic level, this fantasy of a castration-death means resolving the conflict within the personality in favor of the cruel superego: the ego would give up its claims entirely and allow itself to be annihilated by guilt. The pattern of all levels is one of total submission to authority, of annihilation and absorption by it.

This resolution seems to be exactly the reverse of the narcissistic triumph achieved in the ecstasy of the epileptic aura, in which the superego, the internal authority, is overthrown and absorbed by the omnipotent ego. Actually the problem here is the same, and the same goal is achieved, although by different means. The ego, under the assault of rising instinctual impulses and threatened by the superego, can no longer tolerate the conflict with the superego. It submits to being overwhelmed and absorbed by the superego, as though in this way to participate in the superego's omnipotence. Thus the same goal of omnipotence is achieved, this time paradoxically through submission. The intrapsychic transaction does not seem particularly mysterious when one thinks of the joyful sense of release with which individuals regularly renounce their autonomy in favor of authoritarian religions or governments: the fantasy of the devotee is always one of an enormous increase of power through absorption by and participation in the power of the deity or the state.

In the firing squad scene, the image of this transformation appears in the light flashing from the gilded church dome: "It seemed to him that those rays were his new nature and that in three minutes he would somehow melt into them" (pt. 1, chap. 5). The imagery of light and of melting resembles the flashes and floods of radiance during the aura. This merging into radiance is regarded here, however, with aversion: the price to be paid for omnipotence is, after all, terrible.

The epileptic scenes and the descriptions of execution are the points in the novel at which experience reaches its highest intensity: these episodes are in a sense the prototypes of the emotional experience of *The Idiot*. In the great scenes of climactic emotion or violent confrontation, the reader is led to participate in a kind of loss of control: the ego of the protagonist, under the assault of repressed impulses, gives way to energies and fantasies usually inaccessible to it and undergoes an enormous expansion of its capacity for perception and feeling. But this momentary expansion also exposes it to the possibility of annihilation through the savage force of id energies and the retaliation of superego: the result is the collapse of the ego in frenzy, loss of consciousness, or epileptic convulsions.

This characteristic mode of emotional response is what might be called the "epileptic pattern" in the novel. Its positive value is in one sense enormous: at its most acute, in the aura, it constitutes the claim that may be made for the "mystical" quality of Myshkin's insight and personality. These moments of heightened consciousness represent a breakthrough beyond the barriers of repression that define the normal conditions of the ego into a state in which the darker regions of personality usually inaccessible to consciousness are illuminated and the sense of existence is immeasurably intensified. The ego experiences these states as an enormous expansion of its capacity: the conscious mind appears to be offered the possibility of penetrating a limitless reality. In these scenes the reader feels as if he is being forced to *know* more and more, as if the mind is being wrenched out of its limits and into those areas of experience of which no rational understanding is possible. The aim of these passages seems to be to push consciousness to and beyond the breaking point, as if to attain something like the state of that head severed on the guillotine: freed from the limitations of its normal state, perhaps that isolated head achieves some last awful moment of total comprehension, some final transcendence of the barrier between the conscious and the unconscious mind, even between life and death.

The condition of this final knowledge is, of course, annihilation. This is the ambiguity and the fundamental paradox of the moments of greatest intensity in the novel: the most piercing sense of the existence of the conscious self comes at the point of the destruction of personality, at the moment when the ego is about to give way and the mind to return to a primitive and undifferentiated mode of response. The moments of highest meaning in Myshkin's experience—the brilliant awareness of the texture of existence itself—are also the very moments when existence is on the verge of collapse into meaningless emptiness. Myshkin himself knows this: "he often said to himself that all these gleams and flashes of the highest sensation of life and self-consciousness, and therefore also of the highest form of existence, were nothing but disease, the interruption of the normal conditions; and if so, it was not at all the highest form of being, but on the contrary must be reckoned the lowest." And later: "Stupefaction, spiritual darkness, idiocy stood before him conspicuously as the consequence of these 'higher moments'"; but "for the infinite happiness he had felt in it, that second really might well be worth the whole of life" (pt. 2, chap. 5).

This mysticism is an extremely dubious phenomenon: it offers a conception of spiritual experience based on a kind of gambler's dialectic of all or nothing, a compulsion toward extreme mental states that is a continual courting of loss of control. In this compulsive gamble, the ego itself is the stake, and the outcome is omnipotence or annihilation. It might be argued that the character of Myshkin's mental life is imposed on him by his disease, that therefore he cannot be said to "court" or to "gamble" anything. But the point is that this kind of mental excitement, whether chosen or inflicted, is presented in the novel as having an incalculable advantage. Nor is it confined to Myshkin. Myshkin's is only the most extreme form of an experience undergone by other characters as well, all of whom participate to some extent in this "epileptic mode of being," which is at the formal and experiential core of the novel, and which is a continual gamble with the precarious structure of personality.

It is into the darkness that lies beyond the controls of the ego, the perilous region of unmodified instinct and savage retaliation, that we are invited by the great scenes of mounting tension and final frenzy and collapse. Nowhere else in Dostoevsky are we taken so far beyond intellectual speculation about and description of these states into the actual experience itself. The wild beauty and terror of the great scenes, the suffocating excitement that we feel through identification with the protagonists and through the dramatic rhythms of tension and abrupt release, are our own experience of the loosening of ego controls as we read; they register our advance into the realm of dangerous fantasies of forbidden sexual gratification and of reunion with omnipotent authority through awful punishment. Again and again the novel leads us out onto this treacherous ground; beyond this precipice is the abyss of total abandonment in frenzy or stupor—the loss of the ego and all its complicated negotiations between the inner world of instinctual drives and the outer world of external reality.

In the compulsion to lean out over that abyss, to abandon differentiated ego controls for the excitement of more primitive mental states, the novel also risks its own existence as an aesthetic object. The aesthetic experience involves a special kind of mental, and to some degree physical, activity in which id and ego responses are alternated and integrated in a particularly satisfying way that provides the opportunity for both release and mastery. The work of art is a sort of artificial world with built-in formal controls that permit the ego of the reader or spectator to relax its own controls temporarily, to enjoy in the safety of the created world the release of repressed instinctual energies and forbidden fantasies. This id aspect of the aesthetic experience goes on largely without specific conscious awareness. The reader typically feels it only as an excitement or pleasure that may be difficult to explain in terms of the explicit content of the work, for the greatest art often deals with experiences of a kind that are painful, repellent, or frightening in real life. The pleasure afforded by this kind of art implies some dim preconscious or unconscious recognition of the content of the work, however unpleasant it might be in real life, as in some way corresponding to the reader's own internal world.

Moreover, the greatest works engage the whole being of the reader, not simply his conscious mind: at deeper levels of personality the reader is responding unconsciously to symbolic transformations of repressed wishes, to disguised representations of forbidden acts, and to repeated patterns that suggest the structure of primal relationships and fantasies about them. This whole aspect of the aesthetic experience, in which pleasure is often mixed with much that is painful or frightening, may be brought to the level of conscious awareness only in some vaguely articulated way, perhaps as a sense of heightened and expanded life, a feeling that the world is more various, more dangerous, more beautiful than it appears in our everyday lives, that it is richer in meanings for us if we could only know them.

But the ego also has its demands: it requires of the work the pleasures of conscious recognition, of internally consistent and plausible representation, of a harmonious image and a controlled form through which the work defines itself against the relatively formless background of real life and offers a coherent vision of that life. Of course, these two aspects of the aesthetic experience shade off into each other continuously and imperceptibly in ways far too complex to be fully described. But the point here is that the work of art cannot *only* provide an opportunity for regressive fantasy and the release of repressed energies; it must also satisfy the demands of the ego. And in fact the deeper levels of personality can only be involved, paradoxically, by a work that is sufficiently under the control of the ego to allow the ego to relax its controls. That is, if the regression induced by the work feels too deep, too violent, or too real, the ego will experience it as unpleasant and will muster its defenses, turning from the work in aversion, boredom, or incomprehension.

In a work of fiction rooted basically in the realistic mode, the ego is

likely to make its demands felt in the specific expectation of an interesting
and coherent plot, as well as the more general aesthetic expectation of
coherent form, of a sense that every part of the work has some necessary
connection with every other part. It is here, with the formal controls that
satisfy ego demands, that *The Idiot* takes its greatest risks. First, and most
obviously, it deals largely with states that are alien and threatening to the
ego: dream, hallucination, delirium, madness, epilepsy, death. But what is
more significant, it deals with these states not simply by means of objective
description and external observation; the truth of *The Idiot* is the truth that
is "proved upon our pulses," in Keats's phrase. Dostoevsky is not content
to describe the man on the scaffold as he appears from outside; he gives us
the very particles of the condemned man's thought and feeling, his every
fugitive impression and sensation as his time runs out, up to the moment
when the blade descends on his neck—and even after. The language of the
scene evokes a stream of preconscious imagery in the reader in which his
own fears and fantasies of extinction are contained. Through the power of
language to transfer and mediate such preconscious and unconscious thought
and imagery, the prisoner's experience takes on the power of the reader's
deepest emotions—the terror of the man on the scaffold is fused with the
reader's own most primitive fears. Thus the reader is made to share to an
extraordinary degree in the subjective experience of extreme states, even being
led to imagine having his head cut off.

The compulsion to introduce this kind of excitement into the novel nearly
destroys it as an aesthetic experience. The anxieties aroused mobilize the
defenses of the reader's ego, which may protect itself by finding the book
"unbearable," or "overwritten," or "ridiculous." Moreover, in their explosive
force, the great scenes threaten to escape the control of the plot, to disrupt
the continuity of the narrative and drive it into incoherence. This dangerous
flirtation with loss of form is the analogue in the structure of the novel itself
to the courting of loss of ego control in the protagonists, especially Myshkin.
Thus the novel in its terrible fidelity to moral and psychological experience
almost loses itself in the gamble.

Almost, but not quite. Form and meaning are salvaged perilously, like
the hundred thousand roubles Nastasya pulls from the fire at the last moment.
It is not the novel but the protagonists who disappear into the abyss—in
madness, death, and idiocy. What they find there we cannot know: it is not
finally possible for us, or for the novel, to take that last plunge beyond all
language and control. But we have been led as far as a meaningful aesthetic
structure can take us into the darkest areas of personality and experience.
In the brilliance of the great scenes, even that chaotic darkness is lit up for

an instant, so that we recognize in it the outlines of meaning. For out of chaos the book does finally achieve the coherence of meaning, although it does not always give its meanings their true names. Like all dark forces, they must sometimes be called holy, as the Furies were named Gracious Ones. In those unfamiliar shapes of suffering and violence, in that fitfully illuminated landscape of illness, we must finally recognize something of our own dark interior, of the roots of our compassion, our identification with suffering, our fascination with pain. Through Myshkin and all that destroys him, we learn again the lesson of tragedy: that the apparently random and cruel external world of things that we suffer, the world that happens to us, is in some mysterious way integral to the world we experience as necessary and inevitable, the internal world of what we desire and what we are.

ROBERT LOUIS JACKSON

Polina and Lady Luck
in The Gambler

Lucky in cards, unlucky in love.
—ENGLISH SAYING

In a letter written to N. N. Strakhov from Rome in September 1863 Dostoevsky projected the idea of a story that was to evolve later into the novel *The Gambler* (*From the Notes of a Young Man*) (1866). The story, he wrote, would reflect the "contemporary moment (as far as possible, of course) of our inner life." The central character would be "a certain type of Russian abroad":

> I take a straightforward nature, a man, however, highly educated, but in all respects immature, who has lost his faith and *does not dare not to believe*, who revolts against the authorities and fears them. He sets his mind at rest with the thought that for him there is *nothing to do* in Russia and consequently there is bitter criticism of people in Russia summoning back our Russians living abroad. . . . He's a live character—(he stands before me almost in his entirety). . . . The main thing about him is that his living juices, forces, impetuosity, daring have gone into *roulette*. He is a gambler, and not a mere gambler, just as Pushkin's miserly knight is not a simple miser. . . . He is a poet in his own way, but the point is that he himself is ashamed of this poetry, because he deeply feels its baseness, although the need for *risk* also ennobles him in his own eyes. . . . If *House of the Dead* drew the attention

From *The Art of Dostoevsky: Deliriums and Nocturnes*. © 1981 by Princeton University Press.

187

of the public as a depiction of the convicts whom nobody had depicted *vividly* before it, then this story without fail will attract attention as a *vivid* and detailed depiction of the game of roulette.

Dostoevsky's comparison of this story with *House of the Dead* is of particular interest. The link between *The Gambler* and the earlier work goes beyond the fact that both works provide engaging descriptions of novel institutions— the worlds of the prison and the gambling house. In his letter to Strakhov, Dostoevsky indirectly hints at a deeper relationship between these two institutions, or, in any case, between the people who inhabit them. "The piece perhaps is not at all half bad. Why, *House of the Dead* was of real interest. And this is a description of a special kind of hell, a special kind of prison 'bath.'"

The allusion to the world of the gambler as a kind of hell points to the basic similarity in the situations of the convict and the gambler: both are prisoners in what appears to be an enclosed fate-bound universe. But whereas the convict lives in a prison world not of his own choice, a world from which, moreover, there is really no way out, the gambler lives in a dead house, or underground, of his own making. In the gambler's world everybody is possessed by the illusion of freedom, but nobody is really free. Through chance, risk, the turn of the wheel, the gambler challenges fate and seeks to escape its tyranny. Alternatives are offered to Dostoevsky's gambler, Aleksey Ivanovich, in his friend Polina and in lady luck. But in the end, he condemns himself to hurling himself eternally against the walls of his universe. He becomes an inveterate gambler, doomed to permanent unfreedom and to an endless process of trying to change his lot.

The tragedy of the gambler in Dostoevsky's view is that of a man who has uprooted himself from his nation and people and who has lost faith in God. "The cause of evil is lack of faith," Dostoevsky insisted in a letter to A. F. Blagonravov in December 1880, "but he who negates the folk element also negates faith." The gambler finds a surrogate father or mother in fate, chance, luck. Yet the abandonment of self to fate is an unmitigated moral and spiritual disaster for man.

The amoral character of gambling is posited by Dostoevsky on three levels. First, gambling is directly equated with the capitalist market. "Why," asks Aleksey, "should gambling be worse than other means of making money—for instance, commerce?" Everything is relative, a "matter of proportion. What is a trifle to Rothschild is really wealth to me, and as for profits and winnings, people everywhere, and not only at roulette, are doing nothing but gaining or taking away something from each other. Whether profits and gain are vile is another question. But I'm not trying to resolve it here."

Gambling is evil, in the second sense, in that it awakens predatory instincts, chiefly greed and the desire for power. The casino strikes Aleksey as "dirty, somehow morally disgusting and dirty." He notes the greedy faces around him. But since he himself was "overcome by the desire for gain, all this covetousness, and all this covetous filth, if you like, were in a sense natural and congenial to me as soon as I entered the hall."

Yet the ultimate evil that preoccupies Dostoevsky in gambling is the evil that is immanent, psychologically speaking, in the gambling itself. The very act of gambling becomes a conscious or unconscious affirmation of the meaninglessness of the universe, the emptiness of all human choice. "All's nonsense on earth!" declares one of the seconds before Pechorin kills Grushnitski in a duel in Lermontov's *Hero of Our Time* (1840). "Nature is a ninny, fate is a henny and life is a penny." The gambler is a fatalist. Moreover, he challenges the very fate he affirms and seeks to find out if he is favored or unfavored by it. The game, the gamble, the risk itself is by its very nature a dangerous inquiry into the sources of power and an arrogant form of self-assertion; making chance king, the gambler in essence strives to become the king of chance.

The moral correlative of the belief that everything is possible is that all is permissible. Not without reason does the folk language of the market speak of "making a killing." Dostoevsky's gambler speaks of his "hidden moral convictions," but insists that in the gambling halls "there is no place for them": "I notice one thing that of late it has become repugnant for me to test my thoughts and actions by any moral standards whatsoever. I was guided by something else." That something else is fate.

I

The action of *The Gambler* takes place in a kind of no man's land or hell, Roulettenburg. As the fictitious name suggests, the city is nowhere or anywhere in Europe. The mixed French and German components of the name suggest the illegitimate and rootless character of the place. This is the land of Babel, a place without a national language or culture. The gambling salon—the heart of Roulettenburg—is situated, symbolically, in a railway station where people are coming and going, where all is in continuous movement. Everything is in flux in this city: people, languages, currencies, values.

Roulettenburg is the classical city of capitalism: the market is supreme and everyone is engaged in accumulation. Everyone risks money to make money, and what he wins or loses wipes out what he has staked; there are no absolute values, material or moral; everything is relative and changing.

Even people, like stakes at the table, move upward or downward in the eyes of other people according to the value judgment of the roulette wheel. Nowhere is the "cash nexus" that Marx discovered in human relations and affairs in bourgeois society more nakedly visible than in Roulettenburg. Aleksey hopes to redeem himself in the eyes of Polina by winning at roulette. "Money is everything," he declares. "It's nothing more than that with money I shall be a different person to you, not a slave." He is convinced that Polina despises him, sees him as a "cipher" and a "zero." To "rise from the dead" to him means to become a millionaire and to reverse the slave-master relationship that he feels exists between Polina and him.

But there are no permanent plateaus in social or psychological status in Roulettenburg. There are no social realities that are not subject to change. Nothing is what it seems. General Zagoryansky, considered by everybody an extremely wealthy magnate, is in fact not a magnate at all; he is a pompous muddled man who dyes his beard and moustache and is heavily in debt. The Marquis de Grieux is not a marquis, but an imposter. Madame Blanche de Cominges is not a respectable woman, but a courtesan masquerading as a de Cominges. Polina's Russian name is Praskovya, but she uses the Latinized form of her name. The inner Praskovya is not quite the same as the outer Polina. She has been in love with the Marquis de Grieux, but has taken his outer refined form for his inner soul. Aleksey sees through de Grieux, but takes Polina for somebody else.

At the outset Aleksey seems to be an objective and trustworthy observer of this strange world. The prestige of the narrative voice is overwhelming, and, initially, we accept his version of Polina as cruel and manipulative and of himself as a jilted lover. But our confidence is misplaced. Midway in his notes he remarks upon the "whirl" that has caught him up and suggests what we have already begun to suspect—that his view of things, people and events, has not been lucid or wholly rational: "Wasn't I really out of my mind last month, and wasn't I sitting all that time in a madhouse somewhere, and am I not still there perhaps—so that it only seemed to me to have happened, and still only *seems* so?" The whirl of events, at the center of which both figuratively and literally is the whirling roulette wheel, has jolted him "out of all sense of proportion and feeling for measure" and sent him "spinning, spinning, spinning." Nothing is what it seems in Roulettenburg. All is deception.

Roulettenburg lies in the shadow of Schlangenberg, that is, "Snake Mountain," the highest elevation in the area. The ominous allusions of the mountain's name are not out of place. The city, in the symbolism of the novel, is in the power of the devil; people have lost their moral and spiritual freedom here. Belief in fate has replaced belief in God, and people are continually

yielding to temptation in their pursuit of gold. Furthermore, Dostoevsky identifies the act of gambling, or risk, with a suicidal leap, or "plunge." In *House
of the Dead* he speaks of the murderer's feverish delirium and enjoyment of
the "most unbridled and limitless freedom." He adds, significantly, that all
this is "perhaps similar to the sensation of a man who gazes down from a
high tower into the depths below until finally he would be glad to hurl himself
headlong down, as soon as possible, anything to put an end to it all!" In
his delirium, in his craving for risk, the gambler, like the raging murderer
or rebellious convict challenging their fate-bound universe, is overcome by
the same passion for the abyss. At the gambling tables, Aleksey experiences
an "instant of suspense, perhaps, sensation for sensation similar to that
experienced by Madame Blanchard in Paris when she plunged to the earth
from the balloon." He offers to leap off the Schlangenberg—a one-thousand-
foot drop—if Polina but gives the word. "Someday I will pronounce that
word," she remarks, "if only to see how you will pay up."

She tests him later when she suggests that he publicly insult the Baron
and Baroness Wurmerhelm, an act that for Aleksey is psychologically
analogous to leaping off the Schlangenberg: "You swore that you would leap
off the Schlangenberg; you swear that you are ready to murder if I order
it. Instead of all these murders and tragedies I want only to laugh." Aleksey
accepts her "challenge" and agrees to carry out that "crazy fancy." "Madame
la baronne," he exclaims in the confrontation scene, *"j'ai l'honneur d'être
votre esclave."* "The devil knows what urged me on?" Aleksey writes of this
incident. "It was as though I were flying down from a mountain." "I can't
understand what has happened to me," Aleksey writes again in imagery that
recalls the convict or murderer who runs amok, "whether I am really in a
frenzied state or simply have bolted from the road and am carrying on in
a vile way until I am tied up. Sometimes it seems to me that my mind is
disturbed."

Aleksey's reference to the devil—he is mentioned a number of times in
The Gambler—is not without deeper significance in the novel's symbolic
religious-philosophical context. The devil, indeed, may be said to have
prompted Aleksey to abandon all sense of measure and control and make
his leap into the abyss, his irrational underground challenge to fate. Later
he suggests, significantly, that he committed his capricious act out of
"despair."

The deeper meaning of this episode may be illuminated in part by
reference to the second temptation of Jesus in the legend of the Grand
Inquisitor. The devil suggests that Jesus cast himself down from the pinnacle
of the temple to prove that he is the son of God, "because it is said that the

angels would take hold and lift him up and he would not fall and hurt himself." But Jesus refuses to prove his faith in this way and thus buy men's allegiance. "O, Thou didst know then," declares the Grand Inquisitor, "that in taking one step, in making one movement to cast Thyself down, Thou wouldst be tempting God and have lost all thy faith in Him and wouldst have been dashed to pieces against the earth which Thou didst come to save." But the Grand Inquisitor insists that there are not many like Jesus. "And couldst Thou believe for one moment that men, too, could face such a temptation?" In refusing to leap, in refusing to tempt God and buy men's faith with miracle, Jesus affirms the "free decision of the heart," the principle of freedom that Dostoevsky found at the core of Christian faith.

Aleksey stands in relation to Polina as Jesus to the devil. But Aleksey fails the test that Jesus passes. "The devil knows what urged me on?" he wonders apropos of his irrational underground behaviour in the confrontation scene with the baron and baroness. Polina, like the devil in the "legend," certainly plays the role of temptress. Even if we assume (as does the Englishman Astley who may, indeed, reflect Polina's view) that she does not anticipate that Aleksey will "literally carry out her jesting wish," her suggestion nonetheless has the character of a challenge, and Aleksey is put to the test. But while Polina may be the devil's advocate, the ultimate responsibility rests with Aleksey. He *asks* his deity, his devil, to tempt him; and when she gives the command, he leaps—and falls. Aleksey's leap symbolizes his renunciation of free will. It is an act of despair that is comparable in its psychological and philosophical content to the Underground Man's irrational revolt against his "twice two is four" universe. It is an indication of his loss of faith in God and, therefore, in a universe in which man is free to choose between good and evil.

In a conversation with his employer, General Zagoryansky, who is outraged by Aleksey's behavior toward the baron and baroness, Aleksey bridles at the idea that he is answerable in his conduct to the general: "I only wish to clear up the insulting suggestion that I am under the tutelage of a person who supposedly has authority over my free will." The irony of Aleksey's remark—and Dostoevsky's intent is quite clear—is that he is lacking precisely in free will; in all his acts and behavior, he is caught up in an underground syndrome of negation and self-negation. His remark to the general signals indirectly his psychological dilemma: his subservience to Polina and, at the same time, his resentment over that state. "Please observe that I don't speak of my slavery because I wish to be your slave," he remarks to her, "but simply speak of it as a fact that doesn't depend upon me at all." Aleksey relates to Polina in the same rebellious yet rationalizing way that the Underground Man relates to the laws of nature that have been humiliating him.

As D. S. Savage has rightly observed, Aleksey "invests Polina with an authority which he refuses to invest in God. Polina must become God in relation to him or he must become God in relation to Polina—and God is the fatal demiurge of cosmic Necessity" ("Dostoevski: The Idea of *The Gambler*," *The Sewanee Review* 58 [1950]). We need only add that this god, in Dostoevsky's view, is not the God of Christianity, but the devil. And, in fact, Polina has become for Aleksey the surrogate for an implacable deterministic fate and as such arouses in him the opposing feelings of love and hate, adoration and revenge. Aleksey is a person who has forfeited his freedom to fate, and his underground relationship with Polina defines that disaster. His symbolic leap from Schlangenberg anticipates his leap at the gambling tables, his transformation into a compulsive gambler and convinced fatalist. At the end of his notes, the penniless gambler, who has renounced "every goal in life excepting winning at roulette," has driven even his memories from his head. He insists, "I shall rise from the dead." But there can be no future without a past. And just as Polina is not the devil—that is Aleksey's illusion—so Aleksey has no hope of salvation. He will never, like Jesus, "rise from the dead." He will never escape the tyranny of his self-created dead universe.

II

"Polina Aleksandrovna, on seeing me, asked why I had been so long, and without waiting for an answer went off somewhere. Of course, she did this deliberately," remarks Aleksey at the end of the first paragraph of the novel. "All the same, we must have an explanation. A lot of things have accumulated." The movement of *The Gambler*, on levels of plot, theme, character, and psychology, takes the reader from accumulated mystery and complication ("a lot of things have accumulated") through tension and expectation to release and disclosure. The center of everyone's concern is the accumulation of money.

At the outset of the novel everyone in General Zagoryansky's "retinue"— Polina, the Marquis de Grieux, Blanche de Cominges, and others—is waiting "in expectation" for news of the death of "Grandmamma" in Moscow and of a windfall legacy. Grandmamma arrives in place of the anticipated telegram, however, and loses huge sums of money at roulette, but she leaves the gambling tables at last and returns to Moscow. Zagoryansky's little retinue then begins to disintegrate. Blanche, who had been preparing to marry into a fortune, abandons the general and attaches herself to Aleksey who has made colossal winnings at the tables. The Marquis de Grieux, who had been anticipating Polina's legacy and had hoped to get back money he loaned to the general, deserts her. Polina, ill, goes off with the family of the Englishman Astley to live in the north of England. And the now confirmed gambler Aleksey, after a period of dissipation in Paris with Blanche and a "number of absurd blows of fate," finds himself back at zero dreaming of rising from the dead "tomorrow": "Let Polina know that I can still be a man."

Grandmamma is the structural and ideological center of *The Gambler*. She appears on the scene in the ninth chapter—the exact center of the novel—and dominates everybody around her. Like the roulette wheel, she is the center of attention of the main characters in the general's retinue, from the beginning to the end of the novel. All are gambling, as it were, on her death, hoping to resurrect their flagging fortunes. "*Il a du chance*," Blanche remarks apropos of the general toward the end of the novel. "Grandmamma is now really quite ill and will certainly die." Fate and death are joined in everybody's aspirations. The idea of hope in death in the fate-ruled universe of Roulettenburg parodies, of course, the truth of death and resurrection in Dostoevsky's Christian universe. But there is no resurrection for anybody in Roulettenburg; there is only moral and spiritual death, immersion in the river of Lethe where all memories are washed away.

Grandmamma is the only person in the novel who, figuratively speaking, rises from the dead. Her unexpected appearance on the scene, alive, foreshadows her ultimate escape from Roulettenburg and its moral and spiritual chaos. A dominating, imperial figure to all, she is humbled, finally, in her wilful attempt to conquer fate at the gambling tables. "Truly," she remarks, "God seeks out and punishes pride even in the old." But in her naive, simple, and earthy Russian way, she survives the storm of gambling passions, masters her own fate, and returns to Russia, where, significantly, she vows to carry out a promise she had made—to build a church. Like nature, she is full of excess, but also full of the powers of restoration. Grandmamma is for Dostoevsky both symbol and embodiment of Russia's wild abundance, its "breadth," and, at the same time, its rootedness and residual spiritual health.

The relationship between Aleksey and Polina forms the axis of the novel. The work begins with the enigma of their relationship and ends with its clarification. Their lives are complex and portrayed in a moment of crisis and transformation. At the outset of the novel the two characters are enigmas not only to the reader but to each other. Aleksey is continually puzzled by Polina's personality and behavior toward him: "Polina has always been an enigma to me." In turn, Polina's repeated questioning glances at Aleksey point to her deep puzzlement over his character and motivations as they pertain to her. In a certain sense Aleksey speaks for both of them when he confesses that "there was scarcely anything precise and definite" that he could say about his relations with her. The reader who turns to *The Gambler* for the first time would certainly share Aleksey's view of the relationship as "strange" and "incomprehensible." Yet there is no confusion in Dostoevsky's understanding of his characters.

At the outset of the story Aleksey and Polina face remarkably similar situations and relate to each other in quite similar ways. Both are in a state of dependency in the retinue of General Zagoryansky; both are in need of money, though for different reasons; and both place their hopes in roulette. Aleksey is hateful to Polina, but she needs him and is drawn toward him. Polina is hateful to Aleksey, but he is irresistibly drawn toward her and needs her for some deeper psychological reasons.

Polina, robbed of monies rightfully hers by her stepfather General Zagoryansky, in debt and in some kind of psychological or emotional bondage to de Grieux, is in desperate need of money: "I need some money at all costs; it must be got; otherwise I am simply lost." "I place almost all hope on roulette," she remarks pensively at one point. She has evidently borrowed some money and wants to return it. Polina's belief that she will win at roulette is linked with her feeling that she has "no other choice left." She wishes to settle accounts, literally and figuratively, with de Grieux, a man whom she had loved and idealized, but whom "for a long, long time" she has found "detestable." "Oh, he was not the same man before, a thousand times no, but now, but now!" she exclaims to Aleksey when she brings him the letter in which de Grieux as a parting gesture crudely pays her off, as it were, with a fifty thousand franc I.O.U. note. Could she have expected any other outcome, Aleksey asks. "I expected nothing," she replies in a quiet but trembling voice. "I made up my mind long ago; I read his mind and knew what he was thinking. He thought I would seek . . . that I would insist . . . I deliberately redoubled my contempt for him."

Wounded pride, contempt, and disillusionment (still touched by the dying fires of an infatuation) mark Polina's attitude toward de Grieux. Her reliance on roulette derives not only from her objective plight but from the despair of disillusionment. This despair is the origin of her need for Aleksey on the deepest level of their relationship. "Some time back, really a good two months ago," Aleksey notes, "I began to notice that she wanted to make a friend and confidante of me, and to a certain extent really made a try at it. But for some reason things never took off with us at that time; in fact we ended up instead with our present strange relations." In seeking a friend and confidante in Aleksey, Polina made a first step toward self-knowledge and recovery of her inner freedom. Yet it was not a friend that Aleksey sought in Polina. And her cool and at times even cruel behavior toward him was in large part a recognition of this, as it was also in part a reflex of the resentment and frustration she experienced in her relations with another egoist, de Grieux.

Aleksey, like Polina, sees in roulette his "only escape and salvation." For him, as for Polina, winning seems the "only solution." His need for money, too, is linked with a deep feeling of humiliation and entrapment. Polina's relationship toward de Grieux finds a parallel in Aleksey's toward Polina. But his sense of bondage and need for liberation has a particularly disturbing character; it points to a profound feeling of weakness and inadequacy. He seeks in roulette a "radical and decisive change" in his fate. Money for him is not an end in itself but a means. What he seeks in gambling is the restoration of a lost sense of being, self-determination, and mastery. Through money, through gambling, he imagines he will become a different man to Polina, will no longer be a zero and a slave. Yet it is precisely the craving for power, the need to "challenge fate," that poisons his relationship with Polina.

Dostoevsky, then, emphasizes the similarities in the psychological states of Aleksey and Polina. Both find themselves deeply humiliated: Polina before de Grieux and Aleksey before Polina and fate over which he wishes to triumph. Both are drawn toward each other, but the relationship is disfigured by psychological wounds, humiliations, and resentments on both sides. The key to a positive relationship lies in overcoming wounded pride, self-assertion, and the desire to inflict pain. The denouement of the story indicates that Polina is capable of taking this step but that Aleksey is doomed forever to remain in his underground.

III

It is possible to single out in the first pages of *The Gambler* Aleksey's two unconsummated passions: the first, his feverish passion for Polina; the second, his obsession with roulette (like Hermann in Pushkin's "Queen of Spades," Aleksey has never gambled before). But in a schematic way, we might say that Aleksey has an affair with Polina and an affair with lady luck. Toward the end of the story both affairs are consummated: Aleksey momentarily conquers lady luck in what amounts to an orgy at the gambling tables, and he spends a night with Polina. Both victories are fleeting, however, and they end in reversal and disaster for Aleksey. These two affairs or passions constitute in their interaction the psychological drama of Aleksey.

The reader easily distinguishes between Aleksey's two passions. What is far less apparent, initially, is their overlapping character in Aleksey's subconscious, that is, the manner in which Polina is drawn into the orbit of Aleksey's gambling obsession and made to serve as a surrogate for the lady luck he seeks to conquer. In a word, the image of Polina that emerges in Aleksey's notes is not merely a biased one; it is, as it were, clouded over by somebody else. "When we are awake we also do what we do in our dreams," remarks Nietzsche [in *Beyond Good and Evil*], "we invent and make up the person with whom we associate—and immediately forget it." The idea of Polina as a surrogate for an imperious, tantalizing, and, at the same time, cruelly inaccessible lady luck, or fate, is broadly hinted at the end of the first chapter in *The Gambler*. Aleksey ruminates on the nature of his feelings for Polina:

> And now once more I ask myself the question: do I love her? And once more I am not able to answer it, that is, rather, I answered once more for the hundredth time that I hated her. Yes, she had become hateful to me. There were moments (and precisely at the end of every one of our conversations) when I would have given half my life to strangle her! I swear if it had been possible slowly to sink a sharp knife in her breast, I think I would have seized it with pleasure. And yet I swear by all that is holy that if on that fashionable peak of the Schlangenberg she had indeed said to me, "cast yourself down," I should have done so immediately and with pleasure. I know this. One way or another the matter must be settled. She understands all this amazingly well, and the thought that I am clearly and thoroughly conscious of all her inaccessibility to me, of all the impossibility of fulfillment of my dreams—this thought, I am sure, gives her the most extraordinary pleasure; otherwise, could she, cautious and clever as she is, be on such terms of intimacy and frankness with me? I think that up to now she has looked upon me in the manner of the ancient empress who would disrobe in the presence of her slave, not considering him a man.

Aleksey's psychological portrait of Polina here scarcely accords with the real Polina. Her efforts, two months earlier, to establish more intimate and frank relations with him were certainly not based on a desire to humiliate him. She had sought in him a friend and confidante but had found instead a man who neither respected himself nor her, who cast himself in the role of an obedient but deeply resentful slave. "I can't endure that 'slave' theory of yours," she remarks. Aleksey is in the grip of an obsession that only nominally involves the real Polina. He regards her as inaccessible. She is, of course, not inaccessible to the Aleksey she imagines, or hopes, him to be. But she is certainly inaccessible to the Aleksey who cannot relate to her in any other way than that of a slave or despot. She certainly finds hateful the vindictive slave who sees in her an almost impersonal object of love and hate, who sees her as an imperious ancient empress who has been humiliating him and whom he must vanquish in order to become a different man. *That* ancient empress is not some Cleopatra, but fate—lady luck who flaunts her riches before the rabble. Aleksey's passion for this empress psychologically structures and defines his erotic passion for Polina.

Abjectly and resentfully—characteristically in Joban terms—Aleksey speaks of his relationship with Polina: "Since I am her slave and completely insignificant in her eyes, she feels no offense at my coarse curiosity. But the point is that while she permits me to ask questions, she does not answer them. At times she doesn't even take notice of them. That's how things are between us!" That is how things are between the despairing Job and God. But while Job ultimately recognizes the true face of God, Aleksey in his spiritual rebellion and psychological blindness never really recognizes the real Polina, at least not until the fatal resolution of his crisis when it is too late.

The psychological character of Aleksey's relationship to Polina and the ancient empress, fate, may be elucidated against the background of Hermann's relationship to the old countess and her maid-in-waiting Lizaveta in Pushkin's profound and seminal work, *Queen of Spades*. The impact of this work upon *The Gambler* is at least as deep as it is upon *Crime and Punishment*. At the center of Pushkin's story is an affair that Hermann—an ambitious but parsimonious officer who has the "soul of a gambler"—has with a servant girl and with fate. In Pushkin's story fate is incarnated in the figure of an aged countess (the image of a grotesque card queen of spades) who possesses the secret of three winning cards. In order to gain entrance to the bedroom quarters of the old countess, Hermann strikes up an outwardly passionate, though spurious love affair with the countess's maid-in-waiting, Lizaveta. In a midnight encounter with the countess (the result of arranging a rendezvous with Lizaveta) Hermann implores her to give him her secret of the winning cards, importunes her, waves his pistol before her, but to no avail. The countess dies of fright. Later she comes to him in a dream and tells him the secret. The story ends with Hermann's defeat—following two victories—at the gambling tables. "The queen of spades signifies secret ill will," reads Pushkin's epigraph to his story.

The amoral character of Hermann's gambling passion is manifested not only in his encounter with the old countess—a meeting that discloses his disordered psychology and utilitarian outlook—but in his heartless manipulation of the feelings of Lizaveta. "You are a monster!" she cries to him in their arranged tryst immediately after the countess's death. His motives have become apparent to her. "I did not wish her death," he replies, indifferent to the girl who but a little while earlier had been the object of passionate avowals of love. For the egotist Hermann, Lizaveta is but an incidental sacrifice in his quest for power and wealth. This "hardened soul" feels no pangs of conscience either for the old countess or for Lizaveta.

Hermann masks his gambling passion under a simulated passion for Lizaveta. He quite consciously employs this deception to gain entrance to the dwelling of his real lover—lady luck, fate, the old countess. The object of Aleksey's passion is also lady luck, but she is not incarnated in any independent figure or symbol in his drama (there is an allusion to her, of course, in the reference to the ancient empress). Pushkin's play with the fantastic—or play with the real and fantastic—becomes pure theater of the unconscious in Dostoevsky. What Dostoevsky does in *The Gambler* is endow Polina with the function of a fate-figure in Aleksey's unconscious. Lizaveta and the old countess, as it were, merge there into one person.

Aleksey's relation to Polina as a fate-figure is almost identical with Hermann's relation to the mysterious countess. Both Polina and the countess, in the view of their suitors, withhold their favor. Aleksey's comparison of Polina with the imperious ancient empress who expresses her contempt for her slave by calmly undressing in front of him defines what he feels to be Polina's attitude toward him as a lover and—on the plane of his unconscious —as a fate-figure. This is an obvious reminiscence on Dostoevsky's part of the midnight scene in "Queen of Spades" in which Hermann, concealed in the countess's bedroom, is witness to the "repulsive mysteries of her toilet" as she undresses before her mirror.

In a variety of ways Pushkin brings out the unconscious erotic dimension in this episode; indeed, Hermann is compared to a lover of the countess's youth. Hermann now slavishly petitions the countess on his knees, now despotically threatens her with his pistol in his quest for a "favor," the "happiness of his life," the secret of the three cards. He appeals to the countess as "wife, lover, and mother." Though he recognizes that her secret may be linked with a "terrible sin, with the ruination of eternal bliss, with a devil's contract," he announces that he is prepared to take on her sin. As we have noted, the countess does not yield her riches to her impassioned and frustrated suitor. He is not rewarded at this moment by lady luck any more than Aleksey's erotic interests are rewarded immediately by Polina. Hermann is rewarded by the countess when she comes to him in a dream and tells him the secret of the three cards. Aleksey, too, wants his "empress" to come to him. "I was not at all troubled by her fate," he remarks about Polina apropos of the moment Grandmamma was about to gamble away her fortune. "I wanted to fathom her secrets. I wanted her to come to me and say, 'I really love you.'" Polina will, indeed, come to Aleksey and provide the psychological motive for him to rush off confidently to the gambling tables and make his colossal winnings. His erotic strivings will be consummated when he returns to his room where Polina is waiting for him.

In outwardly different but psychologically analogous ways, then, Pushkin and Dostoevsky recognize the interaction of the erotic and gambling impulses in their heroes. In *The Gambler*, the psychosexual dimension of Aleksey's gambling passion is openly expressed in his relationship with Polina. Yet in the deepest sense, Aleksey's passion for Polina is no greater than Hermann's interest in Lizaveta. Hermann simulates a passion for Lizaveta; when she no longer serves as an accessory to his gambling passion, he becomes indifferent to her. It seems to Aleksey that he is in love with Polina and that he cannot live without her. But in fact she is only a stand-in for lady luck. When he recognizes lady luck, when he recognizes his gambling passion and succumbs to it at the tables, his passion for Polina vanishes. He no longer needs the real Polina. He has found lady luck.

IV

The dramatic denouement of Aleksey's affair with Polina and lady luck is as brilliant in execution as in conception. At a critical moment in Polina's destiny, after Grandmamma's huge losses at the tables and at the time de Grieux abandons Polina, Aleksey pens the following note to her:

> Polina Aleksandrovna, I see clearly that the denouement is at hand which will of course affect you too. For the last time I repeat: do you or do you not need my life? If I can be of use, be it *in any way*—dispose of me as you see fit, and meanwhile I will remain in my room, most of the time at least, and not go out anywhere. If it is necessary, write or send for me.
>
> (chap. 13)

Shortly after this note is delivered, Polina turns up in Aleksey's room, pale and somber. He cries out, startled, amazed. "What's the matter? What's the matter?" Polina asks. "You ask what's the matter?" he replies. "You? here, in my room!" Aleksey's expression of amazement inaugurates a scene—the climax of their relationship—which is marked by a dramatic reversal of his whole notion of her attitude toward him. "If I come, then I come in my *entirety*," Polina remarks. "It's a habit with me."

The scene is a significant one. At a critical moment in Polina's life Aleksey impulsively offers her everything that a lover could offer, the maximum of devotion: his life. In turn, Polina comes to him in her entirety and offers him her life. In the language of the gambling tables both are staking or risking all. But are the wagers equal in value? The action that follows clearly points to the radically different values of the wagers. Polina's gamble, at its deepest level, involves a throwing off of pride, a breaking out from the underground tangle of her relationship with de Grieux and Aleksey, an attempt to find salvation not in roulette, but in a human relationship based upon mutual respect. Her earlier offers to share her winnings at the gambling table were symbolic of the kind of relationship she sought. In coming to Aleksey she is making herself vulnerable—the sine qua non in any genuine human relationship—she is risking annihilation to gain a friend, that is, to win Aleksey. Her gamble contemplates neither a play for power nor the annihilation of somebody else's wager.

Aleksey's gamble, on the other hand, on the psychological plane, turns out to be the same as all his other gambles: an affirmation of ego. He wishes only a signal from Polina and he will make his suicidal and murderous leap. His offer to help Polina only masks his desire to win the favor of lady luck and obtain a momentary illusion of freedom and power. Recalling his triumphant win at the gambling tables, he remarks significantly: "I staked my whole life." His pledge of his life to Polina, then, involves not only a symbolic self-annihilation but the annihilation of Polina, her hopes and her high stakes, her last desperate gamble on his love.

In his room Polina shows Aleksey the letter from de Grieux in which he offers her her stepfather's I.O.U. note to be used against him. "Oh," Polina cries out, "with what happiness would I now throw into his vile face those fifty thousand francs and spit at them . . . and grind the spit in!" Aleksey, groping for ways in which Polina can settle accounts with de Grieux, comes up with, among other things, the proposal that she turn to Astley for fifty thousand francs. "What, dost thou thyself really want me to go from thee to that Englishman?" she cries, looking into Aleksey's face with "a piercing glance" and smiling bitterly. "She called me 'thou' for the first time in my life," he recalls. "It seemed to me that she was dizzy with emotion at that moment, and she sat down suddenly on the sofa, as if worn out." Aleksey remembers thinking at this point, "Why, she loves me! She came *to me* and not to Mr. Astley." The inner content of Polina's gamble for Aleksey is manifested, of course, in her use of the familiar pronoun "thou." But the desperate nature of her gamble is evidenced by her dizziness; literally, "her head was spinning."

Aleksey's notion that Polina is hostile to him is shattered here. The foundations are laid, we might imagine, for a positive denouement to this strange relationship: the slave is loved and there is no longer any need for self-assertion. Yet Aleksey's actions at this crucial point only confirm that his conception of himself as a slave and of Polina as some kind of arrogant ancient empress is rooted in deep, ineradicable psychological necessities. He does not want the love of Polina on the terms of equality that she offers. He does not desire a real human partnership. "She came to me," he recalls. "I still don't understand it." Like the Underground Man, Aleksey can understand love only as a slave or despot. In part, Aleksey had invented Polina. He had mistaken the surface Polina for the real Praskovya, just as Polina had mistaken de Grieux—in the sarcastic words of Aleksey—for an "Apollo of Belvedere."

In order to distinguish "beauty of soul and originality of personality," Aleksey rightly observes, a person needs "independence and freedom." The inexperienced and basically unsophisticated Russian girl Praskovya is attracted to the external elegance and form of the counterfeit Marquis de Grieux even though this beauty is only a part of her imagination. She "takes this form as his own soul," Aleksey remarks, "as the natural form of his heart and soul, and not as dress that he has inherited." But this elegant, "finished, beautiful form," in the deepest spiritual sense, is "no form at all." Aleksey correctly diagnoses the debacle of Polina's affair with de Grieux: she has been carried away by a false notion of beauty and form, but what another hero of Dostoevsky, the ridiculous man, has called the "beauty of the lie." "It is only among Frenchmen," Aleksey remarks sarcastically, "that form has been so well defined that it is possible to appear with extraordinary dignity and yet be quite a scoundrel."

Polina's near loss of identity in the face of the assault of superficial Western culture, her spiritual immaturity, and, to a certain extent, her corruption are signaled in the novel by her use of the Latinized form of her name, Polina. Yet in the case of the Russian heroine, authentic form—all that relates to organic Russian nature and intelligence—lies within. Significantly, it is Grandmamma, the only character in the novel who embodies the element of Muscovite directness and naturalness, who addresses Polina as "Praskovya." "I might get fond of you, Praskovya. . . . You're a fine girl, better than all the others, and you sure have a strong will, I'll say! Well, I have a will, too; now turn around: that's not a switch you're wearing, is it?" Polina answers that it is her own hair, and Grandmamma puts in: "Good,

I don't like the silly fashions that are current. You're very pretty. I would fall in love with you if I were a young gentleman. Why don't you get married?"

It is Grandmamma who recognizes the authentic Praskovya beneath the surface Polina. Aleksey, who clearly perceives that Polina was taken in by de Grieux's elegant form, ironically is unable to respond to the authentic Praskovya when she turns to him for help. Polina seeks out in him a friend and confidante at a moment when her relationship with de Grieux is crumbling; later she turns to him in desperation and reveals her deep attraction to him. But in her moment of crucial need he deserts her. Polina is necessary to Aleksey, ultimately, only as ground for a limitless egoism. Thus, when she reaches out to him in need and offers him the possibility of love, he instinctively interprets her gesture as a signal from his deity to make his long-awaited leap for power. A "wild idea" flashed through his mind: "Polina! Give me only one hour! Wait here only an hour and . . . I will return! It's . . . it's necessary! You will see!" Aleksey's idea, significantly, is linked with an inner feeling of something "fatal, necessary, predestined."

Polina, of course, has already offered Aleksey his hour by publicly compromising herself and coming to his room. But what Aleksey wants is an hour with lady luck. What he wants is what only gambling can give him: the momentary illusion of power. In essence, Aleksey exchanges happiness with Polina for luck at the tables. "And I rushed out of the room without answering her astonished, questioning glance; she called out something after me, but I did not go back." That questioning glance is one of many that Polina directs at Aleksey, particularly in their last meeting. These glances reveal the extent of Polina's own perplexity over the nature of Aleksey's strange behavior and psychology. More than any words, they reveal to the reader not a domineering ancient empress sadistically bent on tormenting a passionate lover, but a confused and troubled Russian girl who has not yet fully learned to look beneath surface appearances into the moral-psychological underground.

V

Aleksey's state of mind at the gambling tables is frenzied to the point of madness. There is an intoxicated, orgiastic quality about these moments. His winnings are colossal. This kind of storming of the heavens evokes fear in those around him. Two Jews standing by him warn him to leave: "You are bold! You are very bold!" But Aleksey, like the Underground Man rushing off in pursuit of Zverkov, is "driven on by fate"; he speaks of the "arrogance of chance," the "craving for risk." As he sets off for the hotel, finally, in the darkness, staggering under the sheer weight of the gold he is carrying, he has no thoughts in his head: "I experienced only some kind of fearful sense of pleasure—of success, victory, power." He is conscious that he is going back to Polina, but only "to tell her, show her . . . but I scarcely remembered what she had been saying to me a while ago, and why I had gone, and all those recent feelings of just an hour and a half before seemed to me now something long past, long since taken care of, obsolete—which we would no longer remember because now everything would begin anew."

Aleksey is not thinking as he emerges from the gambling halls. Rather he is feeling the sum total of his experience. The image of Polina, significantly, rises out of the sensations of success, victory, power; he is going to show her the gold, the symbol of his achievement, the evidence that he is no longer a zero. There is an infantile exhibitionism about Aleksey's actions here. There is also a sense of change in his life, as though the experience at the gambling tables had been traumatic and had opened up a new phase in his psychic existence. The words "now everything will begin anew" are ambiguous: seemingly directed toward Polina, they actually point toward an awareness of a radical internal crisis and transformation. Not without reason does Aleksey later remark: "My life has broken into two."

Returning to his hotel room, Aleksey throws the money on the table before Polina. "I remembered she looked into my face with frightful intentness." These words, which open chapter fifteen, strike the keynote for the unfolding scene as far as Polina is concerned: her increasing doubt about Aleksey and about the real nature of his feelings and words. Her glance literally pursues Aleksey throughout their last encounter. As he rushes about, almost completely oblivious of her, tidying up his piles of money and gold, Aleksey notes, she is "attentively" watching him, with a strange expression on her face. "I did not like that look! I do not err in saying that there was hatred in it." When Aleksey suggests that Polina take fifty thousand francs and throw it in de Grieux's face, she does not answer but bursts into the kind of mocking laughter that had always greeted his "most passionate declarations." Her laughter, always defensive in character, now points to her growing disillusionment and despair with Aleksey. At last, he writes, she stops and frowns, looking at Aleksey sternly. De Grieux had sought to cancel his sense of obligation to Polina with an I.O.U. note. Aleksey's proposal, in turn, seems to put the cash sign before their relationship. "You think you can buy my respect with money, if not me myself," Polina had remarked to Aleksey in an earlier episode in the novel. Polina refuses the money.

Aleksey seems incapable of understanding Polina's refusal, however. Puzzled by her response, he counters: "I offer it to you as a friend; I offer you my life." But life is not to be measured by the weight of gold or the gambler's bravado at the tables. Again, Aleksey notes, "she looked at me with a long and searching glance, as if she wanted to transfix me with it." Polina is not a commodity to be bought and sold. "You are setting a high price," she says with a bitter smile, "de Grieux's lover is not worth fifty thousand francs," "Polina, how can you talk that way with me?" Aleksey cries reproachfully. "Am I de Grieux?" Of course, that is precisely the question Polina has been trying to resolve: is he any different from de Grieux? "I hate you! Yes . . . yes!" she exlaims. But then she equates him with de Grieux in another way: "I don't love you any more than I love de Grieux." Her paradoxical manner of expressing her hate reveals her deeply conflicting feelings over Aleksey, and indeed even over de Grieux, the man toward whom she had "redoubled her contempt."

In this last encounter with Aleksey, however, it is not hatred, contempt, or even wounded pride that emerges as the dominant note, but a desperate appeal for love, for support, for a genuine human partnership. This is not the Polina that the reader first perceived through the eyes of Aleksey at the beginning of his notes. In this last encounter with him she seems delirious, ill. For a brief moment, under the strain of an emotional crisis as profound as that of Aleksey's, she reveals both her inner wounded pride and her deepest, hitherto concealed, hopes. "Buy me! Do you want to? Do you want to? for fifty thousand francs, like de Grieux?" she gasped between convulsive sobs. But, significantly, she continues to use the familiar form "thou." Aleksey embraces her, kisses her hands, feet, falls on his knees before her. Her hysteria passes. "She placed both her hands on my shoulders and examined me intently; it seemed that she wanted to read something in my face. . . . An expression of concern and contemplation appeared on her face." Polina draws him toward her, and then pushes him away, and again "took up examining me with a somber look." Then she suddenly embraces him:

> "But you do love me, you do love me, don't you?" she said; "after all, after all you . . . you wanted to fight with the baron for me!" And suddenly she burst out into laughter, as though something amusing and nice suddenly flickered in her memory. She was crying and laughing all at once. Well, what could I do. I was myself almost delirious. I remember she began to say something to me, but I could understand almost nothing of what she said. It was a kind of delirium, a kind of incoherent babble, as though she wanted to tell me something as quickly as possible, delirium interrupted sometimes by the merriest laughter, which began to

frighten me. "No, no, you are sweet, sweet!" she repeated. "You are my faithful one!" And again she put her hands on my shoulders, again began looking at me closely and repeated: "You love me . . . love me . . . You will love me?" I did not take my eyes off her; I had never before seen her in these fits of tenderness and love; it is true, of course, that this was delirium, but . . . on noticing my look of passion she suddenly began to smile slyly.

(chap. 15)

This extraordinary scene lays bare the pro and contra of Polina's feelings toward Aleksey. Her words express tenderness and love, but her questioning glances express her deep doubts and uncertainties—all that she had previously masked in coldness and contempt. Polina's swan song of love— for that is what it is—is full of a frenzied will to believe something that she knows in her heart to be false; it is a last delirious gamble, a last gambler's illusion that forms a counterpart to Aleksey's delirious gamble at the tables— his passionate wooing of lady luck. For his part, Aleksey can understand almost nothing of what she is saying. But his problem in understanding is not merely due to Polina's incoherence; it is deeply rooted in a neurotic gambling passion that has consumed all his psychic energies.

Polina's half-believing, half-despairing lovemaking evokes no reciprocal mood of love or tenderness in Aleksey—only a "look of passion." The protestations of love, the impulsive gestures of tenderness, the physical advances come almost entirely from Polina. Except for one moment when he tries to calm her and falls on his knees before her (the gesture is symbolic), his behavior is passive and his mood almost disbelieving. "I wanted her to come to me and say, 'I really love you,'" Aleksey confided earlier in his notebook. "And if not, if this madness is unthinkable, well then, . . . well, what was I to wish for? Do I really know what I wish? I'm like a person without any perspectives; all I want is to be near her, in her aura, in her radiance, eternally, always, all my life. More than this I don't know! And could I possibly go away from her?" Polina does come and say "I love you." But Aleksey goes off to gamble, and when he returns for the last time, he does not understand her words. Aleksey's whole response to Polina in this episode suggests that he has confused her with the aura of radiance of somebody else, that is, with the dazzling ancient empress, lady luck.

At one point in the episode Polina impulsively embraces Aleksey and exclaims, "We'll go away, we really will go away tomorrow, won't we? And we'll catch up with Grandmamma, don't you think?" To catch up with Grandmamma, of course, is to go back to Moscow—back to Russian soil, Russian nationality, Russian identity, and away from the artificial, rootless, spiritually dead world of Roulettenburg. Russia, in Dostoevsky's ideological design, means spiritual salvation. Polina's hope that Aleksey will take her back to Russia is an illusion. He will be heading not to Moscow, but to the Sodom and Gomorrah of Paris—and not with Polina, but with the radiant Blanche. Polina is, indeed, delirious, on the brink of illness. After another fit of laughter, Aleksey writes, "she suddenly was kissing and embracing me again, passionately and tenderly pressing her face to mine. I no longer thought of anything or heard anything. My head was spinning. . . . I think it was about seven in the morning when I came to my senses."

The night of sex, clearly, does not dissolve the underlying tensions between Aleksey and Polina: conjunctive, physically, it gives expression to a thoroughly disjunctive emotional relationship. For both, it is the denouement of a delusion in which each has mistaken the other for somebody else. In the morning, after three minutes of looking out of the window, Polina turns to Aleksey with loathing and fury, flings the money in his face, and leaves. This action not only points eloquently to the tragedy of loveless sex but climaxes a relationship that on every level must be considered a paradigm of human understanding. Aleksey, characteristically, does not comprehend her behavior. He can only conclude that Polina is "out of her mind." Was it "wounded pride" or "despair," he wonders, that brought her to him. Vanity, he is sure, prompted her "not to trust in me and to insult me." And then, of course, it all happened in a "state of delirium."

Aleksey's ponderings are deeply evasive, egotistical, and lacking in any insight into Polina. What is chiefly noticeable is the absence of any feeling for her. His last act before leaving his room—he hurriedly tucks his whole heap of gold into his bed and covers it—symbolizes the change that has taken place in him since winning at the gambling tables. When he later learns of Polina's illness and of the possibility of her death, he takes account of the changes in himself:

> I was sorry for Polina, I swear, but it's strange—from the very moment I touched the gambling table last night and began to rake in packs of money, my love retreated, as it were, into the background. I say this now, but at the time I still didn't see all this clearly. Is it possible that I really am a gambler, is it possible that I really . . . love Polina so strangely? No, to this day I still love her, as God will witness.
>
> (chap. 15)

Aleksey's orgy at the gambling tables engulfs him completely. He becomes an obsessive gambler. He discovers his true passion—the pursuit of lady luck—and with that discovery, his driving passion for Polina vanishes.

Aleksey's gamble for lady luck and his emotional crisis are paralleled by Polina's gamble for Aleksey and her ensuing crisis and illness. Yet the outcomes of these crises are different. Aleksey wins his gamble at the tables and "breaks in two"; the conflict between the man with hidden moral convictions and the pathological gambler ends in the victory of the latter. In a certain sense, Aleksey does become a different man. Polina, for her part, loses her gamble for Aleksey but retains her integrity. At the very moment Aleksey ceases to regard her as a fate-figure, the incubus of demonism is lifted from her. The hopeful, though by no means optimally positive resolution of her drama—for Dostoevsky this would mean a return to Russia and to her roots—is suggested by her joining the family of the eminently decent Astley in England and, later, in Switzerland.

In contrast, the psychological and spiritual catastrophe of Aleksey is symbolized by his capitulation to the courtesan Blanche, a carnivalesque embodiment of lady luck, a new fate-figure in his life. He goes with her to Paris, where he spends much of his time lying on a couch. "Is it possible I am such a child?" he wonders at the end of his notes. The slave of Polina becomes the "*vil esclave*," the "*fils*," and the "*bon enfant*" of Blanche, the truly infernal woman of the novel. Not without reason does Aleksey refer to Blanche as a "devil" and speak of her face as "diabolical." She is indeed the very incarnation of the beauty of the lie. Aleksey, who so clearly perceives that Polina had been taken in by the superficial elegance and form of de Grieux, is himself taken in by the demon of emptiness and banality, Blanche. She was "beautiful to look at," Aleksey observes. But he remarks further that "she has one of those faces that can be terrifying . . . her eyes are black, with yellowing whites, her glance is bold, her teeth extremely white, and her lips always painted; her perfume is musky. . . . She sometimes laughs aloud, showing all her teeth, but usually sits silent with an insolent stare."

Aleksey's capitulation to Blanche symbolizes on the religious-philosophical plane of the novel his falling away from God. "For as soon as the human soul despairs of God," Vyacheslav Ivanov has written, "it is irresistibly drawn to chaos: it finds joy in all that is ugly and warped, and is greeted, from the deepest ravines of Sodom, by the smile of a beauty that seeks to rival the beauty of Our Lady" (*Freedom and the Tragic Life*, trans. Norman Cameron).

Aleksey, now basically indifferent to anything outside of gambling, does not stay long with Blanche. In a final encounter with the Englishman Astley, Aleksey learns that Polina had loved him. "You are a lost man," Astley tells him. "You've grown numb, you have not only renounced your life, your own interests, and those of society, your duty as a citizen and a man, your friends . . . you have not only renounced every goal except that of winning, but you have even renounced your memories." The special mention of memory here is significant. "Insofar as it is 'forgotten,' the 'past'—historical or primordial—is homologized with death," Mircea Eliade has written in connection with the ancient Greek understanding of memory and forgetting. "The fountain Lethe, 'forgetfulness,' is a necessary part of the realm of Death. The dead are those who have lost their memories" ("Mythologies of Memory and Forgetting," *History of Religions* 11, no. 2 [1963]). For Dostoevsky lss of memory implies a static view of the universe and, ultimately, moral and spiritual death. In turn, restoration of memory—recollection—is linked with a dynamic understanding of human destiny and ultimately a vision of Christian truth and a perception of eternal renewal.

Aleksey's renunciation of his memories is symptomatic of his spiritual disintegration. He speaks of himself as dead but can conceive of resurrection only in terms that parody Christian theological reality. "Tomorrow," he insists, "I can be resurrected from the dead and once again begin to live." But he is dying in a spiritual sense. "Is it possible that I do not realize that I myself am a lost man?" The terminology of Christian salvation, however, returns to his lips (in the deepest regions of his unconscious, of course, he has not forgotten the vision of truth). He is certain that he can "rise again." "In one hour I can change my whole fate." He has in mind, however, salvation at the gambling tables, a new challenge to fate. His final words and the final words of the novel, "tomorrow, tomorrow all will be over," testify to his determination once again, like the Underground Man, to hurl himself against the wall of fate. But on the deeper plane of the novel's meaning, these same words signify the despair of unbelief and the unconscious recognition that in a fate-ruled universe there is no tomorrow, but only a meaningless finality: death without resurrection. Not without reason did Dostoevsky speak of the gambler's world as "a special kind of hell, a special kind of prison 'bath.'"

SERGEI HACKEL

The Religious Dimension: Vision or Evasion? Zosima's Discourse in The Brothers Karamazov

THE PROPHET ACCLAIMED

Dostoevsky took pleasure in telling his wife that he had been acclaimed as a prophet by at least some of his Muscovite audience on 8 June 1880, when he gave his celebrated Pushkin speech. He had conjured up an atmosphere of euphoria and exultation: the epithet was not necessarily intended to survive the occasion. And yet it has survived. In various contexts and with various qualifications Dostoevsky's "gift for prophecy" is still discussed. Although Dostoevsky himself occasionally felt impelled to speak of a capacity for foresight, it is more often a gift for prophetic insight which will be attributed to him. But whatever the nature of the gift, its mere possession would not guarantee judicious use of it. The best heresies are likely to be propagated by prophets, whose identity as "false prophets in sheep's clothing" may not be perceived until it is too late. If Dostoevsky is indeed to be designated as prophet in some sense, how Orthodox—indeed, how Christian—was his message? Questions of this kind were already being posed by such contemporaries of his as Konstantin Leontyev. A century later there is still room for a fresh consideration of them.

The cry "prophet" could not have startled Dostoevsky unduly on 8 June since he had already been receiving some acclaim as such on the eve. Members of the audience, so he told his wife, came crowding in on him during the interval of yet another ceremonial meeting. "You are our prophet," they told him. "You made us into better people when we read the

From New Essays on Dostoevsky, edited by Malcolm V. Jones and Garth M. Terry. © 1983 by Cambridge University Press.

Karamazovs." "In a word," added Dostoevsky in his letter home, "I was left convinced that the Karamazovs have colossal significance."

Dostoevsky's own association of the designation "prophet" with *The Brothers Karamazov*, the nature of the book, the place it occupies at the very peak of his career, together help to justify its being singled out for study when his religious views require to be discussed. In its turn, that section of the novel which Dostoevsky—in an unprecedented fashion—segregated from the narrative proper and limited largely to religious discourse cannot but provide a natural focus for a discussion of this kind.

THE TEXT WITHIN THE TEXT

The passage in question, which consists of the elder Zosima's memoirs and admonitions, is exceptional also in its undisguised didacticism. At several removes the speaker may be said to participate in some kind of dialogue and dialectic with other characters in the novel. But in itself the passage manifestly lacks that vitality and polyphonic richness in which the novel as a whole abounds. Bakhtin attempted to define the section as "hagiographical": Dostoevsky was using his "*zhitiynoye slovo*" ("hagiographical discourse"). The phrase presumably referred less to the form of the section than to its manner and assumptions. In particular Bakhtin might have noted the author's manifest dependence on the credulity of his readers or, equally important, his manifest aim to make them into "better people."

Dostoevsky himself certainly claimed to have such an aim. The blasphemy of Ivan Karamazov, he assured N. A. Lyubimov on 10 May 1879, was to be "triumphantly rejected": he was working on its refutation ("The Russian monk") with "fear, trepidation and awe," for his task was to be considered as nothing other than "a civic feat" ("*grazhdanskim podvigom*"). Statements of this kind could be quoted from other letters of the time, some addressed to the same correspondent (his publisher's editor), others to K. P. Pobedonostsev, all of them commanding some respect.

Dostoevsky's "fear, trepidation and awe" involved a certain anxiety about his future audience. In one of his letters to Pobedonostsev, written in August 1879 when "The Russian monk" was about to appear, he mentioned Zosima's teachings "at which people will simply shout that they are absurd, since too elated." He added, "They are of course absurd in the everyday sense, but in another, inner sense, they seem justified." But he concluded, "In any case I am very worried." It may have been this worry which led him to wrap up his elder's text in layer upon layer of narrative devices.

It could be said that the neighbouring and closely related "Legend of the Grand Inquisitor" is also cocooned. But at least that has a single narrator, who is also its "author," while the novel's official narrator plays no part in its presentation. By contrast, Zosima's discourse is introduced by this narrator; it comprises Alyosha Karamazov's written, revised and retrospective account of what Zosima may have said on more than one occasion; and it in turn introduces Zosima's retrospective account of conversations with Markel, the young man in the woods, or the Mysterious Visitor. Thus introduced, the Mysterious Visitor dwells on his own distant past. The authenticity and effectiveness of each layer are reduced the further each is removed from Zosima's cell and the time of his impending death. Given the nineteenth-century attitude to the revelatory character of "last words," this distancing could well have been avoided. In all respects there is a curious, untypical and untoward dissipation of intensity involved. It is almost as if the ultimate narrator, Dostoevsky himself, is seeking to absolve himself from at least some responsibility for his elder's teaching, however much he claimed "completely" to agree with it.

Even to interrupt and so retard the narration was hardly typical of Dostoevsky. Although one or another of his literary models may have suggested and sanctioned the device, Dostoevsky must still have willed to use it for reasons of his own. One of these models may have been the monk Parfeny's travel tales, which Dostoevsky both possessed and treasured (*Skazaniye o stranstvii i puteshestvii po Rossii, Moldavii, Turtsii i Svyatoy Zemli* . . . [Moscow, 1856]): certainly Zosima's style owed something to Parfeny, as Dostoevsky openly acknowledged. In the third volume of Parfeny's work the evenly paced narration is suddenly interrupted by a heading in Gothic type: this paves the way for a "separate" discourse, thirty-four pages long, on a Siberian starets, Daniil. The heading itself contains at least one phrase which is echoed in the heading of Alyosha's piece. But it is the formal rather than the thematic parallel which deserves to be noted. Of equal interest is the break in the narrative of Hugo's *Les Misérables* to which S. Linnér has drawn attention [in *Starets Zosima in* The Brothers Karamazov]. Hugo's device is all the more pertinent since it is employed to give prominence to the teachings of a saintly cleric: these are allotted two short chapters entitled "Ce qu'il croyait" and "Ce qu'il pensait." It is well known that Dostoevsky loved *Les Misérables*. But whether or not Hugo influenced the form adopted for Zosima's teachings is ultimately of minor importance compared with the influence which he may have had on other aspects of the work. These remain to be discussed below.

AMVROSY'S BOOKS AND OTHER SOURCES

The separateness of Zosima's teachings is modified to some degree by the way in which they are anchored in the early pages of the novel, where the character of Zosima is established and a setting is provided for him. The setting, at least, gained considerably in authenticity since a significant proportion of the circumstantial and atmospheric detail is derived from Dostoevsky's visit to the monastery at Optina Pustyn in the summer of 1877. The visit was brief (26–27 June), he had only three occasions to encounter the famous starets Amvrosy (two of them, admittedly, in semi-private), and it could hardly be said that he emerged from Optino as an expert on monasticism in general or on *startsy* in particular. But as always there were books to supplement his experience. He acquired two general books on the monastery. He could also draw on Parfeny's account of an earlier pilgrimage on which the itinerant monk was able to meet starets Leonid. On Leonid himself he possessed the standard biography. As important, at one time or another he obtained some of the spiritual writings which were published, popularized or (at the very least) approved by the community at Optino, among them sermons by Symeon the New Theologian, a work on repentance by Mark the Ascetic, and a commentary on Psalm 6 by Anastasios of Sinai. It seems likely that many of these works, if not all, were gifts from starets Amvrosy, who always had copies of them available for his "more honoured visitors." More important of all may have been Dostoevsky's acquisition of Isaac of Syria's Ascetic Discourses, elegantly translated into Russian from the Greek under the title *Slova podvizhnicheskiya*. Mere possession of such works did not necessarily safeguard him against a distorted presentation of Orthodox monastic life or attitudes any more than his brief and exceptional visit to Optino. But at least he was in a position to draw on some primary sources of considerable dignity and importance when he felt impelled to do so.

The same may be said of Biblical texts. In view of Zosima's own insistence that Bible readings should play a greater part in the spiritual education of the Russian people, it is not surprising that he himself incorporates at least some scriptural quotations and, more often, references into his discourse. He dwells for some time on the story of Job, and mention is made of several other narratives from the Old Testament. The New Testament is also used as a point of reference. The parable of Lazarus and the rich man plays a significant part in Zosima's discussion of hell, and several of his sayings involve a paraphrase of New Testament texts. Two sentences are quoted in the young Zosima's discussion with the Mysterious Visitor; and one of these, indeed, provides the entire novel with its epigraph. Even so, the list is surprisingly short. The text is hardly saturated with scriptural material, and Zosima cannot be said to depend on such material for his text's coordinates or even for its validation. It may be that at least some knowledge of the Christian scriptures could have been taken for granted even in such an educated audience as Dostoevsky addressed. On the other hand he may have had his own reasons for being reticent when dealing with material like this.

ARGUMENT BY IMAGE

Certainly, he did not intend to refute Ivan's atheistic propositions "point by point," as he explained in a letter to Pobedonostsev of 24 August NS 1879: the answer had to be given "indirectly" by means of "an artistic picture." In this respect he was at one with his correspondent. Pobedonostsev himself had written to him in June that year to say that it was "madness to ask: *prove* your faith to me. What should be said is: *show* me your faith." And he had gone on to say that "this faith is not to be made manifest in some abstract formula, but in the living image of a live man and of a live endeavor—in the image of God, which is that of Adam the man—and more than man, that is Christ the Son of God." Both correspondents would thus have agreed with Renan's judgement to the effect that Jesus himself "put forward no rational demonstration to his disciples and demanded no intellectual concentration on their part. It was not his conviction that he preached, but his very self." Dostoevsky was certainly intrigued by Renan and (prompted by Renan) himself planned to have his prince (that is, Stavrogin) say in *The Devils* that Christ puts forward "no teaching" as such: "the main thing is Christ's image, from which any teaching devolves." Hence the importance of harbouring this image, the responsibility (according to Zosima) both of the Russian monk and, by extension, of the Russian people.

But if Christ's teaching is not to be propounded point by point, the image needs to be all the more vivid and convincing. The utterly (and impressive) silent Christ of the Grand Inquisitor Legend (cf. Mark 15:3–5) needs to be brought more clearly into focus through Zosima's discourse or, better, through his person. It was after all Dostoevsky's cherished ambition to create the "utterly" of "positively beautiful man." But it can hardly be argued that Zosima is an effective *alter Christus*, still less Alyosha Karamazov; while the Russian monk in general (and, even more, the Russian people as a whole) are themselves altogether out of focus and in any case beyond the novelist's control.

ARGUMENT SUPERSEDED BY ELATION

If reason is not to the point, if the authority of scripture is not invoked, and a beautiful (that is, convincing) image difficult to sustain, the role of emotion as a path to cognition, insight or revelation may need to be enhanced. When Alyosha, in an early draft for *The Brothers Karamazov*, "understood that knowledge and faith [were] different and opposed to one another," Dostoevsky carefully supplemented the entry with a marginal note on the way in which Alyosha came to realize that there are "other worlds" and also links with them: in the process he gave a tentative picture of how such understanding was achieved. In Dostoevsky's words, "he understood—at least, attained or even only felt" these things. But even though he "only" felt, his perception was apparently authentic and profound. Dostoevsky was to devote much care to the depiction of such feeling. And although he felt that Zosima's discourse, in particular, would be found "absurd since too elated" by his reader, he clearly hoped that the reader himself would ultimately experience at least some of this elation and so be convinced.

The most obvious circumstantial expressions of such elation are three. The first is the all-important shedding of tears. The second involves the rather more mysterious kissing of the earth. The third, a subdivision of the first, involves a combination of the first and second: the watering of the earth with tears. In other words, a cult of the earth is served by the cultivation of tears: in Zosima's words, "fall on the earth and kiss it, water it with your tears, and the earth will bear fruit from your tears, even though no one saw you or heard you in your isolation."

Starets Amvrosy of Optino possessed the gift of tears, though there is no indication that Dostoevsky saw him demonstrate the fact during his brief visit to Optina Pustyn. Dostoevsky rarely visited other monasteries, if ever, and thus had few opportunities to observe such tears. Nevertheless it should not be assumed that his concern for them is due merely to his being "brought up on Karamzin."

Once more, Parfeny's travels may have provided him with stimulus, the more so since Parfeny speaks of tears at Optino itself. Furthermore, the engraving which forms the frontispiece to Parfeny's fourth volume shows an Athonite monk (*iyeroskhimonakh* Arseny) actually shedding copious tears. But for a richer and more systematic treatment of the subject Dostoevsky had only to turn to his copy of St Isaac of Syria's seventh-century classic, *Slova podvizhnicheskiya*.

ISAAC OF SYRIA AND THE CULT OF TEARS

Not only is its author mentioned in Dostoevsky's notebooks for *The Brothers Karamazov*: the work itself appears more than once on the actual pages of the finished novel. Admittedly, it is given a negative and even dismal context. The first owner of Isaac's text to be mentioned is Grigory Vasilyevich Kutuzov, who possessed a manuscript copy. He at least "read it stubbornly over many years." For all that "he understood virtually nothing of it, though for this very reason maybe loved and valued this book more than any other." His adopted son, Smerdyakov, is eventually found to have a printed version of the same work on his bedside table. It is first mentioned as "some fat book or other in a yellow cover": Smerdyakov "was not reading it, he was apparently sitting down and doing nothing." Only later is the book brought into play, and then merely as a hiding place for the booty derived from the murder of Fyodor Pavlovich Karamazov: "Smerdyakov pressed the money down with it." Smerdyakov's visitor, Ivan, "managed mechanically to read the title": it is given to the reader in Ivan's simplified version as *Svyatago ottsa nashego Isaaka Sirina slova (The Discourses of our Holy Father Isaac of Syria)*, rather than *Tvoreniya izhe vo svyatykh ottsa nashego avvy Isaaka Siriyanina, podvizhnika i otshel'nika . . . Slova podvizhnicheskiya (Ascetic Discourses, a Work of our Father among the Saints Isaac of Syria, Ascetic and Recluse)*. But however misused the book or garbled its title, there is no doubt as to its identity. And whereas its function here is to underline Smerdyakov's (and by extension Ivan's) lack of concern for the spiritual values embodied in it, there may be a more positive, albeit anonymous, role for it elsewhere in the novel.

Isaac of Syria has no doubt about the value of tears. They are the fruit of penitence and spiritual perception, the precondition for a revelation. Zosima's advocacy of tears may be said to have its foundation in such teachings as these. But there are two important factors which prevent an identification of the two.

Isaac is careful to stress that tears have a limited place in monastic spirituality. They are the accompaniment of an infant's spiritual birth, they lead him to spiritual maturation, and "they are a sure sign that the mind has left this world and has experienced that spiritual world." Yet at the same time the progress continues, for silence (*hesychia*) is beyond tears, and the ascetic's eyes "may be likened to a spring of water for up to two years or more; and that is when he achieves a stilling of his thoughts, while after the stilling of his thoughts, insofar as human nature can partially encompass it, he enters on that rest of which St Paul has spoken (Heb. 4:3). And after this peaceful rest the mind begins to contemplate mysteries." Tears are thus no more than a stage in the progress to divinization, not a self-sufficient peak. Furthermore they are themselves the result of a process. There can be no decision to shed tears, only a decision to repent and to practise ascesis. Tears are the by-product of such a decision. By contrast, Zosima suggests that they themselves must be zealously pursued. There is no suggestion that they should be treated as a passing phenomenon, or that their value is ultimately a limited one. Nor, unlike Isaac, does he attempt to differentiate between different stages or types of weeping.

Dostoevsky–Zosima thus accepts an element of Isaac's vocabulary, while giving it a specific and a limited application. But with the injunction that tears be mingled with the ground, still more with the injunction that the earth be kissed, he moves far beyond Isaac and indeed beyond the whole tradition of which Isaac is a part.

This is not to say that exultation in the created order is itself treated with mistrust by Orthodox writers. On the contrary, such exultation may be particularly intense insofar as the Orthodox world since patristic times has preserved an understanding of Creation which involves no rigid separation between nature and grace. "Man cannot create a space-interval between himself and God," as Paulos Gregorios has recently put it: "God is the reality which sustains both man and nature, and it is through man himself and through nature that God presents himself to man. In this sense, it is foolish to see God and nature as alternative poles placed so that if man turns towards one he must turn his back on the other" (*The Human Presence: An Orthodox View of Nature*). Moreover, man is neither utterly nor irremediably fallen, and can act both as a microcosm and a mediator: consequently, as one Cypriot saint has written, "creation does not venerate the Maker directly and by itself . . . it is through me that the heavens declare the glory of God, through me the moon worships God, through me the waters and showers of rain, the dews and all creation, venerate God and give glory."

Isaac himself has a powerful passage which may have provided Dostoevsky with an insight into this aspect of Orthodox tradition. The passage has been quoted by several writers, though simplistic conclusions about Isaac's writings and, more particularly, Dostoevsky's dependence on them, have too often accompanied such quotations. Nevertheless it requires (and deserves) to be quoted once again.

"What is purity?" asks Isaac by way of introduction, and responds, "a heart which is mercifully disposed to all created nature." A few lines later he poses the supplementary question, "what is a merciful heart?" It is this which prompts his well-known answer:

> When a man's heart is aflame on behalf of all creation, of all people, of birds, of animals, of demons and of any creature. Whenever they are remembered or whenever they are seen a man's eyes will shed tears. His heart will grow tender (*umilyayetsya*) from the

intense and great compassion which engulfs it; and it is incapable
of bearing or hearing or seeing any harm whatsoever or [any]
minor injury which may be suffered by creation.

Zosima's heart is indeed aflame in a comparable manner, as are his brother's
and his disciple's. However Isaac is once more describing the symptoms of
a spiritual state, and not its *raison d'être*. His description relates to a larger
context, which modifies its impact. Within its context, moreover, it constitutes
an exception rather than the rule. It required a determined and eclectic
reader—a "reader of genius"—to remove it from this context and to use it
as the kernel of what is beginning to reveal itself as a personal and altogether
different system. Yet even this key passage provides no model for the actual
veneration of the earth.

THE VENERATION OF THE EARTH

Is there something in the Franciscan tradition which might do so? The
question is not asked without good reason. "Pater Seraphicus" is used more
than once as a description of Zosima, and it is Alyosha himself who prompts
the reader to ask why: " 'Pater Seraphicus'—he took that name from somewhere or other—from where?" It is a curiously positive term, for all its
Latin (which makes it stand out starkly against a page of Cyrillic type), its
Western provenance, and its introduction by Ivan: almost inevitably it refers
to Francis of Assisi. The surviving lists of Dostoevsky's library holdings give
no indication of an interest in St Francis, and it remains to be established
whether he pursued any reading in this sphere. But at least it may be said
that had he done so he would have found support for Zosima's attitude to
nature. In particular he would have been struck by Francis's use of the term
"*sora nostra mater Terra*"—"our sister, mother Earth"—in his renowned
Canticle of brother Sun; indeed, the lyrical exultation of the canticle as a
whole would have been congenial to him. The occasions on which Francis
shed tears on mother Earth are few, but they may be significant. Thus one
of the earliest Lives of the saint, the *Legenda Maior* by St Bonaventure, states
that he once "moistened the place with his tears." It is a phrase which is
remarkably close (in Russian translation it could have been closer still) to
Zosima's injunction, "Soak the earth with the tears of your joy," as well as
to Alyosha's subsequent action in "watering" it with his tears. Even in Francis however there is no question of kissing the earth as well.

The kissing of the earth was not a new subject for Dostoevsky. Such
kissing is present in his work at least since *Crime and Punishment*, and he
was to return to it in *The Devils*. In the first of these, Raskolnikov's kiss

involves an act of repentance and reconciliation: Sonya has urged him to kiss the earth which he had defiled by his murders. In the second, Marya Timofeyevna Lebyadkina speaks of an equally mysterious veneration of the earth: the earth is perceived by her at one and the same time as the type of the *Bogoroditsa* (Theotokos; Birthgiver of God), the great mother, and as Mother-damp-earth: to water the earth with one's tears brings joy in all things and leads naturally to the kissing of the earth.

Marya Timofeyevna's approach is closer to Zosima's than is Sonya's. Zosima's shedding of tears and kissing of the earth are also an expression of joy and *umileniye* ("tender emotion") at the integrity, beauty and sanctity of the cosmos. And yet it is Sonya's type of earth veneration, rather than Marya Timofeyevna's, for which a parallel is to be found in Russian sectarian or popular religious practices. Thus, confession to the earth was a widespread phenomenon from at least the time of the fourteenth-century Strigolnik heresy in Pskov and Novgorod. This could naturally involve a desire for reconciliation with the earth, which would have been harmed and defiled by man's sin. Since the earth was treated as sacred, oaths might be taken by it: in this connection the earth might be kissed or even ingested.

However, this is far removed from Zosima's joyful kissing of the earth. Parallels for such behaviour are difficult to trace. For the present only one has come to my attention. An account of the 1860s describes the peregrinations of a certain pilgrim Darya or Daryushka. In the course of her travels she once "kissed the earth in an impulse of joy and gratitude to God, who created this earth and walked upon it." The account was published during the 1860s in the St Petersburg periodical *Strannik*. Three issues of this periodical (for the years 1880 and 1881) are now known to have been in Dostoevsky's library. But it is not known whether Dostoevsky read the relevant issue of two decades earlier. In any case it may be doubted whether Daryushka's one impulsive gesture could have been sufficient to provide the framework and justification for Zosima's system. Nor by itself does it provide evidence of a specifically Orthodox or Russian custom.

ZOSIMA AND THE CHURCH

The tears, prostrations and the kissing of the earth have one feature in common, their intense immediacy. Moreover their character is personal and individualistic rather than ecclesial. There is some desultory talk of the Church in the early chapters of the novel: Paisy makes a clear and positive statement on the Church's role in man's salvific progress and Zosima himself speaks briefly of the Church as an agent of reconciliation in society. In one sentence he even mentions her sacraments. But in general, and certainly in respect of the devotional practices advocated by him, the Church is not involved, recollected or (apparently) required. Nor do the discourses, which might be expected to contain the essence of Zosima's teachings, refer to sacraments or services, the normal manifestations of Orthodox church life. By way of an exception a single Holy Week service (the Liturgy of the Presanctified for Great Tuesday) is mentioned: but this is remembered as part of Zosima's childhood, and Zosima looks back to it with nostalgia, almost as if it no longer referred to the present. And even though Zosima's role as confessor is mentioned, the reader is not shown him practising as such. Zosima, moreover, is a priest, as is made plain by his title *iyeroskhimonakh*, his capacity to bless and the funeral rites which are his due. Yet there is no suggestion that he participates in any service, either at the monastery proper (which his health might prevent) or even—and in this he differs from Amvrosy—at his more secluded scete. Nor does he experience any regret on this score.

It is therefore not altogether inappropriate that his own sacramental needs are ignored by his immediate entourage. Even though all his associates were well aware that his death was imminent and Zosima himself spoke openly about it no thought was given to the administration of confession, unction or communion. As if by way of compensation, Dostoevsky had made special efforts to secure the necessary texts and advice concerning the laying-out of a newly deceased monk. The future Over Procurator of the Holy Synod, Pobedonostsev, ensured that his friend should be given the required support. Yet Dostoevsky was well aware that he also needed details of the rite for unction and communion: he reminded himself of the need in his notebooks. It is therefore the same Dostoevsky who must be held responsible for not acting on this reminder and for his eventual failure to heed the premortem needs of his Pater Seraphicus. Was he perhaps seeking to manipulate his dying so that the last sacraments would not overshadow or displace Zosima's final prostration, the final kissing of the earth? For it would not have been proper for Zosima to prostrate himself that day after communion and thus to diminish a communicant's God-given dignity. Be that as it may, the death of Zosima, "unhousel'd . . . unanel'd," is yet one more expression of his separateness from the sacred structures and prescriptions of his Church.

Zosima's recommended path to salvation therefore involves heightened intensity; and it concerns the individual rather than the group, the body or the Church. At the same time, it is a path which does not necessarily demand a lifelong discipline on the part of those that tread it. In this respect Zosima differs markedly from Isaac of Syria and the elders of Optina Pustyn. Admittedly, he makes some judicious remarks about the lasting effort required to sustain love. He even mentions "obedience, fasting, prayer" as the only way towards "freedom and joy." Yet Zosima himself shows no sign of the spiritual struggle which led him to his present state, nor does he mention such a struggle even for didactic reasons. By contrast, the traditionalist ascetic Ferapont is presented as a ridiculously whited sepulchre and his stance, in effect, is condemned. Zosima is less concerned for disciplined and barely perceptible progress than for immediate transformations.

"LIFE IS PARADISE, THE KEYS ARE IN OUR KEEPING"

Such transformations are within the individual's reach. Zosima's brother is the first to suggest that they can virtually be willed: "Life is paradise, and we are all in paradise, yet we do not want to know it, but if we did want to know it, paradise would begin tomorrow the whole world over." Zosima is to remember these words and to paraphrase them. The Mysterious Visitor is likewise to speak along these lines: "Paradise, he said, is hidden in each of us, here it is hidden within me also, and I have only to wish it, and it will come about the very next day in actual fact and immediately for the whole of my life."

No argument is actually put forward against man's cooperation with God (*synergeia*) in seeking to attain this paradise. Yet neither is this Orthodox principle advanced or even mentioned. On the contrary, the assumption that man himself determines the inauguration of his paradise would effectively preclude any such cooperation. According to one of Dostoevsky's notebook entries for the novel, "Life is paradise, the keys are in our keeping."

In making such a statement he was at one with an obscure scholar, some of whose writings had been submitted to him anonymously in December 1877. He was never to learn the name of their author, N. F. Fyodorov. But he read them "as if they were my own," and they were to inform his thinking in later chapters of the novel. In respect to paradise however the evidence suggests a striking parallel, rather than an influence. Difficult as it is to establish the exact identity of the text at Dostoevsky's disposal, this is not likely to have contained the passage in which Fyodorov most explicitly asserts that "the kingdom of God or paradise must be created only by men themselves." Even so, it is of interest to note that Fyodorov's paradise will be the product not only of people's "full perception" and their "strength of will," but also of their "depth of *feeling*." Nevertheless, Fyodorov is at variance with Dostoevsky in one respect: those who achieve this paradise do so not as individuals, but by deploying "all the means [at the disposal] of all people in their togetherness."

For Dostoevsky's separate individual, the attainment of paradise does not necessarily involve transfiguration. Dostoevsky was evidently not ignorant of the Orthodox teaching on the ultimate divinization of man, on man's striving towards theosis (*obózheniye*). In one of his notebook entries for Zosima's discourse he makes specific reference to it. In the Orthodox world, and in particular since the fourteenth-century councils which upheld the teachings of Gregory Palamas, the light of Christ's Transfiguration on Mount Tabor had long been accepted as a model and an assurance of man's theosis. Hence the burden of Dostoevsky's fourfold notebook entry: "Your flesh will be transformed. (Light of Tabor.) Life is paradise, the keys are in our keeping." Yet the established text does not retain the first two statements, and the concept of life as paradise is thus deprived of an important gloss and validation.

PARADISE OR HEAVEN?

As it is, Zosima's paradise is predominantly a terrestrial condition. Zosima repeatedly uses the term *ray* for its designation. In the Russian translation of the Bible (favoured by Zosima) *ray* stands for the garden (*paradeisos*) of Eden, as well as for the paradise ("an intermediate state between death and resurrection" for the redeemed) to which the Good Thief is promised entry (Luke 23:43). Occasionally it may also be used as a synonym for "heaven": Zosima himself seems to use it in this sense when he applies it (as Luke does not) to the parable of Lazarus and the rich man. But this is not necessarily its primary or most appropriate connotation in the context of the novel (and Constance Garnett was ill-advised to opt for it *passim*). Fyodorov had spoken insistently of the necessity for "paradise on earth"; in his support he could have cited Old Testament apocalyptic writings, in which "the site of the reopened Paradise is almost without exception the earth or the New Jerusalem." Yet once this paradise becomes an earthly prospect, a Fyodorov or a Dostoevsky may transfer its expected realization from the ultimate to the comparatively immediate future and significantly reduce its eschatological implications in the process. Even the exceptional use of the phrase "kingdom of heaven" (or "heavenly kingdom") by the Mysterious Visitor does not swing the balance in an otherworldly direction since such a kingdom in the New Testament is itself perceived largely as a present reality, as the sovereignty of God "over the lives and actions of men here, with a view to their entrance into the perfect Kingdom of God in the hereafter." The orientation of the "here" towards the "hereafter" should distinguish this kingdom from merely utopian states: it is thus of some importance to gauge the strength of such orientation.

LOVE AND MUTUAL RESPONSIBILITY

The most important key to this *ray* is love. Had not Isaac of Syria stated that "paradise [*ray*] is love of God"? This finds its echo in Zosima. But the echo is muted. Zosima speaks less specifically of man's love for God, more of love for man (however sinful he may be) and—insistently and poignantly—of love for all Creation. "Brothers, do not fear sin," says Zosima, "love man even in his sin, for this is the likeness of divine love and the peak of love on earth. Love all God's Creation, [Creation] as a whole and every grain of sand [within it]. Love each leaf, each of God's rays. Love the animals, love the vegetation, love anything that is. When you love everything, then shall you penetrate to God's mystery in things."

The immediate consequence, if not the concomitant of this love is a man's recognition of responsibility for the sins of his fellows. Both Markel and Zosima propound the formula (anticipated by Shatov in *The Devils*) that "anyone is culpable before all for everyone and for anything"; or (more interestingly) "for each [m.] and for all [f.]"—"*za vsyekh i za vsya.*" The latter phrase carries overtones of a sacrificial acceptance of such responsibility: the eucharistic offering in the Liturgy of St John Chrysostom is made in almost identical terms, "*o vsyekh i za vsya.*" The same Liturgy—celebrated in Russian churches virtually throughout the year—would have familiarized Dostoevsky with the communicant's prayer about "sinners of whom I am first" (a phrase borrowed from 1 Timothy 1:15). Dostoevsky would have encountered the same message in Isaac of Syria. For Isaac had urged each reader of his work to consider himself "responsible and culpable in respect of everything."

If a man loves his fellows and is indeed responsible for their sins he is impelled to seek their forgiveness. They for their part would also seek forgiveness for their sins. In the words of Zosima's dying brother, "Even though I am sinful in respect of all, they will in turn forgive me, there's paradise for you. Am I not in paradise now?" Another key to paradise therefore is the mutual forgiveness of sins.

THE PROBLEM OF HELL

Sin is not to be feared: it is never beyond forgiveness. There is only one exception to this rule. In the words of Isaac, "no sin is unforgivable—apart from unrepented sin." Isaac's axiom is to be elaborated in Zosima's text. Its first part is implied throughout; its second informs the final section of Zosima's discourse. But if Isaac could be said to provide an epigraph, it is another (and in this case newly canonized) saint who may have provided at least some of the substance for this text: Tikhon Zadonsky, former Bishop of Voronezh.

Dostoevsky had a longstanding interest in Tikhon. In 1870 he could already speak of having welcomed him enthusiastically into his heart "long ago." He also welcomed him into his library. The recently discovered list of its contents refers to no less than *twenty-one* editions of a short work by Tikhon on repentance. Such an avid collector of one work by this author is not likely to have ignored the remainder; and although he does not seem to have possessed the handsome second edition of Tikhon's collected works in fifteen volumes which appeared in 1860, it would be wrong to assume that he had no familiarity with it. Dostoevsky went out of his way to acknowledge that parts of Zosima's discourse were based on "certain homilies by Tikhon Zadonsky," and referred particularly to the section on sacred scripture. But the final section also bears a marked resemblance to some of Tikhon's work.

Tikhon insists, with Isaac, that no sins are beyond forgiveness for the penitent: "no matter how numerous, great or burdensome they may be, God possesses a still greater abundance of mercy." Tikhon, together with Zosima, also dwells on the fate of those who fail or refuse to repent. Thus both discuss the role of hell and both ponder the anguish of those who realize, too late, that they could and should have acted otherwise before their death. Each refers to the parable of Lazarus and the rich man by way of illustration.

Yet if Tikhon may be said to provide Dostoevsky with a model and a stimulus, this is not to say that the two writers are at one in all respects. Indeed, the difference between them are of as much interest as the similarities.

Tikhon speaks consistently of the sinner's deviation from God and of God's judgment in respect of this. By contrast, God is not mentioned at all in the main part of Zosima's discourse on hell, except insofar as the Lazarus parable requires two mentions of "the Lord." The sinner has deviated not so much from God, as from love: hell is "suffering caused by the fact that it is no longer possible to love." Whereas the capacity to love was given as man's birthright at the time of Creation: "I am and I love" is Zosima's non-Descartean gloss on Genesis. The emphasis is on man's psyche rather than on God's grace. The quotation "God is love" (1 John 4:8) is conspicuous by its absence. Some references to God towards the very end of the passage hardly compensate for his absence hitherto; the less so since he is given a peculiarly negative context. The unrepentant "cannot contemplate the living God without hate and demand that there should be no God of life, that God should destroy himself and all that He created." Yet even they are said to "curse [? only] themselves in cursing God and life": their target is an elusive one.

Only in the case of those who so condemn themselves does Zosima foresee the eternal torment which Tikhon presumes to be the lot of all the condemned without distinction. This is another significant difference between them. For tentatively, and with apologies for lack of clarity, Zosima postulates that many if not most condemned sinners are not utterly lost. The damned may yet come to a realization that the righteous still extend their love towards them. Simultaneously they will become ever more aware of their inability to reciprocate it. This in turn could generate humility. And it is this which eventually prompts "a certain form of that active love which they spurned on earth and, as it were, some action in conformity with it." Zosima thus provides the foundation for Grushenka's more explicit (and certainly more picturesque) folk-legend of the onion, which is soon to follow.

In yet one other respect does Zosima go his own way. Tikhon does not speak of suicides. Zosima not only considers them, but makes a point of questioning the rigidity of Orthodox practices in their regard. "The Church in its outward expression seems to reject them": however, Zosima (like Makar in *A Raw Youth*) daily offers prayers on their behalf. The positive improvement even of their lot is therefore postulated. In the five sentences devoted to this subject, Zosima may be preparing the reader for the suicide of the charmless Smerdyakov.

Zosima's presentation of hell is consistent with his humanitarian and his humanistic train of thought, and he differs from Tikhon to a marked extent. Yet in his brief discussion of suicide he is curiously close to yet another spiritual authority, the subject of that biography which Dostoevsky may have received at the hands of Amvrosy in 1877 and in any case possessed: the starets Leonid, in effect the founder of eldership (*starchestvo*) at Optina Pustyn. For information on Leonid, Dostoevsky could draw not only on this work, but also on his familiar Parfeny, several of whose pages are devoted to starets Leonid.

It has already been noted that Leonid's eventual successor Amvrosy provided much of the circumstantial detail for the portrait of Zosima. But Leonid could have helped to fill it out. He too was cheerful, calm, direct and simple; he too shed tears of joy. Like Amvrosy (and Zosima) after him, he too would receive "people of every walk of life" in his cell, "gentry, merchants and simple folk" alike. The cell itself was to be found "half a verst from the monastery, in the midst of a wood," not unlike Zosima's ("four hundred paces from the monastery, through a little wood," according to the instructions given to F. P. Karamazov). But none of this is as important as the correspondence between Leonid's attitude to suicides and Zosima's. Leonid's is expressed in a prayer which he composed for a disciple whose father had committed suicide. It began with the words, "Take to task, O Lord the fallen soul of my father and if it be possible, have mercy." The phrase "if it be possible" kept the prayer within the bounds of propriety, as presumably did Zosima's private and silent practice of similar prayers. In any case, the censorship left both accounts in place. For once Dostoevsky's deviation from accepted standards of Orthodoxy could be justified by reference to an authentic monastic source.

THE RUSSIAN PEOPLE AND THE SALVATION OF THE WORLD

Prayer for suicides and for the denizens of hell is the natural expression of that mutual love and forgiveness which Zosima preaches. If these can help to overcome the problems of the world beyond, so much more obviously can they resolve the social problems of the here and now. Thus, the reconciliation of the rich and poor is to be brought about by shame on the part of the rich, matched by the humility and tenderness of the poor: psychological and spiritual, rather than political or economic factors are at issue. The source and the guarantee of such a reconciliation are something mysterious which is latent, waiting to be realized, in the common people of Russia and in those who are at one with them, the monks: the image (*obraz*) of Christ. The existence of this image is an article of faith. No definition of it is attempted. Yet it is the people's possession of the image which renders them sacred. In Zosima's words, "This is a people that bears God" within itself: "*sei narod—bogonosets.*"

Therefore, as he asserts, "God will save Russia"; "The Lord will save Russia, as He has repeatedly saved her before"; "God will save His people, for Russia is great in her humility." No other nation is mentioned in this connection: no other nation, so it appears, has comparable potential. Other nations are merely in the background as future beneficiaries of Russia's own salvation.

Zosima can claim to possess a peculiar insight into this problem since it is the Russian monk (specifically *Russian*) who has succeeded in preserving this image of Christ "gloriously and undistorted . . . in continuity with the ancient fathers, the apostles and martyrs." This is the star which is now to "shine forth from the East," the precious diamond which is to shine forth to the whole world. Yet the "God-bearing" nation as a whole is to play an all-important part in its diffusion. Salvation is to "derive from the people, its humility and faith." Thus what seemed to begin as an assertion of the age-old tradition of Orthodoxy is unobtrusively transformed into an expression of nineteenth-century Russian nationalism, if not messianism. No longer is the Church the guardian of the truth, nor even (as the Slavophiles might have expressed it) the members of the Church, but the members of a particular nation. This is hardly to be distinguished from what the recent Constantinopolitan Church Council of 1872 had condemned as *phyletismos*, a teaching whereby nationalistic concepts distort and challenge the Church's universal mission.

Indeed, there is a danger not only of the Church but of God becoming a function of nationality. "Whoever does not believe in God is not going to believe in God's people," says Zosima: his statement almost suggests that belief in God has its justification insofar as it has that particular outcome. Once more God is not presented as an absolute but rather (in Stavrogin's words) as "a simple attribute of nationality"; and the reader may well be reminded of Shatov's hesitant credo, formulated in response to Stavrogin's questions in *The Devils*. Shatov had also asserted that the Russians were "the only 'God-bearing' people." He was challenged as to his own beliefs in God. "I believe in Russia," he replied. "I believe in her Orthodoxy . . . I believe in the body of Christ . . . I believe that the new [second] coming will take place in Russia." "But in God? In God?" "I . . . I shall believe in God."

Is Zosima's credo significantly different? He could proclaim his belief in joy, love, mutual forgiveness, the beauty of Creation, the image of Christ as cherished and propagated by the Russian people, a terrestrial and immediately attainable paradise. If he had been challenged with the question, "But in God?" he might have had no answer other than an evasive counter-question, "Surely that amounts to God?" It is not altogether surprising that the Russian censorship at one time prohibited the separate publication of Zosima's discourse. It was felt that the circulation of such "mystical-social teachings" among the lower classes would be harmful since they display "only an apparent similarity to the teachings of Christ, while being essentially opposed to the doctrine of the Orthodox faith." In the minutes of the censorship committee (3 December 1886), the passages dealing with "paradise on earth" were quoted with evident scorn. Doubts about Zosima's orthodoxy (his teachings were compared with Tolstoy's) were clearly reinforced by an appreciation of Dostoevsky's powers to convince. He was, after all, a "gifted belletrist." Repeated appeals against the decision were of no avail.

ALYOSHA "WAKEFUL AND YET NOT AWAKE"

But whatever the nature of Zosima's credo in the abstract, it is to receive its testing and (Dostoevsky would have hoped) its vindication in Alyosha's experience immediately after the elder's death. Alyosha had left the monastery for a confrontation with Grushenka. He had returned towards the end of the day and was reintroduced to the vigil over Zosima's body by the Gospel reading which had begun immediately after the first requiem service (*panikhida*) and which was to continue throughout the coming night.

There is a new vigour in the exposition. The Zosima insert with its elaborate narrative devices, its deliberately stylized speech, its generous time-scale on the one hand and its pretensions to timelessness on the other, is replaced by a straightforward "eyewitness" account of Alyosha's activities and conversations; this is eventually to merge into a "first-hand" account of his inner experiences. This "first-hand" account is to occupy the greater part of only one short chapter ("Cana of Galilee"), hardly three pages of print. Nevertheless Dostoevsky had no hesitation in describing it as "the most significant in the whole book, and possibly in the novel as well."

As the title of the chapter suggests, it is the narrative of the marriage of Cana (John 2:1–11) which Alyosha hears when he arrives back at the cell. But he is on the verge of sleep after a tiring and disturbing day, and his mind easily wanders. The wedding feast merges imperceptibly into a messianic banquet for which other Gospel passages (such as Matt. 22:1–10) provide the framework and the raw material. These in turn provoke reminiscences of related homiletic material: Dostoevsky borrows several phrases from a paschal homily attributed to St John Chrysostom, thus fulfilling an intention (expressed as early as Eastertide 1876) "to end with the sermon of Chryso-stom, 'If anyone come at the ninth hour.'"

Dostoevsky was by no means inexperienced in the description of dreams. Even so, it may be that in the case of so significant a dream-vision as Alyosha's was to prove, he may have been glad once more of some guidance or support from Isaac of Syria. At least it may be noted that there are two passages in Isaac which could be used to place Alyosha's experience in the context of monastic spirituality.

Isaac speaks of two kinds of rapture which may overtake the monk. The first is experienced "sometimes at the hour of prayer, sometimes during a reading," while the other may occur "during the night, when you find yourself between sleep and wakefulness, somehow sleeping yet not asleep, wakeful yet not awake." In either case, "when this delight comes upon a person and vibrates throughout his body, then is the hour when he thinks that the kingdom of heaven itself is nothing other than this very same thing." At least something of Alyosha's condition is anticipated here.

Equally applicable is another passage in which Isaac suggests that "vision" (which he distinguishes from "revelation") can be experienced in a variety of ways, "in sleep or else at times of waking, sometimes with all clarity, at other times as if in an apparition and somewhat unclearly; for which reason even the recipient of the vision often does not know himself whether he sees the vision in a waking or somnolent state." Moreover, "it is possible to hear a voice asking for assistance, sometimes to see someone clearly face to face, to engage in conversation, to ask questions and to receive replies." It is certainly not difficult to relate Alyosha's conversation with Zosima at the messianic banquet to such words as these.

Alyosha's rapture is divided into two parts. The first involves his vision of the marriage feast, the second his experience of the cosmos in Zosima's garden.

The reader's own expectations—supported by Isaac's comments—would prepare him for some lack of definition. Alyosha's dreams, visions and contemplations are effectively presented as they evolve, and there is no room for the kind of clarification (or attempt at clarification) which a retrospective narrative might prompt. Even so, an acceptance of a narrative device, a reader's willing suspension of disbelief, should not preclude subsequent examination of the vision's substance, a search for its core.

THE MESSIANIC BANQUET

Alyosha's first visionary experience involves a fresh presentation of some of Zosima's principal concerns. Particular emphasis is given to joy and forgiveness. It appears that even Zosima himself, in common with many of his fellow guests at the banquet, has escaped from the possibility of damnation only by virtue of a single "onion," the exceptional good deed which has counted in his favour. All the more reason, therefore, to make merry at the messianic feast.

Yet the feast is curiously presented. The messiah himself, the great host, is not to be seen at first hand. Nor is he to be named, except obliquely. In what may be a reference to such texts as Malachi 4:2 or Revelation 21:33, Zosima speaks of him as "our Sun." Zosima himself presumably sees him, since he asks Alyosha "Do you see our Sun, do you see Him?" But Alyosha avoids the challenge with a whispered, "I am afraid. I do not dare to look." Therefore neither can the reader look at the mysterious presence. Zosima provides a brief comment on some of his host's qualities but the single sentence devoted to this hardly compensates for the effective absence of the Jesus who was explicitly named and presented on the previous page within the framework of the Gospel reading and Alyosha's preliminary musings on it. There is a degree of evasiveness here, and censorship restrictions (which Dostoevsky shows no sign of anticipating in his notebooks) can provide only a partial explanation for it.

ALYOSHA IN ZOSIMA'S GARDEN

But there is more evasiveness to come. For what does Alyosha experience when he leaves the elder's cell?

> His soul, replete with rapture, thirsted for freedom, space, expanse. Above him was inversed the heavenly dome, generous and unfathomable, full of silent glowing stars. From zenith to horizon stretched the Milky Way, as yet indistinct and out of focus. . . . The luxuriant autumn flowers in the beds had gone to sleep until morning. The silence of the earth seemed to merge with that of the heavens, the mystery of the earth with that of the stars. . . . Alyosha stood, watched and suddenly threw himself to the earth as if he had been cut down.

It is at this moment that Zosima's counsels are followed to the letter. Alyosha kisses the earth and waters it (or to follow the Russian literally, her) with his tears:

> He had no idea why he embraced her, he made no attempt to assess why he was so irresistibly impelled to kiss her, to kiss the whole of her, but kiss her he did, weeping, sobbing and watering her with his tears, and he vowed in his elation to love her, to love her for ever. "Water the earth with your tears of joy and love those tears of yours" resounded in his soul.

Not only the earth, but the entire cosmos is brought closer through such tears.

> What was he weeping for? Oh, he wept in his rapture even for these very stars, which shone out to him from the abyss; and "he was not ashamed of such ecstasy." It seemed as if threads from all those countless worlds of God had simultaneously come together in his soul, and it was all a-tremble, "coming into contact with [these] other worlds." He wanted to forgive everyone and for everything and to seek forgiveness, no, not for himself but

for all, for everything and for everyone, while "there are also others interceding for me" came another echo from within his soul.

Alyosha was left under no illusion that he was under the sway of some superior force.

> With every passing minute he could feel clearly and as it were tangibly that something as firm and as immutable as that heavenly vault was entering his soul. Some kind of idea had somehow come to dominate his mind, and from this moment, moreover, for his whole life, and for ever. He fell to the ground a weak youth, but he rose as a warrior, fortified for the rest of his life, and he sensed this immediately, that very moment of his rapture. Never was Alyosha able to forget that moment later, not for so long as he lived, never. "Someone visited my soul that hour," he would say later, with firm conviction in his words.

And so, at one fell swoop, Dostoevsky brings together the kissing of the earth, joy, tears and mutual forgiveness. The mutual forgiveness, moreover, is given a cosmic dimension. It is prompted, justified and sustained by that cosmic harmony of which Alyosha has received such palpable intimations.

It is undoubtedly a high-water mark in the novel, as Dostoevsky himself suggested. At the very least it is a watershed in the life of the character whom Dostoevsky's narrator designated as "my hero." For we witness his initiation into mysteries which leave him marked for life.

Yet what these mysteries mean is left frustratingly unclear. No vaguer terms could have been chosen to describe them. "Some kind of idea" comes to dominate Alyosha's mind "somehow." It is "something firm and immutable" which enters his soul. Only in retrospect does Alyosha come to correct the impression given by these imprecise and markedly impersonal phrases: it is only then that "someone" is said to have visited his soul. But the fact that this supplementary and retrospective account needs to be fortified by reference to his "firm convictions" can provoke as much scepticism as it allays. In any case "someone" hardly does duty as one of the divine names. The same must be said *a fortiori* about "something."

The image (*obraz*) which Dostoevsky had hoped to present has become hopelessly diluted and probably distorted. Certainly Alyosha's experience could never be described as a theophany. If anything it is a cosmophany. From another point of view it may be seen as the expression of cosmolatry. A parallel for it is thus not to be sought in Isaac of Syria, Tikhon of Voronezh, Amvrosy of Optino or Francis of Assisi.

THE GARDEN OF BISHOP BIENVENU

But this is not to say that there is no clerical figure to be cited as a possible source or stimulus for Dostoevsky. The most obvious such cleric however was not the product of the Syrian desert nor of the Russian *pustyn'* (monastery). Like Zosima himself, he was a nineteenth-century novelist's creation. His author was that "great poet, whose genius [as Dostoevsky acknowledged at the beginning of that critical summer of 1879] has exercised so powerful an influence on me ever since my childhood," Victor Hugo. His home is *Les Misérables*, which Dostoevsky reread at least as recently as 1874, and of which he possessed three complete editions. His name is Monseigneur Bienvenu (more correctly, Charles-François Bienvenu Myriel), Bishop of Digne.

Dostoevsky's own regard for this bishop is demonstrated in a letter of 1877, in which he takes pleasure in a friend's positive appreciation of him. It seems likely that Dostoevsky also demonstrated his regard for him in those pages of *The Brothers Karamazov* which have just been examined. For not only does Hugo's hero (Jean Valjean) experience an ecstatic vision of the bishop, his spiritual sponsor, and shed copious tears at the conclusion of it: the bishop himself has many characteristics which are also to be found in Zosima. Moreover, and most important, he is familiar with an experience which closely resembles that of Alyosha in the garden.

Monseigneur Bienvenu "had an excess of love." The essence of his teaching was "*Love one another.*" Indeed, he declared this to be "complete": "he wished for nothing more, and this was the whole of his doctrine." His beliefs in other matters were less clear, certainly less explicit. But he possessed a childlike gaiety, and "it seemed as if joy emanated from the whole of his personality." Nevertheless, stories of his youth suggested that—like Zosima— he had once been a passionate and possibly a violent man. This could not have been suspected at his present age, sixty-five, an age which he shares with Zosima, and also, at the time of Dostoevsky's visit to Optino, with another of Zosima's putative models, Amvrosy. In view of what was said above, Hugo's comparison of Bienvenu with Francis of Assisi is of some interest, although it is not developed by him.

Some of Bienvenu's attitudes and experiences are shared by Alyosha Karamazov. Particularly striking is the way in which Hugo's bishop relates to the night sky. He would engage in a kind of ritual before sleep which involved a visit to his carefully tended garden and contemplation "in the presence of the great spectacles [provided] by the night sky": "He would be there alone with himself, collected, peaceful, full of adoration, comparing the serenity of his own heart with the serenity of the ether, moved in the shadows by the visible splendours of the constellations and the invisible splendours of God, opening his soul to the thoughts which descended from the Unknown."

Unlike Alyosha, therefore, the bishop goes beyond the stars to thoughts (at least) of their creator:

> He mused on the grandeur and the presence of God; on the eternity to come, that strange mystery; on past eternity, that stranger mystery still; on all the infinities which were yet to be discovered by his eyes in all directions; and without seeking to comprehend the incomprehensible, he observed it. He did not study God; rather was he overwhelmed by him.

Yet even here, the Creator is to be apprehended mainly, if not only, through his works. Bienvenu divided his leisure time between "gardening by day and contemplation by night": "was this narrow enclosure [his garden], with the skies for its ceiling, not enough to be able to adore God alternately in his most charming and in his most sublime creation?" Consequently here also a certain depersonalization of the divinity is likely to occur which links Bienvenu's experience most closely with Alyosha's. For that "something" which entered Alyosha's soul during his ecstatic moments in the monastic garden finds its parallel, perhaps its explanation, in the following words:

> In moments like these, offering up his heart at the hour when the nocturnal flowers offer up their scent, illumined like a lamp in the midst of the star-spangled night, welling over in ecstasy, amidst the universal radiance of Creation, he himself probably could not have said what was taking place in his mind; he felt something escape from him and something descend into him. Mysterious exchanges between the depths of the soul and the depths of the universe.

Are Alyosha's "exchanges" substantially to be distinguished from the bishop's? The parallel ought not to be ignored. At the very least it provides yet one more reminder that Alyosha's experience is not necessarily nor yet obviously the fruit or the foundation of a Christian Orthodox commitment. His tears, prostrations, kissing of the earth and communing with the cosmos may still intrigue, impress or even move the reader with their innocent intensity. But despite the Christian cosmetics which Dostoevsky has partially applied, they speak of little more than nature mysticism.

THE PROPHET AND HIS UNBELIEF

The would-be prophet had attained his "hosanna," his faith, "through a great *furnace of doubt*." Yet the doubt had not been left behind. It informs the arguments of Ivan, it gives Zosima's counterweight, that Western monk, the Grand Inquisitor, his haunting and his lasting power. Dostoevsky thus had good reason to emulate the possessed boy's father in the Gospels and to pray, "Lord, I believe; help thou mine unbelief" (Mark 9:24).

In the case of Zosima and Alyosha, who could have been, respectively, the proponent and the champion of belief, the unbelief is not so far to seek as might have been expected. And in the case of either, but especially Alyosha, the reader is ultimately confronted with what A. B. Gibson [in *The Religion of Dostoyevsky*] has succinctly termed "the combination of the sincerest piety with the apparent absence of its object."

JOHN JONES

The Possessed

On first consideration it seems odd that in the early days of planning *The Possessed* Dostoevsky should write to his friend Maikov and describe his new venture as "like *Crime and Punishment* but even nearer to reality, even more urgent, and directly concerned with the most important contemporary question." "Like *Crime and Punishment*"—another murder story—is obvious enough. What falls less easily into place is the judgment about relative importance, urgency, contemporary relevance, nearness to reality; because Raskolnikov comes over as a very grand and accessible conception, a nineteenth-century bohemian Hamlet was one way of putting it, whereas Verkhovensky is just a wrecker.

That is our starting point. It could be said as brusquely of Iago that he is just a wrecker. And of a terrorist in today's headlines: one of those inscrutable middle-class Germans, for example. Thus what I called *Crime and Punishment*'s apocalyptic naturalism is its most vital link with *The Possessed*; I mean, when Dostoevsky read about that gang murder in the *Moscow Record* his mind's eye was caught not by a bizarre and therefore very newsworthy incident but by the seed of a foul commonplace: the seed in eternity, in the deepest realism, though also in the mere mundane future, for Dostoevsky did imagine a time when only the most spectacular acts of terrorism would get headline treatment. Shatov's murder, in the world of this novel, is momentous because it is potentially unremarkable.

Crime and Punishment was different in that Dostoevsky never supposed lots of people would begin committing Raskolnikov-type murders; Danilov

From *Dostoevsky*. © 1983 by John Jones. Oxford University Press, 1983.

doing so was enough to produce from him the exclamation "It has happened!" For Raskolnikov is incorrigibly patrician and rare at heart (which is one reason why the Epilogue does not convince), even if I have overstressed the Hamletish side to him. Nevertheless his crime, like the tawdry footloose elimination of Shatov, springs from unsteadiness (*shatost*). The word appears twice in Dostoevsky's letter to Katkov outlining *Crime and Punishment*, in the phrase "unsteadiness of ideas"—which is natural since a drama of reflection is about to unfold: thinking is Raskolnikov's work, as he tells the maid Nastasya. Unsteady work, we might add. Moreover the surname Shatov appears once in the notebooks relating to *Crime and Punishment*. But nothing further. It's as if the name were waiting for the man, and for the novel which will transpersonalize or socialize the murderous concept: "social unsteadiness, as Shatov says" and as we read in the *Possessed* notebooks.

And in his definitive text the novelist voices social unsteadiness as empty groupings and vapid motions. Von Lemke's cut-outs are phantom human concourses (theatre, station, church), and they are mobile. The quintet is Peter Verkhovensky's plaything. He tricks its members into thinking they are part of a revolutionary network extending across Russia, and at the local level he generates pseudo-purposeful activities which culminate in Shatov's murder. There's a littleness about it all: again it must not be seen as mere chance that we encounter Swift's Lilliput on the first page of the novel.

This littleness is at once paltry and menacing and never in repose. One of the members of the quintet bears the quaint name of Tolkachenko. Dostoevsky followed the trial proceedings closely, and I think the Soviet editor is right to put his finger on the verb *tolkatsya*, to loaf or lounge about, which occurs in a speech by the prosecuting lawyer. The editor might also have noted the colloquial sense of roaming around which the verb *shatatsya* carries, for this may perhaps have encouraged the switch from Shaposhnikov to Shatov as the novel began to define itself. Loafing and roaming cohere into a larger whole, together with such imaginative furniture as hats and travelling rugs and passports and foreign restaurant bills and trashy pamphlets printed abroad and incompetently circulated. This novel seems, but only seems, but does seem insistently, to come from a man who knew nothing but was very opinionated, who checked no facts and guzzled rumour scraps, whose mind was uncouth, raggity, raucous, florid. For it is a condition of Dostoevsky's art to arouse our longing for the settled and the normal and the beautiful itself.

The Possessed swarms with amateurism and with fooling about and make-believe just as childish as Von Lemke's, but dangerous. And if not immediately dangerous, then wanton and sinister in its curious evil comedy. Another member of the quintet, one Lyamshin, a post-office clerk, gets himself asked to parties where "he would give imitations of a pig, a thunder storm, a confinement, with the first cry of the baby, etc., etc.; that was what he was invited for"; and later we hear of him "mimicking, when requested, various types of Jews, a deaf peasant woman making her confession, or the birth of a child." Note the single common element, Lyamshin's confinement act. Masked by the apparently careless tumble of examples ("etc., etc.") is a calculated insistence on the sore spot, on what Shatov in the notebook calls social unsteadiness, a small but virulent secular profanity standing over against the noble, perhaps the noblest sequence in *The Possessed*, where Marie Shatov returns to her husband to give birth to another man's child.

Peter Verkhovensky can't be fitted into this picture because his *raison d'être* is outside it, manipulating. He plays with the quintet in a quite different sense from that in which they play at revolutionary politics; though, bemused by him, set at odds, their purposes deflected and their fantasies fed and coaxed along, it doesn't seem like playing to them. One of the quintet not only means business but high-minded, selfless business. Virginsky—the surname once more points the way—is a utopian socialist of "rare purity of heart" and "honest fervour"; Horace would have called him *candidus*. " 'I will never, never abandon these bright hopes,' he used to say to me with shining eyes. Of his 'bright hopes' he always spoke quietly, in a blissful half-whisper, as it were secretly." And of the tribulations of his personal life, which were in fact grievous: " 'It's of no consequence. It's just one particular case. It won't interfere with the "cause" in the least, not in the least.' " One senses a rush of creative warmth as this lonely rapt figure is conjured in a few sentences. Virginsky will always belong to the Petrashevsky Circle of Dostoevsky's own youth, as well as to the ill-assorted group that dances to Verkhovensky's tune in the late 1860s.

How to describe that tune? I called Peter Verkhovensky a wrecker. I might also have said a nihilist. Nihilist is the case but it risks confusion between Dostoevsky and Turgenev who may not have invented the word but certainly gave it very wide currency. In his novel *Fathers and Children* which (as the title suggests) is about the generation gap, Turgenev pinned "nihilist" to the son Bazarov. The heart of this new word and new conception is a humane, scientific, and Germany-focused enlightenment, a delayed *Aufklärung* hitting Russia's young elite of the 1860s. Bazarov is an idealist and a brave man, and his aims are rational. Verkhovensky has courage (though in its lower forms of which Plato speaks), but otherwise there is nothing in common between the two young men except the times they live in.

After the non-fictional *Sportsman's Sketches*, *Fathers and Children* is Turgenev's best book, and the best thing in it, apart perhaps from the bereaved old couple at the end, is the sensitive give-and-take marriage of its hero's idealism to his scepticism, a questing, generous idealism and an undestroying scepticism. So the novel strikes me, and at one time Dostoevsky thought so too. At least he said he did. One can't be sure. He was at his most two-faced in his dealings with Turgenev. Anyhow, he praised *Fathers and Children* to its author, and in his own *Winter Notes* he remarked Bazarov's "greatness of spirit, in spite of all his nihilism."

Then later, in the *Possessed* notebooks, we read: "Bazarov was created by a man of the 1840s, and was created as a figure without affectation, which means that a man of the 1840s could not create Bazarov without violating the truth." A remarkable statement, and a difficult one. It needn't mean that Dostoevsky had been telling lies and is now telling the truth in the privacy of his own notebooks. He may very well have changed his mind. But if he has, I don't think it follows that *Fathers and Children* has become a bad book in his eyes, but rather, it is now not all that good. A rift has opened between realism and something beyond, and at the same time a link has been forged between Dostoevsky's favourite phrase, the deeper realism, and my own apocalyptic naturalism.

If Turgenev is a man of the 1840s (which he is), what is he supposed to do about it? And if Turgenev were to object that one could not find a more typical product of the 1840s than the Petrashevsky Circle to which Dostoevsky belonged, how would the other men reply? Over both questions, and over all plausible answers to them, I see hovering those common Dostoevsky ideas of split and break and rent. The *raskol* of Raskolnikov means split with a further specialized religious sense of schism. Raskolnikov is self-divided and also separated from the human family in a way which for Dostoevsky is both social and religious. But, as Porfiry tells him, "*You can't do without us.*" Nor can he do without his undivided self. And that is how the body of the novel leaves the matter. It's only in the *Crime and Punishment* notebooks that we read "Love and Sonya broke him." Confusion—the sundering of *raskol*—was thus itself confounded; and the crisis or breaking point of his illness followed by his "regeneration" (*voskresenie*) and his "passing from one world to another" and his "acquaintance with a new and hitherto unknown reality" are merely affirmed at the end of the Epilogue.

Just as *raskol* means split and religious schism, so *voskresenie* means regeneration and theological Resurrection. Both areas, breaking and mending, engrossed Dostoevsky from the time when the shared convict existence of prison snapped him like a dry biscuit yet also made him new, so that in the closing words of *The House of the Dead*, with the knocking off of his fetters, the narrator greets "a new life, *voskresenie* from the dead." Of his attempts to realize this experience over again in his post-Siberian fiction, the bald Epilogue to *Crime and Punishment* is an early and unpromising instance. We have here perhaps the most delicate of all points of contact between his life and his art: hence the impression that further and very private issues are involved in, even shielded by, the assertion that "a man of the 1840s could not create Bazarov." As I suggested apropos the Petrashevsky Circle, one feels an urge to smoke Dostoevsky out with the question, who's talking?

"The epileptic" makes a neat reply, again touching life and art simultaneously: the author and hero of *The Idiot*. I have in mind the experience of being suddenly thrust outside time, which constitutes in *The Idiot* and elsewhere the epileptic aura. When this and the regeneration/resurrection theme are brought to bear upon the remark about Bazarov and the 1840s, what seemed a difference of degree turns out to be one of a kind. The criticism of Turgenev is only incidentally that he is stuck in the 1840s and not far-sighted enough. New-sightedness, the timeless standpoint, "hitherto unknown reality"—these have an air of mystical hubris when dragged into the open, but they are what Dostoevsky is really talking about.

And so while he sat in a German public library and the story of the murder in the park unfolded before him in the newspapers, a novel began to stir. Or, in mystic vein, an order of being was glimpsed in which the 1840s, the 1860s, nihilism, Bazarov, found themselves apocalyptically and teleologically disposed—those two polysyllabic adverbs embracing and transcending all nature, including futurity. As one would expect, pre-existing material got sucked into this new world. First, the murdered man: he turned out to be a student at the Petrine Agricultural Academy, and his name was Ivanov. It so happened that the novelist's wife had a younger brother at this Academy who knew Ivanov. Now the remarkable circumstance, recorded by Anna Dostoevsky in her memoirs, is that her husband had a foreboding of political disturbances at the Academy, and fearing that his brother-in-law "because of his youthfulness and weakness of character might take an active part in them," he persuaded Anna's mother it would be a good thing if the young man came to them in Dresden: which he did in October of 1869, the month before Ivanov was murdered.

Next the murderer, the original of Peter Verkhovensky. He was Sergei Nechaev. In defensive mood, and not with complete truth, Dostoevsky wrote to Katkov: "I do not know and never have known either Nechaev or Ivanov, or the circumstances of the murder, except from the newspapers. And even if I had, I would not have begun copying them." He had reason to be touchy about Nechaev. This ascetic, strong-willed young man, dominating yet dull-toned in personality to the point of satanic flatness, captured as if in his own despite the imagination of the day. Ordinary people talked about him. He even disquieted the hardened revolutionaries he moved among, most notably old Bakunin. His *Catechism of a Revolutionary* is a classic in the tactics of terrorism, and it came with an agreeable click of fittingness to learn recently that this work earned a place on the bookshelves of Stalin.

Dostoevsky wanted to stifle the thought that he was riding on the back of Nechaev's perverse glamour. Thus Nechaev forms the most important part, but still only a part, of the perennial parajournalistic debate about actuality and fiction. In the same letter to Katkov Dostoevsky also claimed that the murder was itself the merest peg; "I am only taking the accomplished fact"; and he went on to assert that the human type "which corresponds to this crime" was the creature of his imagination. At one level, he got there first. At another, we are still getting there, and the man whose bomb explodes at Bologna railway station one summer day in 1980 while I am pulling this page into shape falls straight back inside *The Possessed*. At yet another, we will never get there since a stream of tendency has been caught and held in new-visioned (as opposed to far-sighted) iconic stasis, and there can be no movement on out of the world we live in into the book we read.

Katkov, therefore, is being asked to accept that "my Peter Verkhovensky may in no way resemble Nechaev." This of course won't do. The identities need switching and the whole statement inverting, thus: "The historical wrecker and terrorist, whether in Petersburg or Bologna, must bear the mark of the fiction and thereby confirm it." For the moment Dostoevsky has been sidetracked by his immediate anxieties. As I say, he had reason to feel touchy about Nechaev.

It is also important to note the time gap of nearly a year between the murder and the letter to Katkov. Initially, a swift, artistically rough job was contemplated, a "tendentious piece" which would take a few months to write and would enrage "the nihilists and Westerners" and set them "howling about me that I'm a *retrograde*. Well, to hell with them, but I will say everything to the last word." It was to be topical and polemical, and among other things a direct challenge to *Fathers and Children*. The enlightened Bazarov had inherited, was continuous with, took a stage further, the liberal and Westernizing impulse of the 1840s which itself followed the Decembrist uprising of 1825, an aristocratic bid for reform by men who had chased Napoleon out of Russia and had later felt the civilizing influence of Paris. But Verkhovensky the wrecker is unrelated to anything that had gone before, except in the new-seeing eye of his creator. He articulates the Dostoevsky split (*raskol*) in terms of a generation-gap story. Obviously the other side

of the gap had to be blocked in, and to represent the 1840s the choice fell
on Timofey Granovsky, in his time a renowned liberal professor and public
speaker, and to a lesser extent a man of letters. Dostoevsky wrote for
Stankevich's published critical study of Granovsky—"material absolutely
indispensable for my work," a life-and-death necessity "like air." All was bustle
and confidence. In the earlier *Possessed* notebooks Granovsky appears under
his own name, and Peter Verkhovensky (it must be recorded) is often
Nechaev. The "tendentious" story would soon be out of the way, making
possible a return to what Dostoevsky thought was much more important,
the *Life of a Great Sinner* project. But it didn't come out like that. He found
he had taken on more than he bargained for.

Painfully—for no work cost him more or perhaps as much as this one—
Dostoevsky came to see that *The Possessed* wasn't a sideshow. In its essentials
it wasn't a diversion of any kind. It proved in due course, and in its own
degree, the *Life of a Great Sinner* itself. Looked at another way, *The Possessed*
and the two remaining novels he had in him to write, *A Raw Youth* and
The Brothers Karamazov, are all generation-gap stories, and for Dostoevsky
the generation gap is only subordinately topical and tendentious and mixed
up with Turgenev. How much of the great-sinner project remained unachieved
and how much dissolved itself into the books that in fact got written, can
be debated endlessly. His own discussion of the project tended to be vague
and large. In any event the last three novels juxtapose fathers and sons in
an effort to gain access to or leverage upon some further thing.

The October letter to Katkov envisages this world beyond *The
Possessed*'s initial scope in forthright great-sinner terms. Nicholas Stavrogin
has arrived during the summer months of 1870s, and has established himself
as the one "who might really be called the chief character of the novel." He
is "a villain," but "tragic," and Dostoevsky continues in his most pushy vein,
anxious that Katkov shall take notice, "I have taken him from my heart."

He means the heart of his creative instinct. There is nowhere else to take
Stavrogin from, no other link between the middle-aged overdriven novelist
and his idle young well-connected "chief character." Dostoevsky also calls
him his "real hero" and his "new hero," and I think he might not object to
"antihero" if the suggestion were put to him. For Stavrogin reaches back,
or rather Dostoevsky reaches back in himself, brushing against Raskolnikov
and Svidrigailov as he does so, and makes common cause with the
underground man. Let me try and bring this out by means of a single phrase
in Stavrogin's suicide letter. The final text has "When all's said and done

I've got the habits of a decent man." Five drafts of the relevant passage survive, the first reading "When all's said and done I'm a decent man." The simple end-product arrives only at the fifth attempt.

With hindsight one can point to the underground man complaining that if he could manage even to loaf and idle around wholeheartedly he would be able to call himself a lazy man. This is the rationale of the movement from "a decent man" to "the habits of a decent man." Stavrogin can't, and in our definitive text doesn't, claim to be a decent man or to have any other thing to be; all his letter indicates is a deathlike mime or sleepwalk within behaviour patterns determined by upbringing, class, and kind.

This must appear implausibly neat. But so do many things once the dust of composition has settled and the builder's yard of notebooks and rejected drafts can be studied at leisure. The neatness comes afterwards; it gets imposed when a long and laborious and very untidy process is shortcircuited by the observation (which Dostoevsky himself may never have made) of a direct link between Stavrogin and the underground man. Fumbling after phrases in the suicide letter and a thousand other places, the novelist strives to clarify an idea, but also to purge his understanding of great-sinner preconceptions and ambitions which the developing *Possessed* refuses to accommodate. It isn't because Stavrogin is *not* a decent man that the form of words has to be changed; he also says "I'm bored" in the earliest draft of the letter, and this assertion goes completely. The reason is the underground one I have just stated. Stavrogin acts bored, other people call him bored: he *is* bored! But he lacks the minimal ontological ballast to call himself bored. Or anything else. He writes in that same letter "I can't hate anything," and he admits he can't even own to "despair." And so he drifts towards vanishing point: "One may argue about everything endlessly, but from me nothing has come but negation, with no magnanimity and no force. Even negation has not come from me." Only negation. But really not even negation. Nothing.

Which leads one to ask what becomes of the sinner—let alone the great sinner. What counts as sinning greatly? Or, what does sinning greatly count as? One recalls Svidrigailov and Raskolnikov, the potential suicide twitting the actual murderer with "well, you can certainly do a lot." Stavrogin writes: "I've tried the depths of debauchery and wasted my strength over it; but I don't like debauchery and never wanted it." It doesn't and didn't amount to anything. There is nothing (so to say) deedy in his actions. This crablike sidling away from all he is and does catches the tune of the achieved, fully formed Stavrogin; unlike Svidrigailov, who incidentally makes great play with the fact that he's bored, he would—could—never call himself a debauchee. He is a different sort of great sinner, or essay upon the great-sinner theme, which is why I stress the aspect of return to the vicious and tragic antihero who can't even call himself lazy. The underground man's heart is no more in being idle than in anything else, however much, as he himself puts it, he "wants to want." Stavrogin naturalizes this thought by observing "My desires are too weak." But the suicide letter also keeps a foot in the abstract world, the world of metaphysics in my extended sense. Between them Stavrogin and Dasha Shatov, Shatov's sister, the girl to whom the letter is addressed, have conjured the word "nurse" which is a term of art as metaphysical as anything in *Notes from Underground* and impossible to match in the other post-Siberian novels. "Nurse" is a sort of code between them. She invented it and he picks it up. He has promised that in extremity he will send for her, and she will come and be his nurse. He is perching on the railway, six stops down the line, with a stationmaster he got to know somehow when he was on the town in Petersburg—the Dostoevsky no-home at its most stripped and strange in this novel of aimless movement. She never comes because he hangs himself, she has nobody to be nurse to, but her journey—were she to have made it—would prove as nugatory as his. The letter declares Stavrogin's fear of killing himself. It comes no closer than that to threatening suicide. Nor does it have to: we know his fears are as weak as his desires. Nature is likely to follow art, art here being the pure abstraction of Stavrogin's remark that even negation is more than he can manage.

Svidrigailov would never have said that; he would have gone on making jokes about America. And how different the tone of the two men and their two suicides! The nurse trope, I admit, shares America's power to open human doors the further side of whimsicality, but that is because the suicide letter has only one foot in the completely flat uncomic abstract world of negation talk. The other foot remains in Dostoevskian nature. Dasha actually wants to come and look after Stavrogin, as actually as Svidrigailov is bored— "especially now," he says, as America looms. The two worlds of nature and abstraction meet when Stavrogin asks Dashsa whether by coming to be his nurse "you hope to set up some aim for me at last." This thought combines the antihero wanting to want and Svidrigailov trying sex, balloon-travel, good works even, in his struggle to latch on to life. As a nurse, Dasha's *aim* would be to give Stavrogin an *aim*—simultaneously an underground and an American idea. In the *Possessed* notebooks Dostoevsky tries a snatch of dialogue in which Stavrogin is asked "Why don't you just simply live?"; and he replies "Ah, that's the hardest thing of all." The novel itself foregoes many such touches which aren't quite true because they betray a teasing Svidrigailov-like zest, or, if you prefer, counterzest; just as, on the secondary plane, Lebyadkin's reply to the man who tells him to stop getting drunk is

wonderfully funny but wrong. "What a strange demand!" says Lebyadkin
with an effrontery beyond the man we have been given, though not of course
beyond old Karamazov. The long disciplining process of notebooks and drafts
reduces Stavrogin to a state very near automatism: the *habits* of a decent
man. In rejecting drafts he is constantly saying he's bored. In the book we
have in front of us—and it is a long one—he never does. But, as I say, he
acts bored. Peter Verkhovensky is telling him about a religious conversation
among some army officers. The mood of the party, according to
Verkhovensky, was atheistic. As a group "they gave God short shrift." But

> One grey-haired captain, a rough old chap, sat and sat not saying
> a word, mute as a mackerel, then suddenly got up in the middle
> of the room and, you know, said aloud as if speaking to himself,
> "If there's no God then what sort of a Captain am I after that?"
> and seized his cap and threw up his arms and went out.
> "He expressed a rather sensible idea," said Stavrogin, and
> yawned for the third time.

A wine-breath intellectualism hangs over the sturdy little comedy of the
captain who has found his own words for declaring God to be the ground
of his being. And if there is no God? That brings us to Stavrogin's third yawn.
He has grasped the neat theological and ontological crux implicit in the
captain's statement, and has acted bored at it. If he could help himself this
would be mental vandalism; but he can't; Stavrogin's are yawns that refuse
to be stifled; automatism and involuntarism are finally one, and the tragic
villain-hero who at once apprehends the "sensible idea" and yawns at it betrays
a high but helpless intelligence recalling Raskolnikov as well as Svidrigailov.

Stavrogin is no more an atheist than Raskolnikov was, but his belief—
all his beliefs—are weak, as the suicide letter to Dasha Shatov makes plain,
and their weakness corresponds to the instability (*shatost*) of Raskolnikov's.
Equally, to yawn is to act bored, to admit and even to flaunt kinship with
Svidrigailov, and the evil-omened word *listless* (*vyali*) that dogs Stavrogin,
though he never uses it himself, corresponds to the other man's terminal
boredom. This is what it means to say that Dostoevsky brushes against
Rasknolnikov and Svidrigailov as he reaches back towards the underground
man.

The object of the reaching exercise is of course to arrive at Stavrogin.
It holds more true of some of us than of others, that in the struggle to make
it new we are writing the same book all our lives; and with Dostoevsky this
truth is very true. His post-Siberian great-sinner project won't convincingly

disengage from his interest in the confessional form, and, as we have seen, the Dostoevsky Confession was afoot before Siberia. With Stavrogin, confession and the great sinner come together in the chapter "At Tikhon's," often referred to as Stavrogin's Confession. Dostoevsky set great store by this chapter which marks the acutest phase of his tribulations over *The Possessed*, because his editor Katkov refused to print it. We recall the same editor's objection to the debate about Christianity between Raskolnikov and Sonya Marmeladov in *Crime and Punishment*, and, before that again, the censor's blocking of the positive Christian counter-affirmations in *Notes from Underground*. But this time the rejected text survives: we have the galley proofs of "At Tikhon's" submitted to the magazine *Russian Herald*, and Dostoevsky's alterations to those proofs, and his widow's list of further variants.

Therefore it becomes possible at last to read and evaluate what was earnestly planned, executed, fought for, tinkered with in a vain attempt to propitiate Katkov (but also, as we shall see, for another reason), and finally surrendered. Furthermore, "At Tikhon's" provides the chance to get a look at the figure named by me Dostoevsky's good angel, because here again, as in the two earlier cases, the novelist took no steps to restore the deleted material at some future date when he was his own master; and I think he was right. My proposition, embracing *The House of the Dead, Notes from Underground, Crime and Punishment, The Possessed, Karamazov,* and, negatively, by way of relative failure, *The Idiot,* is that Dostoevsky could only promote his dearest values by creeping up on their blind side: in other words that he had an urge towards crisis and clarity which he could only satisfy by yielding it to the enemy—to the horror of the flogging routine in the "Thy kingdom come" episode in the Dead House at one chronological extreme, and to Ivan Karamazov's showdown with the Religion Swindle at the other.

Clarity appears in those self-directed exhortations of the novelist to elucidate Raskolnikov's motive for murder. The novel itself ignores them. Crisis introduces the word *podvig,* translated "exploit" or "feat," though Jacques Catteau remarks that *avancement* sometimes renders it best. *Podvig,* also prominent in the *Crime and Punishment* notebooks, gets relegated in the final text to the Epilogue where it is seen at its simplest in the mitigating circumstance that the murderer is discovered at his trial to have burnt himself rescuing two little children from a blazing house. With both the motive for the murder and the brave rescue *Crime and Punishment* sets the pattern for later Dostoevsky; his post-Siberian notebooks swarm with admonitions like "Decide the matter definitely one way or the other," and with the X marks the spot of "Here a *podvig* is achieved"; and in the other novels, as in *Crime and Punishment*, the actual outcome of such promptings makes an interesting study.

Crisis and clarity are notebook froth whipped up by a single hidden energy. I ask, what does Dostoevsky's gambling mania aspire towards? And I answer, breaking the bank of all banks, busting Plato's very Idea of a bank; and also being cleaned out absolutely—but absolutely: body, mind, immortal soul: in fact the Dostoevsky apocalypse where all shall be revealed, where crisis *is* clarity. And obviously the novelist's apocalypse is by no means identical with his received Christian one; hence, in part, the divergence of his art from the things his notebooks show him wanting to say. It's a reflection on sadomasochism, and on negation, and on the Underground throughout these novels, that the true gambler's urge to lose is as strong as and not ultimately separable from its opposite.

All this bears closely on Stavrogin and his so-called confession. In "At Tikhon's" he goes to the holy man with a document which he gives him to read, and which he does read, and which Stavrogin next proposes to publish. I see the whole chapter as a subtle but misconceived footnote to *Crime and Punishment*; in these pages, instead of brushing past Raskolnikov and Svidrigailov in his return upon the underground man, Dostoevsky has allowed himself to be obstructed by them, and the result is a Stavrogin who compounds Raskolnikov's bracing himself to enter the police station *"as a man"* and confess with Svidrigailov's reaching out in all directions, including the far extremes of moral and physical debauchery, in the hope that something, it doesn't matter what, will make him unbored.

After a sleepless night Stavrogin sets forth. Then outside the monastery where Bishop Tikhon lives, "he stopped, hastily and anxiously felt something in his side pocket and—smiled." That is Raskolnikov's smile. We know it well. And the gesture is Raskolnikov's too, for example when he feels for the axe slung inside his overcoat. Even the sudden stopping is tell-tale. Stavrogin would never stop in the street like that, his psychophysical being is other. This is not a *Possessed* moment, not a *Possessed* sentence. At the outset we are aware that the chapter "At Tikhon's" is going wrong. Not bad but wrong.

When, driven by unbearable mental torment, Raskolnikov enters the building and climbs the stairs, a splendidly ample and imaginative *podvig* seems to be in prospect, *un avancement spirituel*. It's only afterwards, in the Epilogue, that we learn with surprise and perhaps some vexation that repentance and acceptance of suffering come to him not then but much later, in prison; his confession was not the decisive moral feat we took it for. It was not a heart-and-soul confession but an admission of guilt. And what about Stavrogin as he stands smiling, not of course a happy smile, no kind of unambiguous smile, about to enter the monastery, fingering the pages in his pocket? The man as I say is all Raskolnikov. The document which Bishop Tikhon will read puts Raskolnikov in Svidrigailov's shoes because it is a record of the excesses a mortally jaded palate has got up to.

And as Stavrogin describes his search after new and ever stronger and more bizarre sensations, and as he laments his boredom, and as suicide is touched on, tracts of *Crime and Punishment* open up again: but without the astral, feathering humour of America, anatomy, and ordinary ghosts. And as he mulls over his reasons for behaving as he has and for writing and publishing this record, the footnote status of "At Tikhon's" causes it to embrace a wide range of familiar themes. To loose them off together, scatter-gun fashion: Stavrogin says "I am making this statement, incidentally, to prove I am in full possession of my mental faculties and understand my position"; "I want to forgive myself, this is my chief aim, my whole aim"; "I want everyone to look at me"; "I fall back on this as my last resource"; "The thing about me then was I felt bored with life, sick and tired of it"; "I am seeking boundless suffering"; "I took it into my head to mutilate my life somehow" (not necessarily the same thing as seeking suffering, any more than seeking suffering need entail accepting it).

Let us pause for a moment over "I want everyone to look at me." And I would also like to add yet another "reason" to the already formidable pile, which is that Stavrogin intends a "challenge to society." Now the first is one of Dostoevsky's alterations to the galley proofs of "At Tikhon's," and the second is a variant recorded by his widow. I draw attention to their provenance because commentators have focused on the family-magazine question, on the attempt, that is, to get the chapter past Katkov in some shape or form, and I think this is only half the story. I think in all this textual fussing Dostoevsky was also—and increasingly—troubled by the chapter's footnote status and by the problem which I picture as obstruction by Raskolnikov and Svidrigailov in his backward groping towards the underground man. The sharpened exhibitionism of Stavrogin's wanting everybody to look at him will not have helped Dostoevsky with Katkov, but it does mark a step away from *Crime and Punishment* and closer to *Notes from Underground*. The "challenge to society" seems to fit Raskolnikov's Napoleonic idea—until we read on in Anna Dostoevsky's manuscript where it is at once and directly linked to "the governor's bitten ear," that is to one of those sudden sallies of Stavrogin's elsewhere in *The Possessed*, sallies hovering between outrage and prank. The instance here is of Stavrogin pretending to the provincial governor that he has a secret to communicate to him, and, when the unsuspecting old man "hastily and trustfully" inclines his head, seizing his ear in his teeth and holding on to it, biting hard.

"Nicholas, what kind of joke is this?" moaned the governor mechanically in a voice unlike his own.

It is a *Possessed* kind of joke, inconceivable in *Crime and Punishment*, and there was no reference to it in the version of "At Tikhon's" submitted to Katkov initially. Once again the change can have nothing to do with making the chapter more acceptable. This incident of the bitten ear, presented explicitly as "a challenge to society," has no tonal affinity whatever with Raskolnikov's murder, its home is with the underground man sticking his tongue out; the hesitant backward movement toward the world under the floor is also a forward fumble towards Stavrogin and *The Possessed*.

And what of the document itself? Since "At Tikhon's" is constantly referred to in Russia and the West as Stavrogin's Confession, it occurs to me to note that the word confession does not appear anywhere in the chapter. That the written statement and its publication add up to a true Dostoevsky confession, to repentance and acceptance of suffering, to "a wonderful *podvig*" in Tikhon's words, is one possibility among many. Stavrogin's prodigal scattering of reasons does more than leave the question open. It leaves all questioning behind. It muddies the waters of speculation utterly. If we take wanting everybody to look at him as the "real" reason, then the case of Stavrogin is (in the lawyer's phrase) on all fours with that of the underground man's indecent exposure of consciousness. However, "I invite nobody into my soul" he declares, as if to banish the exhibitionist thought. And then if the search for suffering is allowed to eclipse the rest, we are back with Marmeladov squinnying into the bottom of his vodka jug; whereas Stavrogin saying he wants to forgive himself might be Raskolnikov pondering retrospectively, self-critically, on his admission of guilt at the police station.

To Marmeladov, Raskolnikov, and the underground man, I now add Svidrigailov, because the chief enormity which is being confessed, or merely admitted to, or flaunted, or feigned, binds Stavrogin to the America-minded debauchee no less tightly than does the boredom theme of the "At Tikhon's" chapter. As with the highly misleading phrase Stavrogin's Confession, critics and commentators behave as if they had got into a huddle. Everybody, including the present Soviet editor, talks about Stavrogin's forcing or rape of a young girl. So to sort the thing out: Stavrogin has designs on the child; he kisses her hand, puts her on his knee, whispers to her. She is in terror. Then

> At last there occurred, suddenly, a most strange event which I shall never forget and which astonished me: the little girl flung her arms round my neck and in a rush began kissing me frenziedly. Her face expressed complete rapture. I nearly got up and went

away out of pity, I found this so unpleasant in a slip of a child.
But I overcame my immediate fearful feeling, and I stayed.

And that's that. The next sentence begins a new paragraph: "When all was over, she was covered in confusion." Therefore no rape occurs. The child is sexually responsive and perhaps dominant. Hence her smile "as if ashamed, a kind of twisted smile" after her terror and immediately before the passage I have just quoted. Hence, later, her words "I have killed God," and her suicide. Getting this right obviously matters in itself, but also for its bearing on two further issues.

First, it drives Stavrogin even closer to Svidrigailov than I have suggested so far. The episode with the child is a reworking of Svidrigailov's nightmare immediately before his suicide, in which he finds an abandoned little girl and carries her upstairs and puts her in his bed, and goes back later to see how she is.

> Now, without any further concealment, she opened both her eyes;
> they turned a blazing, shameless glance upon him, they invited
> him, they laughed. . . . "Damn you!" Svidrigailov cried in horror,
> raising his hand to strike her. But at that moment he woke up.

Second, it discredits those—and again the Soviet editor is among them—who seek to explain Dostoevsky's failure to reinstate "At Tikhon's" solely by the prevailing conditions of censorship. He got Svidrigailov's nightmare past the censor, and there is a good deal more to that horror than I have quoted; and "At Tikhon's" could have been got past him too. It is unsound to argue that Svidrigailov's experience was only a bad dream, because the manuscript variants prove that Dostoevsky was prepared at one stage to forego the actuality of the sexual outcome between Stavrogin and the child. "It was just a psychological misunderstanding," so Stavrogin reassures the bishop in Anna's text:

> "Nothing happened. Not a thing."
> "Well, God be praised," said Tikhon, and crossed himself.

Amidst this confusion, my view of "At Tikhon's" as a hyper-lucid footnote to *Crime and Punishment*, as misconceived crisis and clarity, needs justifying: the very point of Stavrogin's scattering of "reasons" is that he and his document shall not come clear or clinch anything. But, as to clinching things, Stavrogin is not Tikhon, which evokes another of my dicta: Dostoevsky could only satisfy his urge towards crisis and clarity by surrendering it to the enemy. For sure he takes pains to make Tikhon a human puzzle so that he shan't in any obvious way speak God's truth. He looks a bit ill, smiles vaguely, and has a strange rather shy expression. His furniture is a jumble of good and bad; a magnificent Bokhara carpet lies next to straw mats, and engravings of fashionable society and sacred icons confront one another. He appears to enjoy light reading. Perhaps even salacious reading.

But nothing, and certainly not articulating his words "cheerfully and artlessly," can muffle Tikhon's diagnosis which is that Stavrogin suffers from "indifference." At once the two of them fall into a kind of trance. Stavrogin asks the bishop (in cool reason a preposterous question) if he has read the Christian Apocalypse. He then directs him to the message to the angel of the church at Laodicea in the third chapter of Revelation. Tikhon knows the passage by heart and recites it word for word. Its burden is:

> I know thy works, that thou art neither hot nor cold: I would
> that thou wert hot or cold. So then because thou art lukewarm
> and neither hot nor cold, I will spew thee out of my mouth.

The "lukewarm" state is of course a biblical and transcendental and authoritative anchoring of "indifference." It isolates and ratifies the reason among so many reasons which Stavrogin himself gives: "the disease of indifference." Tikhon and Stavrogin have both got it right. But this *it* cannot be said, can only be shown forth as in the suicide letter where Stavrogin writes "My desires are too weak; they cannot guide me." We aim straight at the art of *The Possessed* by observing that the follow-up, I'm a lukewarm man, or I'm an indifferent, an apathetic man, is beyond Stavrogin. All self-definition, as Dostoevsky finally shaped and gave Stavrogin to the world, is beyond him. That is why, instead of taking the weakness of his desires to himself, Stavrogin continues in figurative, musing vein, sad and free, very beautiful in context: "You can cross a river on a tree-trunk, but not on a chip of wood." This is the same young man who bit the ear of the governor—and we can only meet and get to know him in the novel itself.

Get to know as opposed to get at. The "At Tikhon's" chapter, rejected by the editor and finally abandoned by the novelist, gets at, ponders the case of, somebody we never even meet there: the smiling man outside the monastery is Raskolnikov, and the document in his pocket recounts Svidrigailov's deeds. The pondering, the getting at the absent Stavrogin, proves successful; many acute observations buttress the central "lukewarm" truth about him, and analysis spills over into the notebooks where Tikhon's God's-voice function appears at its clearest. "Try to hold something sacred, no matter what it be," he exhorts Stavrogin who replies "What for?" And then the punch line: "This isn't done *for something*, it is done *just so*." At which moment we can sense the warm breath of composition coming off the page, for Dostoevsky first had Tikhon continue "It carries its own reward" and then crossed these words out in his notebook, no doubt because they are too obvious and touched by the world's wisdom. They aren't worthy of the silent spiritual gesture made by that italicized *"just so."* Nor is Stavrogin's pert Svidrigailov-like "What for?" worthy of it, or of himself. And Tikhon's own further move isn't right either: "If you do not feel a need, and if you love nothing, it follows you are incapable of it." To this severe driving home of the issue in pursuit of crisis and clarity, Stavrogin might fairly reply that he didn't create himself lukewarm. He would never have had it so. "I want to want," the underground man's lonely cry, is also his though he doesn't utter it, and biting the governor's ear, like sticking the tongue out, is a one-against-all drumming of the heels of consciousness—but again with a difference which is that the biting extends beyond the notional; it happens and it hurts, though it's a minor foray compared with Raskolnikov's spectacular eruption into actuality with the murder. And at the same time, since Svidrigailov too has been brushed against in this reaching back which is also a reaching forward, the incident of the governor's ear can be understood in all its matchless comedy as a desperate man's recourse against boredom.

The mere mention of the biting in Anna's manuscript record of "At Tikhon's" variants is enough to pull the reader back into *The Possessed*, and he can't experience the sudden fierce tug of that novel without realizing simultaneously that the whole "At Tikhon's" chapter belongs elsewhere, to a different masterpiece. Its footnote status in relation to *Crime and Punishment* constitutes, I admit, a funny sort of belonging, as does the obstructive force of Raskolnikov and Svidrigailov upon Dostoevsky's attempt to give decisively new shape to the Great Sinner of his notebooks and letters and fondest creative hopes. A negative belonging, if you like. But narrative tone is a different and affirmative matter.

> A minute later I looked at my watch and noted the time. Evening was drawing in. A fly was buzzing over my head and kept settling on my face. I caught it, held it in my fingers and put it out of the window. A cart drove very loudly into the yard below. Very loudly (and for some time before), a tailor had been singing as he sat at a window in a corner of the yard. He sat at his work and I could see him. It occurred to me that as I had met nobody as I walked through the gate and went upstairs, there was no need to encounter anyone now, going down, and I moved my chair from the window. I picked up a book, but put it down again and

began looking at a tiny red spider on the leaf of a geranium, and
lost count of time. I remember everything to the very last moment.

This sequence could not occur in *The Possessed*—a dangerous thing to say
about a very long and diverse book, but true. Despite the fact that spiders
are all over the place in Dostoevsky, not just in Svidrigailov's dirty bathhouse
vision of Eternity, and that urban potted plants go back to the beginning
in *Poor People*, we are here firmly inside *Crime and Punishment* in its abandoned first-person narrative form ("I am on trial and will tell all"): Petersburg
evenings and their hanging summer light, noises from below, happy workmen,
blessed "living life" elsewhere, a lonely man in pain passing through gates,
over thresholds, slipping up and down staircases, the buzzing fly of
Raskolnikov's dream and his awakening, intense time-consciousness alternating with time-oblivion.

"At Tikhon's" has strayed out of a metropolitan novel into a provincial
one which won't accommodate it. To take one's finger off the bounding
narrative pulse of *Crime and Punishment* and to open *The Possessed*—to open
it anywhere—is to find oneself out in the sticks once again: the "our town"
of the novel and the voice relating its affairs bring back the "we" of convict
life in *The House of the Dead* and the more sketchy collective of that remote
Siberian community outside the prison walls. The same dilating and con-
tracting principle informs both novels, a first-person narrator who moves
between "we all thought" and "it was just my hunch," though the swing
is greater in *The Possessed* and its figuration much more complex. If any
House of the Dead notebooks had survived I would expect them to contain sudden leaps of discovery and creative arrivals like "Most important—
it's a chronicle " and

> "I've had breakfast.
> I'll keep the secret.
> I am a character."

By drawing a rectangle round "*it's a chronicle*" Dostoevsky suggests a framed
narrative for *The Possessed* like the story found by the frame narrator among
a deceased ex-convict's effects in *The House of the Dead*; and by declaring
"I am a character" (*kharakter*: a person, not a literary *personazh*) he puts
himself inside that frame. The result, therefore, is a framed narrative without
a frame narrator—not that he reached the two sides of this conclusion
simultaneously. The first came early and firmly, in February of 1870: "From
a provincial chronicle . . . The system I have adopted is that of a CHRONI-
CLE." The second was an untidy and protracted business, stretching on
through the spring and summer and coinciding with the refusal of *The*

Possessed to be contained within the limits of a "tendentious" sideshow. The novel insisted on reverting to the ampler great-sinner pattern; hence Stavrogin's emergence as "chief character," "tragic villain" and so forth during this period, and Peter Verkhovensky's withdrawal to the second rank: Verkhovensky the mere wrecker, the nihilist, the man of the 1860s, the deeper realist's answer to Turgenev.

I look in the same direction to account for the charming note "Granovsky has got a bit out of hand." Taken more or less straight from life, Granovsky was to have represented the liberal 1840s in a crisp, neat, polemical generation-gap story. In *The Possessed* he becomes Stepan Trofimovich Verkhovensky (hereafter Stepan), Peter's father and one of the best things Dostoevsky ever did. But in the mean time, whose hand has Granovsky escaped from? This pinpoints the issue of Dostoevsky as author and as "a character" in the provincial chronicle, the framed narrative. Again we are at the tip of his pen as he draws a box to put himself inside, and as the most private and informative area of the *Possessed* notebooks begins to open up. At first he hadn't even settled on first-person narration; the voice from inside the frame is sometimes "the chronicler's" or "the author's," sometimes "mine." A double stance develops—inevitably, since the figure inside the frame can't wish away the novelist bent over his notebooks. Thus: "ABOUT NECHAEV [Peter Verkhovensky]: NECHAEV PLAYS TWO ROLES, THE SECOND OF WHICH I, THE CHRONICLER, DON'T KNOW AT ALL AND AM NOT PRESENTING." Sometimes we catch the novelist positively shaping and manipulating the narrator: "The chronicler pretends for his part that he feels the sorrow of a Christian." And from, or nearly from, the outset there is the hint of a three-cornered relationship in which the future reader of the as yet unwritten *Possessed* joins novelist and narrator in a conspiracy to uphold the truth of the fiction: "Altogether, when I describe conversations, even *tête-à-tête* conversations between two people—don't worry: either I have hard facts, or perhaps I am *inventing* them myself—but in any case rest assured that everything is true."

The man being reassured is the reader. The man reassuring him is, or has the authority of, the omniscient and omnipotent novelist. The "I" describing conversations he hasn't direct access to, which he wasn't present at, which he may not even have been told about and so may be inventing, is the "character" Dostoevsky has turned himself into for the purpose of narrating the provincial chronicle. This one sentence from the notebooks goes straight home to the novel which eventually got written. And the novel which got written breathes life into this sentence's very unpromising warrant for the "truth" of what is being told, namely that there are hard facts or perhaps it is just being made up.

Reassurance is another matter, except at the level where all great art reassures; for a spirit of slippage presides over *The Possessed*. In the opening paragraphs we are introduced to Stepan Verkhovensky:

> Nevertheless he was a most intelligent and gifted man, even, so to say, a scholar, though, as far as his scholarship was concerned, well, in a word, his scholarship didn't amount to much, to nothing at all, I think.

A scholar. Not much of a scholar. Really no scholar. Recall Stavrogin's suicide letter. Only negation. Not even negation. Nothing. Doubling in Dostoevsky, which goes back to the very beginning, to Mr Devushkin living and not living in the kitchen, which has its post-Siberian developments in the underground man's now-you-see-me-now-you-don't "flashing" of his consciousness, in Raskolnikov's and Svidrigailov's different ways of being among but not with us and Porfiry's torture tune of "There's nothing here, precisely nothing, perhaps absolutely nothing"—doubling takes on a new form in *The Possessed*, closer to the I/We/They/Everybody/Nobody shifts of *The House of the Dead* than anything else before it or to come.

The slippage sentence just quoted concludes with an "I think." This "I" is the first-person narrator inside the frame of the provincial chronicle, the "character" Dostoevsky has turned himself into. He is a young friend of Stepan Verkhovensky, and when the notebooks record that Granovsky (Stepan's prototype) has got out of hand they are also heralding the novelist's escape into a fictional mode of enormous suppleness. That Stepan's scholarship amounts to nothing is only what "I think." Others may and do think otherwise. A freedom is generated which has its phases of indiscipline, licence, chaos. The book is a stampede, faithful to its title and its epigraph which is the story of the Gadarene swine possessed by devils and rushing into the lake of Galilee and drowning themselves.

The fury, the energy of *The Possessed* seems quite magically unconvenanted. The slippage principle should make for enervation and a general whittling away. But on the contrary, this world of "it was rumoured" and "that may well have been so" followed at once by "it is more likely that nothing of the sort happened"—again in the opening paragraphs—is as exhilarating as the challenge of life's opacities to a healthy curiosity. Indeed the overall triumph of art in this case is that the novel walks out into our fact rather than ourselves entering its fiction: a very primitive and absolute form of consumer capitulation. Dostoevsky has an impudent way of making his narrator declare "As a chronicler I confine myself to presenting events exactly as they happened, and it's not my fault if they appear incredible"—like the son of the house writing home about his time on the northwest frontier of India. The imperial-provincial *idée* is a sovereign one. We read about the governor's bitten ear with the fascination of doting remoteness. Likewise the Audenesque opprobrious act which precedes it.

> One of the most respected of our club members, on our committee of management, Pavel Pavlovich Gaganov, an elderly man and highly esteemed, had formed the innocent habit of following anything he had to say with the vehement addition, "No, sir, you can't lead me by the nose!" Well, there's no harm in that. But one day at the club when he trotted out this phrase during some heated discussion in the midst of a little group of members (all of them persons of some consequence), Nicholas Stavrogin who was standing to one side alone and unnoticed, suddenly went up to Mr. Gaganov and, taking him unexpectedly and firmly with two fingers by the nose, managed to drag him two or three steps across the room.

Cantonment goings-on in Peshawar! Goings-on of cruel and rootless hilarity. This is how there is no getting at Stavrogin, and how getting to know him proceeds. And this is what happens to the *podvig* tic which obsesses the notebooks and the "At Tikhon's" chapter: it becomes deflected and surrealized into eruptive impenetrable little freaks. Or Dostoevsky holds firm to a certain grandness and climactic force, while inverting the *podvig* and rendering it passive, when Stavrogin "endures" a tremendous punch in the face from Shatov. Stavrogin is a killer—or can be—but he does nothing: "the light in his eyes seemed to go out." Though untalkative, he is as inspectable as Hamlet, and no less inscrutable. Quite late in his notebooks Dostoevsky puts the matter thus: Stavrogin "confides in nobody and is a mystery all round." Then a few lines further on: Stavrogin "reveals himself gradually through the action without any explanations." But the self that gets revealed in the novel's action is a bundle of contradictions, like some people we know well. So there's no inconsistency when Dostoevsky says that what is *"most important"* is the *"special tone of the narrative"* whereby *"everything will be saved,"* and that the tone of the narrative rests in Stavrogin "not being elucidated."

Stavrogin's ear-biting and nose-pulling present two small samples of this all-important narrative tone. The first of these revelations which elucidate nothing is introduced as "completely unthinkable but from another point of view and in one respect all too easy to envisage." Slippage again: the crumbling, self-thwarting surface of the prose. From what "point of view" and in

which "respect"? We are never told. Furthermore, unthinkable to whom and
envisageable by whom? The chronicler wasn't present at the incident. As with
large tracts of *The Possessed* this is in effect third-person narrative, recalling
the notebook assurance that whether "my" story is based on hard facts or
has simply been made up, it is all "true."

Nor does the chronicler say whether he was present at the nose-pulling.
But nor does it matter; "our club" will have been seething with talk for days,
and "I" am bound to have heard about Stavrogin's escapade. And the "they"
of more or less the whole town will have heard too. Here *The Possessed* draws
close to the I/We/They/Everybody shifts of *The House of the Dead*, and
the tone of the narrative, which (Dostoevsky said) is to save everything,
demonstrates its airy yet potent, rather Proustian anecdotal scope. "Our club"
presumably overlaps while being smaller than "the best circles" of this society,
whereas the "they" of "the whole town" is sometimes, but only sometimes,
the "we" of "our town"; and "our group" which springs out of "my" special
relationship with Stepan Verkhovensky and which gathers round Mrs
Stavrogin, Nicholas's mother and Stepan's patroness, is different again and
again overlapping; and the "all" buried inside the phrase "our 'old man'—
as we all used to call Stepan Trofimovich among ourselves" is probably though
not certainly synonymous with this "group"; while Dostoevsky delights in
sly collective evocations like "civic grief" and in parcellings-out like "the
poorest expectant mothers of the town," and in fouling the whole snobbish
provincial nest with such carefully calculated absurdities as "almost the whole
town, that is of course the entire top stratum of our society."

So there is no difficulty in imagining how the news of the senior citizen's
pulled nose got around. In the general excitement—the novel has scarcely
begun—it gets borne in upon the reader that Stavrogin's conduct is not the
only thing to be puzzled by. Not one of "us" in the whole town ascribes his
action to madness. "That means we were inclined to expect such behaviour
even from a sane Stavrogin." *That means*—the unsettling authorial logic is
neutrally deployed, with no follow-up. Something has bitten "us." "Our" men-
tality is odd too. The reader must make what he can of it. Everybody in
"our town" feels indignant about the insult to the respected old gentleman,
and a proposal gets off the ground to give a subscription dinner in his honour;
but finally "we" think better of it, "perhaps realizing at last that a man had,
after all, been pulled by the nose, so there really wasn't any cause for a
celebration."

"Social unsteadiness (*shatost*), as Shatov says" What has bitten "us,"
the transpersonal Gadarene motif of *The Possessed*, manifests itself through
the dotty plan for a dinner just as eloquently as through the murder in the

park. It's a mistake to have a narrowly political view of the novel, as it is to regard its comedy as somehow decorative. The lightness of its light relief is *shatost* too. "We," the provincial society, display all the loose-end symptoms of Peter the Great's reforms—though Dostoevsky's overt theorizing about Peter gets left behind in the notebooks. The novel articulates the loose end as boredom, again transpersonalized. "I find it strange looking at you all," says Marya Lebyadkin, the crazed visionary cripple, the fool-in-Christ (*yurodivaya*), in a touchstone meditation; "I don't understand how it is people are bored."

Uniting boredom, provinciality, the Gadarene stampede, and paper people, Peter Verkhovensky says: "I realize that in this godforsaken town you are bored, so you make a rush for any piece of paper with something written on it." This boredom rotates upon a frivolous-menacing, frenetic-slack, comic-terrible axis which is the book's living principle. In itself the dim complacency of gossip and cards at "our club" would seem harmless, familiar, merely social; but "in itself" denatures *The Possessed* where groupings dissolve or collapse into each other, and where the "merely" social has no place. On his death-bed Stepan Verkhovensky returns to the swine of the gospel story and paraphrases the devils which enter them as a disease afflicting all Russia. In Eternity, like the madman in the story who got rid of his devils when they were driven out of him and into the swine, Russia will sit healed at the feet of Jesus. This dubious eschatology need not worry us because the novel makes no attempt to encompass it. Jesus and Holy Russia at his feet remain harmlessly, hypothetically beyond the apocalyptic naturalism which is everything the book is about: the devils, the disease, the all-pervading unsteadiness.

Those "poorest expectant mothers of the town" are the objects of Mrs Stavrogin's competitive philanthropy. She and the new governor's wife, Mrs von Lemke, enter upon a tussle for local ascendancy through their rival charitable undertakings. In the end Mrs Stavrogin and her expectant mothers lose out—if indeed there was ever any winning—while Mrs von Lemke's needy governesses bring that determined woman victory, but then defeat. The fundraising fête for the governesses is the biggest set-piece *skandal* in all Dostoevsky. Drunks and gatecrashers move in. Grotesque isolated figures—"a huge pock-marked retired captain"—loom out of the chaos and disappear again. Humble clerks who have gone a bust on clothes for marriageable daughters are outraged but too timid to protest. The book itself seems to go mad. Its flickering epidemic relish at the expense of clerks and governesses and expectant mothers is wilder than irresponsibility and more furious than

Saturnalian record. Out of sight, shielded by riot and revelry and now a quarter of a century older, lurks the poet who boasted he had not shown his young mug in *Poor People*: the sober laborious craftsman determined that his tone shall save everything.

> An extraordinary number of subscribers and donors had turned up, all the select society of the town; but even the most unselect were admitted, provided they brought the cash.

Trouble ahead! Trouble conveyed in one exactly placed slippage sentence. That is before the fête begins. And at the end, after twelve cancelled variants in one short paragraph, a single sentence, itself the third attempt, tells us "They would not let the orchestra go, and musicians who attempted to leave were beaten up," which says all we need to know about the unstated "Keep playing!" whereby the liveliness of the small hours will have been sustained.

On the other hand this skulking novelist told himself in a notebook, as we recall, "I am a character"; and there is every reason why the narrating "I" of *The Possessed* should be perfectly visible. Sometimes he is just a secondary figure floating in the novel's bloodstream, as at the fête where he has got roped in with a few other young men to be a marshal and make sure everything goes smoothly. Of course he is incompetent, and as well as being swept along in the muddle and uproar he shares "our town's" positive transpersonal complicities in what goes on here. All over the place, not only at the fête, a psychic infection rages and erupts in small ugly-comic jests— "They put a dead cat in my trunk"—but also in affronts to the human self as massive and immemorial as those Homer describes. A very young man has shot himself and "we" ride off in an inquisitive Gadarene "cavalcade" ("our ladies had never seen a suicide") to view the corpse; "everything's so boring"—recall Marya Lebyadkin's words—"one can't afford to be squeamish about one's amusements so long as they are fun"; and Lyamshin, the man who gets himself asked to parties to mimic women in labour, newborn babies, and peasants in the confessional, steals a bunch of grapes from the room of death.

It's not easy to say what the narrating "I" is doing at such a scene. Again and again he seems to be in and yet dubiously of the party. In fact the chronicle succeeds in having its cake and eating it, all the way back to the stir caused by Nicholas Stavrogin's arrival in "our town," when it is recorded among other things that he seemed to know a lot—"But of course it didn't take much knowledge to astonish us." Isolated, that looks like straightforward double focus: the first-person narrator inside the chronicle box, unaware of his provincial limitations; and Dostoevsky outside it. One's overall sense of *The*

Possessed absolutely refuses to confirm any such duality, and one can pay the novel no simpler or fuller tribute than by saying so.

The slippage principle which should, I remarked, enervate but in truth exhilarates, has a way of positioning the reader on the side of the narrative against the narrator. The troubles of the new governor are being described. Cattle plague is rife. Fires keep breaking out. Rumours—that Fama of *The Possessed* which can swell to a raging flood but equally can sink into a hoarse inward whisper—rumours of incendiarism abound. "Cases of robbery were twice as numerous as usual. But all this, of course, would have been perfectly normal had there not been other more weighty reasons which disturbed the composure of the hitherto cheerful von Lemke."

How can twice as many robberies as usual be perfectly normal? Of course they can't. Simultaneously the reader responds to the transpersonal unsteadiness, the possessed state of the book, and feels an urge to thrust aside the irresolute self-contradictory narrator and repose upon the story of von Lemke with his cut-out toys and yellow autumn flower. "However hard it may be to imagine, it was so." Thus speaks the fool narrator. But this incomparable narrative needs no shoring-up by him. He might as well ask the reader to believe in those supremely credible terrorized musicians scraping and blowing through the small hours.

The intrusive chronicling "I" can't even make up his mind about numbers. Once the rosetted marshals at the fête are six, and once they are twelve. Very few readers will notice this discrepancy, but all are flicked and jabbed at and irritated—those circling insects—by contradiction, by undetermination followed by overdetermination of reasons, by the narrator's fuss over details which don't matter, his youthful sententiousness about women ("the depths of the female heart") and other irrelevancies, his moralizing, his way of wantonly bleeding a robust narrative with "However, that may only have seemed so," his "I have already described" when he hasn't, his promises to explain later which aren't kept when the reader doesn't want explanation anyhow, he wants the story. Once and once only in six hundred and seventeen pages the narrator gives his readership a disconcerting, impertinent prod by addressing it directly as "Gentlemen." These things add up.

They add up to a novel of leaking secrets and amputated thoughts, of wildly comic material sometimes dully, almost dutifully deployed, as if the humour had escaped the teller; of people "missing" each other in dialogue

"Perhaps he didn't go out of his mind at all."
"Oh you mean because he started biting people?"

and clashing head-on unforgettably

"But I'm your uncle; I carried you about in my arms when you
were a baby."

"What do I care what you carried? I didn't ask you to carry me."

A novel scatty yet dense, as when events are badly related in real life. A novel
of little sprouting aphorisms: "Every man is worth an umbrella." And
enchanted ghost-voice exchanges of extremist purity:

"What's that? An allegory?"

"N-no—why? Not an allegory, just a leaf, one leaf."

A novel where actions get unhooked from their (or any) waking rationale:

The prince too looked at the German, turning his head and collar towards him and putting on his pince-nez, though without the
slightest curiosity.

And words as well as actions:

"Suppose you had lived on the moon," Stavrogin interrupted. . . .

"I don't know," replied Kirillov. "I've not been on the moon,"
he added, without any irony, simply as a statement of fact.

And here's another fact:

"Nowadays they carry corpses by rail," said one of the most
insignificant young men unexpectedly.

A toneless, disjunctive fact, droll and very uneasy, one of those amputated
thoughts I have just mentioned and also a sensation, a crawling sensation
of the time being out of joint; there is more *Hamlet* to *The Possessed* than
what is personal to Stavrogin, "the Prince" as he first appears, though on
the surface of his mind Dostoevsky evidently meant Prince Hal, not the Prince
of Denmark.

Nevertheless Stavrogin does contemplate suicide, and the notebook
entry "to be or not to be" bears the date 16 August, so it belongs to the summer when the "tendentious" political story gets tugged back into great-sinner
orbit, growing physically and imaginatively larger and more formidable all
the time. Dostoevsky's main troubles were with Stavrogin himself, his new-
found "chief character." His first and continuing urge was to drive him toward
crisis and clarity, which involved, one might almost say which meant, finding a *podvig* that would satisfy his idea of Stavrogin.

And thus suicide comes in. Now the underground man would have
extinguished his consciousness if he could, but since the fable of life under the

floorboards renders him bodiless and one can't kill consciousness without laying hands on one's body, the matter doesn't arise. Svidrigailov possesses a body, and destroys it. Whether the suicide who teases the murderer about his ability to do something is himself achieving anything deedy by going to his America—that question *Crime and Punishment* never voices, and it is a crucial and inspired omission. And now, writing the same novel all his life, Dostoevsky finds himself doomed to confront suicide as deed, perhaps life's one deed and therefore the *podvig* he is seeking.

During his struggle to get *The Possessed* into shape he came to see that his conception of Stavrogin, as well as obsessed by crisis and clarity, was hopelessly overcrowded. With cornucopian largesse and ramification the notebooks polarize the emerging hero into a man indulging all vileness and in love with the good. In the novel he stays polarized, but without bulk and in a tragic sense without force; he goes through the motions ("the habits of a decent man" and so forth) while his great-sinner infamies are unloaded upon a past which he cannot even renounce. The final letter declares: "Indignation and shame I can never feel; therefore not despair, either." His inability to despair makes the soaped rope and spare nail of his suicide at once meticulous and completely open-ended. The doctors rule out insanity, God knows why, just as the club and other circles of "our town" think a sane Stavrogin capable of ear-biting and nose-pulling.

One recalls the disease of indifference in the abandoned "At Tikhon's" chapter and observes how odd its symptoms are; or one quotes Stavrogin's notebook rejoinder that simply to live is the hardest thing of all. Anyhow, he kills himself and there is no more to be said. Suicide as *podvig*, on the other hand, must drag a verbalized freight of theory behind it. So the novel frees Stavrogin from "to be or not to be" and all other trammels of the notebooks, and transfers them to Kirillov. Like Svidrigailov, Kirillov comes to the fore very late and very fast in the process of composition, but unlike *Crime and Punishment*'s self-slaughterer the man in *The Possessed* parades an entire philosophy and theology of suicide. This theorizing is the last thing of all to arrive. Initially, in November, which is three months after Stavrogin was quoting Hamlet, Kirillov's "*ROLE IS A FACTUAL ONE*"—by which Dostoevsky means he "volunteered to shoot himself for the common cause" and leave a letter claiming responsibility for Shatov's murder, thus diverting the attention of the police from Peter Verkhovensky and the quintet. This framework of suicide and untruthful self-incriminating letter remains. But at the last minute, apparently under the immediate pressure of writing the magazine version of the novel, Dostoevsky realised that "*FACTUAL*" is precisely what Kirillov's role must not, in essence and impact, be.

Kirillov is needed to give *The Possessed* its strand of theoretic absolutism. He is as Gadarene, as possessed, as any one, but at the level of total ideal obsession. While Shatov expounds and disputes ardently, and incidentally takes a lot of good- and God-focused material off the shoulders of the notebook Stavrogin ("'Shatov must be tied up before you can argue with him,' Stepan Verkhovensky sometimes joked"), only to Kirillov can it be said and is it said, "you haven't swallowed an idea, but an idea has swallowed you"—to which he responds delightedly with "That's good. You've got a bit of sense."

The idea which has swallowed Kirillov is suicide, not suicide for the common cause of the quintet as Dostoevsky first proposed, but to achieve a metaphysical and religious purpose; and thus he plays a big part in the transformation of a neat political generation-gap story into a larger, more complicated object. He writes the self-incriminating letter because he has promised to. He kills himself, as innumerable commentators have paraphrased and elaborated, in order to kill God. Suicide for this reason—to free mankind of the consoling yet imprisoning fictions of religion—is the highest expression of self-will, a perfectly free action, a divine gesture. The man who kills himself *thus*, becomes god. More exactly, he becomes man-god as opposed to God-man who is the Christ of Christianity. There have been millions of suicides in the history of the world, but none, according to Kirillov, for *this* reason. Therefore mankind, history, eternity, God, all wait upon him and his deed.

While doing rough justice to what Kirillov says, to his brand of mystical atheism, this more or less agreed summary is not convincingly inward with Dostoevsky's creation. In trying to improve on it, perhaps the best plan is to enter where Kirillov does. He is introduced as a "structural engineer." I think we should prick our ears at that. Dostoevsky's groping backwards past *Crime and Punishment* towards *Notes from Underground* is not just a matter of arriving at Stavrogin. The seed-bed of Kirillov's structural engineering is the underground man's image of normal human beings as roadbuilders: being somebody, doing something, going somewhere. Of course Kirillov is anything but a normal human being; and that is just the point. His structural engineering never happens. He has arrived from abroad, yet another bird of passage, "in the hope of getting a job building our railway bridge." But, so Stepan Verkhovensky tells him, "They won't let you build our bridge." Why not? And who are "they"? A sudden whiff of Kafka. This is the world of the underground man's eruptive and unexplained "They won't let me—I can't be—good"; which world is itself continuous with that of the pre-Siberian stories, particularly *The Double* where Dostoevsky says he found his underground type. As to "our bridge" (which is never mentioned again), the reader can if he likes reflect that Kirillov is an odd fish and will no doubt prove himself *persona non grata* in "our town," or that the local bureaucrats are an officious and/or corrupt lot, or that the central authority thousands of miles away in Petersburg enjoys throwing its weight about. But this would be moving in and making up the message in the style of the "missing" letters in *Poor People*, the first story of all.

The fact is that *The Possessed*, which can be circumstantial to a calculated fault when it chooses, in this case chooses to say nothing. The novel proposes a man who has been swallowed by a theory of suicide. He lives for us, we can feel him kicking inside the idea's belly, because the bridge-builder who does no bridge-building is vitalized by the nobody to be and nowhere to go of Dostoevsky's inexhaustible inventive fascination. Here, self-exclusion from the feast of life takes a fresh turn. And a new twist is given to the urge to be a Napoleon. In the immediate context of *The Possessed* Kirillov delights even while he is dismaying us by pushing theory—the novel's Paper Person motif, that is—to the very limit, the born gambler's limit. He may be mad. Stavrogin says he is. If so, he is incidentally mad in accord with Kafka's piercing throw-off. He embraces suicide as deed, as the one true act in a false world, as supreme *podvig*, as feat to end feats, God-killing, god-making; and in doing so he exemplifies, as others before and Ivan Karamazov after him, the truth that Dostoevsky can only satisfy his hunger for crisis and clarity by bestowing it on the enemy.

No jokes about America from Kirillov. He has actually been to the actual America—and come back. It was a failure. The novel handles the subject brusquely, whereas a notebook entry about Stavrogin back in the spring of 1870 suggests a position midway between Svidrigailov and Kirillov: "Sometimes he complains all of a sudden: 'I'm bored!' The S. S. Alabama: 'I'll get there!' (dream)." But an unmetaphorical America in *The Possessed* does not mean an unwitty treatment of suicide. What makes the commentators on man-godhood and related themes misleading, why they fail to evoke the real thing, is that they suggest an object which is stable and personal (as opposed to volatile and transpersonal). The obsession has become Kirillov's alone. But the sunrise of impending suicide bathes him and others in fiery metaphysical comedy; "be as free as you like," Peter Verkhovensky tells him, "so long as you don't change your mind"—that is "so long as your entirely free intention is carried out." "Free intention" is the crux. As Kirillov puts it, "I am killing myself to show my rebelliousness and my new terrible freedom." He asks rhetorically, apropos the idea which has swallowed him, "Who will prove it?" and answers "I." But Kirillov has himself pointedly ruled out life after death: "the laws of nature did not spare even *Him*"—Jesus, that

is. Then what of this proof and this freedom? Kirillov alive has proved
nothing, and Kirillov dead will himself be nothing. Stepan Verkhovensky's
naked transcendental "They won't let you" turns out to be a very suitable
preface to a logical joke about time and identity.

Stepan's forward-pointing negative "won't" is no less important than his
collective "they." As *The Possessed* is a novel of groups, circles, sets, quintets,
real and imagined, so it is a novel of empty or baffled futurity. Bridge-building
is empty because it never happens, God-killing and god-making suicide is
baffled because there is only a corpse to point at, there is nobody to attach
a fulfilled "free intention" to. Peter Verkhovensky attacks this bafflement
from the other end, from the standpoint of afterwards, as well as that of
the not-yet-dead Kirillov who is arguing with him here and now. How is
the world going to know it has received a boundless freedom at the hands
of an obscure young man lying in some back room in a provincial Russian
town? Kirillov replies: "There is nothing secret that will not be made known.
He said so." And with these words he points towards an icon of the Saviour
before which he has lighted a lamp—"to be on the safe side," Peter suggests.
But in response to this Voltairean jest, the lonely, agonized, perhaps crazed
man "made no answer." He was no doubt contemplating not futurity but
baffled Eternity itself: a universal Revelation outside nature guaranteed by
a Christ whom the laws of nature did not spare.

When Stavrogin, who "poisoned" Kirillov, and who also kills himself,
wrote that letter to Dasha Shatov asking her to come and be his nurse, his
mind won't have been bent either on or away from suicide; he was neutrally
wondering whether she hoped "to set up some aim for me at last." He is
both rudderless and becalmed, and the futurity conjured by his letter blends
the metaphysical frustration of a brilliant unhoused intellectual torpor with
human impossibility: you can't cross a river on a chip of wood. This single
great emptiness before him has lots of smaller ones inside it. For example,
when Dostoevsky abandons the "At Tikhon's" chapter but retains the brief
exchange in which Shatov urges Stavrogin to go to Bishop Tikhon, and
Stavrogin replies "Thank you, I will," let nobody persuade us the novelist
has made a mistake.

And the same future tense—"I will"—has Shatov in its grip. Stavrogin,
needling away, elicits from him that he believes in Russia and the Orthodox
Church and the body of Christ. "But in God? In God?" Stavrogin persists.
"I—I will believe in God," says Shatov. While Stavrogin never gets to see
Tikhon, the immediate future holds murder in store for Shatov. One of his
killers is the high-minded Virginsky who "*will* never, never abandon these
bright hopes" (my italics), and another member of the quintet is Shigalov

who pulls out of the affair at the very last moment, not from fear or pity or remorse but because the murder "is in direct contradiction of my programme"—of Shigalov's own brand of revolutionary ideology. He's not going to warn Shatov or tell the police, he's going to make a statement "for general edification"—words but no deeds, a turn toward sanity and life that *might have been*, and a horrific-comic *Possessed* moment of subtlest art.

Shigalov does make his statement. The murder goes forward. Thus some things that are said to be going to happen, do happen. "But they will lose their reason," says Peter Verkhovensky's lieutenant when Peter has argued that the quintet will hold together after the murder "unless they've lost their reason." And sure enough they do panic and run amok, and "the almost mystical terror which suddenly took hold of our authorities" completes the ruinous and negative side of the Gadarene story.

Chronology

1821   Fyodor Mikhailovich Dostoevsky born October 30 in a Moscow hospital for the poor, where his father was a resident surgeon.

1837   Dostoevsky's mother dies.

1838   Dostoevsky enters military engineering school in St. Petersburg.

1839   In the wake of increasingly harsh and abusive treatment, Dostoevsky believes, the serfs on Dostoevsky's father's estate castrate and murder their master. Recent evidence, however, casts doubts on the circumstances of his father's death.

1843   Dostoevsky finishes engineering course; joins engineering department of the War Ministry.

1844   Resigns from his post. Publishes his translation of *Eugenie Grandet*.

1845   Finishes his first novel, *Poor Folk*, which wins the acclaim of radical critic Belinsky.

1846   *Poor Folk* published in *St. Petersburg Miscellany*. *The Double* published in *Notes from the Fatherland* two weeks later.

1847   "A Novel in Nine Letters" published in *The Contemporary*. Dostoevsky frequents meetings of the Petrashevsky circle, a clandestine society of progressive thinkers. Publishes pamphlets in the *St. Petersburg Chronicle* and the *St. Petersburg News*.

1848   Publication of *A Strange Wife, A Faint Heart*, "The Stories of a Veteran," *The Christmas Tree and the Wedding, White Nights, The Jealous Husband*, and *The Landlady*, all in *Notes from the Fatherland.* The latter work draws harsh criticism from Belinsky.

1849 Dostoevsky arrested for his role in the Petrashevsky circle, and imprisoned in St. Petersburg's Peter and Paul Fortress. Sentenced to death, but at the last minute the sentence is commuted to four years of forced labor in Siberia. Sent to Omsk, where he remains until 1854.

1854 Dostoevsky enlists in the army as a private and is sent to Semipalatinsk, near the Mongolian border.

1856 Promoted to lieutenant.

1857 Marries Maria Dmitrievna Isaeva, a widow. *A Little Hero* published anonymously in *Notes from the Fatherland.*

1858 Released from army; leaves Semipalatinsk for Tver.

1859 Is permitted to return to St. Petersburg. "Uncle's Dream" published in *The Russian Word; A Friend of the Family* published in *Notes from the Fatherland.*

1860 Introduction and first chapter to *Notes from the House of the Dead* are published. Work meets opposition from the censor at *The Russian World.*

1861 *Notes from the House of the Dead* in its entirety and *The Insulted and the Injured* are published in *Time,* a journal recently started by Dostoevsky's brother Mikhail.

1862 First trip abroad. "An Unpleasant Predicament" published in *Time.*

1863 "Winter Notes on Summer Impressions" published in *Time. Time* is suppressed. Second trip abroad.

1864 Publishes magazine, *Epoch,* with brother Mikhail. *Notes from Underground* published in *Epoch.* Dostoevsky's wife and brother die within months of each other.

1865 *Epoch* ceases publication. Third trip abroad.

1866 *Crime and Punishment* serialized in *The Russian Herald.* Anna Grigorievna Snitkina comes to work for Dostoevsky as a stenographer. *The Gambler* published.

1867	Marries Snitkina. The couple goes abroad to live for the next four years.
1868	*The Idiot* serialized in *The Russian Herald*. A daughter, Sofia, is born, but dies two months later.
1869	Daughter Lyubov' born in Dresden.
1870	*The Eternal Husband* published in *Dawn*.
1871–72	Returns to St. Petersburg. Son Fyodor born. *The Possessed* serialized in *The Russian Herald*.
1873–74	Editor of *The Citizen*. *Diary of a Writer* begins publication.
1875	Son Alexey (Alyosha) born. *A Raw Youth* serialized in *Notes from the Fatherland*.
1876	"A Gentle Spirit" published in *Diary of a Writer*.
1877	"Dream of a Ridiculous Man" published in *Diary of a Writer*.
1878	Death of son Alyosha. Dostoevsky visits Optina monastery with Vladimir Solov'yov; they meet Starets Amvrozy.
1879–80	*The Brothers Karamazov* serialized in *The Russian Herald*.
1881	Dostoevsky dies on January 28.

Contributors

HAROLD BLOOM, Sterling Professor of the Humanities at Yale University, is the author of *The Anxiety of Influence, Poetry and Repression*, and many other volumes of literary criticism. His forthcoming study, *Freud: Transference and Authority*, attempts a full-scale reading of all of Freud's major writings. A MacArthur Prize Fellow, he is general editor of five series of literary criticism published by Chelsea House. During 1987–88, he served as Charles Eliot Norton Professor of Poetry at Harvard University.

MIKHAIL BAKHTIN, Russian scholar and literary theorist, is the author of *The Dialogic Imagination* and of influential studies of Rabelais and Dostoevsky.

JOSEPH FRANK is Professor of Comparative Literature Emeritus at Princeton University. He is the author of *Dostoevsky: The Seeds of Revolt, 1821–1849; Dostoevsky: The Years of Ordeal, 1850–1859;* and *Dostoevsky: The Stir of Liberation, 1860–1865.*

DONALD FANGER is Professor of Slavic Languages and Comparative Literature at Harvard University. He is best known for *The Creation of Nikolai Gogol* and *Dostoevsky and Romantic Realism.*

GARY S. MORSON, Professor of Russian at Northwestern University, is the author of *The Boundaries of Genre: Dostoevsky's* Diary of a Writer *and the Traditions of Literary Utopia.*

MICHAEL HOLQUIST has taught Russian literature at the University of Texas at Austin and Indiana University, and is currently Professor of Comparative Literature at Yale University. He is the author of *Dostoevsky and the Novel.*

ROBERT L. BELKNAP, Professor of Russian Language and Literature at Columbia University, has written *The Structure of* The Brothers Karamazov.

A. D. NUTTALL is Professor of English at Sussex University and is the author of *A Common Sky, A New Mimesis*, and Crime and Punishment: *Murder as Philosophic Experiment.*

ELIZABETH DALTON, Professor of English at Columbia University–Barnard College, has written *Unconscious Structure in Dostoevsky's* The Idiot: *A Study in Literature and Psychoanalysis.*

ROBERT LOUIS JACKSON, Professor of Russian Literature at Yale University, has published several books on Dostoevsky and edited a reader on Russian formalism.

SERGEI HACKEL is a Reader in Russian Studies at Sussex University.

JOHN JONES, Fellow of New College, Oxford, is the author of books on Wordsworth, Keats, Dostoevsky, and others.

Bibliography

Adamovich, Ales'. "Dostoevsky after Dostoevsky." *Soviet Literature* 12 (1981): 70–81.

Alexander, Alex E. "The Two Ivans' Sexual Underpinnings." *Slavic and East European Journal* 25 (1981): 24–37.

Alm, Brian M. "The Four Horsemen and the Lamb: Structure and Balance in *Crime and Punishment*." *McNeese Review* 21 (1974–75): 72–79.

Anderson, Roger B. "*Crime and Punishment*: Psycho-Myth and the Making of a Hero." *California Slavic Studies* 11 (1977): 523–38.

———. "The Meaning of Carnival in *The Brothers Karamazov*." *Slavic and East European Journal* 23 (1979): 458–78.

———. "Mythical Implications of Father Zosima's Religious Teachings." *Slavic Review* 38 (1979): 272–89.

———. "Raskolnikov and the Myth Experience." *Slavic and East European Journal* 20 (1976): 1–17.

Arbery, Glenn. "The Violated Ikon: Dostoevsky and the Riddle of Beauty." *Renascence* 36 (1984): 182–202.

Axthelm, P. M. "Origins of the Modern Confessional Novel: Dostoevsky." In *The Modern Confessional Novel*, 13–53. New Haven: Yale University Press, 1967.

Bakhtin, Mikhail. *Problems of Dostoevsky's Poetics*. Minneapolis: University of Minnesota Press, 1984.

Banerjee, Maria. " 'The American Revolver': An Essay on Dostoevsky's *The Devils*." *Modern Fiction Studies* 27 (1981): 278–83.

Barstow, Jane. "Dostoevsky's *Notes from Underground* versus Chernyshevsky's *What Is to Be Done?*" *College Literature* 5 (1978): 24–33.

Batchelor, R. E. "Dostoevskii and Camus: Similarities and Contrasts." *Journal of European Studies* 5 (1975): 111–52.

———. "Malraux's Debt to Dostoevskii." *Journal of European Studies* 6 (1976): 153–71.

Beatty, Joseph. "From Rebellion and Alienation to Salutary Freedom: A Study in *Notes from Underground*." *Soundings* 61 (1978): 182–205.

Belknap, Robert. "The Origins of Alesa Karamazov." In *American Contributions to the Sixth International Congress of Slavists, Prague, 1963, August 7–13*, vol. 2, edited by William Harkins. The Hague: Mouton, 1968.

———. *The Structure of* The Brothers Karamazov. Ann Arbor, Mich.: University Microfilms, 1967.

Berdyaev, N. A. *Dostoevsky*. Translated by Donald Attwater. New York: Sheed & Ward, 1934.

Berry, Thomas E. "Dostoevsky and Spiritualism." *Dostoevsky Studies* 2 (1981): 43–49.

———. *Plots and Characters in Major Russian Fiction*. Vol. 2. Hamden, Conn.: Archon Books, 1978.

Bethea, David M. "Structure versus Symmetry in *Crime and Punishment*." In *Fearful Symmetry: Doubles and Doubling in Literature and Film*, edited by Eugene J. Crook, 41–64. Tallahassee: University Press of Florida, 1982.

Beyer, Thomas R., Jr. "Dostoevsky's *Crime and Punishment*." *Explicator* 41, no. 1 (Fall 1982): 33–36.

Burnett, Leon, ed. *F. M. Dostoevsky (1821–1881): A Centenary Collection*. Colchester: University of Essex, 1981.

Calder, Angus. *Russia Discovered: Nineteenth-Century Fiction from Pushkin to Chekhov*. London: Heinemann, 1976.

Camus, Albert. *The Possessed: A Play in Three Parts*. Translated by Justin O'Brien. New York: Knopf, 1960.

Carr, Edward Hallet. *Dostoevskij: 1821–1881*. London: Allen & Unwin, 1931.

Carroll, J. *Break-Out for the Crystal Palace: The Anarcho-Psychological Critique—Stirner, Nietzsche, Dostoevsky*. London: Routledge & Kegan Paul, 1974.

Carter, Geoffrey. "Freud and *The Brothers Karamazov*." *Literature and Psychology* 31, no. 3 (1981): 15–32.

Cassedy, Steven. "The Formal Problem of the Epilogue in *Crime and Punishment*: The Logic of Tragic and Christian Structures." *Dostoevsky Studies* 3 (1982): 171–90.

Chavkin, Allan. "Ivan Karamazov's Rebellion and Bellow's *The Victim*." *Papers on Language and Literature* 16 (1980): 316–20.

Clive, Geoffrey. "Dostoevsky and the Intellectuals." In *The Broken Icon: Intuitive Existentialism in Classical Russian Fiction*. New York: Macmillan, 1972.

Consigny, Scott. "The Paradox of Textuality: Writing as Entrapment and Deliverance in *Notes from the Underground*." *California Slavic Studies* 12 (1978): 341–52.

Correa Vasques, Pedro. "Mirror of Conscience." *Soviet Literature* 12 (1981): 139–40.

Costa, Richard Hauer. "Notes from a Dark Heller: Bob Slocum and the Underground Man." *Texas Studies in Literature and Language* 23 (1981): 159–82.

Cox, Gary D. "D. H. Lawrence and F. M. Dostoevsky: Mirror Images of Murderous Aggression." *Modern Fiction Studies* 29 (1983): 175–82.

Cox, Roger L. "Dostoevsky and the Ridiculous." *Dostoevsky Studies* 1 (1980): 103–9.

———. "Stavrogin and Prince Hal." *Canadian Slavonic Papers* 26 (1984): 121–26.

Dalton, Elizabeth. "Myshkin's Epilepsy." *Partisan Review* 45 (1978): 595–610.

———. *Unconscious Structure in Dostoevsky's* The Idiot: *A Study in Literature and Psychoanalysis*. Princeton: Princeton University Press, 1979.

Danow, David K. "A Note on the Internal Dynamics of the Dostoevskian Conclave." *Dostoevsky Studies* 2 (1981): 61–68.

———. "Notes on Generating a Text: *The Brothers Karamazov*." *Modern Language Studies* 11 (1980–81): 75–95.

———. "Semiotics of Gesture in Dostoevskian Dialogue." *Russian Literature* 8 (1980): 41–75.

——. "Subtexts of *The Brothers Karamazov*." *Russian Literature* 11 (1982): 173–208.

Davie, Donald, ed. *Russian Literature and Modern English Fiction*. Chicago: University of Chicago Press, 1965.

Davydov, Sergei. "Dostoevsky and Nabokov: The Morality of Structure in *Crime and Punishment* and *Despair*." *Dostoevsky Studies* 3 (1982): 157–70.

Debreczeny, Paul. "Dostoevskij's Use of *Manon Lescaut* in *The Gambler*." *Comparative Literature* 28 (1976): 1–18.

deJonge, Alex. *Dostoevsky and the Age of Intensity*. New York: St. Martin's, 1975.

Dev, Jai. "The Function of *The Idiot* Motifs in *As If by Magic*." *Twentieth-Century Literature* 29 (1983): 223–30.

Dilman, Ilham. "Dostoyevsky: Psychology and the Novelist." In *Philosophy and Literature*, edited by A. Phillips Griffiths, 95–114. Cambridge: Cambridge University Press, 1984.

Dolan, Paul J. *Of War and War's Alarms: Fiction and Politics in the Modern World*. New York: Free Press, 1976.

Dostoevsky, Anna. *Dostoevsky: Reminiscences*. Translated and edited by B. Stillman. New York: Liveright, 1975.

Dryzhakova, Elena. "Dostoevsky, Chernyshevsky, and the Rejection of Nihilism." *Oxford Slavonic Papers* 13 (1980): 58–79.

Edgerton, William B. "Spanish and Portuguese Responses to Dostoevskij." *Revue de Littérature Comparée* (1981): 419–38.

Erlich, Victor. "Two Concepts of the Dostoevsky Novel." *International Journal of Slavic Linguistics and Poetics* 25–26 (1982): 127–36.

Falen, James E. "The Meaning of Dostoevskian Narrative." *International Dostoevsky Society Bulletin* 8 (1978): 42–55.

Fanger, D. *Dostoevsky and Romantic Realism: A Study of Dostoevsky in Relation to Balzac, Dickens and Gogol*. Harvard Studies in Comparative Literature 27. Cambridge, Mass. Harvard University Press, 1965.

Fasting, Sigurd. "Dostoevskij and George Sand." *Russian Literature* 4, no. 3 (1976): 309–21.

Fiderer, Gerald. "Raskolnikov's Confession." *Literature and Psychology* 30 (1980): 62–71.

Fiene, Donald M. "Elements of Dostoevsky in the Novels of Kurt Vonnegut." *Dostoevsky Studies* 2 (1981): 129–42.

——. "Pushkin's 'Poor Knight': The Key to Perceiving Dostoevsky's *Idiot* as Allegory." *International Dostoevsky Society Bulletin* 8 (1978): 10–21.

Fitzgerald, Gene D. "Anton Lavrent'evič G-v: The Narrator as Re-Creator in Dostoevskij's *The Possessed*." In *New Perspectives on Nineteenth-Century Russian Prose*, edited by George J. Gutsche and Lauren G. Leighton, 121–34. Columbus: Slavica, 1982.

Fortin, Rene E. "Responsive Form: Dostoevsky's *Notes from Underground* and the Confessional Tradition." *Essays in Literature* 7 (1980): 225–45.

Frank, Joseph. *Dostoevsky: The Seeds of Revolt, 1821–1849*. Princeton: Princeton University Press, 1976.

——. "Dostoevsky's Realism." *Encounter* 40, no. 3 (March 1973): 31–38.

————. "The Masks of Stavrogin." *The Sewanee Review* 77 (1969): 660–91.

————. "Ralph Ellison and a Literary 'Ancestor': Dostoevsky." *New Criterion* 2, no. 1 (September 1983): 11–21.

————. "The World of Raskolnikov." *Encounter* 26, no. 6 (June 1966): 30–35.

Freeborn, Richard. *"Crime and Punishment."* In *The Rise of the Russian Novel: Studies in the Russian Novel from* Eugene Onegin *to* War and Peace. Cambridge: Cambridge University Press, 157–207.

————. "Dostoevsky." In *Russian Literary Attitudes from Pushkin to Solzhenitsyn,* edited by Richard Freeborn, Georgette Donchin, and N. J. Anning, 39–59. London: Macmillan, 1976.

Friedman, M. S. *Problematic Rebel: Melville, Dostoievsky, Kafka, Camus.* Rev. ed. Chicago: University of Chicago Press, 1970.

Fuchs, Daniel. "Saul Bellow and the Example of Dostoevsky." In *The Stoic Strain in American Literature: Essays in Honour of Marston La-France,* edited by Duane J. MacMillan, 157–76. Toronto: University of Toronto, 1979.

Futrell, Michael. "Dostoevsky and Islam (and Chokan Valikhanov)." *The Slavonic and East European Review* 57 (1979): 16–31.

Gibson, A. B. *The Religion of Dostoevsky.* London: S.C.M. Press, 1973.

Gide, A. P. G. *Dostoevsky.* Westport, Conn.: Greenwood, 1981.

Gifford, H. "Dostoevsky: The Dialectic of Resistance." In *The Novel in Russia from Pushkin to Pasternak.* London: Hutchinson University Library, 1964.

Gill, Richard. "The Bridges of St. Petersburg: A Motif in *Crime and Punishment.*" *Dostoevsky Studies* 3 (1982): 145–55.

————. "*The Rime of the Ancient Mariner* and *Crime and Punishment:* Existential Parables." *Philosophy and Literature* 5 (1981): 131–49.

Goerner, Tatiana. "The Theme of Art and Aesthetics in Dostoevsky's *The Idiot.*" *Ulbandus Review* 2, no. 2 (1982): 79–95.

Goldstein, David I. *Dostoyevsky and the Jews.* Austin: University of Texas Press, 1981.

Goodheart, E. "Dostoevsky and the Hubris of the Immoralist." In *The Cult of the Ego: The Self in Modern Literature,* 90–113. Chicago: University of Chicago Press, 1968.

Goryaev, Vitali, and Nikita Ivanov. "In Dostoevsky's World." *Soviet Literature* 12 (1981): 186–91.

Gregg, R. A. "Two Adams and Eve in the Crystal Palace: Dostoevsky, the Bible, and *We.*" In *Major Soviet Writers: Essays in Criticism,* edited by E. J. Brown, 202–8. Oxford: Oxford University Press, 1973.

Gregory, Serge V. "Dostoevsky's *The Devils* and the Antinihilist Novel." *Slavic Review* 38 (1979): 444–55.

Grossman, Leonid. "About *The Meek One.*" *Soviet Literature* 12 (1981): 57–59.

————. *Dostoevsky: A Biography.* Translated by Mary Mackler. London: Allen Lane, 1974.

Guerard, Albert J. *The Triumph of the Novel: Dickens, Dostoevsky, Faulkner.* New York: Oxford University Press, 1976.

Hackel, Sergei. "F. M. Dostoevsky (1821–1881): Prophet Manqué?" *Dostoevsky Studies* 3 (1982): 5–25.

Hall, J. R. "Abstraction in Dostoyevsky's *Notes from the Underground.*" *Modern Language Review* 76 (1981): 129–37.

Hanak, Miroslav J. "Hegel's 'Frenzy of Self-Conceit' as Key to the Annihilation of Individuality in Dostoevsky's *Possessed.*" *Dostoevsky Studies* 2 (1981): 147–54.

Hingley, Ronald. *Dostoyevsky: His Life and Work.* New York: Scribner's, 1978.

Holquist, Michael. *Dostoevsky and the Novel.* Princeton: Princeton University Press, 1977.

Ivanits, Linda J. "Dostoevsky's Mar'ja Lebjadkina." *Slavic and East European Journal* 22, no. 2 (1978): 127–140.

———. "Folk Beliefs about the 'Unclean Force' in Dostoevskij's *The Brothers Karamazov.*" In *New Perspectives on Nineteenth-Century Russian Prose*, edited by George J. Gutsche and Lauren G. Leighton, 135–46. Columbus: Slavica, 1982.

Ivanov, Vyacheslav. *Freedom and the Tragic Life: A Study in Dostoevsky.* Translated by Norman Cameron. London: Harrill Press, 1952.

Jackson, Robert Louis. *The Art of Dostoevsky: Deliriums and Nocturnes.* Princeton: Princeton University Press, 1981.

———. "Dostoevskii and the Marquis de Sade." *Russian Literature* 4 (1976): 27–45.

———. "Dostoevsky in the Twentieth Century." *Dostoevsky Studies* 1 (1980): 3–10.

———. *Dostoevsky: New Perspectives:* Englewood Cliffs, N.J.: Prentice-Hall, 1984.

———. *Dostoevsky's Quest for Form: A Study of His Philosophy of Art.* Yale Russian and East European Studies 1. New Haven: Yale University Press, 1966.

———. "The Garden of Eden in Dostoevsky's 'A Christmas Party and a Wedding' and Chekhov's 'Because of Little Apples.' " *Revue de Littérature Comparée* 55 (1981): 331–41.

———. "The Triple Vision: Dostoevsky's 'The Peasant Mercy.' " *The Yale Review* 67 (1978): 225–35.

———, ed. *Twentieth Century Interpretations of* Crime and Punishment: *A Collection of Critical Essays.* Englewood Cliffs, N.J.: Prentice-Hall, 1974.

Jones, Malcolm V. "Dostoyevsky and an Aspect of Schiller's Psychology." *The Slavonic and East European Review* 52 (1974): 337–54.

———. "Dostoevsky and Europe: Travels in the Mind." *Renaissance and Modern Studies* 24 (1980): 38–57.

———. *Dostoevsky: The Novel of Discord.* New York: Barnes & Noble, 1976.

———. "Dostoyevsky's Conception of the Idea." *Renaissance and Modern Studies* 13 (1969): 106–31.

———. *Philosophy and the Novel: Philosophical Aspects of* Middlemarch, Anna Karenina, The Brothers Karamazov, A la recherche du temps perdu *and of* Methods of Criticism. Oxford: Clarendon Press, 1975.

———. "Some Echoes of Hegel in Dostoyevsky." *The Slavonic and East European Review* 49 (1971): 500–520.

———, and Garth M. Terry, eds. *New Essays on Dostoevsky.* Cambridge: Cambridge University Press, 1983.

Kabat, Geoffrey C. *Ideology and Imagination: The Image of Society in Dostoevsky.* New York: Columbia University Press, 1978.

Kaufmann, Walter. "Dostoevsky: *Notes from Underground.*" In *Existentialism from Dostoevsky to Sartre.* New York: New American Library, 1956.

Khrapchenko, Mikhail. "Dostoevsky and His Literary Legacy." *Soviet Literature* 12 (1981): 7–20.

Kiremidjian, David. "*Crime and Punishment:* Matricide and the Woman Question." *America Imago* 33 (1976): 403–33.

Klotz, Kenneth. "Dostoevsky and *The Old Curiosity Shop*." *Yale University Library Gazette* 50 (1976): 237–47.

Koehler, Ludmila. "*The Little Hero* of a Great Writer." *International Dostoevsky Society Bulletin* 8 (1978): 22–30.

Koprince, Ralph G. "The Question of Raskol'nikov's Suicide." *Canadian-American Slavic Studies* 16, no. 1 (1982): 73–81.

Krag, Erik. *Dostoevsky: The Literary Artist*. New York: Humanities Press, 1976.

Krasnov, V. *Solzhenitsyn and Dostoevsky: A Study in the Polyphonic Novel*. Athens: University of Georgia Press, 1980.

Lary, E. "Dostoevsky," In *Nineteenth-Century Russian Literature*, edited by J. F. I. Fennell, 225–60. London: Faber & Faber, 1973.

Lavrin, J. "Dostoevsky and Tolstoy." In *A Panorama of Russian Literature*, 130–46. London: London University Press, 1973.

Lawrence, D. H. "The Grand Inquisitor." In *Selected Literary Criticism*, edited by Anthony Beal, 233–41. London: Heinemann, 1955.

Leatherbarrow, W. J. "The Aesthetic Louse: Ethics and Aesthetics in Dostoevsky's *Prestupleniye i nakazaniye*." *Modern Language Review* 71 (1976): 857–66.

———. "Apocalyptic Imagery in *The Idiot* and *The Devils*." *Dostoevsky Studies* 3 (1982): 43–51.

———. "Dostoevsky's Treatment of the Theme of Romantic Dreaming in *Hozyayka* and *Belyye Nochi'*." *Modern Language Review* 69 (1974): 584–95.

———. "Idealism and Utopian Socialism in Dostoevsky's *Gospodin Prokharchin* and *Slaboye serdtse*." *Slavic and East European Studies* 58 (1980): 524–40.

———. "Pushkin and the Early Dostoevsky." *Modern Language Review* 74 (1979): 68–85.

———. "The Rag with Ambition: The Problem of Self-Will in Dostoevsky's *Bednyye Lyudi* and *Dvoybnik*." *Modern Language Review* 68 (1973): 607–18.

———. "Raskolnikov and the 'Enigma of His Personality.'" *Forum for Modern Language Studies* 9 (1973): 153–65.

Leighton, Lauren G. "The Crime and Punishment of Monstrous Coincidence." *Mosaic* 12, no. 1 (1978): 93–106.

Levitsky, Igor. "Dreams of a Golden Age: A Recurrent Theme in Dostoevsky's Later Fiction." In *Crisis and Commitment: Studies in German and Russian Literature in Honour of J. W. Dyck*, edited by John Whiton and Harry Loewen, 148–55. Waterloo: University of Waterloo Press, 1983.

Lindenmeyr, Adele. "Raskolnikov's City and the Napoleonic Plan." *Slavic Review* 35 (1976): 37–47.

Lindstrom, Thaïs S. "The Great Truth-Tellers: Tolstoy and Dostoyevsky." In *A Concise History of Russian Literature*, vol. 1, 164–99. New York: New York University Press, 1966.

Linner, Sven. *Starets Zosima in* The Brothers Karamazov: *A Study in the Mimesis of Virtue*. Stockholm: Almqvist & Wiksell, 1976.

Loewen, Harry. "Freedom and Rebellion in Dostoevsky's 'The Grand Inquisitor' and Nietzsche's *The Antichrist*." In *Crisis and Commitment: Studies in German and Russian Literature in Honour of J. W. Dyck*, edited by John Whiton and Harry Loewen, 156–67. Waterloo: University of Waterloo Press, 1983.

Lord, R. *Dostoevsky: Essays and Perspectives*. London: Chatto & Windus, 1970.

McKinney, David M. "*Notes from Underground:* A Dostoevskean Faust." *California Slavic Studies* 12 (1978): 189–229.

MacPike, Loralee. *Dostoevsky's Dickens: A Study of Literary Influence.* New York: Barnes & Noble, 1981.

Magarshack, David. *Dostoevsky.* London: Secker & Warburg, 1962.

Mann, Robert. "Elijah the Prophet in *Crime and Punishment.*" *Canadian Slavonic Papers* 23 (1981): 261–72.

Maze, J. R. "Dostoyevsky: Epilepsy, Mysticism, and Homosexuality." *American Imago* 38 (1981): 155–83.

Meijer, Jan M. "The Development of Dostoevskij's Hero." *Russian Literature* 4, (1976): 257–71.

Merrill, Reed B. "Brain Fever in the Novels of Dostoevsky." *The Texas Quarterly* 19, no. 3 (1976): 29–50.

Meyer, Priscilla. "Dostoevskij, Naturalist Poetics and 'Mr. Procharcin.' " *Russian Literature* 10 (1981): 163–90.

Mihajlov, M. *Russian Themes.* New York: Farrar, Straus & Giroux, 1968.

Miller, Karl. *Doubles.* Oxford: Oxford University Press, 1985.

Miller, Richard C. "The Biblical Story of Joseph in Dostoevskii's *The Brothers Karamazov.*" *Slavic Review* 41 (1982): 653–65.

Miller, Robin Feuer. *Dostoevsky and* The Idiot: *Author, Narrator, and Reader.* Cambridge, Mass.: Harvard University Press, 1981.

———. "Dostoevsky and the Tale of Terror." In *The Russian Novel from Pushkin to Pasternak,* edited by John Garrard, 103–21. New Haven: Yale University Press, 1983.

———. "The Function of Inserted Narratives in *The Idiot.*" *Ulbandus Review* 1, no. 1 (1977): 15–27.

———. "Notions of Narrative in the Notebooks for *The Idiot.*" *Ulbandus Review* 2, no. 1 (1979): 160–74.

Mishra, Vijay. "White's Poetics: Patrick White through Mikhail Bakhtin." *SPAN* 18 (April 1984): 54–75.

Mochul'skii, K. D. *Dostoevsky, His Life and Work.* Translated by Michael Minihan. Princeton: Princeton University Press, 1967.

Moravcevich, Nicholas. "The Romantization of the Prostitute in Dostoevskij's Fiction." *Russian Literature* 4 (1976): 229–307.

Morson, Gary S. *The Boundaries of Genre: Dostoevsky's* Diary of a Writer *and the Traditions of Literary Utopia.* Austin: University of Texas Press, 1981.

———. "Literary Theory, Psychoanalysis, and the Creative Process: A Review Article." *Slavic and East European Journal* 25, no. 4 (Winter 1981): 62–75.

———. "Reading between the Genres: Dostoevsky's *Diary of a Writer* as Metafiction." *The Yale Review* 68 (1979): 224–34.

———. "State of the Field." *The Slavic and East European Journal* 22 (1978): 203–7.

———. "Verbal Pollution in *The Brothers Karamazov.*" *PTL: A Journal for Descriptive Poetics and Theory* 3 (1978): 223–33.

Moser, Charles A. "Dostoevsky and the Aesthetics of Journalism." *Dostoevsky Studies* 3 (1982): 27–41.

———. "Nihilism, Aesthetics, and *The Idiot.*" *Russian Literature* 11 (1982): 377–88.

Motyleva, Tamara. "New Works about Dostoevsky Abroad." *Soviet Literature* 12

(1981): 98–122.

Murry, J. Middleton. *Fyodor Dostoevsky: A Critical Study.* London: Martin Secker, 1916.

Nuttall, A. D. *Dostoevsky's* Crime and Punishment: *Murder as Philosophic Experiment.* Atlantic Highlands, N.J.: Humanities Press, 1978.

Oates, Joyce Carol. "The Tragic Vision of *The Possessed.*" *The Georgia Review* 32 (1978): 868–93.

Offord, Derek. "Dostoyevsky and Chernyshevsky." *The Slavonic and East European Review* 57 (1979): 509–30.

Orr, John. "The Demonic Tendency, Politics and Society in Dostoevsky's *The Devils.*" In *The Sociology of Literature: Applied Studies*, edited by Diana Laurenson, 271–83. Keele, England: University of Keele, 1978.

Pachmuss, Telmira. *F. M. Dostoevsky.* Carbondale: Southern Illinois University Press, 1963.

———. "Prometheus and Job Reincarnated: Melville and Dostoevskij." *The Slavic and East European Journal* 23 (1979): 25–37.

Panichas, George A. *The Burden of Vision: Dostoevsky's Spiritual Art.* Grand Rapids, Mich.: Eerdmans, 1977.

———. "The World of Dostoevsky." *Modern Age* 22 (1978): 346–57.

Paris, Bernard J. *A Psychological Approach to Fiction: Studies in Thackeray, Stendhal, George Eliot, Dostoevsky and Conrad.* Bloomington: Indiana University Press, 1974.

Peace, Richard. "Dostoevsky and 'the Golden Age.' " *Dostoevsky Studies* 3 (1982): 61–78.

———. *Dostoyevsky: An Examination of the Major Novels.* Cambridge: Cambridge University Press, 1971.

———. "Dostoevsky's *The Eternal Husband* and Literary Polemics." *Essays in Poetics* 33, no. 2 (1978): 22–40.

Pearce, R. "Transformation: Dostoyevsky's *Idiot* and Kafka's 'Metamorphosis.' " In *Stages of the Clown: Perspectives on Modern Fiction from Dostoyevsky to Beckett.* Carbondale: Southern Illinois University Press, 1970.

Pritchett. V. S. "The Early Dostoevsky." In *The Myth Makers: Essays on European, Russian and South American Novelists.* London: Chatto & Windus, 1980.

Rabinowitz, Peter J. "The Click of the Spring: The Detective Story as Parallel Structure in Dostoyevsky and Faulkner." *Modern Philology* 76 (1979): 355–69.

Radoyce, Lubomir. "Writer in Hell: Notes on Dostoevsky's Letters." *California Slavic Studies* 9 (1976): 71–123.

Rahv, Philip. "Dostoevsky: Two Short Novels." In *Literature and the Sixth Sense.* Boston: Houghton Mifflin, 1969.

Rancour-Laferriere, Daniel. "All the World's a *Vertep*: The Personification/Depersonification Complex in Gogol's *Sorocinskaja jarmarka.*" *Harvard Ukrainian Studies* 6 (1982): 339–71.

Rayfield, Donald. "Dostoyevsky's *Eugenie Grandet.*" *Forum for Modern Language Studies* 20 (1984): 133–42.

Reeve, F. D. "*Crime and Punishment.*" In *The Russian Novel*, 159–204. New York: McGraw-Hill, 1966.

Rice, James, L. "Raskol'nikov and Tsar Gorox." *Slavic and East European Journal* 25, no. 3 (1981): 38–53.

Richards, Sylvie L. F. "The Eye and the Portrait: The Fantastic in Poe, Hawthorne, and Gogol." *Studies in Short Fiction* 20 (1983): 307–15.

Rosen, Nathan. "The Defective Memory of the Ridiculous Man." *California Slavic Studies* 12 (1978): 323–38.

Rosenshield, Gary. "Artistic Consistency in *Notes from the Underground*—Part One." In *Studies in Honor of Xenia Gasiorowska*, edited by Lauren Leighton. 11–21. Columbus: Slavica, 1982.

———. Crime and Punishment: *The Techniques of the Omniscient Author*. Atlantic Highlands, N.J.: Humanities Press, 1978.

———. "The Fate of Dostoevskij's Underground Man: The Case for an Open Ending." *Slavic and East European Journal* 28, no. 3 (1984): 161–72.

———. "Old Pokrovskij: Technique and Meaning in a Character Foil in Dostoevskij's *Poor Folk*." In *New Perspectives on Nineteenth-Century Russian Prose*, edited by George J. Gutsche and Lauren G. Leighton, 99–110. Columbus: Slavica, 1982.

———. "Point of View and the Imagination in Dostoevskij's 'White Nights.' " *Slavic and East European Journal* 21 (1977): 191–203.

———. "Rationalism, Motivation, and Time in Dostoevsky's *Notes from the Underground*." *Dostoevsky Studies* 3 (1982): 87–100.

Rosenthal, Richard J. "Dostoevsky's Use of Projection: Psychic Mechanism as Literary Form in *The Double*." *Dostoevsky Studies* 3 (1982): 79–86.

Rothe, Hans. "Quotations in Dostoyevsky's *A Raw Youth*." *Modern Language Review* 79 (1984): 131–41.

Rowe, W. W. *Dostoevsky: Child and Man in His Works*. New York: New York University Press, 1968.

Rozanov, V. V. *Dostoevsky and the Legend of the Grand Inquisitor*. Ithaca, N.Y.: Cornell University Press, 1972.

Russian Literature 4, no. 1 (1976). Special Dostoevsky issue.

Saunders, D. B. "Contemporary Critics of Gogol's *Vechera* and the Debate about Russian *narodnost*." *Harvard Ukrainian Studies* 5, no. 1 (March 1981): 66–82.

Savage, D. S. "Dostoevski: The Idea of *The Gambler*." *The Sewanee Review* 58 (1950): 281–98.

Seduro, Vladimir. *Dostoevski's Image in Russia Today*. Belmont, Mass.: Nordland, 1975.

———. *Dostoyevski in Russian Literary Criticism, 1946–1956*. New York: Columbia University Press, 1957.

Seeley, Frank Friedberg. "Dostoyevsky's Women." *The Slavonic and East European Review* 39 (1961): 291–313.

———. "The Two Faces of Svidrigailov." *Canadian-American Slavic Studies* 12 (1978): 413–17.

Simmons, Ernest J. *Dostoevsky: The Making of a Novelist*. New York: Oxford University Press, 1940.

———. *Feodor Dostoevsky*. Columbia Essays on Modern Writers 40. New York: Columbia University Press, 1969.

Slattery, Dennis P. "The Frame Tale: Temporality, Fantasy and Innocence in *The Idiot.*" *International Dostoevsky Society Bulletin* 9 (1979): 6–25.

——. *"The Idiot: Dostoevsky's Fantastic Prince: A Phenomenological Approach.* New York: Lang, 1983.

Snow, C. P. "Dostoevsky." In *The Realists: Portraits of Eight Novelists*, 84–138. London: Macmillan, 1978.

Steiner, G. *Tolstoy or Dostoevsky: An Essay in Contrast.* London: Faber & Faber, 1960.

Struc, Roman S. "Dostoevsky's 'Confessions' as Critique of Literature." *Research Studies* 46 (1978): 79–89.

——. "Kafka and Dostoevsky as 'Blood Relatives.' " *Dostoevsky Studies* 2 (1981): 111–17.

Sutherland, Stewart R. *Atheism and the Rejection of God: Contemporary Philosophy and* The Brothers Karamazov. Oxford: Basil Blackwell, 1977.

——. "Death and Fulfillment, or Would the Real Mr. Dostoyevsky Stand Up?" In *Philosophy and Literature*, edited by A. Phillips Griffiths, 15–27. Cambridge: Cambridge University Press, 1984.

——. "Dostoevsky and the Grand Inquisitor: A Study in Atheism." *The Yale Review* 66 (1976): 364–73.

——. "Language and Interpretation in *Crime and Punishment.*" *Philosophy and Literature* 2 (1978): 223–36.

Terras, Victor. "Dostoevsky's Aesthetics and Its Relationship to Romanticism." *Russian Literature* 4, no. 1 (1976): 15–26.

——. *F. M. Dostoevsky: Life, Work, and Criticism.* Fredericton, N.B.: York, 1984.

——. *A Karamazov Companion: Commentary on the Genesis, Language and Style of Dostoevsky's Novel.* Madison: University of Wisconsin Press, 1981.

——. *The Young Dostoevsky (1846–1849).* The Hague: Mouton, 1969.

——, ed. *American Contributions to the Eighth International Congress of Slavists.* Vol. 2. Columbus: Slavica, 1978.

Thomas, George. "Aspects of the Study of Dostoyevsky's Vocabulary." *Modern Language Review* 77 (1982): 670–78.

Todd, William Mills, III, ed. *Literature and Society in Imperial Russia: 1800–1914.* Stanford: Stanford University Press, 1978.

Troyat, H. *Firebrand: The Life of Dostoievsky.* New York: Roy Publishers, 1946.

Van Holk, A. G. F. "Verbal Aggression and Offended Honour in Dostoevskij's *Selo Stepancikogo i ego obitateli*: A Text-Grammatical Approach." *Russian Literature* 4, no. 1 (1976): 67–107.

Vladiv, Slobodanka. *Narrative Principles in Dostoevkij's Besy: A Structural Analysis.* European University Studies 16, 10. Bern: Lang, 1979.

——. "The Use of Circumstantial Evidence in Dostoevskii's Works." *California Slavic Studies* 12 (1978): 53–70.

Wasiolek, Edward. *Dostoevsky: The Major Fiction.* Cambridge, Mass.: MIT Press, 1964.

——, ed. Crime and Punishment *and the Critics.* San Francisco: Wadsworth, 1961.

Weisberg, Richard H. *The Failure of the Word: The Protagonist as Lawyer in Modern Fiction.* New Haven: Yale University Press, 1984.

Welch, Lois M. "Luzhin's Crime and the Advantages of Melodrama in Dostoevsky's

Crime and Punishment." *Texas Studies in Literature and Language* 18 (1976): 135–46.

Wellek, René. "Bakhtin's View of Dostoevsky: 'Polyphony' and 'Carnivalesque.'" *Dostoevsky Studies* 1 (1980): 31–39.

———, ed. *Dostoevsky: A Collection of Critical Essays.* Englewood Cliffs, N.J.: Prentice-Hall, 1962.

Wilson, Edmund. "Dostoevsky Abroad." In *The Shores of Light: A Literary Chronicle of the Twenties and Thirties,* 408–14. New York: Farrar, Strauss & Young, 1952.

Wilson, Raymond J., III. "Raskolnikov's Dream in *Crime and Punishment.*" *Literature and Psychology* 26 (1976): 159–66.

Winfield, William. "Reflection/Negation/Reality: Dostoyevsky and Hegel." *Comparative Literature Studies* 17 (1980): 399–409.

Yule, Robert. "Numbered with the Transgressors: Dostoyevsky's Image of Christ." In *From Dante to Solzhenitsyn: Essays on Christianity and Literature,* edited by Robert M. Yule, 111–38. Wellington: Tertiary Christian Studies Program, Victoria University of Wellington, 1978.

Acknowledgments

"The Hero's Monologic Discourse and Narrational Discourse in Dostoevsky's Early Novels" by Mikhail Bakhtin (excerpt from *Problems of Dostoevsky's Poetics*, translated by R. W. Rostel) from *Dostoevsky and Gogol*, edited by Priscilla Meyer and Stephen Rudy, © 1979 by Ardis Publishers, Ann Arbor, Michigan. Reprinted by permission of Ardis Publishers.

"Nihilism and *Notes from Underground*" by Joseph Frank from *The Sewanee Review* 69, no. 1 (January–March 1961), © 1961 by the University of the South. Reprinted by permission of the editor.

"Apogee: *Crime and Punishment*" by Donald Fanger from *Dostoevsky and Romantic Realism: A Study of Dostoevsky in Relation to Balzac, Dickens and Gogol* by Donald Fanger, © 1967 by the President and Fellows of Harvard College. Reprinted by permission of Harvard University Press.

"Dostoevsky's *Writer's Diary* as Literature of Process" by Gary S. Morson from *Russian Literature* 4, no. 1 (January 1976), © 1976 by North-Holland Publishing Co. Reprinted by permission of North-Holland Publishing Co., Elsevier Science Publishers B. V.

"The Search for a Story: *White Nights, Winter Notes on Summer Impressions*, and *Notes from Underground*" by Michael Holquist from *Dostoevsky and the Novel* by Michael Holquist, © 1977 by Princeton University Press. Reprinted by permission of Princeton University Press.

"The Rhetoric of an Ideological Novel" by Robert L. Belknap from *Literature and Society in Imperial Russia, 1800–1914*, edited by William Mills Todd III, © 1978 by the Board of Trustees of the Leland Stanford Junior University. Reprinted by permission of Stamford University Press.

"*Crime and Punishment*: The Psychological Problem" (originally entitled "The Psychological Problem") by A. D. Nuttall from Crime and Punishment: *Murder as Philosophic Experiment* by A. D. Nuttall, © 1978 by A. D. Nuttall. Reprinted by permission.

"The Epileptic Mode of Being" by Elizabeth Dalton from *Unconscious Structure in Dostoevsky's* The Idiot: *A Study in Literature and Psychoanalysis* by Elizabeth

Dalton, © 1979 by Princeton University Press. Reprinted by permission of Princeton University Press.

"Polina and Lady Luck in *The Gambler*" by Robert Louis Jackson from *The Art of Dostoevsky: Deliriums and Nocturnes* by Robert Louis Jackson, © 1981 by Princeton University Press. Reprinted by permission of Princeton University Press.

"The Religious Dimension: Vision or Evasion? Zosima's Discourse in *The Brothers Karamazov*" by Sergei Hackel from *New Essays on Dostoyevsky*, edited by Malcolm V. Jones and Garth M. Terry, © 1983 by Cambridge University Press. Reprinted by permission of Cambridge University Press.

"*The Possessed*" by John Jones from *Dostoevsky* by John Jones, © 1983 by John Jones. Reprinted by permission.

Index